C000197286

THE ULTIMATE GDPR PRACTITIONER GUIDE:
DEMYSTIFYING PRIVACY & DATA PROTECTION

STEPHEN MASSEY MSc FIP CISSP

STEPHEN MASSEY

Fox Red Risk Publishing is an Imprint of Fox Red Risk Solutions Ltd (9997987)
27 Old Gloucester Street, LONDON, WC1N 3AX, UNITED KINGDOM

#ultimateGDPRguide

ISBN-13: 978-1999827205 (Print)
ISBN-13: 978-1-9998272-1-2 (Kindle)
ISBN-13: 978-1-9998272-2-9 (ePUB)

DEDICATION

I dedicate this book to the two most inspirational people in my life:

My late wife Kate and, my best boy Cooper

CONTENTS

ACKNOWLEDGMENTS

This work would not have been possible without all the people I have interacted with over my career as an information security and data protection professional. The questions I have asked and have been asked of me; the projects I have worked on or supported and; the curve balls batted at me or batted away; have all shaped the content of this book in some way. Without these experiences, this book would not be quite so 'Ultimate'.

I would, however, like to single out some people who have been especially noteworthy in regards to making this book possible.

I would like to thank Judith Milne, for scrutinising the copy of this book with a hawk-like eye. There is only so much automated grammar, and spell checkers can do – and they can never tell you whether the content actually makes sense!

I would like to thank my father-in-law, Alasdair. Thank you for all the support, the interest you take means a lot!

I would like to thank Andy Johnson for proof-reading the information security and data protection by design and default sections. Without his input, who knows what I would be classifying as encryption!

I would also like to thank the keen legal minds that are Elly Rich & Richard Pooley for their contributions to the Data Protection Policies and Privacy Notices, Outsourcing and Third Country Transfers chapters.

A worthy mention must go out to all the Data Protection and Information Security Practitioners on sites such as LinkedIn who have inspired some of the content of this book and have also give me regular pause to contemplate 'have I covered that?'

While this book is dedicated to my late wife Kate, without her enduring support (and tolerance), it simply would not have been possible. The world has lost a truly amazing, kind and loving woman who is missed by many, not just me!

PART I: THE ULTIMATE PRACTITIONER - (THE BASICS)

1. INTRODUCTION

Welcome Practitioner!

Hi Reader. Thank you for taking the time to read my book on the EU General Data Protection Regulation. I know your time is precious so I will try and keep this introduction reasonably short. This book aims to give Practitioners a 'one-stop' reference guide for implementing the requirements of GDPR within their organisation. The style of the book is somewhat conversational. I have read a lot of stuffy textbooks, and they often do not encourage engagement with the material. I have read a lot of academic books too which talk about the ideas behind something but don't offer the reader a lot in the way of practical help.

I hope to bring my personality and experience into this material and provide something that is both engaging but more importantly, useful! So who am I? Well, I am a practical, pragmatic, problem-solving, personable, passionate and (sometimes) playful Practitioner who wants to share my knowledge on the subject of Data Protection. This experience has been gained over the last 20 years from when I was initially introduced to the data protection back in 1998. Before we get properly going, a quick disclaimer: Reading this book alone will not make you compliant with GDPR. As you read each chapter, it is highly likely you will identify things you need to change with regards to the way your organisation processes personal data. Every organisation will have its way of meeting the spirit of the regulation, and it would not be practical for me to cover every possible way you could achieve compliance in a single book. Additionally, there are some things in the Regulation which we will not discuss in great detail because it is not relevant in an organisational context. A good example, I am not going to spend too much time waffling about things such as article 97's requirement for the European Commission to write a report on GDPR every four years. What this book aims to do is serve to show you what your obligations are and then suggest ways you can meet these obligations.

Why Should I Care about Privacy?

Ok, so now we have got the disclaimers out of the way, I just wanted to say: It is often common to think of regulatory compliance as a dull and boring tick-box exercise, but I hope you feel privacy is different. Here in Europe, it is an important human right we must strive to protect. When we get privacy and data protection wrong, real lives are affected. When privacy is invaded, it can often leave people feeling violated and distressed. This sense of foreboding is precisely why the governments of Europe have strengthened privacy laws and enhanced the enforcement action which can be imposed on an organisation when rights are violated.

1

Now, enforcement action, such as a fine, means something has already gone wrong. I am keen to help as many organisations as possible avoid a situation where they are going to be issued a fine or suffer some other form of enforcement action, and that is why I have decided to write this book…but also because they say everyone has at least one book in them…it's definitely not to make money as a book like this is highly unlikely to end up in the New York Times Bestsellers list!

> **DID YOU KNOW: Privacy is only mentioned twice in the text of General Data Protection Regulation, and that is in reference to the Directive on Privacy and Electronic Communications.**

I am not even in the EU, so I definitely shouldn't care…should I?

Hang on a minute; my company is not based in the European Union; GDPR is not something I need to pay much attention. Well, maybe and maybe not. If you are operating in an organisation – anywhere in the world – that processes personal data relating to an EU citizen, you need to sit up and take note. The reason you must take GDPR seriously is that GDPR has 'extra-territorial applicability'. Extra-territorial applicability means the Regulation applies to the processing of EU personal data by Controllers that are not established in the Union, but in a place where Member State law applies by virtue of public international law. So essentially, if you are in a country where the rule of law applies, and you have EU customers, your data processing activities are in scope of GDPR.

Using this Book

Naturally, I would recommend reading the whole book first before doing anything but I know not everybody will do that, so I have laid this book into three main parts. The aim is to give three different types of Practitioner the best possible experience. If you are the kind of Practitioner who is completely new to the topic, then you can keep to PART I and work on the principle the Practitioner guidance aims to implement the Regulation in a relatively generic way. Once you have got to the stage where you have a basic, boilerplate programme, I would then recommend reading PART I in conjunction with PART II and PART III to tweak your basic programme to better suit the needs of your organisation. Don't worry too much if you keep to just this part of the book as there are references to the other parts where relevant.

If you are a more experienced Practitioner or the kind of Practitioner who wants to check the regulation as you go, in order to tweak and modify the guidance in PART I, you can delve into PART II. This part of the book contains a replication of the General Data Protection Regulation (GDPR) text – all ninety-nine articles! In this part of the book, you can get the exact wording of the Regulation, so you can make your own interpretations as to how you should implement a specific clause, in a way that best suits your organisation. As mentioned earlier, it is not possible to give a perfect solution to every scenario in one book, so it is important, as a more experienced Practitioner, to be able to delve into the text of the Regulation.

It is also useful to have a physical copy of the text available because having the ability to show someone in your organisation offline can be a lifesaver. Just showing a person precisely what the text says, can be the simplest way to clarify why you are asking them to do something in a certain way. I did toy with the idea of merely referencing to the online locations of the GDPR and associated recitals, but with the kind permission of the Publications Office of the European Union, I have included them in full. It is not to pad out the pages but because many of us read on the train on the way into work or, may not be near an Internet connection when the 'challenging' question gets raised.

The final audience I had in mind for this book is the Zen Practitioner. If you are a Zen Practitioner, you not only want to know the letter of the Regulation but, also the spirit of the Regulation and how it has been interpreted thus far. As such you should use all sections of the book including: 'PART III: THE RECITALS'. Part III explains what the lawmakers, who created the GDPR, intended when they included specific prose. A Zen Practitioner understands when you combine all parts of the book you get a deeper understanding of the GDPR and how it is most likely to affect you and your organisation. Throughout the book, I have placed some questions and short summaries in boxes. These are to encourage self-reflection or drive home the importance of a particular concept. In addition to these boxes, there are also grey boxes 'Did you know' items and examples. These nuggets of information, identified during the research for this book are included for interest and deeper understanding. Whichever Practitioner type you are, and however you use this book, I am sure you will get at the very least something out this book so without further ado, let's get started!

What type of Practitioner do you want to be?

Key Terms

The following definitions are crucial to understanding the General Data Protection Regulation. When dealing with personal data, you must keep the following definitions in mind as they will be vital to understanding your data protection roles and responsibilities. This list is not exhaustive and more terms will be described throughout the book but initially, the most useful are as follows:

Natural Person: Essentially an EU citizen who is alive. A Natural Person may also be referred to as a Data Subject.

Child: For the purposes of GDPR is a Natural person who requires parental consent, usually if they are below 16. The EU Member States can, however, reduce the requirement for consent to those no younger than 13 (i.e. if the Natural Person is over 13 parental consent would not be required).

Personal Data: any information relating to an identified or identifiable Natural Person (or 'Data Subject'); an identifiable Natural Person is one who can be identified, directly or indirectly, in particular by reference to an identifier such as a name, an identification number, location data, an online identifier or to one or more factors specific to the physical, physiological, genetic, mental, economic, cultural or social identity of that Natural Person.

Sensitive Data: special categories of information relating to an identified or identifiable Natural Person (or 'Data Subject'). Examples include racial or ethnic origin, political opinions, religious or philosophical beliefs, or trade union membership, genetic data, biometric data, sex life of sexual orientation.

Processing: any operation or set of operations which is performed on personal data or on sets of personal data, whether or not by automated means, such as collection, recording, organisation, structuring, storage, adaptation or alteration, retrieval, consultation, use, disclosure by transmission, dissemination or otherwise making available, alignment or combination, restriction, erasure or destruction.

Profiling: any form of automated processing of personal data consisting of the use of personal data to evaluate certain personal aspects relating to a Natural Person, in particular to analyse or predict aspects concerning that Natural Person's performance at work, economic situation, health, personal preferences, interests, reliability, behaviour, location or movements.

Consent: any freely given, specific, informed and unambiguous indication of the Data Subject's wishes by which he or she, by a statement or by a clear affirmative action, signifies agreement to the processing of personal data relating to him or her.

Controller: the natural or legal person, public authority, agency or other body which, alone or jointly with others, determines the purposes and means of the processing of personal data; where the purposes and means of such processing are determined by Union or Member State law, the Controller or the specific criteria for its nomination may be provided for by Union or Member State law.

Processor: a natural or legal person, public authority, agency or other body which processes personal data on behalf of the Controller.

EU Member State: any country party to the founding treaties of the European Union (EU) and thereby subject to the privileges and obligations of membership. Member States are subject to binding laws in exchange for representation within the common legislative and judicial institutions.

Third Country: any country which is not an EU Member State (e.g. USA, India, China or the Philippines)

Supervisory Authority: the regulator within a European country who will provide regulatory oversight for GDPR, provide guidance and advice and, where necessary impose corrective actions or administrative fines.

Information Security: The protection of information and information systems from unauthorized access, use, disclosure, disruption, modification, or destruction in order to provide confidentiality, integrity, and availability.

Personal Data Breach: a breach of security leading to the accidental or unlawful destruction, loss, alteration, unauthorised disclosure of, or access to, personal data transmitted, stored or otherwise processed.

Data Protection Impact Assessment (DPIA): An assessment of the impact of the envisaged processing operations on the protection of personal data and the rights and freedoms of natural persons.

Subject Access Request (SAR): A request, made by a natural person, to access personal data held by a Controller or Processor,

Data Protection Officer (DPO): a person with expert knowledge of data protection law and practices who assists the Controller or Processor to monitor internal compliance with GDPR. Such data protection officers, whether or not they are an employee of the Controller, should be in a position to perform their duties and tasks in an independent manner.

2. WHAT IS THE GENERAL DATA PROTECTION REGULATION (GDPR)?

In this chapter, we will look at the General Data Protection Regulation in more detail. We will look at the origins of privacy and how data protection developed from idea to legislation. We will look at the key changes GDPR brings into European Law and discuss the structure and related instruments. We will then look at the criteria an organisation must use to confirm their processing activities are lawful. Finally, we will delve into the consequences should processing be determined unlawful.

History of Privacy & Data Protection

Before diving into the GDPR itself, it is useful to understand how we got to a stage whereby we need such a comprehensive piece of legislation. It is essential to know why is privacy so important to EU citizens and others across the world. People may be surprised to know that the concept of privacy is not new. Privacy concerns, in reasonably crude form, can be traced back to at least 1499 C.E. in terms of an old axiom which purports *"An Englishman's home is his castle"*. The premise is that a person – well at that time an English man – was protected by the law of the land from a servant of the Crown entering their property and either confiscating items or taking their liberty. A case in the 17th century, Semayne v Gresham [01 January 1604] clarified the Crown did have the right to enter a person's house but should let the resident know they are coming and the reason - before breaking down the doors! At this stage in history, citizen's concerns about privacy tended to focus on issues such as trespass. People were not typically concerned about privacy in regards to information. There are many reasons which could explain this, but it is possible literacy played the most prominent part.

Johannes Gutenberg had invented the printing press circa 1440, which dramatically increased the spread of information across the world. However, illiteracy rates remained as high as 50% well into the mid-18th century for men, and women's illiteracy was, dreadfully, a lot higher at 75%[1]. As literacy rates improved at the turn of the 20th century, so too did people's attitudes to the paradigm of information privacy. It is no coincidence at the same time governments realised both the importance of information and the need to protect information. The idea of data protection as a component of privacy had now been conceived.

---

[1] The Cambridge Economic History of Modern Britain, Floud & Johnson, 2004

Johannes Gutenberg (1398-1468) – Father of Mass Communication [2]

For those with a global view, privacy is not an issue solely in Europe. In the United States, census data has been collected since at least 1790[3], and at that time there were only four questions on the form. By 1890 the number of questions had mushroomed considerably, becoming more and more intrusive in nature. What made this issue concerning at the time was the practice of making copies of the census data freely available to facilitate error checking. Given census information contained significant amounts of personal data, it was not too long before people began to raise concerns resulting in the practice of publishing census data becoming illegal in 1919. As history went on to show, it is clear the concerns of US citizens were valid. 1930s Europe saw what is probably the clearest example of how personal data in the wrong hands can lead to unspeakable atrocity. According to the book 'IBM and the Holocaust'[4] by Edwin Black, Nazi Germany formed a strategic alliance with IBM, which involved the leasing, custom design and support of a punch card and card sorting 'computer' to organise census data to identify Jewish citizens systematically.

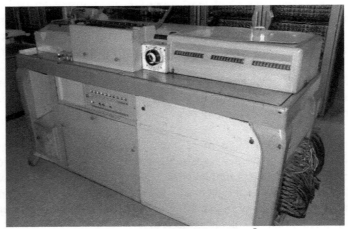

Hollerith D-11 Card Sorting Machine[5]

---

2 By LoretoLeon9 CC BY-SA 4.0
3 A Population History of the United States, Herbert S Klein, 2012
4 IBM and the Holocaust: The Strategic Alliance Between Nazi Germany and America's Most Powerful Corporation, Edwin Black, 2012
5 By Dr Bernd Gross (Own work) Creative Commons, CC BY-SA 4.0

This automated data processing enabled Nazi Germany to dramatically increase the efficiency of their extermination campaign to the extent approximately six million Jews were killed. It cannot be understated how much this event shapes the way Europeans value privacy.

Shortly after the war on the 10 December 1948, the UN General Assembly adopted the Universal Declaration of Human Rights. Within the declaration is Article 12, which enshrined the right to privacy. In 1950 this right to privacy was also enshrined within Article 8 of the European Convention on Human Rights (ECHR). The ECHR introduced a means for seeking judicial remedy through the European Court of Human Rights. Data protection was by then at the embryonic stage. Up until the 1960s, privacy was still very much centred around family life and a person's home. There was, however, growing concern a person's privacy in the home could now be interfered with through the use of technology, namely through phone-tapping and other forms of surreptitious observation. These concerns ultimately led in 1968 to the publication of Recommendation 509 which recommended a study, the topic of which was whether the Member States adequately protected its citizens' rights under Article 8 of the ECHR and if the Member States did not, what courses of action should be taken. The proceeding study identified multiple issues which led to resolutions 73 (22)[6] and 74 (29)[7]. Around the same time, a US Advisory Committee Report on Automated Data Systems was published making similar recommendations. From this point Data Protection as we know it today was born.

In 1980 the Organisation for Economic Co-Operation and Development (OECD), understanding the economic potential of data, issued guidelines on how privacy rights could be protected in the context of data flowing between nation states (not just those in Europe). Following shortly on from the OECD guidelines, in 1981 the Council of Europe published Convention 108, Convention for the Protection of Individuals with regard to Automatic Processing of Personal Data. Convention 108 was the first international legal instrument designed solely for Data Protection. It introduced into European law a formal definition of personal and sensitive data, lawful processing and retention limitations. The convention included Data Subjects' rights to access and rectification, and limited data flows to countries which did not offer Data Subjects sufficient legal protections. Technology progress in the 1980s rapidly changed the world, and it was clear data protection legislation needed to be updated to keep pace. Not only that, because the Treaty of Rome codified the four freedoms relating to the movement of goods, services, capital and people, it was becoming more and more challenging for companies to operate without equivalence in data protection legislation. To answer this challenge, the European Union published the 1995 EU Data Protection Directive. The 1995 Directive has since been translated into Member State law, but over the last 22 years, technology has once again marched on ahead of the legislation. While other legal instruments have been introduced to offer additional protections, it was not enough, and so, in 2011, the European Data Protection Supervisor kick-started what was to become the EU General Data Protection Regulation (GDPR). Data Protection had now reached maturity!

---

[6] Resolution 73 (22) on the Protection of the Privacy of Individuals Vis-A-Vis Electronic Data Banks in the Private Sector

[7] Resolution 74 (29) on the Protection of the Privacy of Individuals Vis-A-Vis Electronic Data Banks in the Public Sector

What is GDPR?

The General Data Protection Regulation (GDPR) is a Pan-European piece of legislation implemented by the European Parliament and Council to significantly strengthen Data Subject's rights in regards to how their data is used. GDPR applies[8] to two kinds of data. Personal Data and Sensitive Data. GDPR does not apply to the processing of personal data relating to criminal convictions[9] and offences, and in some instances, restrictions[10] may apply, for example, national security or defence.

As discussed in the previous section, GDPR is the result an evolution in law over some years to bring data protection legislation into line with the way data is used in the 21st Century. Essentially, this update brings data protection kicking and screaming into the modern world we live in where pretty much every aspect of our daily lives requires the processing of personal data in some form or another. Not only did data protection legislation need updating it also required streamlining. All over the EU, national Data Protection Laws exist as a result of Member States translating the 1995 EU Data Protection Directive into local law. GDPR replaces all these local laws and introduces a single piece of legislation. GDPR now has sharp teeth too. The regulation adds harsher fines for non-compliance and breaches but also gives people much more say over what companies can do with their data.

The primary motivations behind the GDPR are: Firstly, the EU wants to give people more control over how their personal data is used, bearing in mind that many companies like Google and LinkedIn swap access to people's data for the use of their products. Current legislation was drafted before the internet and cloud technology created the novel ways of exploiting data which are ubiquitous in our lives. GDPR seeks to address this imbalance. By strengthening legislation and introducing stricter enforcement measures, the EU is striving to improve consumer trust. Secondly, the EU wants to give businesses a more straightforward, more explicit legal environment in which to operate, making data protection law identical throughout the single market. The GDPR will apply in all EU Member States from 25 May 2018. Because GDPR is a regulation, not a directive, EU nations do not need to draw up new legislation - instead, it will apply automatically. While it came into force on 24 May 2016, businesses and organisations, whether operating physically in the EU or not, have until 25 May 2018 until the law applies. The clock is ticking!

Key Changes

Your exposure to Data Protection legislation will likely depend on what your organisation does and your role within the organisation. If you skipped the history section, you might not know this, but there has been legislation to protect personal data for well over 20 years, however, at the time the current legislation was drafted, the world was quite different. GDPR aims to protect all EU citizens from privacy and data breaches in an increasingly data-driven world that is vastly different from the time in which the previous 1995 directive was established. So what has changed in the legislation? Well, the key changes included in GDPR are as follows:

Increased Territorial Scope (extra-territorial applicability): One of the most significant changes to EU data privacy comes with the extended jurisdiction of the GDPR - it now applies to all companies processing the personal data of Data Subjects residing in the EU, *regardless* of the company's location. If you thought the prior legislation was ambiguous, GPDR now makes its applicability very clear - it will apply to the processing of personal data by Controllers and Processors in the EU, regardless of whether the processing takes place in the EU or not. GDPR will apply to the processing of personal data of Data Subjects in the EU by a Controller or Processor not established in the EU, where the activities relate to offering goods or services to EU citizens - irrespective of whether payment is

---

[8] Article 2: Material Scope
[9] Article 10: Processing of personal data relating to criminal convictions and offences
[10] Article 23: Restrictions

required. For example, if your organisation provides an app for free but monetises users' personal data. In addition, Non-EU businesses processing the data of EU citizens will also have to appoint a representative in the EU. (See Chapter 14).

Consent & Withdrawal of Consent: The conditions for consent have been strengthened, and companies will no longer be able to use long illegible terms and conditions full of legalese, as the request for consent must be given in an intelligible and easily accessible form, with the purpose of the data processing attached to that consent. Consent must be explicit and distinguishable from other matters and must use clear language. GDPR introduces a material change to consent making it a requirement for consent to be as easy to withdraw[11] as it is to give.

Children and Consent: When it comes to children, there are additional requirements. A child is a Natural person who requires parental consent, usually if they are below 16 years of age. You must make reasonable efforts to confirm parental consent is provided by a person who holds parental responsibility for the child (e.g. the biological mother or father).

Other Additional Rights: In addition to the already mentioned changes, there are also increased rights for EU citizens which we will discuss a little later but include the following:

1. Breach notification: the right to be informed if their data has been compromised
2. Expanded Subject Access: in addition to current rights, rights also include access to information about how their data is being processed, where and for what purpose.
3. Right to be Forgotten: entitles the Data Subject to have the data Controller erase his/her personal data, cease further dissemination of the data, and potentially have third parties halt processing of the data.
4. Data Portability: the right for a Data Subject to receive the personal data concerning them, which they have previously provided in a 'commonly used and machine-readable format' and have the right to transmit that data to another Controller.

So as you can see, there are quite a few changes, and that is going to mean you and your organisation are going to have to work out how this will impact the way you process data and what you need to do to make sure you are compliant with the new regulation.

Structure of GDPR

The General Data Protection Regulation is a legal instrument drafted by the European Parliament. As it is a Regulation, it is not required to be converted into Member State Law. The Regulation replaces[12] Directive 95/46/EC of the European Parliament and of the Council of 24 October 1995 on the 'protection of individuals with regard to the processing of personal data and on the free movement of such data'. GDPR makes it explicitly clear the processing of data for criminal offences is outside its material[13] (and territorial) scope. Accompanying GDPR is a separate legal instrument. Directive (EU) 2016/680 on the 'protection of Natural Persons with regard to the processing of personal data by competent authorities for the purposes of the prevention, investigation, detection or prosecution of criminal offences or the execution of criminal penalties, and on the free movement of such data'. This Directive has been drafted because the Member States wish to retain more control over the processing of personal data about criminal activity. However, whilst out of the scope of GDPR, GDPR does recommend there should be equivalency in the protection of relevant personal data across all Member States.

---

[11] Article 7(3): Conditions for consent
[12] Article 94: Repeal of Directive 95/46/EC
[13] Article 2(2): Material Scope

DID YOU KNOW: Because 95/46/EC was a Directive, Member States were required to create new legislation or update existing laws. In the case of the United Kingdom, this needed an update of the 1984 Data Protection Act which then became the 1998 Data Protection Act. Local laws also provided the opportunity for the Member States enshrine into the statute books derogations from the Directive and in some cases enhancements. For example, the UK chose not to include a Data Protection Official and Germany decided to make the Data Protection Official a protected role.

In addition to 2016/680, Practitioners should also be aware of 2002/58/EC concerning the processing of personal data and the protection of privacy in the electronic communications sector (Directive on privacy and electronic communications). You may not be aware of the directive by name, but you are most likely aware of its impact on every website you visit with those lovely cookie notifications. This Directive is due to be replaced with a new ePrivacy Regulation (so again will not require transposition into Member State law) and aims to ensure the same privacy controls, that apply to telecommunications providers currently, will apply to electronic messaging services (e.g. Skype or WhatsApp). The proposed regulation will also introduce the requirement to gain consent for a messaging service to collect metadata (e.g. when and where a message was sent or received), require marketing callers to identify who they are (e.g. through caller ID) and, thankfully, improve the way end users are informed about cookies! Regarding interaction, the ePrivacy Regulation will be *lex specialis* to GDPR, which means its provisions will override those within GDPR. While it is useful to know Directives 2016/680, 2002/58/EC and the proposed ePrivacy Regulation exist and, how they relate to GDPR, further discussion on content and application is out of the scope of this book.

Now to the primary legislation of this book. GDPR is split into 99 Articles across 11 chapters. The first chapters focus on the Data Subject and rules for data processing. Chapter I deals with general provisions such as scope and definitions. Chapter II covers the data protection principles. Chapter III sets out Data Subjects' Rights. Chapter IV details the roles and responsibilities of Data Processors and Controllers. This chapter also covers the designation, position and tasks of the Data Protection Officer. Chapter V contains the requirements relating to data transfers to Third Countries outside the European Union. The latter chapters focus more on governance and oversight activities. Chapter VI discusses the roles and responsibilities of the Supervisory Authorities and how an Authority can enforce the Regulation. Chapter VII discusses how the Member States are to cooperate to ensure the regulation is consistently applied and enforced. Chapter VIII details remedies, liability and fines. Chapter IX sets out rules relating to specific situations such as the use of personal data in an employment context or where there are obligations of secrecy. Chapter X codifies certain delegated acts and committee procedural elements. Finally, Chapter IX contains administrative prose relating to the repeal of previous legislation and dates whereby GDPR will come into force and subsequently apply.

What is Personal Data?

Personal Data[14] is: "any information relating to an identified or identifiable Natural Person (or 'Data Subject'); an identifiable Natural Person is one who can be identified, directly or indirectly, in particular by reference to an identifier such as a name, an identification number, location data, an online identifier or to one or more factors specific to the physical, physiological, genetic, mental, economic, cultural or social identity of that Natural Person." So what does this mean in practice? Let's look at through the lens of fields in a database table. All the values below could be considered Personal Data:

Field	Example	Field	Example	Field	Example
FName	Joe	SName	Bloggs	Store-Card No.	1234 5468 1234
DOB	01/01/1970	Address	1 The Road	Fingerprint	JB01011970.fpf
PostCode	EC41 4AT	Phone No.	020 1234 5678	Interview Notes	JBloggsNotes1-1-17.docx
Email	Joe.bloggs @foxredrisk.com	Driving Licence No.	MORGA657054SM9IJ	NI Number	PQ 12 34 56 A
Passport	925665416	IP Address	37.187.129.177	DNA	JB01011970.genome
Gender	Female	IMEI	351066060926230	Salary	€40,000pa
Photo	JBloggs.jpg	CV	JBloggsCV.docx	MAC Address	00:30:6E:F5:E0:7D
VRN	MA 55 EYS				

Examples of Personal Data

The field list is not exhaustive, but it should give you food-for-thought as to the far-reaching scope of GDPR. When you look at the definition, it states Directly or Indirectly. Directly Identifiable Personal Data would be something like a unique identifier (e.g. Passport or Driving Licence No.) because these identifiers are typically linked to only one person. Indirectly Identifiable Personal Data would be data points that can be pieced together to identify the Data Subject. For example, Post Code and Date of Birth would be enough in most cases to uniquely identify an individual. Care must also be taken with file name taxonomy. If an organisation collects data on an individual whereby the content is pseudonymised but then names the file using a combination of personal data, then pseudonymisation is invalidated. In addition to direct and indirect data points, profiling or scoring derived from personal data, in itself, becomes personal data.

What is Sensitive Data?

Sensitive Data is: "special categories of information relating to an identified or identifiable Natural Person (or 'Data Subject'). Examples include racial or ethnic origin, political opinions, religious or philosophical beliefs, or trade union membership, genetic data, biometric data, sex life of sexual orientation." If you have ever filled out a diversity monitoring questionnaire, you will have a good understanding of the types of data which are classified as sensitive data. The reason why this information is so sensitive is that people have been negatively targeted throughout history because of where they sit in these sensitive categories. Imagine if someone were to get hold of a database full of personal data which he or she used to send out hate mail or target people for physical violence, or worse.

This is why GDPR prohibits[15] processing of such sensitive data unless under very specific conditions and only under the obligation of professional secrecy (e.g. A Doctor, a Lawyer or a Journalist). The conditions are:

1. The Data Subject has given explicit consent
2. processing is necessary for the purposes of carrying out the obligations and exercising specific rights.
3. processing is necessary to protect the vital interests of the data subject or of another natural person where

---

[14] Article 4: Definitions
[15] Article 9(1): Processing of special categories of personal data

the data subject is physically or legally incapable of giving consent
4. processing is carried out in the course of its legitimate activities with appropriate safeguards
5. Processing relates to data which is already public
6. Processing relates to legal action
7. There is substantial public interest
8. Processing relates to Medical or Social Care including public health
9. Archiving purposes in the public interest or for scientific or historical research purposes.

Comparison with US Privacy Legislation

Given the international reach of Silicon Valley, it is useful to have some insight into the way privacy is regulated in the US. It may surprise many Practitioners to know that EU privacy legislation bears some of its origins in US privacy legislation. However, the way US citizens' privacy rights are protected is different in many fundamental ways. The first significant difference is that there is no single federal-level data protection act. Instead, there are some national-level legal instruments which govern data protection. One instrument is the Federal Trade Commission (FTC) Act. Introduced initially into law 1914, the FTC Act is primarily aimed at protecting consumers from unfair commercial practices. The next instrument is the Financial Services Modernization Act[16]. Again while broader in terms of scope, this Act protects customers of financial services organisations (e.g. Banks and Insurance Companies). Another federal level instrument is the Health Insurance Portability and Accountability Act (HIPAA) which regulates medical information used and shared in hospitals, health insurance companies, pharmacies and associated Processors. There is also the CAN-SPAM Act[17] which is similar to the PECR[18] in that it governs the collection and use of telephone numbers and email addresses for the purposes of marketing.

As a result of such a legislative collage, there is not a single federal data protection regulator, which means US Data Subjects need to go to different regulators, dependent on the complaint and type of data affected – and sometimes that can involve more than one regulator as there is overlap. The second significant difference is about Data Subjects' rights. US citizen's data protection rights are light touch, to say the least. For example, there is no single federal law which gives US Data Subjects a right to access the information a Data Controller or Processor holds. HIPAA does provide a right of access to health data, but it is limited to personal health information. US citizens are not able to make a subject access request to an employer in the same way an EU Data Subject is able. Other rights such as portability and the right to be forgotten are also absent from the US statute books. The third significant difference relates to cross-border data flow. The US has no equivalent restriction regarding transferring data across national boundaries. The US does not require Controllers to notify a federal Supervisory Authority before moving data outside the US and does not place any restriction on the onward transfer of data to a third (or fourth) national boundary.

Finally, there are State laws governing data protection. Yes, fifty different states worth of additional legal complexity. A common question asked is which jurisdiction has the best data protection regime. The 'best regime' question is complex and in any case, falls out of the scope of this book (as it would probably require a book of its own). The author's personal opinion is that due to the lessons of history, enshrining in law explicit privacy rights, harmonising and simplifying data protection legislation, appears *prima facie,* a better approach. GDPR is the way forward!

---

[16] Also known as the Gramm-Leach-Bliley Act (GLBA) after the three Republican Senators who were involved in bring the Act into law.
[17] Controlling the Assault of Non-Solicited Pornography and Marketing Act
[18] Privacy and Electronic Communications Directive (2002/58/EC)

Establishing Lawful Grounds for Processing

You and your organisation (including any third parties processing data on your behalf) must have lawful grounds for processing personal data, and you must be able to prove your processing is lawful. Processing is lawful if at least one of the following applies:

1. The Data Subject has given consent to the processing of his or her personal data for one or more specific purposes; This could be through a checkbox on your website where they enter their data.
2. processing is necessary for the performance of a contract to which the Data Subject is party or in order to take steps at the request of the Data Subject prior to entering into a contract; An example of this could be your name and address would be required in order to make a purchase.
3. processing is necessary for compliance with a legal obligation to which the Controller is subject; an example of this could be in carrying out background checks before hiring a new employee.
4. processing is necessary in order to protect the vital interests of the Data Subject or of another Natural Person; This could be in relation to a medical information where data is needed to support the treatment of an unconscious person.
5. processing is necessary for the performance of a task carried out in the public interest or in the exercise of official authority vested in the Controller; A good example of this would be a census.
6. processing is necessary for the purposes of the legitimate interests pursued by the Controller or by a third party, except where such interests are overridden by the interests or fundamental rights and freedoms of the Data Subject which require protection of personal data, in particular where the Data Subject is a child.

Consent

When it comes to consent, you must be able to prove the Data Subject has provided consent for their data to be used for each specific purpose. If each specific purpose does not have specific consent, some or all of the processing may not be considered lawful. The Data Subject must also be provided with the ability to withdraw consent in a manner that is equally as easy as when consent was provided. If it is not, the processing activities may also be considered unlawful. Care must also be taken when it comes to requiring consent for processing activities in a contract which are not required to perform the primary contracted service. The Regulator is likely to uphold the right of the Data Subject in these cases and find against the Controller organisation.

Consent and Children

When it comes to children, there are additional requirements[19] relating to consent. A child is a Natural person who requires parental consent, usually if they are below 16. The Controller or Processor must make reasonable efforts to confirm parental consent is provided by a person who holds parental responsibility for the child (e.g. the biological mother or father) before Processing commences.

The Controller & the Processor

In Chapter One, the terms Controller and Processor were introduced; let's look at the two concepts in a little more detail. As previously described, the Controller is the natural or legal person, public authority, agency or other body which, alone or jointly with others, determines the purposes and means of the processing of personal data. The Controller will need to ensure Data Subjects' rights are upheld. The Controller will be a coordinator for Subject

---

[19] Article 8: Conditions applicable to child's consent in relation to information society services

Access Requests (See Chapter 13) and must ensure information is provided within the statutory deadline of 30 days – even if the information requested is only available at a Third Party Processor (e.g. an Outsourced Service Provider). The Controller will be required to ensure personal and sensitive data is processed securely, how long data is to be retained and whether data can be disclosed to a third party. The Controller is ultimately accountable for upholding Data Subjects' rights as they apply to the data the Controller (and any Processors acting lawfully on their behalf) processes.

Example: Holling & Milne LLC (the Controller) provide a research agency, Davenport-Wrensome LLC (the Processor) with employee names, email addresses, job titles and departments. The data is provided solely to conduct an employee engagement survey. Davenport-Wrensome also has a recruitment wing which is always on the lookout for unhappy employees who could perhaps be persuaded to make a move to another opportunity.

Davenport-Wrensome would not be permitted to share this data with their recruitment wing as this type of processing would not have been authorised by the Data Controller, Holling & Milne.

There may be times when two or more organisations determine the purposes and means of processing. In these cases, the organisations are considered to be Joint Controllers[20]. Joint Controllers are responsible for ensuring their responsibilities for upholding the rights and freedoms of Data Subjects and whilst the Regulation does not explicitly state this must be in writing or legally binding, Article 26 goes on to state *"The essence of the arrangement shall be made available to the data subject"*. Joint Controllers organisation should therefore consider taking legal advice to determine an appropriate approach. Irrespective of the roles and responsibilities arrangement agreed by the Joint Controllers, Data Subjects can still exercise their rights under GDPR against any of the Joint Controllers.

EXAMPLE: Holling & Milne LLC and Davenport Wrensome LLC are Joint Controllers. Under an arrangement as described in Article 26 the Joint Controllers agree Davenport Wrensome LLC's Data Protection Officer will act on behalf of both organisations in respect to upholding Data Subjects' Rights. A Data Subject registers on a portal jointly controlled by the above Joint Controllers. A year after registering, the Data Subject wishes to make a Subject Access Request and contacts a representative of Holling & Milne.

The representative of Holling & Milne would be required to forward[21] the request on to the agreed Data Protection Officer and would not be permitted to ask the Data Subject to contact the Davenport Wrensome LLC DPO directly.

---

[20] Article 26: Joint controllers
[21] Article 12: Transparent information for the exercise of the rights of the data subject.

Now a Processor, on the other hand, is a natural or legal person, public authority, agency or other body which processes personal data on behalf of the Controller. A Processor is not permitted to conduct any processing activity on personal data provided by a Controller without the Controller's express permission – and only when that processing is lawful. Processors must also uphold the rights of Data Subjects and in many cases may be both a Controller and a Processor. If you are a Processor, it's important to know you cannot absolve yourself of personal responsibility should a data breach occur which involves a Controller's data – especially if there are no penalties laid out in a Controller-Processor contract. Supervisory Authorities have the power[22] to impose a temporary or definitive limitation including a ban on processing.

> **Example: Davenport-Wrensome is a Processor of Holling & Milne LLC however for the purposes of processing their own employee's data, Davenport-Wrensome is a Controller.**

GDPR now strengthens the requirements for Controllers to supervise Processors and now makes it mandatory for any Controller-Processor relationship to be governed by a legally binding contract. This topic will be discussed in more detail in Chapter 13.

The Supervisory Authority

A Regulation is not going to be very effective without an organisation to monitor and oversee adherence. In terms of GDPR, this oversight role falls to the Supervisory Authority. As you can imagine with a continent of 24 official languages, there is a requirement for each Member State to establish a Supervisory Authority. For reference, there is a list of current Supervisory Authorities as an appendix to this book. The existing Supervisory Authorities are well established, and their websites provide a great deal of useful information. According to Article 51[23], the Supervisory Authority's primary role is to "protect the fundamental rights and freedoms of Natural Persons in relation to processing and to facilitate the free flow of personal data within the Union", and it does this in a number of ways.

A Supervisory Authority must act with independence[24]. This independence is achieved in the regulation using rules forbidding the Member States from interfering with its operations or decisions, prohibiting interference with the hiring of staff and requiring the Member States to provide an appropriate level of funding. While the Supervisory Authority is independent, it must still cooperate with Supervisory Authorities in the other Member States to ensure consistency[25] of application.

> **Example: The Polish Supervisory Authority (The Bureau of the Inspector General for the Protection of Personal Data – GIODO) issues a €10million administrative fine in a specific set of circumstances. Supervisory Authorities in Spain, Austria et al. would all be required to take this decision into consideration when issuing administrative fines in their jurisdiction for a similar violation.**

---

[22] Article 58(2).f: Powers
[23] Article 51: Supervisory authority
[24] Article 52: Independence
[25] Article 63: Consistency mechanism

GDPR mandates a Supervisory Authority carry certain tasks[26]. These tasks include, but are not limited to: promoting awareness, handling complaints, conducting investigations and giving advice. So that a Supervisory Authority may enforce the Regulation, GDPR proffers certain powers[27] to the Supervisory Authority which will be discussed in the next section. One of the tasks of the Supervisory Authority, still in the early stages of development at the time this book went to press, is to encourage the establishment of certification mechanisms[28]. Presently, there are no officially accredited certifications for privacy, but it is expected such certifications will be introduced shortly after GDPR applies. Certification is particularly useful to organisations in that it: demonstrates to data subjects that an organisation takes data protection seriously and; it can be used by organisations during the procurement phase to filter for Processors who have demonstrated they can process data in compliance with the Regulation.

The most important takeaway is that the Supervisory Authority could be your best friend or your worst enemy. They typically have great resources and a wealth of information, so if you are in any doubt about any aspect of data protection compliance, give them a call – they will be only too happy to help!

Consequences of Non-Compliance

Unfortunately, while it would be great to live in a world where reasonable laws were merely adhered to for the greater good, there are times when both the letter and the spirit of the law are not followed. In these cases, Supervisory Bodies under GDPR now have greater powers. They have the authority to investigate issues and conduct audits, they have the authority to require corrective actions be carried out at an organisation processing personal data, and they can impose administrative fines. Additionally, they are the *de facto* source for authorisation and advice about data protection matters within a Member State. A full list of the Supervisory Authority's powers can be found in Article 58 of the GDPR. As mentioned, one of the key powers the Supervisory Authority now has is the ability to impose administrative fines which are much larger than those seen previously. It is worth noting the general feeling amongst Supervisory Authorities are administrative fines are seen as a response of last resort. The approach – thus far – is to take a consensual approach typically seeking to give organisations the opportunity to take corrective action before considering financial penalties.

Given the prevalence of data breaches in recent years it is not clear whether this approach is bearing appropriate fruit and only time will tell if Supervisory Authorities decide to take a more hard-line stance to encourage behavioural change. Whichever legal framework you are operating as the fines are now directly linked to an organisation's revenue, these penalties are now material and are highly likely to have your senior management's attention, so it is worth making sure you know the worst-case scenarios. For a breach of the following, the fines can be up to €20million or 4% of worldwide annual turnover (whichever is higher):

1. A breach of the six GDPR principles (which we shall come to shortly)
2. Issues surrounding the rights of Data Subjects (which we shall come to after the principles)
3. Where data processing was found to be unlawful
4. Where it is found consent cannot be proven or processing was continued after consent has been withdrawn.
5. Breaches of sensitive categories of data
6. Transfers to countries where data privacy rights are not equivalent to those afforded within GDPR
7. Issues surrounding cooperation with a Supervisory Authority during investigations
8. Issues surrounding meeting the requirements of corrective action issued by a Supervisory Authority

While the above is for the most serious of breaches, the Supervisory Authority can also impose fines of up to

---

[26] Article 57: Tasks
[27] Article 58: Powers
[28] Article 42: Certification

€10million or 2% of worldwide annual turnover for lesser violations of GDPR. In addition to the above, any person who has suffered material or non-material damage as a result of an infringement of GDPR will now have the right to seek compensation from the Controller or Processor for the harm sustained. Further detail can be found in Part II, GDPR Chapter VIII (Remedies, Liability and Penalties). A final note on administrative fines for those of you who have outsourced data processing activities. If a breach occurs at a Processor, it is likely that the Controller organisation will receive the penalty and will need to claw the penalty back through any agreed contractual terms from the Processor organisation. Controllers will need to bear this in mind when entering into outsourcing arrangements where personal or sensitive processing is involved. We will discuss third-party relationships such as outsourcing in more detail in Chapter 14.

DID YOU KNOW: For those who have already delved into the Regulation (or are Practitioners from either Denmark or Estonia), the legal systems in these two countries do not allow for administrative fines. Therefore, the rules on administrative fines are likely to be applied in such a manner that in Denmark a fine is imposed by competent national courts as a criminal penalty and in Estonia imposed by the Supervisory Authority in the framework of a misdemeanour procedure.

---

3. QUICK START CHECKLIST

If you have flicked straight to this section, you may just want to get on with implementing the General Data Protection Regulation, and if that is the case, this is an excellent place to start. If not, welcome to the first steps in implementing GDPR! This chapter focusses on the basics and getting you up and running. To get you up and running as quickly as possible, this section draws upon on the 12 Steps which the Irish Data Protection Commissioner recommend you take to get your organisation compliant. Before we get into the 12 steps themselves, there are few things it is worth considering to hopefully reduce the pain involved in rolling out GDPR into your organisation as one thing is pretty sure – people, in general, don't like change!

Appoint a Data Protection Officer (DPO)

If you are reading this, it is possible you have been nominated, or perhaps 'volunteered', to own Data Protection within your organisation, but it is equally plausible you are an independent project manager or consultant who is working with an organisation to help get them compliant with the Regulation. In any case, you need to consider if your organisation needs to appoint a Data Protection Officer formally. Appointing a Data Protection Officer is not mandatory unless you fall into one of the following three categories:

1. the processing is carried out by a public authority or body, except for courts acting in their judicial capacity;
2. the core activities of the Controller or the Processor consist of processing operations which, by virtue of their nature, their scope and/or their purposes, require regular and systematic monitoring of Data Subjects on a large scale; or
3. the core activities of the Controller or the Processor consist of processing on a large scale of special categories of data pursuant to GDPR Article 9 and personal data relating to criminal convictions and offences referred to in GDPR Article 10.

Even if you do not fall into one of the above categories, you may find it is worth appointing a DPO to ensure your organisation remains compliant. We will discuss the DPO role in more detail in Chapter 05 so for now, let's park the concept.

A Project Approach

I recommend taking a project approach. You may want to look at conducting a primary gap analysis too. While project management is outside the scope of this book, you should consider using a methodology such as PRINCE2[29] or PMBOK[30]. I will be honest, unless you are going to use AGILE properly I would stay clear. It is not a criticism of the methodology but more to do with the way I have seen it implemented where it is often thought of a methodology whereby you do not have to write anything down. In most cases, GDPR is going to require that organisations maintain good and accurate records of processing activities so it is best to start off on the right foot. If your organisation does have a preferred methodology, you should arrange a meeting with whoever runs your Project Management Office (PMO).

A GDPR project is going to require resources from all over the business so if you are not an experienced Project Manager you may try and plan out your project in isolation. It is imperative to understand the 'Change' burden – that is all the different programmes and projects going on in your organisation – as you will need to factor this into your planning. Another aspect people often forget to factor into their project plans are holidays, and IT change freezes – try not to plan your milestones to coincide with month end accounting deadlines or half-term. A PMO may also provide you with a Programme or Project Manager (depending on the size of your organisation) at best or, at the very minimum the project management templates you will need to keep track of your implementation and progress. If you are not tied to a specific methodology, and you do not want to go down the route of a formal methodology such as PRINCE2 or PMBOK then I would recommend at a minimum, you maintain the following project artefacts:

1. Business Case
2. Project Initiation Document (PID)
3. Project Plan
4. Communication Plan
5. Risk Register
6. Progress Report
7. Budget
8. Project Handover & Lessons Learned Report

There are plenty of useful websites on the Internet where you can download templates of the above artefacts. Google is your friend! As with all projects, it is absolutely critical to have a Project Sponsor (called the Executive in PRINCE2) who is ultimately responsible for the business benefits of the GDPR implementation. This person is likely to be at the highest level of management and must be able to exert influence on the entire business and, quite importantly, sign the cheques! Try your best to keep the Sponsor informed and engaged, have regular catch-ups and don't be afraid to ask for what you need!

No (Wo)man is an Island

The next piece of advice I can provide is: do not try and do this alone! I have seen this so many times whereby a Practitioner sets up an entire programme, creates bespoke tools and templates and then goes out to the business requesting they provide reams upon reams of paperwork. Had the Practitioner involved others, they would have found information is either already available or could be collected as part of another initiative. Now many challenges can get in the way of what seems like a mutually beneficial approach to getting things done such as internal politics, competing commitments and the ever-present question: Who is going to pay for this?

---

[29] PRINCE2: Projects in Controlled Environments, AXELOS
[30] PMBOK: Project Management Book of Knowledge, PMI

You are best placed to understand how to get things done in your organisation, but it never hurts to find out what other people are doing. As you work through the requirements of GDPR, it should become clear there are concepts which you should already be familiar. Incident Management is a case in point. I would be astonished if your organisation does not have something in place, so don't try and reinvent the wheel (not pointing any fingers external consultants) but instead integrate GDPR into the existing processes already *in situ*.

Management Systems & Standards

While talking to your colleagues, you may become aware of Management Systems, ideally based on a recognised standard, already operating within your organisation. I strongly recommend seeking to integrate your Data Protection programme with such appropriate Management Systems as it should mean a lot less bureaucracy and complexity for both you and your business units. Common Management Systems which may already be in place in your organisations are:

1. ISO 27001 (or equivalent): Information Security Management System (ISMS)
2. ISO 22301 (or equivalent): Business Continuity Management System (BCMS)
3. ISO 9001 (or equivalent): Quality Management System (QMS)
4. ISO 14001 (or equivalent): Environmental Management System (EMS)

If you do not have any of the above, you may wish to consider working towards implementing BS10012:2017 Personal Information Management System (PIMS), published by the British Standards Institute (BSI). If you have ISO 27001 and 9000, however, to limit the compliance burden, I may be worth considering expanding the scope of those programmes instead of implementing an entirely new standard. It's important to be aware ISO 27001 does not cover all aspects of GDPR, and an organisation cannot rely solely on ISO 27001 compliance/certification (but it will definitely help). The reason why I like standards is that, when executed well, they make the whole process of managing an ongoing, risk-based programme such as GDPR, a lot more straightforward. Using a recognised and commonly used standard provides the following advantages:

1. Lots of online support, tools and templates from those who have already implemented the standard.
2. The benefit of learning from others' lessons learned
3. A framework which can support audits
4. A framework which can support due-diligence activities
5. A structure which can be used to show you have been independently assessed and certified to customers and clients
6. A framework you can use to evaluate your supply chain for cultural and operational fit.

Ultimately, though, it will be a decision you will need to take while being mindful of your organisation's culture and appetite for risk – but in the long run, I believe it is well worth the effort.

Data is King!

I cannot stress this part enough – if the data is already available in a searchable form do not go and ask a human to fill out a spreadsheet with the same data. It is a sure fire way to get people's backs up and more importantly will end up being woefully inaccurate. It may be the cynic in me, but some people will not see the value in what you are trying to achieve and will be obstructive. More commonly, there will be people who are just incredibly busy with their day-to-day work and will want to prioritise their regular tasks over what they see as 'side-of-desk' activities. This is just the way of things, so it is imperative to demonstrate you are not asking people to do things that are a waste of their time. Consider the following:

1. Try not to ask departments to provide lists of Data Sources if your organisation maintains a Configuration Management Database or similar record of systems within your organisation
2. Try not to ask departments for a list of their Third Parties when it is highly likely your organisation's accounts department will have a data source for invoicing purposes.
3. Try not to ask departments, which third parties they send personal data to if you have a Data Leakage Prevention (DLP) tool which could be queried
4. Try not to ask what personal data is stored on file systems when this can be queried using relatively inexpensive tools.

Sometimes, however, when implementing regulatory programmes such as GDPR you may be told there is no budget and that can be why Practitioners end up resorting to asking people to fill in spreadsheets. Before reaching for Excel though, it is worth noting Article 38 (2) states:

'The Controller and Processor shall support the data protection officer in performing the tasks referred to in Article 39 by providing resources necessary to carry out those tasks and access to personal data and processing operations.'

So it might be worth having this in mind when planning your implementation that you are allowed to ask for data...and it is much more likely to be accurate if it comes from a system of record than from the memory of an already busy employee. Even if you cannot get all of the data you need from a system of record it is still a great starting point as sometimes business units will not even realise they are still using a particular supplier – you never know you might save someone some money!

The 12 (initial) Steps to Compliance

Not to be confused with the 12 steps produced by the UK Information Commissioner's Office[31] the 12 steps issued by the Irish Data Protection Commissioner[32] recommends steps organisations should take to prepare for GDPR. While the ICO's 12 steps are also a useful guide, the Irish 12 steps are, in the author's humble opinion, better. In either case, both are a great starting point for a Practitioner to flesh out a skeleton plan. The Irish DPA's 12 steps are as follows:

1. <u>Become Aware</u>: Review and enhance your organisation's risk management processes – identify problem areas now. Chapter 06 discusses this step in more detail.

2. <u>Become Accountable</u>: Make an inventory of all personal data you hold. Why do you hold it? Do you still need it? Is it safe? Chapter 08 discusses this step in more detail.

3. <u>How will Access Requests change</u>: Plan how you will handle requests within the new timescales – requests must be dealt with within one month. Chapter 13 discusses this step in more detail.

4. <u>Personal Privacy Rights</u>: Ensure your procedures cover all the rights individuals are entitled to, including deletion and data portability. Chapter 07 discusses this step in more detail.

5. <u>Communicating with Staff and Service Users</u>: Review all your data privacy notices and make sure you keep service users fully informed about how you use their data. Chapter 07 discusses this step in more detail.

---

[31] Information Commissioner's Office. Preparing for the General Data Protection Regulation – ICO V2.0 20170525, licensed under the OGL.
[32] The GDPR and You: Preparing for 2018, Irish Data Protection Commissioner

THE ULTIMATE GDPR PRACTITIONER GUIDE

6. <u>What we mean when we talk about a 'Legal Basis'</u>: Are you relying on consent, legitimate interests or a legal enactment to collect and process the data? Do you meet the standards of the GDPR? Chapter 02 discusses this step in more detail.

7. <u>Using Customer Consent as grounds to process data</u>: Review how you seek, obtain and record consent, and whether you need to make any changes to be GDPR ready. Chapter 02 discusses this step in more detail.

8. <u>Processing Children's Data</u>: Do you have adequate systems in place to verify individual ages and gather consent from guardians? Chapter 02 discusses this step in more detail.

9. <u>Data Protection Impact Assessments (DPIA) and Data Protection by Design and Default</u>: Data privacy needs to be at the heart of all future projects. Chapter 09 discusses this step in more detail.

10. <u>Reporting Data Breaches</u>: Are you ready for mandatory breach reporting? Make sure you have the procedures in place to detect, report and investigate a data breach. Chapter 12 discusses this step in more detail.

11. <u>Data Protection Officers</u>: Will you be required to designate a DPO? Make sure that it's someone who has the knowledge, support and authority to do the job effectively. Chapter 05 discusses this step in more detail.

12. <u>International Organisations and the GDPR</u>: The GDPR includes a 'one-stop-shop' provision which will assist those data controllers whose companies operate in many member states. Identify where your Main Establishment is located in the EU in order to identify your Lead Supervisory Authority. Chapter 15 discusses this step in more detail.

So, quite a few things to consider. What I would recommend is before fleshing out your skeleton plan, consider using these 12 steps to assess your organisation's current data protection capability in the form of a Gap Analysis and then prioritising the areas where you feel you have the most significant gaps. It is common to try and go first for the 'low-hanging fruit' as it feels like you are making some progress relatively quickly. Beware racking up the quick wins doesn't give you a false sense of comfort. It is essential to get commitment for some of the 'big ticket' items within the programme where it will take time to implement – Data Discovery in terms of Subject Access Requests or implementing systems changes to support just in time privacy notices or data portability are good examples of line items in a privacy programme which may take a lot longer, and cost more, to get over the line.

4. GDPR PRINCIPLES & DATA SUBJECTS' RIGHTS

In order to ensure those organisations entrusted with Personal and Sensitive Data of European Union Data Subjects, the drafters of the General Data Protection Regulation have defined the fundamental principles which organisations must apply when processing data. These six principles enshrine into law how Data Controllers and Processors must treat the Personal and Sensitive Data they process. Data Protection Regulation is not just about protecting Personal and Sensitive Data, but ensuring the rights and freedoms of the Data Subjects themselves. In this chapter we will explore the fundamental principles of GDPR and rights GDPR affords to EU Natural Persons.

The Six Principles

The GDPR has six fundamental principles which underpin how a person or organisation controlling or processing personal data must act.

The principles are:

1. **Processed lawfully**, fairly and in a transparent manner
2. **Collected** for specified, explicit and legitimate purposes
3. **Adequate**, relevant and limited to what is necessary
4. **Accurate** and, where necessary, kept up to date
5. **Retained** only for as long as necessary
6. **Processed securely**, in an appropriate manner to maintain security

Whilst the principles are listed in GDPR order, to remember the principles, you can use the mnemonic **CARPPA** (pronounced: *'Carp-Pa'*) remembering both Ps stand for Processed. Processed lawfully and processed securely. What links these principles together is **accountability**. Your organisation is accountable for ensuring processing activities are conducted in a manner that honours the six principles. Let's look at the six principles in a bit more detail.

Collected for specified, explicit and legitimate purposes: when an organisation collects personal or sensitive data, even if that information is not obtained directly from a Data Subject, or collected without the conscious knowledge of the Data Subject, it must be for a legitimate process. An organisation must not collect personal data stating the data will be used for one purpose and then use that information for another without informing the Data Subject.

Example: XYZ Widgets Ltd collects personal data from users on its website stating the purpose is to enable users to be authenticated to their secure portal. This same data is then used by the marketing department to profile site visitors to target advertising across many different websites. XYZ Widgets Ltd did not explicitly inform Data Subject their data would be used for this purpose.

In this example, XYZ Widgets Ltd is not adhering to this GDPR principle as they have not specifically and explicitly informed the Data Subject how their personal data would be used.

Accurate and, where necessary, kept up to date: organisations must ensure the data they process is correct. Organisations must also be mindful this information will include items relating to the Data Subject too. In some cases, information will change over time too, and so it will be incumbent upon an organisation to make sure personal data is maintained. In terms of inaccurate information, this must be either rectified or erased.

Example: Tarquin's Hot Tub Emporium maintains a list of customers' addresses. The address list is for the specified purpose of sending out a quarterly catalogue detailing new Hot Tub models. Customers can update their details through an online portal however the mailing list is a stored on a separate spreadsheet which is updated before the quarterly catalogue publication. In the last quarter, 30 customers updated their address details and 20 updated their contact preferences stating they now only wished to receive the electronic version of the catalogue via email. Due to a change of staff, the spreadsheet was not updated, and those 30 customers missed out on their catalogue with a further 20 receiving a physical version of the catalogue they did not want.

Tarquin's Hot Tub Emporium failed to adhere to this GDPR principle because they did not keep the personal data is stored accurately in all the places it is processed.

Retained only for as long as necessary: organisations are only permitted to keep information while it is needed to fulfil the legitimate processing activities. When data is no longer required it should be securely deleted.

Example: Zebrowski Digital Inc. is a large US multinational company with over 50,000 employees. In the UK it has 20% of it workforces. Eight years ago it went through a significant restructuring in its London office, cutting the workforce by 16%. An ex-employee who was made redundant at the time made a Subject Access Request and was provided with detailed information about her employment up until she left.

Zebrowski Digital Inc. may be breaking this GDPR principle as, under UK Law, employment records only need to be retained for six years[33]. There may, however, be legitimate reasons to hold this information for a more extended period.

Processed lawfully, fairly and in a transparent manner: organisations must ensure their processing activities are lawful and that they have informed Data Subjects how personal and sensitive data is processed. As discussed in Chapter 2 there are a number of mechanisms in which to determine whether processing is lawful. The most common method to demonstrate transparency is through a privacy notice which is discussed in Chapter 07.

Example: Gluhwein Traumhaft GmbH has purchased an email list from a data broker and has used this list to send unsolicited emails about their amazing line of mulled wines to millions of EU Data Subjects. The emails did not provide a mechanism for recipients to remove themselves from receiving future emails.

Gluhwein Traumhaft GmbH has failed to adhere to this GDPR principle because the Data Subjects are unlikely to have provided their consent to be subjected to such marketing emails. Also, consent must be as easy to withdraw as it is given.

Processed securely, in an appropriate manner to maintain security: personal and sensitive data must be secured during all stages of the processing life-cycle. Data must be collected securely and also securely destroyed when no longer required.

Example: Adolfo Consigliere Bank PLC has decided to outsource its operations function to a Third Party in India. To support a proof of concept, the Bank has transferred its entire customer relationship management database via FTP to the outsourced service provider's Hyderabad office. At this stage, no contractual arrangements have been agreed or signed.

Adolfo Consigliere Bank PLC are violating this GDPR principle in a number of ways. Firstly, FTP is an insecure file transfer protocol. Secondly, there are no contractual arrangements in place between the Controller and Processor. Thirdly, there would be no legitimate reason to send the entire database across to India. Finally, while this is not necessarily a security issue per se, India is considered a Third Country and thus not deemed to have adequate safeguards in place to protect EU Data Subjects.

---

[33] Section 5, Limitation Act 1980

Adequate, relevant and limited to what is necessary: organisations must not ask Data Subjects for more of their personal data than is required to provide the service to which the Data Subject has provided consent (or the Controller has another lawful reason for processing). Organisations cannot ask Data Subjects for personal or sensitive information 'just-in-case' it may be needed for some currently unknown processing activity or because it may become more challenging to gain the information at a later date. Remember the key to meeting this principle is data minimisation.

Example: Narau and Davidson Holdings Ltd ask Data Subjects to provide their DoB, a copy of their Passport and a recent utility bill in order satisfy their Anti-Money Laundering (AML) compliance obligations.

While this information is personal data and collection may seem excessive, it is adequate, relevant and limited to the minimum required to comply with the organisation's other regulatory requirements. Had the organisation requested multiple forms of Identification or address verification, such a request would have violated this GDPR principle.

The examples in this section should hopefully give you an idea of the scenarios you may face within your organisation. The key questions you will need to keep asking are:

1. Why are we collecting this data?
2. Is the processing lawful?
3. Have we been transparent about our processing activities?
4. Is our processing secure?
5. Are we collecting more data than we need?
6. Do we still need to hold this data? Are we still permitted to hold this data?

If the answers to these questions are giving you comfort your organisation is upholding Data Subjects' rights, you are already in a good place. If not, read on!

The Eight Rights

A Natural Person or Data Subject has the following rights which must be upheld when processing their personal data. A breach of these rights can result in the maximum fine

The rights are:

1. The right to be **Informed**
2. The right of **Access**
3. The right to **Rectification**
4. The right to **Erasure**
5. The right to **Restrict** processing
6. The right to data **Portability**
7. The right to **Object**
8. Rights in relation to automated decision making and **Profiling**

Whilst the rights are listed in the order as per GDPR, to remember the rights, you can use the mnemonic **PREPAROI** (pronounced: *'prep-ah-roy'*). There are also four other rights we will discuss in this chapter which relate to how a Data Subject can seek redress where the above rights have been violated. These are the right to lodge a complaint, the right to an effective judicial remedy against a Supervisory authority. The same right [to effective judicial remedy] against a Controller or Processor and the right to compensation and liability. In the following sections, we will look at these rights in more detail

The Right to Data Portability: This is a new right under GDPR and requires an organisation to provide a Data Subject with their data in a 'commonly used and machine-readable format' so they can transfer that data to another organisation in a way which isn't too onerous to upload the data. The most common way is a Comma Separated Values (or CSV) file, but your industry may have a particular standard which could also be used – the main thing to remember is you cannot use a proprietary format that would mean the Data Subject would have to spend money to convert. Now there are a couple of limitations in regards to this right you should be aware. The right only applies to data provided by the Data Subject to a Controller; where the processing is based on consent or a contract and when the processing is automated. If the data does not fall into those categories, then the data portability right does not apply.

> **EXAMPLE: Sarah has been with her electricity provider over a year and wants to provide her meter readings to a comparison site to compare deals with other providers. As Sarah provided the meter readings, her right to portability means the current provider must give her the readings in a commonly used machine-readable form such as a CSV file.**

The Right to Rectification: If a Data Subject becomes aware of a mistake within the processed data, they have the right to have that data corrected. These mistakes could be something like an error in a database inadvertently recording a male person's gender as female, but it could be over time a person's address is no longer correct because they have moved. It could also be incorrect Next of Kin information in an HR system or perhaps an old CV. In any case, where the personal data is inaccurate you must have a process in place to correct the information and let the Data Subject know it has been corrected.

> **EXAMPLE: Jenni works in a large healthcare provider who uses an outsourced service provider for payroll. Part of their service is to post out payslips to employee's home addresses. Jenni has recently moved home, however, while she has updated her address in the HR system, an update has not been provided to the Payroll provider. Jenni has a right to have this information rectified, so her payslips do not get sent to her old home address.**

A word of caution, when making any corrections to personal data, it is essential to verify the person's identity. There is a risk a request to correct could be fraudulent in an attempt to steal a person's identity. It should also be noted any corrections must be promulgated to all the sources of data and this includes Third Parties too.

The Right to Erasure: This is another new right under GDPR. It requires organisations under certain conditions to erase data about a Data Subject. There are a few reasons why a request for data to be erased is made, it could be the processing activity has concluded (e.g. An unsuccessful application to a University) or the Data Subject withdraws consent. Additionally, in the case of a person turning 18 years of age, they have special rights to have their data erased. This latter right has been enshrined in law because it has been felt a child may not have fully understood what they agreed to when they initially provided their personal data. As mentioned, the right to erasure is only under certain circumstances and will need to be balanced against other legislation which requires data to be retained for a specified period.

> **EXAMPLE: Amber was arrested and found guilty of murdering her husband. This case was high profile and courted a lot of media attention. Shortly after the trial, new evidence came to light which proved Amber's innocence, and she was exonerated. Unfortunately, searching Amber's name online, all the original trial news articles appear. Amber has the right for search engines to 'forget' these articles, so they no longer appear in searches for Amber.**

Rights in Relation to Automated Decision Making and Profiling: Profiling, or automated decision making, is the process whereby personal data is used to evaluate certain personal aspects relating to a Natural Person. In particular, to analyse or predict aspects concerning that Natural Person's performance at work, economic situation, health, personal preferences, interests, reliability, behaviour, location or movements. There are many examples of the use of profiling such as Insurance in all its forms where you input your details, and an algorithm determines how much your premium should be or whether you will be insured at all. Loan and Mortgage applications can operate similarly, and there are also systems when you apply for a job that will analyse your CV and score the content based on keywords or in more advanced cases, the reputation of the university you went to or companies you have previously been employed. The challenge with data provided by humans is that spelling and formatting can lead to a system misinterpreting key information. These errors could lead to above excessive insurance premiums, mortgages to be denied or a situation where the perfect candidate for a job application is filtered out because they have used the UK English spelling of a word when the system is looking for the American spelling of the word. In cases like the ones described above, there are requirements under GDPR. The first is you must inform the Data Subject how their data will be used (e.g. This system will use the information you provide and, other information sources available, to automate the decision-making process to determine if you are eligible for a Credit Card). You must also inform them of their rights

THE ULTIMATE GDPR PRACTITIONER GUIDE

In regards having the automated process carried out manually. An excellent way to inform about the manual processing right while maintaining a good user experience would be to have information posted in line with the decision so, if a person is unhappy with the automated decision, they know their options – and everyone else, who are already happy to continue, can then choose to continue. Remember, even if someone is satisfied with the decision you must still inform them of his or her right to have the decision-making process be conducted manually. To fulfil a request to process an automated decision manually, a documented process for manual processing is highly recommended. The manual process mirroring your automated process must be documented so if required you can demonstrate that your process is consistent, repeatable and verifiable. It is also highly recommended your documentation contains explanations of any mathematical scoring models used, and a template report to provide to the Data Subject detailing the results of the manual decision-making process. It is useful if you can ascertain readily which aspect of the automated process has caused a decision to be rejected. A word of caution: identify the problem area of a process should not be used as a shortcut to completing the whole decision-making process as there may be other errors which may be within tolerance in isolation, but could still have an effect on the final decision.

> **EXAMPLE: Diane has been wanting to upgrade her car for some years and has set her heart on a brand new sporty convertible. Diane applies for finance at the dealership and finds the automated loan application declines her on the basis it has assessed her credit score to be too low. Diane has the right to have the application processed manually. During the manual process, a flaw in the scoring mechanism was identified, which had led to Diane's application being declined.**

The Right of Access: This is not a new right under GDPR, as it formed part of the 1995 Directive, but the right has been strengthened. One of the guiding principles is transparency, and so organisations will now have an increased burden regarding letting Data Subjects know what they are doing with their data, and how they are protecting a Data Subject's rights. The primary mechanism to gain access under GDPR is the Subject Access Request (SAR) discussed in Chapter 13 however much can be achieved through privacy notices and privacy by design techniques.

Three of the key changes organisations must be aware. Organisations are no longer permitted (in most cases) to charge. The deadline to respond is now 30 days, down from 40 days. If a Data Subject requests in electronic form[34] (e.g. by email or Twitter), an organisation must respond electronically. Gone are the days of requesting Data Subjects send in a cheque by snail mail and then sending all their data in paper form!

> **EXAMPLE: Julia has been offered a job subject to the provision of satisfactory references. After providing references, Julia is informed the vetting was not satisfactory, and therefore the job offer is rescinded. Julia makes a subject access request to see the information in the reference but is told this information has been provided confidentially. Julia then makes a subject access request to each of the referees and identifies information in one reference relates to a different employee of the same name – which was not so flattering. Julia requests this data be corrected and the new employer reinstates the offer.**

---

[34] Article 15(3): Right of access by the Data Subject

The Right to Restrict Processing: This is a new right under GDPR and basically, requires an organisation to stop processing a person's data – except storing the data. This right could mean if a Data Subject's personal data is used to create a profile of your customer base, an organisation would be required to remove the data relating to the Data Subject from your model or the system creating the model.

> **EXAMPLE: Neville has been informed by a hiring manager a recruitment agency has sent the hiring manager Neville's CV as part of a 'fishing' expedition to see if the hiring manager was interested in Neville as a candidate. Neville has not provided his consent for the recruitment agency to process his personal data in this way. As the processing is unlawful (there is no consent), Neville has the right to restrict this processing.**

If you have a Direct Marketing tool which sends out mail shots to people and a Data Subject requested this processing be stopped, again you would be required to comply. Another issue you may need to consider is the use of third parties to carry out processing activities or where you have passed data to a third party as part of a legal agreement. In both these cases, you would be responsible for making sure the third parties comply with the request and cease processing.

The Right to Object: This is not a new right under GDPR as it was part of the 1995 Directive. It has however been transposed into the new Regulation and gives the Data Subject more or less the same power to object to processing which is considered lawful (so slightly different to the right to restrict processing). In the case where the right to object is exercised, the Controller will in most cases need to demonstrate why their need to process the information is greater than the right of the Data Subject to have the processing activity stopped.

> **EXAMPLE: An ex-girlfriend is stalking Nick. He has moved house and no longer wishes to be on the public version of the electoral roll. Nick may be able to use his right to object to having his name removed, even though his inclusion in the roll would be considered lawful processing.**

The Right to be Informed: while this is not a new right, it has been reinforced under GDPR. Controller organisations must provide Data Subjects with information about data processing activities and how they can exercise their rights. Controllers must give the details of their Data Protection Officer (if applicable). If the organisation is transferring personal data to a Third Country, they must also provide information as to the methods used to safeguard data should there not be an adequacy decision by the European Commission.

Third Country transfers will be discussed in more detail in Chapter 15. Under GDPR, if the information has not been provided directly from the Data Subject a Controller now has an obligation to provide the Data Subject with certain information. The Data subject must be informed, at the latest, within one month of receiving the data. If not in one month, in the first communication or, if the data is likely to be passed on to another party - whichever is first.

> **EXAMPLE: Danielle has applied for a job at a hospital via a jobs board. A recruitment agency has received her CV and has shortlisted her to onward submission to the hiring manager at the hospital. At each stage of this recruitment process where data is transferred from one controller to another, the Data Subject has a right to be informed. The recruitment agency must notify the candidate they are processing the candidate's personal data and before it is sent to the hospital. The hospital must also inform the candidate they are processing the personal data within one month or receipt. It is useful to note in this particular situation, even a CV without a name or contact information is still considered personal information as a person's employment history is typically unique enough to identify a person by cross-referencing with publically available information such as that published on sites like LinkedIn. Removing names and contact information to avoid the requirement to inform Data Subjects would not be sufficient.**

Additional Rights: the eight rights discussed so far are the rights we should expect to have upheld during our day-to-day dealings with an organisation processing our personal data. Sometimes, however, organisations may not be operating as well as we would expect. In such cases, Data Subjects have some options at their disposal to get things back on track.

> **EXAMPLE: DeerStalker & Harris Ltd send daily direct marketing emails to Dafydd, even after he has withdrawn consent and despite Dafydd making multiple complaints about the continued marketing emails. Dafydd has a right to complain to the Supervisory Authority (SA) as he considers this processing to be unlawful.**
>
> **In this case, the SA investigated the complaint and determined the Controller was in breach of GDPR and PECR. The SA subsequently issued an administrative fine to the sum of £50,000 to the offending Controller and required the Controller to take some corrective actions to prevent a repeat of the incident. At appropriate stages the SA kept Dafydd informed about the investigation and its outcome.**

If you have exhausted your primary rights (e.g. by withdrawing consent or requesting processing be restricted or objecting to a lawful processing activity), a Data Subject also has the right to complain to the Supervisory Authority[35]. The Supervisory Authority is required to investigate, keep the complainant informed and ultimately inform the complainant of the outcome of their complaint. If a Data Subject does not think the Supervisory Authority's legally binding decision is correct or fair, the Data Subject has the right to take the Supervisory Authority to court to seek a judicial remedy[36]. Such action can take a data protection issue all the way up to the (European) Court of Justice.

---

[35] Article 77: Right to lodge a complaint with a supervisory authority
[36] Article 78: Right to an effective judicial remedy against a supervisory authority

In addition to the supervisory authority route, a Data Subject can take Controllers and Processors directly to court to seek a judicial remedy[37]Judicial remedy against a Controller is not a new right, but with the strengthening of a Data Subject's rights, there is likely to be an increase – at least in the short term – in legal action against organisations who have failed to prepare. The judicial remedy could include: legally compelling an organisation to comply with a Data Subject's request, payment of compensation for damages (including emotional distress!). If you are reading this book, I am sure you will want to avoid a situation ending up in court so if you are ready, onwards to the Practitioner section!

DID YOU KNOW: A complainant does not necessarily need to make a complaint to the Supervisory Authority in their Member State. A complainant could complain to the Supervisory Authority any Member State.

For example, in the case of Maximillian Schrems v Data Protection Commissioner. The plaintiff was an Austrian citizen but lodged a complaint with the Irish Supervisory Authority against the Irish subsidiary or an American multinational. As you can see, it can get quite complicated!

If you have exhausted your primary rights (e.g. by withdrawing consent or requesting processing be restricted or objecting to a lawful processing activity), a Data Subject also has the right to complain to the Supervisory Authority[38]. The Supervisory Authority is required to investigate, keep the complainant informed and ultimately inform the complainant of the outcome of their complaint. If a Data Subject does not think the Supervisory Authority's legally binding decision is correct or fair, the Data Subject has the right to take the Supervisory Authority to court to seek a judicial remedy[39]. Such action can take a data protection issue all the way up to the (European) Court of Justice. In addition to the Supervisory Authority route, a Data Subject can take Controllers and Processors directly to court to seek a judicial remedy[40]Judicial remedy against a Controller is not a new right, but with the strengthening of a Data Subject's rights, there is likely to be an increase – at least in the short term – in legal action against organisations who have failed to prepare. The judicial remedy could include: legally compelling an organisation to comply with a Data Subject's request or payment of compensation for damages (including emotional distress!). If you are reading this book, I am sure you will want to avoid a situation unnecessarily ending up in court so if you are ready, onwards to the Practitioner section!

---

[37] Article 79: Right to an effective judicial remedy against a controller or processor
[38] Article 77: Right to lodge a complaint with a supervisory authority
[39] Article 78: Right to an effective judicial remedy against a supervisory authority
[40] Article 79: Right to an effective judicial remedy against a controller or processor

5. THE DATA PROTECTION OFFICER (DPO)

GDPR is not going to run itself in an organisation – someone is going to have to oversee the day-to-day governance activities. Someone needs to make sure everyone from the most junior data Processor to the most senior manager understands and, more importantly, acts in a manner commensurate with his or her obligations under the regulation. This person is the Data Protection Officer. In the original 1995 Directive this role was known as the Data Protection Official, and as we had discussed before as the 1995 text was a Directive, Member States had a lot more flexibility in what they included in the local legislation, and many countries chose not to codify the role. For example, in Germany, the Data Protection Official has been a mandatory post since 2001 and is included in the Bundesdatenschutzgesetz[41] but in the UK Data Protection Act 1998 the role is not included in the text. GDPR seeks to standardise the approach, and the role of Data Protection Officer is now universal across the EU and in certain situations it will be mandatory to appoint a DPO. In this chapter, we will look at the role and qualities of a DPO and also discuss how the position could be implemented in your organisation.

What is the DPO?

The Data Protection Officer is a person appointed to oversee a Data Controller or Data Processor and their activities pertaining to the processing of personal data of EU Data Subjects. It is an exciting and challenging role because the DPO is appointed with the primary aim of protecting the interests of Data Subjects. For those of you who have worked in corporate environments, you are no doubt aware this is likely to lead to interesting and potentially tricky conversations due to the nature data is sometimes used. A DPO must be independent and neutral, having a strong knowledge of Data Protection law and associated practices (e.g. Privacy by Design, Data Protection Impact Assessments or Subject Access Requests). If you have already appointed a Data Protection based on the current data protection requirements, a review of the current incumbent is recommended as GDPR prohibits those holding conflicting roles from also holding the role of Data Protection Officer. Having Data Protection knowledge is however not enough. The DPO should also have contextual expertise in regards to the industry or sector they operate. If a DPO works in a regulated industry such as Financial Services, then knowledge of other relevant regulation such as that issued in the UK by the FCA[42] or in Spain by the CNMV[43] will also be essential to know. A good example would be in relation to outsourcing discussed in Chapter 14 where the GDPR requires specific criteria to be in place, and FCA Handbook SYSC 8.1 'General Outsourcing Requirements' includes requirements too. These requirements will in many

---

[41] Germany's Federal Data Protection Act
[42] Financial Conduct Authority (FCA)
[43] Comisión Nacional del Mercado de Valores (CNMV)

cases intersect so one will need to be mindful of both. The Data Protection Officer will not only require knowledge of DP law and sector-specific expertise but will also need a high level of personal integrity and professional ethics. As mentioned earlier the DPO is likely to have some challenging conversations with business units who will want to have a free reign to collect whatever data they want and use it however they please. It will be incumbent on the DPO to act as a trusted advisor who can balance the risks to the Data Subjects they are employed to protect and the needs of the organisation they are working within.

Do I need a DPO?

As first mentioned in Chapter 03, appointing a Data Protection Officer is only mandatory if you fall into one of the following three categories:

1. the processing is carried out by a public authority or body, except for courts acting in their judicial capacity;

2. the core activities of the Controller or the Processor consist of processing operations which, by virtue of their nature, their scope and/or their purposes, require regular and systematic monitoring of Data Subjects on a large scale; or
3. the core activities of the Controller or the Processor consist of processing on a large scale of special categories of data pursuant to GDPR Article 9 and personal data relating to criminal convictions and offences referred to in GDPR Article 10.

You may be wondering if you are part of a giant conglomerate or multinational whether you need a Data Protection Officer for each separate legal entity. The answer is no, provided the DPO is easily accessible to each of the entities and that they have the resources necessary to carry out those tasks and access to personal data and processing operations in each of the entities. You may also be wondering if anyone can be a Data Protection Officer. The answer is maybe. At the time of going to print, there is no specific qualification a DPO requires, before their appointment. That said organisations are supposed to appoint their DPO based on qualities such as a high level of integrity and professional ethics, an expert knowledge of Data Protection Law and associated practices and ability to fulfil the tasks laid out within Article 39 "Tasks of the Data Protection Officer". Organisations are also required to provide resources to support the maintenance of the DPO's expert knowledge – which may mean you could well be eligible to submit an expense claim for this very book...?

Tasks of the DPO?

As mentioned in the previous section, there are mandatory tasks laid out within the GDPR[44] which I shall expand. Firstly, the DPO is to inform and advise the Controller or the Processor and the employees who carry out processing of their obligations under this Regulation and other Union or Member State data protection provisions. You will note this is to 'inform and advise' and not 'do'. As mentioned earlier in this chapter, the DPO is a trusted advisor; it is the responsibility of the business units which are performing the processing activities to ensure their activities are compliant with the regulation. Business Units cannot absolve themselves of their duties or wait to be told what to do – they must actively seek the advice from the DPO. Secondly, the DPO is to monitor compliance with this Regulation, with other Union or Member State data protection provisions and with the policies of the Controller or Processor in relation to the protection of personal data, including the assignment of responsibilities, awareness-raising and training of staff involved in processing operations, and the related audits. What this means is the DPO will need to establish an awareness programme (See Chapter 06), a compliance monitoring programme and ensure there are risk-based, data protection themed audits included in the organisation's audit programme (See Chapter 07). Thirdly,

---

[44] Article 39 – Tasks of the Data Protection Officer

the DPO is to provide advice where requested as regards the Data Protection Impact Assessment (see Chapter 09) and monitor its performance. Again the key words here are 'provide advice' and not 'do' the DPIAs. While the should in the text means the person completing the DPIA does not have to ask for advice the spirit is they would. Advice does not necessarily mean direct consultation every time a DPIA is completed; it could be using an online portal where advice is recorded. Alternatively, an organisation may adopt the approach of requiring 'advice by exception' or adopt risk-based consultation rules within a Data Protection Policy (See Chapter 07). In regards to monitoring, this could be achieved in multiple ways such as incorporating a checkpoint within a project's lifecycle whereby the project involves Personal Data processing or, through a mandatory registration process or, through a sampling exercise where a percentage of DPIAs are reviewed.

Fourthly, the DPO is to cooperate with the Supervisory Authority. There many reasons why the DPO may need to consult with the Supervisory Authority, but in the context of cooperation, is most likely going to be in relation to a complaint or a data breach. GDPR[45] makes it a requirement to cooperate with the Supervisory Authority, and in these cases, a Data Protection Officer is going to rely heavily on the internal processes they have helped establish and the quality of record keeping (See Chapter 08) within their organisation. It will be essential to make this clear to senior management this documentation will be requested, and organisations will be required to provide this documentation to the Supervisory Authority. It will also be critical the DPO make it abundantly clear a failure to cooperate will lead to stricter enforcement action. Finally, the DPO is to act as the contact point for the Supervisory Authority on issues relating to processing, including prior consultation, and to consult, where appropriate, about any other matter. 'Any other matter' is a bit of a catch-all but essentially what this means is where there is a data protection issue, and the business needs clarity which the DPO is not able to provide, the DPO should get a definitive answer from the Supervisory Authority. The DPO is permitted to conduct other tasks within an organisation, but care must be taken to ensure there are no conflicts of interest.

> **EXAMPLE: It would be very difficult to justify appointing the Head of Marketing or Head of HR as a Data Protection Officer given their duties involve managing teams who process personal data on a daily basis. Both of these roles would have material conflicts of interest.**

Qualities of a DPO?

As discussed in the 'Do I need a DPO' section of this chapter, DPOs must have a high level of integrity and professional ethics. These qualities are essential as the DPO will have high levels of access to potentially significant volumes of personal data. During the course of their duties, the DPO may come across activities which fall significantly short of the minimum levels of compliance with GDPR. As such, the DPO will be required to do the right thing where others are not so willing. While these are the explicit qualities stated in the Regulation, it is useful to look at the other qualities a Data Protection Officer should possess or develop.

Resilient: A Data Protection Officer is likely to face a great deal of opposition from the business and affected support functions. This resistance is, predominantly, because people do not like change and, people very rarely like change which is perceived to restrict how they carry out their day-to-day activities. The Data Protection Officer may be seen as the personification of this negative change. Managers at all levels may also try to exert pressure on a DPO to come to a certain point of view which is diametrically opposed the protecting the rights of Data Subjects. In some cases, people may try and undermine the DPO. Business Units may opt to let the DPO know about activities right at the last

---

[45] Article 31 – Cooperation with the Supervisory Authority

minute and then complain the DPO is holding up business critical projects (this can be common in projects already late/over budget where the Project Manager is looking to shift blame away from their team). It will, therefore, be critical for a DPO to be resilient and be able to demonstrate where the true bottlenecks in delivery are located clearly.

Metrics-Driven: what can't be measured, can't be managed. Data Protection Officers are required to monitor a Controller or Processor's compliance with the Regulation and so will need to be able to identify appropriate metrics and ensure they are collected, analysed and reported to senior managers. A metrics-driven mindset goes hand-in-glove with resilience as it is a lot harder to challenge a DPOs assessment if it can be backed up with accurate data.

An Educator: In the next chapter we will look at awareness and, more specifically, awareness through learning. A DPO is the Data Protection Subject Matter Expert, so as part of the role, a DPO is highly likely to be involved in training employees. The DPO will need to be comfortable providing training and education in a workplace environment. The DPO will also need to provide coaching to senior management and mentorship to junior managers, helping them carry out their duties in a manner compliant with GDPR.

There are many other worthy traits one can look for in a DPO too. Confidence, communication skills, a person who is collaborative, and a person who is credible in their knowledge and application of GDPR. The one quality organisations must avoid is a 'Yes Man'. GDPR is explicit that the Data Protection Officer is not accountable for GDPR failings. The Controller or Processor is accountable.

Relationship with the Supervisory Authority

The Data Protection Officer is the conduit between the Controller (or Processor) and the Supervisory Authority. There following are the most likely times when the DPO and the SA may interact:

1. Requesting guidance or clarification on an aspect of GDPR
2. Reading recent decision notices issued by the SA
3. Reading current guidance material published by the SA
4. Consulting on a High-Risk Data Protection Impact Assessment
5. Notification of a security breach
6. Supporting the investigation and resolution of Data Subject complaints
7. Supporting SA initiated Data Protection Audits
8. Ensuring SA required corrective action is implemented within mandated timeframes

For those of you who have held the role of Data Protection Officer under the 1995 Directive, A Data Controller was required to send a Supervisor Authority a set of 'registrable particulars' and a Fee. Under GDPR you are no longer required to notify the Supervisory Authority. The shrewd amongst you may be thinking that means I do not have to maintain the set of particulars OR pay a registration fee. Sadly, you would be wrong on both fronts. While you do not need to send the registrable particulars to the SA, the DPO must still maintain the information within your organisation and make it available to the Supervisory Authority is requested. As for the fee, well, while it may be absent from GDPR, the Supervisory Authorities still require funding so expect it to be included in a different piece of local legislation in your Member State. In the UK, for example, the requirement to pay a fee is included in the Digital Economy Act 2017[46].

---

[46] Digital Economy Act: Section 108. Regulations about charges payable to the Information Commissioner

As an example of the likely fees, your organisation may be required to pay below is a table showing the fees proposed (accurate at the time of publishing) in the UK, it is useful to note, there is an additional fee for those companies involved in direct marketing.

Tier	Description	Fee
Tier 1: Small and medium firms that do not process large volumes of data*	Staff headcount below 250; and Turnover below £50M pa; and Number of records processed under 10,000	Up to £55
Tier 2: Small and medium firms that process large volumes of data*	Staff headcount below 250; and Turnover below £50M pa; and Number of records processed above 10,000	Up to £80
Tier 3: Large businesses*	Staff headcount above 250; and Turnover above £50M pa	Up to £1000
Direct marketing top up	Organisations that carry out electronic marketing activities as part of their business.	£20

ICO Proposed Fee Structure

*Public Authorities should categorise themselves according to staff headcount and number of records only.

A Protected Species

The consensus is the Data Protection Officer will not be considered personally responsible[47] for non-compliance, and GDPR states the DPO: shall not be dismissed or penalised by the Controller or the Processor for performing his tasks. As such the Data Protection Officer is legally protected from those, who may not want to take Data Protection seriously. It is not yet clear how these protections will work in practice across every Member State however given there is a cooperation and consistency mechanism we may be able to draw upon those Member States who already enshrine protected status for their Data Protection Officials. In Germany, for example, section 4f of the Bundesdatenschutzgesetz it states:

"If a data protection official is to be appointed under sub-Section 1, then this appointment shall not be subject to termination unless there is reason for the Controller to terminate the appointment for just cause without complying with a notice period. After the data protection official has been removed from office, he or she cannot be terminated for a year following the end of the appointment unless the responsible body has just cause for termination without complying with a notice period."

Whether this is a model which will be applied universally is yet to be ironed out (and maybe something for an updated edition of this book). What is clear in the Regulation is that penalties shall be effective, proportionate and dissuasive, so it is assessed an organisation trying to impede, harass or punish their Data Protection Officer deliberately is likely to face a hefty penalty. In addition to penalties from the Supervisory Authority, the Data Protection Officer may also have additional protections under local employment legislation.

---

[47] Article 29 Data Protection Working Party: Guidelines on Data Protection Officers ('DPOs'), Revision 5 April 2017

Data Protection Officer as a Service (DPOaaS)

For those organisations that don't have the headroom to employ a Data Protection Officer or, for those organisations which cannot identify a person who doesn't have a conflict of interest (e.g. DPO tasks conflict with their day-to-day activities) then the Regulation does allow for a third party[48] to carry out the role of the Data Protection Officer. Should the Controller wish to employ a third party to perform the role or a Data Protection Officer, there must be a formal, written service contract. The term used to describe such a third party carrying out Data Protection Officer Roles is Data Protection Officer as a Service (DPOaaS) or may also be referred to as Data Protection as a Service (DPaaS). DPOaaS can be an extremely cost-effective way of managing Data Protection Risk, especially where retaining expertise in-house is going to be challenging. DPOaaS can also benefit an organisation in terms of getting access to tried and tested policies, procedures and methodologies. When looking at a DPOaaS, you must still go through the same due-diligence process as you would with any other potential Processor. Due-diligence will be discussed in more detail in Chapter 14, but in the meantime, some of the key items you should ask are:

1. How will the service provider fulfil the statutory duties of the DPO?
2. Will we have a dedicated DPO?
3. What additional services will the DPOaaS provide in addition to the statutory duties (e.g. Gap Analysis, Training)?
4. What tools will the DPOaaS provide the Controller to support service delivery? Are they compatible with existing tools?
5. What is the delivery model (in-house, remote, hybrid)?
6. What is the pricing model (fixed costs, variable costs)?
7. How elastic is the service model (e.g. can it cope with sharp spikes in activity say after a data breach)?
8. How will they report on the effectiveness of the service?

In addition to the pre-engagement questions, organisations should also consider the term of any arrangement and the cultural fit with your organisation. You should also be aware of hidden costs. For example, some DPOaaS providers may mandate the appointment of a dedicated internal Data Protection Representative, which in itself is reasonable, but then require attendance on their training courses at additional cost. If Organisations are not careful, they may find they are paying for a service and, at the same time, doing most of the work themselves! Whether you go out to tender or retain in-house expertise, GDPR is explicit, the Controller or Processor still owns the risk and will be accountable. It is therefore critical to make sure whichever option chosen, the Data Protection Officer is given sufficient resources to perform their tasks and Controller/Processor take the guidance provided by the role holder seriously.

---

[48] Article 37(6): Designation of the Data Protection Officer

PART I: THE ULTIMATE PRACTITIONER (IMPLEMENTATION)

6. AWARENESS

GDPR is going to affect people in different ways. In many cases, there are going to be competing commitments. A good example is where a Controller needs to find the right balance between those who view personal data as a commodity which can be monetized, and those who see personal data as sacrosanct. In this Chapter, we are going do a deep dive into how we create compelling awareness. We will examine different stakeholders to get a sense of how these various groups feel about GDPR. The analysis in this book will be generic, but I would encourage you to conduct a similar exercise within your organisation, tailoring the analysis accordingly. Once you have this analysis, it can be converted into a communication plan. This plan will be an invaluable tool, aiding Data Protection Practitioners in customising their GDPR programmes and in particular how the programme content is communicated efficaciously.

Stakeholder Analysis

A particularly useful way to analyse is to assign stakeholders into a power-impact grid, shown in the table below. This analysis enables you to identify stakeholders regarding interest (i.e. how much they want to know what you are doing) and influence (i.e. how much power they have to affect your programme). Once the type of stakeholder is identified, a strategy for keeping the stakeholder onside can be formulated. For example, a high impact, high influence stakeholder will need to be kept in the loop and positively engaged as they could cause significant disruption to a programme. However, in contrast, low power, low-interest stakeholder is someone who still needs to know what is going on but is likely only to require occasional contact. Before using the power-impact grid, a Practitioner must identify their stakeholders. I recommend listing all stakeholders, as many as you can think of and then getting others to provide their input too. It is common to feel 'such and such won't be interested' and then take a decision not to include this stakeholder in your grid. I would caution against this approach. Stakeholder positions in a power-impact grid can and do, change over time. A CFO who was initially disinterested could suddenly become very interested if a significant sum of money, say to implement new technology, is requested. A newly promoted stakeholder could also have increased influence and will now need to be engaged differently. As a result of the inevitability of such changes, the Practitioner must periodically review stakeholder analysis because knowing which stakeholders are likely to throw you curveballs will give you the best chance of heading off their concerns, ideally before they even realised they had an interest in the first place. So, let us have a look at some of the key stakeholders from the perspective of the Data Protection Practitioner, to give you a feel who will need occasional contact and who will need active engagement. Some people find it practical to look at stakeholders from the perspective of those internal to your organisation and those external, but I prefer to keep them all together because stakeholders interact and it is a lot easier to assess those dependencies if stakeholders are kept together.

		Interest	
		Low	High
Influence	High	Keep Satisfied	Actively Engaged
	Low	Occasionally Contact	Keep Informed

Power-Impact Grid, Office of Government Commerce, 2003

Data Subjects: Arguably, in terms of GDPR, the Data Subject is the most crucial Stakeholder. GDPR gives the Data Subject significantly more influence over how an organisation can process their data. It should be anticipated, given media attention surrounding the regulation, and recent data breaches, interest will be high - at least initially. When it becomes common knowledge the charges relating to Subject Access Requests have been removed, and that a request can now be made in electronic form[49], the interest of Data Subjects to find out what data organisations hold is assessed to be very high. Stakeholder Group: Actively Engaged.

Privacy Groups: Privacy Groups have been battling on behalf of Data Subjects for years to enhance data protection regulation. In some cases, privacy groups have supported plaintiffs via funding, legal advice, research and creating media awareness of a particular issue. For the most part, interest and influence on a specific organisation are assessed to be low. Organisations should be mindful, however, should Data Subject's rights be neglected, interest will increase. Stakeholder Group: Occasionally Contact.

The Media: Media interest in GDPR will ebb and flow, the key for any organisation is to manage their reputation. Getting Data Protection wrong, either by failing to uphold Data Subject's rights or, suffering a security breach, is likely to attract adverse media attention. Companies do not enjoy the Right to be Forgotten[50] so once a breach has made it online, it is going to be there forever! Stakeholder Group: Keep Satisfied.

Hackers & Hacktivists: Certain types of hackers are incredibly interested in personal data as they use it to commit identity theft and other forms of fraud. The more intimate the data held, the more interested hackers would be in your organisation. The less secure your organisation, the more interesting an organisation's systems will be to the Hacker. Hacktivists have a slightly different motivation; they are more interested in causing damage to organisations because they disagree with specific practices. It may be they believe an organisation is a massive polluter or are overcharging for life-saving pharmaceuticals or have just caused millions to lose their homes. Hacktivists will be keen to embarrass and disrupt. The influence of hackers and hacktivists will depend on their capability to attack and your organisation's capacity to defend itself. Stakeholder Group: Keep Satisfied.

---

[49] Article 12: Transparent information, communication and modalities for the exercise of the rights of the Data Subject, Para (3).
[50] Article 17: Right to erasure ('right to be forgotten')

Supervisory Authority: The Supervisory Authority will have a keen interest in organisations who are not upholding the rights of Data Subjects, so it would be wise to keep them in the low-interest box on the power-impact grid as GDPR gives supervisory authorities much greater powers than they have previously enjoyed. A Supervisory Authority can mandate an audit of your organisation, compel corrective action and in the worst case scenario impose significant fines. The Supervisory Authority is a stakeholder whereby if their position on the grid changed from a low to high interest in your organisation, active engagement is going to require much effort. I would recommend keeping to the default. Stakeholder Group (default): Keep Satisfied.

Member States Courts / Judiciary: Naturally, the judiciary will always be a stakeholder when legislative instruments are involved. GDPR gives Data Subjects a number of rights such as the right to a judicial remedy against a Controller, a Processor[51] and even the Supervisory Authority[52]. A Data Subject also has the right to receive compensation from a Controller or Processor[53]. Therefore, the optimal place for this stakeholder is low interest and low influence, but where a Data Subject decides to seek a judicial remedy, interest and influence may become high very quickly. Stakeholder Group: Occasionally Contact.

Organisational Senior Management & The Board: to successfully implement GDPR, senior organisational management and the Board must be interested as ultimately they are accountable[54] for ensuring their organisation can demonstrate compliance with the Regulation. Concurrently, Senior Management has the most influence within the company; they will have the final say on the allocation of resources required for a successful programme. It may be challenging to maintain their interest and benefit from their influence, as you jostle for priority against the organisation's other commitments, but keep at it, as a failure to engage this stakeholder group will lead to disaster! Stakeholder Group: Actively Engage.

Committees: Senior Management, certainly in larger organisations, often establishes committees to oversee different aspects of governance. Examples are Audit, Risk, Compliance, Operations and, more common in recent years, Technology committees. In each committee described above, GDPR is going to become part of the agenda. The minutes and reports generated by these committees will also form part of the evidence required to demonstrate compliance. Stakeholder Group: Keep Informed.

Chief Risk Officer (CRO): Risk is a common theme throughout GDPR. A Controller is required to take into account the risks[55] to the rights and freedoms of Data Subjects and, in doing so, ensure appropriate technical and organisational measures are in place. These measures must be sufficient to demonstrate that processing is performed in accordance with the requirements of GDPR. Given the material impacts a breach of Data Subject's rights could have on an organisation, the CRO will be interested in GDPR and will be a crucial ally in terms of ensuring risks are adequately mitigated. Stakeholder Group: Keep Informed.

Chief Information Security Officer (CISO): Security is also a common theme throughout GDPR. Both Controllers and Processors are required to implement appropriate technical and organisational measures to ensure a level of security appropriate to the risk to the rights and freedoms of Data Subjects. Depending on where the CISO sits in the hierarchical structure of an organisation will have an impact on how they respond to GDPR. If they sit within IT, for example, their objectivity could be compromised due to conflicts of interest with their boss the CIO. However, if the CISO sits outside of technology, they should be a key ally. Nurturing this relationship will be critical. Stakeholder Group: Actively Engage.

---

[51] Article 79: Right to an effective judicial remedy against a controller or processor
[52] Article 78: Right to an effective judicial remedy against a supervisory authority
[53] Article 82: Right to compensation and liability
[54] Article 5: Principles relating to processing of personal data
[55] Article 24: Responsibility of the Controller

Chief Information Officer (CIO) / Head of Technology: From an operational perspective the CIO is, without doubt, a critical internal stakeholder and should have a high interest in GDPR. The CIO typically controls the technology budget and therefore holds much influence in regards to applications and infrastructure where personal data will be processed. It is vital to understand the motivations of the CIO as they could be under significant pressure to keep IT costs down and are an increased regulatory burden could be perceived as an unwanted headache. Stakeholder Group: Actively Engage.

Head of Legal: GDPR is going to make the Legal department busy. Every contract with a Processor is going to require a review and in a percentage of cases will need significant renegotiation. In the event a contract is not in place, work will need to be done to get terms in place as GDPR now makes it a requirement[56]. Additionally, and now fees can no longer be charged for subject access requests, an increased likelihood exists the Legal department will support higher volumes of requests. This increased effort will likely manifest in terms of advising business units on legal risks associated with disclosure, redaction and applicable case law.

Head of HR: Human Resources are big consumers of personal data and not only about employees. HR stores data on candidates, former employees, next of kin, beneficiaries (e.g. pensions or death-in-service payments) and in some cases dependents (e.g. for the provision of private family healthcare). All this data must be processed in a manner which upholds the rights of the Data Subjects[57]. The Head of HR will still need to be interested in Data Protection after GDPR and will have a lot of influence relating to how HR personal data is processed. In recent years, there has been a trend in HR to outsource HR tasks such as recruiting, payroll, employee engagement, learning & development, background screening. Each of these outsourced processing activities must have a contract in place under GDPR. Such a contract must include a requirement to ensure data is processed securely and that a Processor cooperates in demonstrating compliance with GDPR. As HR manage processes relating to candidates, employees and former employees, it is important the Head of HR fully understands these groups are still considered Data Subjects. HR is typically a focal point for Subject Access Requests (See Chapter 13), and as such, HR will need to be on the ball in terms of responding the requests from Data Subjects (e.g. A candidate is entitled to request interview notes if they are not successful after a job interview). Stakeholder Group: Actively Engage.

Head of Marketing: Whichever level of sophistication, marketing is going to be…let's say…interesting! Not only must marketers comply with GDPR, but they must also comply with PECR[58]. Marketers deal with massive volumes of personal data, so there is a high likelihood a lot of work will be required to ensure GDPR compliance. We are already seeing some initial reaction from organisations deleting marketing databases[59] and companies fined for distributing emails to customers without consent[60]. Ironically in one case, a cited reason for a mass email was to comply with GDPR[61]. Stakeholder Group: Actively Engage.

End Users: For GDPR, end users are those employees, contractors and others who are working directly with personal data. They could be a member of an operations team processing a delivery order, a member of an HR team processing candidate CVs / application forms or, a member of a sales team chasing leads. These days it will be pretty much everyone in your organisation with maybe a few exceptions (e.g. cleaners, maintenance engineers). End Users

---

[56] Article 28(3): Processor

[57] Data Protection - The Employment Practices Code, ICO, Nov 2011

[58] The Privacy and Electronic Communications (EC Directive) Regulations 2003

[59] Wetherspoons deletes entire email marketing database (http://www.decisionmarketing.co.uk/news/wetherspoons-deletes-entire-email-marketing-database, 27 June 2017)

[60] Flybe Limited ICO Penalty Notice: https://ico.org.uk/media/action-weve-taken/mpns/2013731/mpn-flybe-limited-20170320.pdf, 20 March 2017)

[61] Honda Motor Europe Limited ICO Penalty Notice: https://ico.org.uk/media/action-weve-taken/mpns/2013732/mpn-honda-europe-20170320.pdf, 20 March 2017)

will often be in direct contact with Data Subjects, and under GDPR a subject access request can be made to anyone within an organisation (including the cleaner!) so End Users will all need to know what they must do to comply. Stakeholder Group: Keep Informed.

Third Parties & Suppliers: Outsourced service providers should be interested because it is going to be a lot more challenging for a buyer to justify choosing an organisation to process their data which has already been breached over an organisation that has a strong data protection culture. Third party suppliers who can demonstrate they are taking GDPR seriously will be in a much better position to influence purchasing decisions. In the case of existing suppliers, there will be existing risk which will require active management and the more suppliers processing personal data, the higher the risk. Stakeholder Group: Actively Engage.

Communications Planning

Understanding stakeholders, and identifying an appropriate engagement strategy, is all well and good at a high level. Sooner or later, you are going to have to follow through and start communicating! Now, you may work in a large multinational with a large internal communications team and, an even larger marketing and Public Relations (PR) team. If that is you, then there is every possibility you can get this work done for you, and I would encourage you to go down this route first. If this is not you, or those teams cannot spare anyone to support you, it is highly likely you are going to need to develop a communications plan.

Communications planning[62] is about keeping everybody informed. The communications planning process concerns defining the types of information you will deliver, who will receive it, the format for communicating it, and the timing of its release and distribution. It is likely 90% of a Practitioner's role will be spent on communication, so it is important to make sure everybody gets the right message at the right time. For those of you who like a template, I have included one at the end of this section, but before we get to that, a good communication plan will consist of the following elements:

1. Identify stakeholders and their expectations
2. Identify necessary communication to satisfy stakeholder expectations
3. Determine frequency of communications
4. Determine message channels
5. Confirm who will communicate messages
6. Document items (e.g. templates, formats, documents)
7. Measure Engagement

As we have already covered point one, let us look at points two to six in a little more detail:

Necessary communication: to determine what is required communication you will need to set out communication goals (i.e. what do you want to communicate). Some useful communications goals for a Data Protection programme could be:

1. Communication of roles and responsibilities to affected employees
2. Communication of changes in deadlines for SARs (30days)
3. Communication of new mandatory breach notification deadline (72hours)
4. Communication of new policy requirements

---

[62] Project Management, Watt A, 2016. ShareAlike 4.0 (CC BY-SA 4.0)

Each of these goals could be broken down further by the audience for example. Remember, what is necessary communication for one person, can be too much or too little for another person. One rule of thumb I have found works well is the more senior a person is in an organisation, the shorter the communication. Take, for example, creating a slide deck. For a relatively junior or broad audience, having a number of slides may be appropriate, for the Board, you should ideally be looking at no more than two – and probably more realistically – just one.

> **If you are not getting the expected response back from your email communication, try the Bottom Line Up Front (BLUF) technique. Write the email as you usually would, then move the last line, your request for action, to the top. Always include words to the effect "would it be possible to get this back to me by…?" Most people writing a business email, do so in the same way they communicate verbally. The email explains (often at length) the background to a situation, presents courses of action and only then, after many paragraphs of supporting analysis, will there be a call to action. The trouble is when busy people see long emails; they often put it in the 'I will read that properly later' folder…which eventually becomes the 'never going to read' folder. If you put the call to action and a deadline at the top of the email, it is more likely you will get a response. If you put a suggested deadline, you will help the person in prioritising when the work needs to be completed.**

Communication should also be appropriate to your intended objective. If you want a decision from someone, then make that explicitly clear. Don't go into the Boardroom saying you have identified a requirement for an eDiscovery tool and it costs £150k and then walk out of there without first ensuring you have explicitly asked the Board for a funding decision.

Frequency & Channels: timing is always going to be important when it comes to communication. In most organisations which have a committee structure, there will be deadlines before standing meetings when materials must be submitted. These deadlines are so committee members can read the meeting pack before the meeting (that is the idea anyway!). When planning your programme's communications, you must take this into account so you can provide stakeholders with the most current information. In terms of written reports, keep to one document which can be expanded/contracted, dependent on the audience. In your master document, avoid complex formatting, this way you can transfer material into the dozens of other people's templates with a lot less effort.

> **EXAMPLE: Computer Based Training is an excellent communication channel for interactive information. As are Town Halls and Workshops.**

In terms of channels, there are too many to list out. So many it can become overwhelming when you think of just how many ways a person can now interact with others. To keep things simple try and group the information you wish to communicate into static, fluid, and interactive and then pick a channel suitable for such information. Static data is items unlikely to change often such as a privacy notice. Fluid information is likely to change over the course of time, such as a project progress report. Interactive information, as the name suggests, will vary based on interaction with an audience such as a social media site.

The Messenger: most people will tell you, if they are honest, they prioritise reading and responding to emails coming from their boss or someone significantly senior like the CEO. This behaviour is of course understandable. A line manager will conduct appraisals and so will assess team members on how well they have performed against tasks they have set. It is likely such assessment will also have a direct impact on any pay rises, promotions or bonuses. Understanding who motivates a person to action is just as important as the message containing the call to action. A word of caution when asking others to communicate on your behalf, be aware they will need guidance. Guidance can include key talking points, frequently asked questions, who can help with more difficult questions and so on. Don't just draft them an email and leave them to it!

Documentation: in addition to the template mentioned at the beginning of this section, the following items should be documented and maintained as part of your communication plan:

1. Communication Plan!
2. Branded Templates (for consistency)
3. Content of emails
4. Wiki Site / Intranet Portal
5. Posters
6. Press Releases
7. Learning Objectives for Training
8. FAQs
9. Guidelines for Line Managers communicating to their teams
10. Policy for communication with external organisations (e.g. Media)
11. Policy for communication with customers and general public

Measure Engagement: Communication is not one way; it requires some form of response. Often inexperienced Practitioners are guilty of thinking sending an email, telling everybody what they must be doing, is communication. These missives are not communication, it is dissemination and is likely to be highly ineffective if the person receiving the information is not a willing participant. An effective communication plan will require multiple forms of measurement to ascertain how successful communication has been in achieving the intended goals.

EXAMPLE: A communication objective is to inform employees of new SAR deadlines via e-Learning. To measure success a question is included in a test at the end. e.g.: Subject Access Requests must be answered in:

A - 40 days
B - 30 days
C - Take as long as you need to be thorough

Raising awareness can be an absolute minefield. If a Practitioner gets communication right, it will make their lives significantly easier. If on the other hand, communication is weak, it can break a programme. Before sending out missives or designing posters, document your communication plan and ask colleagues to sanity check the content.

Communications Plan Template

Communication Plan (Version X.X)		
Programme Name: General Data Protection Awareness		
Comms Plan Owner: *[Insert Name]*		
Stakeholder Analysis		
Name	**Role**	**Engagement**

Communication Objectives		
Ser.	**Objective**	**Talking Points**

Plan					
Issue Date	**Owner**	**Audience**	**Channel**	**Frequency**	**Location of Materials**
Notes:					

Awareness through Learning

Not hearing is not as good as hearing, hearing is not as good as seeing, seeing is not as good as knowing, knowing is not as good as acting; true learning continues until it is put into action[63]. Wise words that have stood the test of time. A wise Practitioner should also incorporate this ancient philosophy in their awareness programme. By combining effective and appropriate learning activities into your awareness programme, there will be a significant increase in your audience's engagement levels. The essential ingredients being effective and appropriate. Learning activities are often executed poorly with a little forethought in terms of the learning process. A typical approach is to look at a topic, add some slides covering the relevant parts and then getting participants in a room in an event often referred to as 'Death by PowerPoint'. Participants are then asked to sign a register for the audit trail and sent off into the world to apply their 'knowledge'. Practitioners often fail to incorporate any pedagogical steps. What the Practitioner should try aim to achieve is for those in scope of learning activities to become unconsciously competent in art and science of data protection. This state of being is where your employees don't consciously think about ensuring something is compliant with GDPR, but do it as an integral part of their duties. A word of caution, as people become consciously competent, there is a tendency for people to forget why they are doing something in a certain way or as new staff join the organisation, the reason behind a certain practice may not be passed on as part of any induction training. It is therefore critical the conscious competency learning framework is seen as cyclical, with practitioners understanding people can regress from consciously competent back to unconsciously incompetent, and any of the stages inbetween.

1. UNCONSCIOUS INCOMPETENT	4. UNCONSCIOUS COMPETENT
You are **not** aware of a skill and your lack of competency	You are able to use a skill without thinking about it
2. CONSCIOUS INCOMPETENT	3. CONSCIOUS COMPETENT
You are aware of a skill and your lack of competency	You are able to use a skill but it takes effort

Conscious Competence Learning Framework[64]

Stages of Learning: Unless you have a machine such as the one used in the Matrix Trilogy (excellent films by the way!), no one becomes an expert in anything overnight. A student goes on a journey to become competent and then onto mastering their chosen speciality. As a Zen Practitioner you are already there but how do you bring everybody else with you on the journey? an excellent way to do this is to customise training according to the different stages of learning. To create an effective training programme for your data protection programme, it is important to understand the stages of learning and how they can be applied. While I will list them, they should not be viewed hierarchically (i.e. you should use a stage appropriate to your intended objective).

---

[63] Xunzi, Xun Kuang, circa 260BCE
[64] The Empathic Communicator. Howell, W.S., 1982

Another factor to consider is the availability of resources. In a corporate environment, you will be competing with many other people when it comes to getting employees to participate in training, so it is important to get the best bang for your buck.

The learning stages[65] are:

1. Remember: Recognising and recalling facts
2. Understand: Understanding what facts mean
3. Apply: Applying the facts, rules, concepts, and ideas
4. Analyse: Breaking down information into components
5. Evaluate: Judging the value of information or ideas
6. Create: Combining parts to make a new whole.

Let's look at how this could be applied to a Data Protection programme training programme:

Learning Stage	Learning Objective	Audience
Remember	Recall the six GDPR principles	All staff
Understand	Paraphrase the Right to Portability	IT Developer
Apply	Calculate the cost of an Administrative Fine of 4% of gross annual turnover	Risk Manager
Analyse	Categorise business processes into those in and out of GDPR scope	Process Owner
Evaluate	Assess the risks to a processing activity	Department Head
Create	Create an updated procedure for dealing with employee related Subject Access Requests (SARs).	HR Manager

Bloom's Revised Taxonomy Applied to Data Protection

While this is a small snapshot of potential learning objectives, there are countless more. Once you have identified the most appropriate learning objectives for your programme, you then need to plan the learning activity to support the learning. Luckily, teaching is a mature profession, and the most commonly used tool is the lesson plan.

[65] A Taxonomy for Learning, Teaching, and Assessing: Pearson New International Edition: A Revision of Bloom's Taxonomy of Educational Objectives, Abridged Edition. Anderson L et al., 2013

The Lesson Plan: a lesson plan's primary purpose is to support an educator in the delivery of a discrete learning activity. It places a structure around the activity in a similar way a communication plan or project plan does for communications and projects. The fundamental components are as follows:

1. Setting Learning Objectives: what are we trying to teach
2. Preliminaries: what is required to meet the objectives
3. Introduction: setting the scene
4. Learning Stages: breaking learning into manageable chunks
5. Guided Practice: supervising the application of knowledge
6. Review: confirm assimilation of knowledge
7. Consolidation: taking the learning back out into the workplace

Learning objectives: In the stages of learning section, we touched upon learning objectives and how they relate to the different learning stages. A good objective will usually have a verb-noun pair of which an output must exist. The output must exist so the learning objective can be confirmed as being achieved by the learner, through evidence-based assessment. If a learning objective cannot be confirmed through evidence-based assessment, it is not a learning objective!

> **EXAMPLE: categorise business processes into those in and out of GDPR scope.**

Preliminaries: before any instruction can take place, there is a certain amount of preparatory work. This work could be as simple as making sure there is a room with enough seats and chairs; through to printing handouts; to more complex preparations such as building an IT laboratory. If you are planning to use multimedia (e.g. PowerPoint) an instructor must, at a minimum, proofread slides, check projectors etc. are working and, sit in the seats of the participant to verify they can see the material. Rehearsing also comes under the prelims banner. As you become more competent in the material, you may not need to rehearse as much but whenever delivering material for the first time (even as an expert), do a dry run before unleashing the material on your real audience. Often, learning in a commercial environment is not going to be classroom based. There are so many different ways. The learning could be computer-based, via video conferencing or even one-to-one at a learner's desk. Whichever location, the basic tenet is proper planning and preparation will prevent poor performance!

Setting the scene: once you have rehearsed, set up your learning environment and are now face-to-face with those you intend to instruct, you now need to set the scene and explain why they are giving up their day jobs to attend your training. The introduction must, therefore, include the following components:

1. Preamble: how did we get to now
2. The challenge: what do we need to achieve
3. The learning objectives: how are we going to get there
4. Question policy: how can people ask for help/clarification

> **EXAMPLE: As we learned in a previous session, our organisation is required to demonstrate the personal data we hold is processed in accordance with GDPR. To do that we must identify which processes are in scope of GDPR.**
>
> **As such, the objective of this session is to teach participants to categorise business processes into those in and out of GDPR scope.**
>
> **The material may raise questions so, in order to get through the material efficiently, we will have Q&A points at each stage. If you have an urgent question, please let me know.**

Learning Stages: this is where the meat of the instruction takes place. If you are combining multiple learning objectives into one lesson, each objective could be considered a learning stage. Each stage has the following component:

1. State the theory/concept
2. Explain the theory in context
3. Discuss a scenario
4. Ask and answer questions

> **EXAMPLE: A processing activity will be in the scope of GDPR is the process involves processing of personal data. Personal Data is [put a definition on slide]. Let's look at the following three scenarios.**
>
> **For each are the processes in or out of scope and why?**
>
> **Scenario 1: [use slide] Processing a loan application. In scope processing involves personal data of applicants.**
>
> **Scenario 2: [use slide] Producing Balance Sheet. Out-of-scope as does not involve personal data.**
>
> **Scenario 3: [Use slide] Monitoring Logs of Customer portal. Discuss what could bring this process into scope.**

If the lesson is practical, such as training someone how to complete a Data Protection Impact Assessment (DPIA) the following approach should be used:

1. Explain the task
2. Demonstrate the task
3. Get participants to copy the task under supervision
4. Get participants to practice the task

When it comes to questions, a useful technique is to Pose, Pause, Pounce. Ask the whole group the question, pause and read the group's body language, and then pounce on someone you think will (or won't) know. Avoid singling a person out and then asking the question, as the rest of the group will switch off. Another good tip is to ask the rest of the group then whether they think the person is correct and ask the group why. The more interaction throughout the learning stages, the more the concepts will be assimilated! In some cases, you will not know the answer (or you have forgotten). The one thing you must never do – don't bluff. If you do not know the answer, explain you will check the regulation and get back to them with a definitive answer. Alternatively, if you have this book on hand – you could always look in the relevant section!

Guided practice: This concept is more appropriate for practical tasks over theory and in workplace learning, there should be lots of opportunities to practice. A good way to carry out guided practice is to create a case study. Get participants to split into smaller groups and give participants a number of questions to answer.

> **EXAMPLE: The HR department of Acme Ltd need assisting in identifying processes involving personal data. In your groups identify ten processes likely to include personal data. For each process what types of personal data are likely to be involved.**

Review & Confirmation: This is where all the learning is summarised, participants ask final questions, and finally, the instructor confirms the learning objective has been achieved. This confirmation can be by a Q&A session or a short written test or an exercise. Whichever option is chosen the instructor needs to ensure the learning objective has been achieved by all participants. The Review section is also a useful time for the instructor to make a note of any questions that could not be answered and point participants in the direction of helpful reference material (e.g. an Intranet portal). It is also helpful to provide contact details as sometimes people are embarrassed to ask the 'stupid' question in front of their peers or a concept suddenly makes sense when they apply it for real and then results in questions they did not have during the course!

> **Objective: Recall the six GDPR principles**
>
> **Confirmation: Participants will be asked to name a principle at random. Other participants will confirm the principle is correct. Alternatively, Instructor will state a principle and participants must confirm if the principle is correct.**

Consolidation: no workplace learning should stop at the classroom; learning needs to be incorporated into day-to-day operational activities. As such, if you are integrating learning activities into your data protection programme, you should catch up with your participants and find out how the learning has helped (or hindered). Often feedback forms are sent out the same day as the course ends, which is pretty useless as how will the instructor know if the concepts are understood until the learning is applied. When seeking feedback, give it at least a couple of weeks! Awareness through learning, in my humble opinion, is the most efficient way of getting a message across to an audience. It is an especially effective medium where the message requires follow-on, and often, continuous application of the content – long after the learning activity has finished.

Lesson Plan Template

Lesson Plan (Version X.X)		
Lesson Name: e.g. Data Protection Impact Analysis		
Instructor: [Insert Name]		
Previous Leaning Activity: e.g. DPIA Theory		
Preliminaries		
Resources		
Location & Equipment		
Introduction		
Preamble		
Challenge		
Learning Objectives		
Question Policy		
Lesson Stages		
Stage	**Content**	**Notes**
1		
2		
3		
4		
5		
Review		
Final Confirmation		
Recap Objectives		
Summary & Look Forward		

7. DATA PROTECTION POLICIES AND PRIVACY NOTICES

Whether you are in a behemoth multinational or a small start-up, you are going to need policies to govern how people within your organisation process Personal and Sensitive data. Your organisation will also need to tell your customers and Data Subjects how their data will be securely processed in a manner that upholds their rights – even if your organisation is not based in the European Union! In this chapter, we will first define some key terminology as, anecdotally, misinterpretation of what a particular term means is the first step to confusion. We will discuss why you should never incorporate a procedure into a policy and the importance of using clear, unambiguous language. We will discuss the process a policy drafter must go through to get a policy approved and once implemented how to ensure compliance is maintained. As this is a Practitioner book, examples of an internal data protection policy and an external privacy notice are included to help Practitioners get a feel for what the content should look like. These are examples only and should not be replicated as a whole on the assumption that using them will automatically lead to compliance; if you are unsure, you should always speak to your legal advisor. So, if you're ready, let's dive in.

Standardised Terminology

Before we continue, it is useful to standardise terminology[66] as the terms we are about to discuss often get confused or conflated. Similar confusion often finds itself in policy, so I'm keen Practitioners start off on a good foot. No matter how the following terms are used within your organisation, for the purposes of this book, the following definitions apply:

Legislation: laws made and maintained by a Member State (or internationally) which an organisation must adhere or suffer judicial action.

Regulation: rules and requirements made and maintained by a Supervisory Authority to which an organisation must adhere or suffer enforcement action.

Risk Appetite: the level of risk, senior management within an organisation, is willing to take to meet their objectives.

---

[66] Writing Effective Policies and Procedures: A Step-by-Step Resource for Clear Communication. Campbell N., 1998

Policy Framework: a set of guiding principles for creating and implementing policies within an organisation.

Organisational Policy: a documented set of rules and requirements adopted by an organisation. An organisational policy provides a mechanism for transposing external legislative or regulatory requirements and defining the management expectations of appropriate conduct throughout the organisation. The organisational policy is also a reflection of organisational risk appetite.

Policy Committee: a group of interested and empowered parties within an organisation who provide the governance and oversight for policy development and implementation.

Policy Owner: a senior member of the organisation responsible for maintaining an organisational policy.

Exception: a deviation from a rule or requirement defined in the organisational policy.

Policy Framework

Before one word of policy is written within an organisation, there must be a framework to govern policy design and implementation. Simply writing a policy will not make it effective. Simply communicating a policy in an email and linking to a copy on the company Intranet portal, equally, will not make it effective. Shockingly, these two approaches are common. In this section, we will look at what is required to make a policy effective. The following are a set of guiding principles for creating and implementing organisational policy.

Costed: every rule and requirement in policy has a cost. For a policy to be effective, there must be an appropriate budget to support implementation. When developing policy, the cost of a requirement must be balanced against management's risk appetite. Taking into account all relevant factors (e.g. Regulatory Censure), a policy requirement should never cost more than the risk it aims to prevent.

EXAMPLE: Which policy requirement is more cost-effective?

A: Every Manager shall review and approve all transactions input by their team

B: Team members must check and sign each other's transactions; managers shall, once a month, review a random sample of transactions amounting to no less than 10% of total transactions.

Authority: a policy is not effective unless it has the backing of the most senior level of management. When a policy is published, it must be understood its content carries the same weight as the CEO walking up to someone's desk and telling them these are the rules with which you must comply. All policies must, therefore, be formally approved at the appropriate management level. The same goes for policy changes and reviews.

Acceptance: even when a policy has the authority of senior management supporting the content, middle management and below may, for a variety of reasons, seek to undermine or ignore policy. There must be a mechanism to ensure policies are accepted across the business. Policy Committee membership, collaboration and good communication can go a long way to improving acceptance.

Oversight: there must be a mechanism in place to ensure the documented requirements are effectively monitored and that compliance is enforced. Everyone in the organisation must know compliance is monitored and there are consequences for non-compliance.

Unambiguous: while procedures and guidelines can be open to interpretation, rules and requirements in policy must not. It must be clear to the intended audience not only what the explicit rule or requirement means but the implicit spirit should also be easily understood.

> **EXAMPLE: In order that the impact of a security breach is minimised, all Databases containing Personal Data must be built using the latest build standard.**

Decoupled: in some organisations, there is an awful tendency to conflate policies and procedures. It is to be avoided at all costs. A policy defines the rules as approved by senior management. Procedures lay out how business processes will operate to ensure the rules are followed, are written by the end users and approved by the Policy Owner. By including procedures in policy documents, the review effort for senior management increases exponentially and thus increases the cost. Don't forget changes to policies require the same scrutiny and approval as the original draft. Keep the senior management time required to review policy to the absolute minimum – they will be very grateful!

> **EXAMPLE: A good policy statement might say:** *"To minimise compromise, Email containing Personal Data must be encrypted using an approved encryption mechanism as documented in the Encryption Standard."*
>
> **A bad policy statement might say:** *"To minimise compromise, Emails containing Personal Data must be sent using enforced TLS."*
>
> **The former gives flexibility in the spirit of mitigating risk. The latter may not even be achievable.**

Another useful item to consider, when documenting policy requirements is, avoid referring to a specific piece of software or a current vendor. Both can change at short notice which means a policy will then require updating.

> **EXAMPLE: Rather than** *"Incidents must be recorded within 24 hours in Fox One owned by Dave Jones."*
>
> **Consider:** *"Incidents must be recorded within 24 hours in the Incident Management System, owned by the Head of Operational Risk Management."*

Owned: a policy must have an Owner. Policy Owners have the final say on the interpretation of policy where its meaning is either ambiguous or contested. Policy Owners endorse or reject exceptions to policy and define the timeframe and any supporting conditions in which the exception is permitted. The Policy Committee would then formally approve the exception taking into consideration the Policy Owner's endorsement (or if appealed, rejection). Policy Owners must also ensure policy content remains relevant, up-to-date and continues to reflect the organisation's risk appetite.

EXAMPLE: A policy owner who currently maintains a Data Protection policy must ensure the policy is updated to reflect the new requirements laid down in GPDR.

Consistent: Policies throughout an organisation should be consistent in structure, format and language. When an employee reads an HR policy, it should have the same structure as an IT policy or a Legal policy. Avoid the tendency to write your policy in isolation, use a standard template to ensure all the relevant information is included. If there is no policy standard, set this as an agenda item and get a standard agreed.

Supported: policies are not standalone documents; they must be supported by other documents. The Policy Owner at a minimum should produce a model process and template set for end users to either adopt or use as the base for customisation. Processes for collecting, analysing and reporting policy compliance must also be defined, created and implemented. A register of exceptions decisions and associated conditions must be maintained to support consistency or establish the context for a requirement to change policy.

EXAMPLE: A policy requirement states 'In order to maintain accurate records, all application forms, submitted by applicants electronically must be printed and archived.' This policy statement was originally drafted when IT systems were more prone to data corruption, and the cost of storage was prohibitive.

Due to a significant increase in customers, physical storage of documents is eating into office space, and Business Units are requesting an exception to the physical storage requirement.

The Policy Owner may decide to review this policy requirement and suggest a change commensurate with the current level of risk of data loss.

Policy Life-Cycle

A policy is a living document which must be governed throughout its life. The following is a description a good practice policy life-cycle.

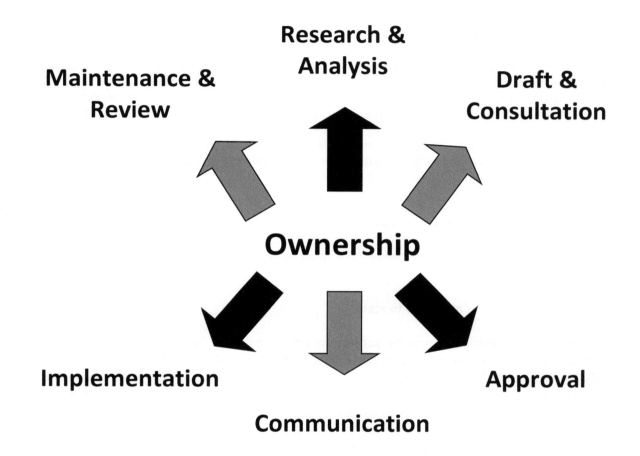

Policy Life-Cycle

Research & Analysis: policy requirements can arise in a number of ways. Proactively, the policy is often developed in response to upcoming legislation or regulation (e.g. GDPR). Sometimes it can come about reactively as a result of an internal issue (e.g. a higher than desired frequency of incidents). Using horizon scanning research or internal metrics, Senior Management will need to assess whether a specific set of rules and requirements must be codified to deal with an issue. Now, senior management is not going to do this work themselves; a Policy Owner will be assigned who will work out what needs to be put in place to bring the issue back to risk appetite. Research and analysis may involve discussing best practice with industry experts or even running pilots using different controls to identify which approach provides the most cost-effective solution. Remember every line in policy is a cost to the business (with the aim of reducing the cost of incidents).

Draft & Consultation: this is where policy is first created, circulated and refined. Policy drafts should go through a staged process of review. The first stage is a technical review whereby subject matter experts ensure the content is appropriate the needs of the organisation. The second stage is a review of the format, structure and spelling to ensure when it hits the senior management team there are no howlers which would immediately destroy your credibility or have the policy rejected for submission for approval. The third is a consultation review which should seek to gain feedback, where possible, from those whom the policy will affect. The Stakeholder review is where policy is likely to meet most resistance, and so it is essential the Policy Owner manages policy communications effectively. When asking stakeholders to review policy, get them to apply the proposed rules to their current processes and report back on any identified issues. This data will aid in more accurately costing the policy. When consulting on policy, it's worth finding the people with the greatest attention to detail you can to review draft policy documents. It is these people who will find the loopholes, the ambiguities and the commas in the wrong places. Get them involved early! When assigning time to this stage, it's important to consider your stakeholders' workload and give them a reasonable period in which to review however it must also clear the consultation period is time-bound right at the beginning of the process. When drafting and consulting on policy, consideration must be given to the impact of your policy on other policies. Will other policy requirements now conflict, or will new rules be required in other policies? In order to support the consultation process, create a Frequently Asked Questions (FAQ) document so you can track common issues or concerns. These questions will be invaluable in validating policy is understood.

EXAMPLE: An Outsourcing Policy may have a statement such as:

All purchasing decisions valued above £10k must go through a formal vendor management process.

which may need to be amended to state:

All purchasing decisions must be subject to risk assessment. The outcome of the risk assessment may require additional due-diligence. Contracts shall not be signed, and data shall not be shared with Third Parties until required due-diligence has been conducted and reviewed by the appropriate oversight body. Vendor Management is responsible for maintaining a list of required due-diligence steps.

NB: Data Protection is not explicitly mentioned in the policy statement as it is likely other due-diligence activities must also be carried out. By not mentioning any specific due-diligence steps, the policy can remain concise and require fewer updates.

Approval: if you have completed the first two steps well, the approval phase should be relatively painless. For policy to be approved it should be either presented directly to the Board or, typically, presented to a Policy Committee who will formally review the policy and then endorse the policy to the Board. Policies submitted to Policy Committee must be circulated in good time to committee members. If a Policy Committee meets monthly, then you should aim to circulate the policy the day after the previous Policy Committee meeting to give member as much time to review the policy as possible. It is a good idea to arrange catch-ups with policy members to iron out any concerns ahead of the endorsement meeting too. What you don't want to happen is concerns raised at the endorsement meeting then derailing implementation until the next policy cycle. Policy Committees may also mandate or recommend implementation conditions. Such conditions could be when the policy goes live, when it applies and when departments can expect to be audited against the content. In multinational organisations, there may be conditions based on Jurisdiction. Policy endorsement must be formally documented in the minutes of the policy committee meeting in which the policy was endorsed. The approval must then be documented in the minutes of the Board meeting the policy was approved.

EXAMPLE: the minutes of a policy meeting may reflect an endorsement of a new Data Protection policy in December 2017, on the condition that while it shall apply from January 2017, business units will have until 31 March 2018 to become compliant. All Front Office Departments, Operations, HR and IT must be audited against the policy requirements before 25 May 2018.

Communication: there are a number of aspects of communication a Practitioner must consider once a policy is approved. Each communication objective should be included in a wider Data Protection Communications Plan (See Chapter 06). Before issuing any all-staff missives it is worth considering the likely impacts of a new policy. People will not know where to find the policy; people will have questions, people will need help translating the policy into meaningful action and people will sometimes need a waiver to a certain aspect of the policy. Policy Owners will need to be able to respond to such issues as when a policy goes live with a fixed deadline; many people may panic!

Where is the policy going to live? If your organisation has a policy portal, then a read-only version (e.g. in PDF) of the approved policy should be uploaded to the portal. It's worth doing one more scan for spelling, punctuation and grammar prior to upload. There should be only one version of the policy live and available at any one time. If you maintain an Intranet site avoid the urge to add a copy of the policy to your own site but instead directly link to the official version. Take full advantage of metadata. Tag your policy with relevant keywords so it can be easily found. Metadata should also include the role of the Policy Owner (e.g. Chief Privacy Officer), the date approved and the next review date. This will aid the Policy Owner and Policy Committee plan future activities and avoid data stagnating should people change roles. How will you deal with questions? If you are issuing a completely new Data Protection Policy or supporting a large user base, questions can quickly overwhelm a team and distract from the day-to-day operational work. Ensure the FAQ (created during the consultation phase) is maintained to improve the efficiency of response. Post model processes and templates (version controlled of course!) on your Intranet Site and don't forget to include guidance on how to complete templates – don't rely on the end user to complete it properly simply because it makes sense to you.

How will you deal with exceptions? If you are operating within a mature organisation, there should be a policy exceptions process which those requiring exception must follow. Create guidelines on what can and cannot be raised as an exception and who must approve an exception in addition to the Policy Owner. Guidelines should also suggest the conditions in which an exception may be granted. Where there are a lot of exception requests for a particular policy point, it is typically an indicator of a systemic issue. If exception requests are coming from all over the business, it may be there is a requirement for a transformation project to be kicked off. Exceptions must never be taken in isolation.

> **EXAMPLE: Consider the following policy requirement:**
>
> *"Personal Data in PROD environments must not be used in DEV, QA, UAT environments."*
>
> **The corresponding (non-public) guidelines for exceptions could include:**
>
> *"Where absolutely unavoidable, exceptions to this requirement may be granted if PROD data is pseudonymised and randomised by a member of the Operational Support Team PRIOR to onward transmission to the DEV or TEST teams. Under no circumstances shall PROD data be provided to DEV and TEST without pseudonymisation and randomisation."*

So, we have our ducks in a row; we can field a million and one questions, we are now ready to unleash our policy into the wild! It is recommended to do this in three ways. The first is a short email from the most senior person in the organisation briefly summarising the policy and the implementation deadlines. The email must direct further questions to the Policy Owner and include a link to the policy (NOT an attachment) and a link to any Intranet Site containing supporting materials such as templates and such like. The second should be filtered down through management channels. Managers should be requested to include details of the new policy in their team meetings. To support this trickle-down communication, Practitioners should create briefing packs as part of their communication plan. The third method is through direct awareness activities. This third type could include posters, screensavers and computer based training.

Implementation: Implementation is where business units convert policy requirements into operational procedures. Ideally, a policy should be supported by a model procedure for businesses to customise however this may not always be practical (e.g. for established processes). Business Units may need to make significant system changes which will, of course, incur costs. When it comes to Data Protection, these systems changes are likely to require significant support from the Data Protection team, and so the Policy Owner must ensure this is factored into the policy implementation. The Policy Owner must be mindful there will be resources outside their direct control which will be impacted by this policy change. Data Protection by Design and Default[67] will add a new element to in-scope projects in terms of the additional tasks required of business analysts, developers and information security. Changes relating to Subject Access Requests[68] may increase departments' workloads. Similarly, the Right to be Forgotten[69] and the Right to Portability[70], may require investment and development.

Maintenance: policy implementation doesn't simply stop once everyone gets to a minimum level of compliance. Compliance with a policy is an ongoing activity. The most common method to monitor compliance is through the use of Key Control Indicators (KCIs). KCIs must be identified, analysed and reported to ensure ongoing compliance. In a mature organisation, KCIs are linked to Key Risk Indicators (KRIs), the theory is, an increase in control failures has a direct impact on chances of a loss occurring. Such metrics, if data is sufficiently granular, are a useful means by which to feed into a risk-based audit program. Where the Policy Owner identifies a particular department is regularly demonstrating non-compliance with policy, a recommendation can be made that Internal Audit carry out a more thorough controls assessment of the errant department.

---

[67] Article 25

[68] Article 15

[69] Article17

[70] Article 20

EXAMPLE: Consider the KCI:

Number of management checks conducted each month

This KCI is linked to the KRI:

Number of input errors recorded per month

This KRI is linked to the KPI:

99.99999% data accuracy rate

If the KCI dropped from 90% (an acceptable level) to 10%, the risk of an input error being missed increases (albeit not necessarily proportionally). The more errors, the less likely the KPI will be met.

Review: The final component in the policy life-cycle is to review policy. Organisations should plan a periodic review of organisational policies of between 1-3 years. For a lot of policies, a three-year policy review cycle may suffice, but Policy Committees should also place a condition that Policy Owners must continually assess policy for adequacy and effectiveness. A Policy Owner should constantly be monitoring changes in legislation and regulation as part of their day job so owners should be aware of any significant changes on the horizon! Another potential catalyst for change in policy is a change in either strategy or risk appetite at the organisational level. Where the organisation takes a material change in direction, a policy review should be triggered.

EXAMPLE: NDH Sp. z o.o. based in Poland is acquired by Drumhaus Faber LLC based in the US. An acquisition would trigger a policy review on both the acquired interest and the new parent company.

By following the above guiding principles, policies stand a greater chance of being followed. As policies are a translation of the organisation's risk appetite too, organisations with well-implemented policies will be well placed to manage their enterprise risk effectively.

Drafting Policy

Now we have our guiding principles and a policy life-cycle what should the policy itself look like? No matter the content, a good policy must have the following core components.

1. Title
2. Classification label and numbering
3. Approvals & Review
4. Version Control
5. Policy Owner
6. Purpose
7. Risk Appetite Statement
8. Glossary of Terms
9. Scope
10. Requirements
11. Roles & Responsibilities
12. Related Policies
13. Links to supporting Templates

Classification label and numbering: as will be discussed in Chapter 11, documents should be clearly labelled with an appropriate information classification. It is also useful to include the current and total page numbers on each page and number each requirement. Numbering individual requirements can make it a lot easier to find items within the policy or aid in linking templates and process back to policy without explicitly replicating the entire requirement in another document or template.

Approvals & Review: in order to demonstrate accountability, policies must be approved and a record of the approval decision clearly visible on the policy. It is good practice to include the data when the policy applies and the data after which it will be enforced. In some cases, organisations may choose to explain the consequences of non-compliance in their policies.

Version Control: in order to ensure transparency, changes to a document must be recorded so the reader can see what has changed since they last read the document. Typically, there are three types of change.

1. Corrections and clarifications – these could be corrections in spelling, punctuation or clarifications due to an identified ambiguity or unintended interpretation.
2. Minor Changes – this could be the introduction of a new rule
3. Major Changes – this would be a significant revision to reflect major changes to legislation (e.g. the change from the 1995 Directive to the 2016 GDPR).

When making a correction or clarification, it would be sensible to communicate the change to relevant stakeholders however approval to make the change would usually not be required. When making minor or major changes, both approval and communication would usually be required. It is also a good idea to include in the document the official location of the policy. Documents are often copied and stored in other locations. Part of your audience may then rely solely on the copy instead of the official version.

Policy Owner: every policy must have a person of sufficient seniority and subject matter expertise to own the policy. It is likely, in terms of a General Data Protection policy, where an organisation is mandated to appoint a Data Protection Officer, the DPO will most likely own the policy, but this may be different in your organisation. Don't put people's names in the policy. Not because it puts the document in the scope of GDPR, but because it is another item which would require review and maintenance. If the policy has a CRO, DPO, CISO, Head of IT, Head of Marketing, Head of HR and so forth, every time one of those people change roles or leaves, the policy will require amendment. Remember, we want to keep the administrative burden as low as possible.

Purpose: this is where the reader finds out why the policy exists. In this section, any legislation or regulation, to which the policy relates or refers, must be included. Including a reference to appropriate legislation or regulation helps the reader understand the nature and origin of the policy requirements. Including the relevant legislation or regulation can also aid in dealing with omissions in policy, whether accidental or deliberate.

> **EXAMPLE: A policy drafter may choose to refer to the tasks of the Data Protection Officer as 'statutory tasks' as opposed to listing the tasks out individually. The inference being there is a list of tasks enacted in a statute, which are unlikely to change frequently or at short notice.**

Risk Appetite Statement: the link between the organisation's risk appetite and the requirements of the policy are an essential ingredient for demonstrating accountability at the highest level. The risk appetite statement should reflect the likely consequences should those in the scope of the policy fail to comply. The statement should also highlight the most likely impacts that would result should the those in scope fail to comply with the policy requirements.

Glossary of Terms: if there are a few terms which need explaining, keep them in the main body of the policy. If there are many terms, as may be the case in a general data protection policy, consider using an appendix which contains a more detailed glossary. Always have in mind, if a policy doesn't contain a glossary specifically defining a term, then it will be interpreted by the reader.

> **EXAMPLE: What does the term 'reasonable steps' mean to you?**

Scope: this section of policy defines who is subject to the policy requirements. Implicitly, employees tend to understand they are in scope of Organisational Policies. Others, may think the policies do not apply to them (e.g. Contractors, Interims) because the consequence of not following the policy requirements may not be so clear. The scope is not limited to the people who must adhere to the requirements of the policy, but systems, geographic locations, types of data and so forth. It is important to make the scope clear and unambiguous. A broad scope increases the cost of the policy. When writing a scope statement, consider which aspects of your organisation should be excluded from the scope of the policy. In terms of a general data protection policy, it is unlikely any part of an organisation is going to be completely out-of-scope. Perhaps save the de-scoping for the first review!

Requirements: This is the core of the policy. For a GDPR related policy, this section is where you place all the specific Data Protection requirements. It is useful to add headings to separate this section further (as seen in the policy example). Anything in this section is a rule which must be adhered to, and it must be possible for evidence to be collected to demonstrate compliance. Have in mind what evidence would be appropriate. When departments, such as Internal Audit, carry out a controls assessment, the evidence requirements will be a useful tool.

> **EXAMPLE: Data Subject access requests shall be completed as soon as possible but no more than 30 calendar days from receipt.**

Try to stick to using the word 'shall' for requirement statements. Only use 'shall **not**' when you wish to explicitly state something must not be done in a certain way or if a statement could be ambiguously interpreted. Examples can also provide clarity but use them sparingly. Examples can often frame a requirement in a way that the reader implicitly de-scopes activities not directly related to the example.

> **EXAMPLE: A System Owner shall be appointed for all Information Systems containing Personal or Sensitive Data. The System Owner shall NOT be from IT unless IT is performing the primary processing activity (e.g. IT operate the Service Desk System and so an IT Manager could be assigned as System Owner).**

Avoid using 'could', 'should' and 'may' as they semantically change a statement from a rule to an optional clause. Remember policy is the minimum requirements, so try to keep content to an absolute minimum. Similarly, avoid ambiguous terms like periodically and instead be specific. The time to be general is in terms of vendors and systems, avoid naming these as should these systems or vendors change, the policy will require updating.

> **EXAMPLE: Rather than:**
>
> **The DPO shall maintain CORUS[71] (the Processes Register)**
>
> **Consider:**
>
> **The DPO shall maintain the Process Register**

Roles & Responsibilities: this is where specific people are assigned specific tasks to ensure those in scope remain in compliance with the policy. This is separate from the requirements because a particular role could potentially interpret their inclusion in the requirements section, as an inference their role only has to comply with the requirements where they are explicitly named.

Related Policies: a question a Practitioner must ask when implementing policy is whether one Data Protection policy is appropriate or should Data Protection requirements be included in existing policies. There is no right or wrong answer to this question as long as it is clearly understood what is required and who owns the oversight of the requirements. That said, no policy lives in isolation and requirements from related policies should not be copied

---

[71] At the time of print, no Processes register was available with the name CORUS.

wholesale into a general data protection policy. The Practitioner should, therefore, identify and explicitly state the related policies. In turn, the related Policy Owners must update their policy to include the General Data Protection policy.

Links to supporting Templates: policies don't operate in isolation. A Policy Owner should be able to demonstrate a method of achieving policy compliance by providing a model solution to each requirement. This could be a template form or process. A bad practice is to include the templates in the policy document itself. This practice is bad because it increases the change management burden of maintaining the policy. Remember policies need senior management approval, but a template doesn't – necessarily – need any approval at such a senior level.

Procedures, Guidelines, Standards, Methodologies & Templates

Anyone who has been a policy owner will know it is tempting to write detailed instructions explaining to the end user exactly how to achieve compliance. This temptation must be resisted. The policy is a place for rules, not procedural steps. There are other document types in which supporting information relating should be maintained. When drafting policy, the policy owner should have in mind additional information end users require and which type of document should be used. The following are common document types

Standard: a predefined set of conditions, measurements or configuration which sets the minimum level of attainment which must be reached to comply with relevant organisational policies. Some examples are:

Server Hardening Standard
Project Management Document Set Standard
Encryption Standard
External Data Transfer Standard
Information Classification Standard

Procedure / Process: a series of actions conducted in a certain order or manner. Procedural steps must incorporate all relevant organisational policy requirements, so those following procedures do not need to cross-reference back to multiple policy documents continually. Policy Owners should seek to identify which requirements of policy need standalone procedures and provide a model procedure for process owners to either adopt, modify or incorporate into their current procedures. Including procedural steps in a policy document should be avoided! Some examples are:

Incident Management Procedures
Subject Access Request Procedure
Data Protection Impact Analysis Process
Notification Procedure
Access Management Process
Change Management Process
New Starters Procedure

Guidelines: a set of principles or advice which, if adhered to, would meet the rules and requirements of a particular aspect of organisational policy. Some examples are:

Guidance on Data Protection by Design & Default
How to create a strong password.
eDiscovery in Office 365: Tips and Tricks
Data Minimisation: SharePoint and Reporting
How to get the best out of Business Objects to avoid downloading data to Spreadsheets

---

Methodology: A system of methods used in a particular area of activity. Methodologies are often used where linear procedural steps lack the depth of structure to deal with complex issues. Often a methodology will include high-level procedural steps. Some examples are:

Information Security Risk Management Methodology
Project Management Methodology
Penetration Testing Methodology
Procurement Methodology
Data Protection Impact Analysis Methodology

Template: a document that serves as a model for others to copy. When creating templates, always combine the template with a guideline on how to complete the template. I have seen (and have been asked to complete) so many templates where it is not clear what the template issuer wants in the completed document. Where possible try and include input validation and just-in-time advice to the support completion of templates. Some examples are:

Supervisory Authority Notification Template
DPIA Template
Monthly Reporting Template
Project Initiation Document Template

In many cases, the documents above may have already been created (e.g. by Information Security or by the Project Management Officer). Where it is the case that others have created material, don't try and reinvent the wheel but work with the document owners to get those templates amended to include the Data Protection elements.

Policy Enforcement

Once a policy is approved and issued the work does not stop there, the policy must now be enforced. In addition to explicitly stating who will be accountable for non-compliance with policies, a policy must include the person(s) responsible for enforcing the policy in the Roles and Responsibilities section to ensure there is no doubt as to why a person or team is requesting tasks be completed in a certain way or information be provided in a certain format and timeframe. There are a number of tools which can be used to enforce a policy which will be discussed in this section.

Automated Policy Enforcement: This is the ideal scenario whereby technical controls actively monitor compliance and, where configured correctly, prohibit non-compliance. Access Management is the most common automated policy control, but other controls include Anti-Virus, Data Leakage Prevention (if combined with Information Classification) and Scheduled Backups. It is common to think of vulnerability scanning as an automated policy enforcement tool. However, this would be only the case where organisations have configured systems to allow automatically respond to the information identified. Security Information and Event Management (SIEM) systems are a case-in-point whereby on detection of a potential security breach can be configured to isolate a system to minimise the potential impact of the security breach.

Key Performance Indicators (KPIs): depending on what is permitted in your Member State, it may be possible to include an objective within employees' annual performance criteria. Such objectives could be tailored to different levels of seniority or department. When defining any objective, it is important to note the objective must be Specific, Measurable, Agreed, Realistic and Time-Bound (SMART) and there must be a mechanism to fairly and consistently report upon agreed performance.

Reporting: this is a passive method of enforcing policy but can often be very effective. The key to enforcing policy through reporting is to ensure the information is presented in a manner which motivates the intended audience. Metrics in reporting can be used negatively; to highlight where one department is letting the side down or positively; to encourage competition.

Negative Metric:	**Positive Metric:**
Total number of incidents per department this year.	Subject Access Request Response Time per department this month.

Disciplinary Actions and Termination of Contract: unfortunately, there will be times when there is no other recourse but to take disciplinary action or terminate a contract. In such serious circumstances, it is incredibly important to ensure there are alternative options for processing ready to go. When enforcing policy at a Third Party, policy requirements will need to be converted into contractual terms[72] and enforced through Service Level Agreements (SLA) which we will discuss in Chapter 14. Consideration should also be taken as to how to enforce policy with temporary resources such as Contractors, Interns and Volunteers. For Contractors, this could involve immediate termination of contract but it is a little more challenging with Interns and Volunteers, and so the risk of allowing Interns and Volunteers access to processing activities must be balanced against the risk to the Data Subjects.

---

[72] Article 29: Processing under the authority of the controller or processor

The Data Protection / Privacy Notice

In addition to internal organisational policies, the Practitioner must ensure information is provided to Data Subjects publically. Typically, the primary method will be the Data Protection Notice or a Privacy Statement. Before we get on to the meat of the Privacy Notice, for clarification, Privacy Policy and Privacy statements are not synonymous terms. It's important for Practitioners to ensure their organisations understand the difference. A Privacy Policy is an internal organisational policy which sets out the requirements related to how an organisation upholds Data Subjects' privacy rights. A Data Protection / Privacy Notice is a statutory public document which provides information showing how an organisation upholds Data Subjects' rights. The Privacy Notice will therefore not be a set of rules but a concise document written in plain English and containing statutory information. Organisations processing Personal or Sensitive Data must have a publically available Privacy Notice under current legislation[73], GDPR will require that Privacy Notices include additional information. It is unlikely there will be a situation where an organisation doesn't require a Privacy Notice because it is unlikely your business could possibly function without processing some form of personal data. If you have a modern website, for example, the site will store cookies on a Data Subject's machine. if you use analytical services, provided by organisations such as LinkedIn and Google, these organisations will collect information about site visitors and combine it with the information they already hold on the user. In short, unless you have coded a static website, with absolutely no functionality and no analytics capability, there must be a Privacy Notice made publically available.

Layering: a favoured approach to providing privacy notices in an intelligible and accessible form to data subjects is the concept of layering. The process of layering privacy notices is where information is provided to data subjects in easily digestible chunks but providing further information as required. The most common approach is to include 'just-in-time' privacy notices at the time of collection, a high-level privacy statement and then a more detailed privacy notice. Just-in-Time privacy notices are discussed in Chapter 11.

High-Level Privacy Statement: a high-level privacy statement is a summary version of the full privacy notice. A good format to follow is to write a paragraph under the following headings with links to the relevant sections of the detailed privacy notices:

1. What is Personal Data collected?
2. Who is collecting it?
3. How is it collected?
4. Why is it being collected?
5. How will it be used?
6. Whom will it be shared with?
7. What will be the effect of this on the individuals concerned?
8. Is the intended use likely to cause individuals to object or complain?

Statutory Privacy Information: If an organisation fails to provide statutory privacy information, it would be exposed to the risk of enforcement action by a Supervisory Authority and, additionally, Data Subjects would have the right to seek a judicial remedy. To remove ambiguity, the statutory information which is to be provided to Data Subjects shall be described as a Privacy Notice in this book, but the document may also be referred to as a Privacy Statement, a Data Protection Notice or a Data Protection Statement. In addition to GDPR requirements, an organisation's privacy notice must still include the statutory information required from other pieces of legislation (e.g. PECR) however those items will not be covered as PECR is out of the scope of this book. So, what must a Privacy Statement under GDPR include? The following is a list of mandatory information which a Privacy Notice must include:

---

[73] Directive 95/46/EC & Directive 2002/58/EC both include a requirement to provide Data Subjects information

Identity and contact details of the controller and where applicable, the controller's representative and the data protection officer: This is an amended requirement under GDPR. The name and details of the Controller were already required however if you are an organisation operating from outside the European Union there is a requirement to appoint a representative and their details must be included in the Privacy Notice. Where an organisation is mandated to appoint a Data Protection Officer, their details must also be included on the site. Under the 95/46/EC directive, many organisations have provided a postal address only for the Data Protection Officer and where a Data Subject enquiry has arrived at the Customer Service email address, Customer Service Representatives have directed Data Subjects to write to the DPO at their postal address. Under GDPR, Data Subjects can make queries to anyone in the organisation and in electronic form too so it may be worth setting up a Data Protection Enquiries email address to cut out the middleman and reduces the chances of a missed deadline.

Purpose of the processing and the legal basis for the processing: there must be a clear statement explaining why the data provided, directly or indirectly, from a user has been collected. An organisation must not state only the primary purpose but all purposes. For example, if a Data Subject provides data to sign up to an online portal but the data will also be used to profile the Data Subject or be used for marketing purposes, these purposes must be clearly stated on the Notice. If all the purposes are not clearly stated, just remember; it may become challenging to prove the undisclosed processing activity is lawful. Within this section of the notice, the organisation must also explain the legal basis for processing which would be one or more of the six reasons stated in Chapter 02.

The legitimate interests of the controller or third party, where applicable: Except where it applies to Public Authorities, legitimate interests hasn't materially changed under GDPR. Organisations' Privacy Notices must include a statement explaining its legitimate interests for processing personal data. You may be thinking this sounds very similar to the first statement concerning the purpose and legal basis. Legitimate interests is a lawful basis for processing however it may not be clear what these legitimate interests are to a Data Subject. It is useful to think of legitimate interests as ancillary processing activities which only come about from processing data for a primary purpose, of which the Controller has a legal basis.

> **EXAMPLE: A Data Subject provides Personal Data for a loan application via an online portal. At the same time, additional Personal Data is collected for fraud prevention purposes. While the additional data collected is not required for the processing of the loan application it is in the Controllers legitimate interests to prevent fraudulent applications**

Legitimate interests are not solely related to data held by the Controller but may also relate to data passed to a third party. Where organisations are relying on legitimate interests as a legal basis for a processing activity which uses a third party, the legitimate interest must clearly state third-party involvement.

> **EXAMPLE: NDH LLC use an outsourced service provider who manages a Security Information and Event Management (SIEM) system. The third party provider has access to logs which contain personal data. A Controller is sharing this information with a Processor, for information security purposes, could be considered a legitimate interest of the Controller.**

When using legitimate interests as a legal basis for processing the Controller must be able to demonstrate they have taken into account the primary processing activity and whether the legitimate interest is compatible. Specifically, this consideration must take into account the link between processing activities, the context in which data was provided by a Data Subject, the Personal and Sensitive data collected, the consequences of these processing activities on the Data Subject and the existence of appropriate safeguards. Where legitimate interests are processed by a Processor, a binding contract would likely be required too.

EXAMPLE: WhackyRolesRUs are a recruitment company who are registered with a Jobs Board and can download Candidate CVs when a Candidate has applied for a particular role. WhackyRolesRUs advertise a position on the Board but do not state the company name in the advert. The Recruiter would have to consider whether their legitimate interest in sharing applicants' CVs with the hiring organisation outweighs the possible consequences of the intended further processing for the applicants, I.e. would the applicant want this, as yet unidentified, organisation to have a copy of their CV.

Any recipient or categories of recipients of the personal data: in a similar fashion to the requirement to publish information concerning personal data categories, Controllers are required to be explicit about whom they share Data Subjects' Personal Data. The following are some of the categories of recipients which could be used in your Privacy Notice:

Family Member	Healthcare Professional	Past Employers	Examining bodies
Credit reference agencies	Central and local government	Persons making an enquiry	Charitable Organisations
Traders in personal data	Recruitment agencies	Ombudsmen and regulatory authorities	Fraud prevention agencies
Police Forces	Suppliers	Claims Investigators	…and more!

Details of transfers to third country and safeguards: this requirement is not new to GDPR, if you intend to transfer EU Data Subjects' Personal or Sensitive Data outside the European Economic Area (EEA) you must make this clear in your privacy notice. The notice must also include details of why you are transferring this data and how you will ensure Personal or Sensitive Data transferred to a third country will be safeguarded.

Retention period or criteria used to determine the retention period: the requirement to inform the Data Subject about the basis for determining how long data is to be retained is new however the requirement to only retain data for the minimum period necessary is not. The Privacy Notice should inform the user how long their data is likely to be retained either by reference to a specific legally required retention period, a legal basis to hold the data (e.g. due to ongoing litigation) or because a Data Subject has provided consent for Personal Data to be held for a specified period of time up to and including indefinitely.

Categories of personal data: this should be fairly straightforward in principle. It is the Personal and Sensitive data you collect in categories a Data Subject is likely to understand. In this section, the Controller must also state the categories of data subject too. The following table should give you an idea of the categories of Personal and Sensitive Date which your organisation may process and the categories of Data Subjects the data may relate.

Personal Data Categories	Sensitive Data Categories	Data Subject Categories
Personal details	Racial or ethnic origin	Employees
Family details	Political opinions	Customers
Financial details	Religious or other beliefs of a similar nature	Beneficiaries, assignees and payees,
Education and employment details	Trade union membership	Professional advisers and consultants
Goods and services provided	Physical or mental health details	Complainants, enquirers
Lifestyle and social circumstances	Sexual life	Members and shareholders
Visual images, personal appearance and behaviour	Offences and alleged offences	Individuals captured by CCTV images
Text of articles and information relevant to the publication	Criminal proceedings, outcomes and sentences	Suppliers and service providers
Business activities of the person whose personal data we are processing		Subjects of publication
		Offenders and suspected offenders

Data Categories

The existence of each of data subject's rights: this section of your policy must clearly state that Data Subjects have rights under the General Data Protection Regulation (as discussed in Chapter 04) and provide information relating to how the Data Subject can exercise those rights.

The right to withdraw consent at any time, where relevant: where consent is relied upon for a processing activity, the data subject has the right to withdraw such consent. This must be made clear in your privacy notice, and you should also provide high-level instructions (or a link to further instructions) explaining how consent can be withdrawn. Remember consent must be as easy to withdraw as it was for the Data Subject to provide.

The right to lodge a complaint with a supervisory authority: privacy notices must provide information to the Data Subject stating their right to lodge a complaint with the Supervisory Authority. It's worth including a Supervisory Authority's contact details but remember, the Data Subject could just as easily ignore this guidance and lodge a complaint with the Supervisory Authority of their Home Member State. The Supervisory Authority of the Member State where the Data Subject resides (i.e. An Austrian National working in Belgium) or Supervisory Authority of their Member State where the organisation is located

The source the personal data originates from and whether it came from publicly accessible sources: you must tell the data subject where you are getting Personal Data from. This could be from the Data Subject themselves either directly (i.e. the data subject consciously fills in a form) or indirectly (the data subject's computer or mobile device provides with information without the data subject's conscious knowledge). It could be from publically available registers such as the electoral roll or perhaps a third party market research organisation.

Whether the provision of personal data forms part of a statutory or contractual requirement or obligation and possible consequences of failing to provide the personal data: if a data subject enters into a contract with a third party, the collection of personal data may be required to fulfil the contractual terms. In these cases, the Data Subject must be told this is why the data is being collected, and the impact should they not provide the contractually required data. Consequences could be that a service cannot be fulfilled or the data subject may experience a reduced service.

> **EXAMPLE: Gary enters into a contract with a dating agency. The contract states the agency will provide three introductions per month. The contract requires Gary to provide specific information in order to maximise the chance of a good match. The dating agency must inform Gary that failure to provide the requested personal or sensitive data could result in more frogs than princesses.**

The existence of automated decision making, including profiling and information about how decisions are made, the significance and the consequences: if an organisation uses automated decision making or profiling techniques as part of their offering then they must state this in their privacy policy. This information must also be complemented by information explaining to a Data Subject they have the right to object to such processing and can instead request a manual alternative.

> **EXAMPLE: Gary is not getting much luck from the dating agency. Rather than believing his poor success rate is down to his poor dress sense and lack of conversational skills, he believes the matching algorithm is the cause. Gary checks the privacy notice and finds he can request the matching process is carried out manually instead. While the manual matching process did identify some further introductions, sadly, Gary was no more successful.**

Example General Data Protection Policy

NB: This policy is for example only and is not intended to be suitable for any particular organisation.

1. Approvals & Review:

1.1   This policy was endorsed by Policy Committee on 19 February 2018 and approved by the Board on 20 March 2018. The policy shall apply 20 March 2018 and will be enforced from 24 May 2018.

1.2   This Policy shall be reviewed by Policy Committee no later than 25 May 2019.

2. Version Control:

2.1 The current official copy of this policy shall be located on the policy portal. If this document was found in any other location, the reader should check the policy portal to confirm they are reading the current requirements. The following version information is as follows:

Ver.	Description	Date	Author	Reviewer
0.1	Initial Draft	01/12/17	DPO	HORM
0.9	Final Draft	05/01/18	DPO	CRO
1.0	Approved for Issue	20/03/18	DPO	Policy Committee

3. Policy Owner:

3.1   The Owner of this policy is the incumbent Data Protection Officer.

4. Purpose:

4.1   An organisation which controls processing activities, involving Personal or Sensitive Data relating to European Union Data Subjects, must comply with the General Data Protection Regulation 2016 ('**GDPR**') and the Privacy & Electronic Communications Regulation 2003 ('**PECR**'). This policy sets out the requirements all those in scope must adhere.

4.2   This Policy is subject to all the laws, rules and regulations that this organisation is governed by. In the event this policy allows the exercise of discretion, such discretion must be exercised within the confines of the organisation's statutory obligations and must not contravene any of its legal, accounting or other regulatory requirements.

5. Risk Appetite Statement:

5.1   The Boards Risk Appetite for a material breach of GDPR compliance is **LOW**.

5.2   The Board has identified personal data breaches, failing to uphold Data Subjects' rights and reputational damage as key data protection risks.

6. Glossary of Terms:

6.1   A glossary of defined terms shall be included in Appendix A to this Policy.

7. Scope:

7.1   The scope of this policy covers all Processing activities and supporting Information Systems involving Personal or Sensitive Data where the organisation acts as the Controller. This includes personal or sensitive data in physical form, stored in a relevant filing system.

7.2   The scope of this policy covers all global geographic territories. For the avoidance of doubt, this includes Third Countries, outside the European Union (EU).

7.3   The scope of this policy covers all Employees, Contractors, Third Parties, Processors or others who process Personal of Sensitive Data on behalf of the organisation.

8. Requirements:

Principles

8.1   All Processing activities shall be:

      I. Collected for specified, explicit and legitimate purposes only
      II. Accurate and, where necessary, kept up to date
      III. Retained only for as long as necessary
      IV. Processed lawfully, fairly and in a transparent manner
      V. Processed securely, in an appropriate manner to maintain security
      VI. Adequate, relevant and limited to what is necessary

Data Protection Officer (DPO)

9.1   A Data Protection Officer (DPO) shall be appointed and report directly to the Board.

9.2   The DPO shall support the organisation in upholding the rights of Data Subjects as it relates to the organisation's processing activities.

9.3   The DPO shall respond to enquiries from Data Subjects in a timely manner.

9.4   The DPO shall establish and maintain a programme to monitor compliance with this policy.

9.5   The DPO shall establish and maintain a General Data Protection training and awareness programme.

9.6   The DPO shall support compliance with this policy by providing support and advice as it relates to complying with the requirements of this policy.

9.7   The DPO shall be provided timely and appropriate access to information and information systems as it relates to the discharge of their duties.

9.8   Details of the DPO, and their contact details shall be made publically available.

9.9   The DPO shall maintain the following registers:

      I. Register of Processing Activities
     II. Register of Data Protection Impact Assessments (DPIA)
    III. Register for Data Protection Metrics
    IV. Register for Data Subject Enquiries

9.10 The DPO shall report personal data breaches to the Supervisory Authority no later than 72 hours after the breach has been detected.

Accountability

10.1 A record of processing activities shall be provided to the Data Protection Officer

10.2 A System Owner shall be appointed for all Information Systems containing Personal or Sensitive Data. The System Owner shall **not** be from IT unless IT is performing the primary processing activity (e.g. IT operate the Service Desk System and so an IT Manager could be assigned as System Owner).

10.3 System Ownership shall **not** be assigned to a person who does not have budgetary responsibility for the Information System.

10.4 System Ownership shall **not** be assigned to a person who does not hold formal authority over those carrying out processing activity within the Information System.

10.5 A System Owner may delegate responsibility for operational tasks relating to this policy but shall **not** delegate accountability.

10.6 A System Owner may seek advice in the discharge of their duties but remains accountable for any subsequent decisions taken (e.g. acceptance of risk).

10.7 Processing activities shall be documented and a Process Owner appointed

10.8 Process Ownership shall **not** be assigned to a person who does not hold formal authority over those carrying out processing activity within the Information System.

Lawfulness of Processing

11.1 Process Owners shall ensure processing is lawful and document the lawful grounds for processing.

11.2 Where processing involves data of Children, parental consent must be sought, provided and documented.

11.3 With the exception of storage, processing shall cease immediately where there are no longer lawful grounds for processing.

Transparency

12.1 Process Owners shall ensure information related to their processing activities is made available to the DPO so that an organisational Data Protection notice may be published.

12.2 Data Subjects shall be informed of processing activities and provided statutory information at the time data is collected.

12.3 Where data is collected from a source other than the Data Subject, they shall be informed of processing activities and provided statutory information as soon as practicable but no less than 10 working days.

12.4 Process Owners shall review the published Data Protection notice quarterly for any inaccuracies relating to their processes. The Process Owner shall report inaccuracies to the DPO within 5 working days.

Data Protection by Design & Default

13.1 Information Systems and Processes shall be designed to comply with the requirements of this policy.

13.2 Process and System Owners shall implement appropriate technical and organisational measures to ensure that data protection is incorporated into processes and systems, by design and default.

13.3 Processing activities and supporting Information Systems shall be designed to ensure the minimum personal data is stored and for the minimum period necessary.

13.4 All Information Systems shall ensure their systems undergo a Data Protection Impact Analysis (DPIA) which contains at a minimum:

I. a systematic description of the envisaged processing operations and the purposes of the processing.
II. an assessment of the necessity and proportionality of the processing operations in relation to the purposes;
III. an assessment of the risks to the rights and freedoms of data subjects
IV. the measures envisaged to address the risks, including safeguards, security measures and mechanisms to ensure the protection of personal data and to demonstrate compliance with this policy taking into account the rights and legitimate interests of data subjects and other persons concerned

13.5 The System Owner shall consult with the DPO in relation to the completion of the DPIA.

13.6 The DPO shall, where the risk to Data Subjects' rights is deemed HIGH, consult with the Supervisory Authority.

13.7 System Owners shall ensure systems are explicitly designed to minimise the impact involved in upholding Data Subjects' rights.

13.8 Process Owners shall ensure processes are explicitly designed to minimise the impact involved in upholding Data Subjects' rights.

Security of Processing

14.1 System Owners shall be accountable for ensuring systems meet the minimum required standards for security, including, but not limited to:

      I. Identity & Access Management
      II. Patch & Vulnerability Management
      III. Change Management
      IV. Backup & Restoration
      V. IT Service Continuity Planning and Testing
      VI. Development and Testing Activities
      VII. Security breach monitoring and detection

14.2 Information Systems, containing personal or sensitive data, exposed to the Internet or a Third Party, shall be subject to an independent, risk-based penetration test to an agreed scope, no less than annually. System Owners shall ensure all issues identified are appropriate treated commensurate with the Board's risk appetite.

14.3 Personal Data Breaches shall be reported to the DPO as soon as possible but no later than 24 hours after detection.

Accuracy of Processing

15.1 Process Owners shall ensure data remains accurate and where inaccurate corrected as soon as possible but no later than 5 working days from when the error is reported and verified.

15.2 Process Owners of processes involving automated decision making or profiling shall document an alternative manual process and ensure appropriate resources are trained to carry out the manual process if required.

15.3 A Data Subject shall have a right not to be subject to an automated decision or profiling. Process Owner shall ensure this right is respected except where statutory exemptions apply.

Retention

16.1 With the exception of data held under statutory exemptions, personal data shall not be retained any longer than necessary.

Data Subject Access

17.1 Process Owners shall ensure those processing data understand how to identify a Data Subject access request

17.2 Data Subject access requests shall be recorded in a register owned by the DPO.

17.3 Data Subject access requests shall be completed as soon as possible but no more than 30 calendar days.

17.4 Data Subject access requests shall **not** incur a charge

17.5 Data Subject access request shall be processed electronically if this is requested by the Data Subject.

17.6 Reasonable steps shall be taken to verify the identity of the Data Subject prior to providing access to their personal data.

17.7 System Owners shall ensure appropriate resource is made available to support Data Subject access requests.

17.8 Reasonable steps shall be made to seek the permission of third parties prior to including their information within an access request. Where permission is not provided, the DPO shall be consulted to determine whether data should be provided or redacted.

17.9 Requested information shall be communicated to the Data Subject securely

Third Party Processing

18.1 Processing activities shall **not** be outsourced to a third party without a binding written contract that sets out the subject-matter and duration of the processing, the nature and purpose of the processing, the type of personal data and categories of Data Subjects and the obligations and rights of this Organisation.

18.2 Process Owners shall use only third-party Processors providing sufficient guarantees to implement appropriate technical and organisational measures in such a manner that processing will meet the requirements of this policy and ensure the protection of the rights of the Data Subject.

18.3 Process and System Owners shall consult with, and attain a written recommendation from the DPO and representatives from Legal, Procurement, Information Security, Business Continuity and Risk **prior** to signing a contract with a third party Processor and with sufficient time to carry out effective due-diligence on the proposed outsourced process and the third party Processors data protection technical and organisational controls.

18.4 Process and System Owners shall engage an independent (internal or external) assessor that is professionally qualified to assess the third party Processor's data protection technical and organisations controls.

18.5 Process and System Owners engaging third-party Processors shall ensure continuing compliance with this policy and maintain accurate records of relevant meetings and compliance visits including supporting evidence of the third party Processor's ongoing compliance.

19. Roles & Responsibilities:

19.1 The Board has overall responsibility for this policy, and for reviewing the effectiveness of actions taken in response to concerns raised in this policy.

19.2 Senior Management shall ensure appropriate resources are made available to support the implementation of this policy throughout all in-scope areas.

19.3 All those in scope of this policy are responsible for adhering to the requirements of this policy

19.4 The Data Protection Officer (DPO) is responsible for monitoring compliance with this policy and shall provide periodic reporting to the Board and Senior Management on the organisation's compliance with this policy.

19.5 The Data Protection Office shall be the contact point for all matters relating to the Supervisory Authority (SA)

19.6 The Chief Information Security Officer (CISO) is responsible for providing information security support as it relates to this policy.

19.7 Those described as Owners of this policy are responsible for ensuring their Processes, and Information Systems meet the minimum requirements of all in-scope policies.

19.8 The Owners of the policies, detailed in 10.1, shall ensure requirements are amended to reflect the requirements of this policy.

19.9 The Head of Human Resources shall ensure Human Resources processing is compliant with the requirements of this policy.

19.10   The Head of Marketing shall ensure processing related to marketing activities is compliant with the requirements of this policy.

19.11   The Head of Procurement shall ensure procurement processes are compliant with the requirements of this policy.

19.12   Internal Audit shall provide the Board with independent assurance that the organisation is adhering to the requirements of this policy.

20. Related Policies

20.1 This policy should not be read in isolation. The following policies also include specific and supporting requirements:

     I. (Enterprise/Operational) Risk Management Policy
    II. Information Security Policy
    III. Incident Response Policy
    IV. Records Management Policy
    V. HR Policy Portfolio
    VI. Change Management Policy
    VII. Project Management Policy
    VIII. Outsourcing Policy
    IX. Fraud Policy

20.2 The policies stated in paras 10.1 can be found in the Policy Portal on the Corporate Intranet Site.

21. Links to supporting Templates

21.1 Templates and other supporting materials can be found in the Data Protection Section of the Organisation's Intranet Site.

Appendix A – Glossary of Terms

This appendix would contain a glossary of terms used in the policy. I am not going to waste valuable pages copying terms already defined elsewhere in this book!

Example Privacy Notice

NB: This policy is for example only and will not be suitable for any particular organisation.

1. Introduction

Fox Red Risk Solutions Ltd takes data protection seriously. The use of the Internet pages of the Fox Red Risk Solutions Ltd is not possible without the provision of some personal data; however, if a Data Subject wishes to use certain services via our website, processing of further personal data could become necessary. If the processing of personal data is necessary and there is no statutory basis for such processing, we will obtain consent from the data subject.

Personal Data processing shall always be in line with the General Data Protection Regulation (GDPR), and in accordance with the country-specific legislation applicable to the Fox Red Risk Publishing. By means of this Privacy Notice, we would like to inform the general public why we collect and process personal data and Data Subjects rights relating to the collection and processing of Personal Data.

2. Definitions:

The data protection notice of the Fox Red Risk Solutions Ltd is based on the terms used by the European legislator for the adoption of the General Data Protection Regulation (GDPR) but for ease of understanding the following definitions apply.

Controller: the natural or legal person, public authority, agency or other body which, alone or jointly with others, determines the purposes and means of the processing of personal data; where the purposes and means of such processing are determined by Union or Member State law, the controller or the specific criteria for its nomination may be provided for by Union or Member State law.

Personal data: any information relating to an identified or identifiable natural person ("Data Subject"). An identifiable natural person is one who can be identified, directly or indirectly, in particular by reference to an identifier such as a name, an identification number, location data, an online identifier or to one or more factors specific to the physical, physiological, genetic, mental, economic, cultural or social identity of that natural person.

Data subject: any identified or identifiable natural person, whose personal data is processed by the controller responsible for the processing.

Processor: a natural or legal person, public authority, agency or other body which processes personal data on behalf of the controller.

Recipient: a natural or legal person, public authority, agency or another body, to which the personal data are disclosed, whether a third party or not. However, public authorities which may receive personal data in the framework of a particular inquiry in accordance with Union or Member State law shall not be regarded as recipients; the processing of those data by those public authorities shall be in compliance with the applicable data protection rules according to the purposes of the processing.

Third Party: a natural or legal person, public authority, agency or body other than the data subject, controller, processor and persons who, under the direct authority of the controller or processor, are authorised to process personal data.

Restriction of processing: the marking of stored personal data with the aim of limiting their processing in the future.

Processing: any operation or set of operations which is performed on personal data or on sets of personal data, whether or not by automated means, such as collection, recording, organisation, structuring, storage, adaptation or alteration, retrieval, consultation, use, disclosure by transmission, dissemination or otherwise making available, alignment or combination, restriction, erasure or destruction.

Profiling: any form of automated processing of personal data consisting of the use of personal data to evaluate certain personal aspects relating to a natural person, in particular to analyse or predict aspects concerning that natural person's performance at work, economic situation, health, personal preferences, interests, reliability, behaviour, location or movements.

Consent: Consent of the data subject is any freely given, specific, informed and unambiguous indication of the data subject's wishes by which he or she, by a statement or by a clear affirmative action, signifies agreement to the processing of personal data relating to him or her.

3. Name and Address of the Controller:

The Controller is:

Fox Red Risk Publishing, 27 Old Gloucester Road, London, WC1N 3AX. Phone: +44 (0) 20 8720 9260. Email: info@foxredrisk.com. Website: https://www.foxredrisk.com

4. Name and Address of the Data Protection Officer:

The Data Protection Officer of the Controller is:

Data Protection Officer, Fox Red Risk Solutions Ltd, 27 Old Gloucester Road, London, WC1N 3AX. Phone: +44 (0) 20 8720 9260. Email: dpo@foxredrisk.com. Website: https://www.foxredrisk.com

A Data Subject may contact our Data Protection Officer directly with any enquiries relating to Data Protection.

5. Name and Address of the Lead Supervisory Authority:

The Lead Supervisory Authority overseeing the Controller is:

Information Commissioner's Office, Wycliffe House, Water Lane, Wilmslow, Cheshire, SK9 5AF, United Kingdom. Phone: +44 (0) 303 123 1113, Email: casework@ico.org.uk. Website: https://ico.org.uk

6. Cookies

The Internet pages of the Fox Red Risk Solutions Ltd use cookies. Cookies are text files that are stored in a computer system via an Internet browser. Many Internet sites and servers use cookies. Many cookies contain a so-called cookie ID. A cookie ID is a unique identifier of the cookie. It consists of a character string through which Internet pages and servers can be assigned to the specific Internet browser in which the cookie was stored. This allows visited Internet sites and servers to differentiate the individual browser of the data subject from other Internet browsers that contain other cookies. A specific Internet browser can be recognised and identified using the unique cookie ID. Through the use of cookies, the Fox Red Risk Solutions Ltd can provide the users of this website with more user-friendly services that would not be possible without the cookie setting.

By means of a cookie, the information and offers on our website can be optimised with the user in mind. Cookies allow us, as previously mentioned, to recognise our website users. The purpose of this recognition is to make it easier for users to utilise our website. The website user that uses cookies e.g. does not have to enter access data each time the website is accessed, because this is taken over by the website, and the cookie is thus stored on the user's computer system. The data subject may, at any time, prevent the setting of cookies through our website by means of a corresponding setting of the Internet browser used, and may thus permanently deny the setting of cookies. Furthermore, already set cookies may be deleted at any time via an Internet browser or other software programs. This is possible in all popular Internet browsers. If the data subject deactivates the setting of cookies in the Internet browser used, not all functions of our website may be entirely usable.

7. Reasons/purposes for processing information

The following is a broad description of the way this organisation/data controller processes personal information. To understand how your own personal information is processed you may also need to refer to any personal communications you have received. We process personal information to enable us to provide Information Security and Data Protection consultancy and advisory services, to promote our services, to maintain our own accounts and records and to support and manage our employees.

We collect information relating to the above reasons/purpose from the following sources:

- The Data Subject directly (e.g. from information entered into forms)
- The Data Subject indirectly (e.g. information collected when you browse our site such as IP address and Operating System)
- Publically Available Registers (e.g. Electoral Roll)
- Social Media (e.g. Twitter, LinkedIn, Facebook)
- Research provided by Third Party Providers including Search Engines

We process information relating to the above reasons/purposes. This information may include:

- personal details
- business activities of the person whose personal information we are processing
- goods and services provided
- financial details
- education details
- employment details

We also process sensitive classes of information that may include:

- offences and alleged offences

We process personal information about our:

- customers
- clients and employees
- complainants and enquirers
- suppliers
- advisers and other professional experts

We sometimes need to share the personal information we process with the individual themselves and also with other organisations. Where this is necessary, we are required to comply with all aspects of the Data Protection Act (DPA), Privacy and Electronic Communications Regulation (PECR) and the EU General Data Protection Regulation (GDPR) as it applies. What follows is a description of the types of organisations we may need to share some of the personal information we process with for one or more reasons.

Where necessary or required we share information with:

- business associates and other professional advisers
- financial organisations
- current, past or prospective employers
- educators and examining bodies
- suppliers and services providers

8. Rights of the data subject

GDPR affords EU Data Subjects with rights. These rights are summarised below. In order to assert any of these rights, the Data Subject may contact the Data Protection Officer designated by the Fox Red Risk Solutions Ltd or another employee at any time.

The right of Confirmation: Each data subject shall have the right to obtain from the controller the confirmation as to whether or not personal data concerning him or her are being processed.

The right of Access: Each data subject shall have the right to obtain from the controller, free information about his or her personal data stored at any time and a copy of this information. Furthermore, the data subject shall have a right to obtain information as to whether personal data are transferred to a third country or to an international organisation. Where this is the case, the data subject shall have the right to be informed of the appropriate safeguards relating to the transfer.

Right to Rectification: Each data subject shall have the right granted by the European legislator to obtain from the controller without undue delay the rectification of inaccurate personal data concerning him or her. Taking into account the purposes of the processing, the data subject shall have the right to have incomplete personal data completed, including by means of providing a supplementary statement.

Right to Erasure (Right to be forgotten): Each data subject shall have the right to obtain from the controller the erasure of personal data concerning him or her without undue delay, and the controller shall have an obligation to erase personal data without undue delay where one of the statutory grounds applies, as long as the processing is not necessary

Right of Restriction of Processing: Each data subject shall have the right granted by the European legislator to obtain from the controller restriction of processing where a statutory reason applies

Right to Data Portability: Each data subject shall have the right granted by the European legislator, to receive the personal data concerning him or her, which was provided to a controller, in a structured, commonly used and machine-readable format.

Right to Object: Each data subject shall have the right to object, on grounds relating to his or her particular situation, at any time, to the processing of personal data concerning him or her.

Automated individual decision-making, including profiling: Each data subject shall have the right not to be subject to a decision based solely on automated processing, including profiling.

Right to Withdraw Consent: Where consent forms the basis for processing, Data Subjects shall have the right to withdraw his or her consent to the processing of his or her personal data at any time. Data Subjects can withdraw consent by logging into the user portal, clicking the privacy link in the menu and then updating the privacy settings as required. Data Subjects can also contact the Data Protection Officer or any other employee to withdraw consent.

Right to Complain to the Supervisory Authority: Where consent forms the basis for processing, Data Subjects shall have the right to withdraw his or her consent to the processing of his or her personal data at any time. The details of the Supervisory Authority are contained at the top of this Privacy Notice.

9. Legal basis for the processing

The legal basis for processing shall be where:

- the data subject has given consent to the processing of his or her personal data for one or more specific purposes;
- processing is necessary for the performance of a contract to which the data subject is party or in order to take steps at the request of the data subject prior to entering into a contract;
- processing is necessary for compliance with a legal obligation to which the controller is subject;
- processing is necessary in order to protect the vital interests of the data subject or of another natural person;
- processing is necessary for the performance of a task carried out in the public interest or in the exercise of official authority vested in the controller;
- processing is necessary for the purposes of the legitimate interests pursued by the controller or by a third party, except where such interests are overridden by the interests or fundamental rights and freedoms of the data subject which require protection of personal data, in particular where the data subject is a child.

10. The Legitimate Interests pursued by the Controller or by a Third Party

Where the processing of personal data is based on our legitimate interest, it is to carry out our business in favour of the well-being of all our employees and the shareholders.

11. Security of Processing

As the Controller, the Fox Red Risk Solutions Ltd has implemented technical and organisational measures to ensure personal data processed remains secure however absolute security cannot be guaranteed. Should a Data Subject have a particular concern about a particular method of data transmission, we will take reasonable steps to provide an alternative method.

12. Transfers

It may sometimes be necessary to transfer personal information overseas. When transfers are needed, information may be transferred to countries or territories around the world. Any transfers made will be in full compliance with all aspects of the General Data Protection Regulation and in accordance with the country-specific legislation applicable to the Fox Red Risk Publishing.

13. Personal Data Retention Periods

The criteria used to determine the retention period of personal data is the respective statutory retention period within the Member State. After the expiration of that period, personal data shall be securely deleted, as long as it is no longer necessary for the fulfilment of the contract, the initiation of a contract, or in relation to other legal proceedings.

14. Contractual obligation of the data subject to provide the personal data and the possible consequences of failure to provide such data

For clarity, the provision of personal data is partly required by law (e.g. tax regulations) or can also result from contractual provisions (e.g. information on the contractual partner). Sometimes it may be necessary to conclude a contract that the data subject provides us with personal data, which must subsequently be processed by us. The data subject is, for example, obliged to provide us with personal data when our company signs a contract with him or her. The non-provision of the personal data would have the consequence that the contract with the data subject could not be concluded.

15. Automated decision-making & Profiling

We do not process personal data for automatic decision-making or profiling.

16. Data protection for Employment & Recruitment Procedures

The data controller shall collect and process the personal data of applicants for the purpose of the processing of the application procedure. The processing may also be carried out electronically. This is the case, in particular, if an applicant submits corresponding application documents by e-mail or by means of a web form on the website to the controller. If the data controller concludes an employment contract with an applicant, the submitted data will be stored for the purpose of processing the employment relationship in compliance with legal requirements. If no employment contract is concluded with the applicant by the Controller, the application documents shall be automatically erased two months after notification of the refusal decision, provided that no other legitimate interests of the controller are opposed to the erasure. Other legitimate interests could be complying with country-specific legislation, e.g. the UK Equality Act 2010.

17. Data protection notification concerning the use of [*Insert Service / Application*]

On this website, the controller has integrated the component of a third party service called [*Insert Name*]. This service performs the following functions [*Describe Functionality*].

The operator of the Service is [Insert Operator] whose Registered Address is [Insert Address]

Further information and the applicable data protection provisions of the service can be found here: [*Insert Details to the service-specific Privacy Notice(s)*]

18. General

You may not transfer any of your rights under this privacy notice to any other person. We may transfer our rights under this privacy notice where we reasonably believe your rights will not be affected.

If any court or competent authority finds that any provision of this privacy notice (or part of any provision) is invalid, illegal or unenforceable, that provision or part-provision will, to the extent required, be deemed to be deleted, and the validity and enforceability of the other provisions of this privacy notice will not be affected.

Unless otherwise agreed, no delay, act or omission by a party in exercising any right or remedy will be deemed a waiver of that, or any other, right or remedy.

This notice will be governed by and interpreted according to the law of England and Wales. All disputes arising under the notice will be subject to the exclusive jurisdiction of the English and Welsh courts.

19. Changes to this notice

This notice was last updated on 24/05/2018. We may change this policy by updating this page to reflect changes in the law or our privacy practices. However, we will not use your Personal Data in any new ways without your consent.

8. INFORMATION AUDITS & PROCESS MAPPING

In the previous two chapters, communication and awareness have been discussed and also data protection policy and notices. What this means is once you have successfully implemented the content described in these preceding chapters, the people in your organisation will now be aware and will need advice and guidance in meeting policy requirements. The first thing they will likely need help with is identifying and documenting their processing activities. In the first part of this chapter, we will discuss techniques which can be used to discover processing activities which are in scope of the GDPR. This discovery process is more commonly referred to as an Information Audit. Once the Practitioner has identified the processing activities in the scope of GDPR, there is information which organisations must record and maintain as part of GDPR recordkeeping requirements[74]. As you will find throughout the implementation section of this book, there are already mature methodologies out there which, often without any modification, can aid the Practitioner to meet the requirements of GDPR negating the need to develop a whole toolset from scratch. In the second part of this chapter, we will discuss how to map a process using a common process mapping methodologies. If the Practitioner is acquainted with a project management methodology or business analysis techniques, it is likely the recordkeeping requirements will be familiar. This is because a number of the techniques to document information related to processing activities are more commonly used in change and transformation projects, or within a Quality Management System such as ISO 9000.

The Information Audit

The information audit is an exercise which involves every aspect of the business. An organisation must go through all its systems with a fine toothcomb to identify sources of Personal and Sensitive Data. Practitioners should consider running this exercise as a discrete project because this is likely to involve quite a bit of work. The following guidance should hopefully help things move a little quicker. It is also useful to clarify before we go on that an Information Audit is not the same as a Data Protection Audit which must be against your data protection policy or the regulation applicable in the country(ies) your organisation operates.

Scope the Audit: there are a few different ways the information audit could be performed. At the very basic level, the minimum scope would be to confirm where data resides, confirm data ownership and whether the lawfulness of related processing can be ascertained. Depending on resources, the next stage would be to assess compliance to retention requirements – this way anything which doesn't need to be retained can be securely destroyed and at the

---

[74] Article 30: Records of processing activities

same time reducing the size of the compliance burden! The next stage would be to assess the quality of the data. It is a requirement for a Controller to maintain accurate and up-to-date[75] Personal Data so the Information Audit could include in its scope an assessment of the quality and completeness of data currently held. The final stage of the audit would include an assessment of the security[76] risks to processing activities. Ultimately, organisations will need to work through all stages of information audit, but for now, we shall concentrate on identifying data in the scope of GDPR.

Combine with a CMDB project: Configuration Management Databases (CMDB) are databases[77] that contain details about the attributes and history of each Configuration Item (or Information Asset) in your organisation's IT infrastructure and details of the important relationships between the Information Assets. The information held may be in a variety of formats, textual, diagrammatic, photographic, etc.; effectively a data map of the physical reality of IT Infrastructure. CMDBs are tailor-made to support an information audit and the ongoing maintenance of what data is located in what database. If your organisation hasn't seen the value in implementing a CMDB for other aspects of IT Service Management (of which there are many), perhaps GDPR can provide a more compelling business case. Most CMDBs have an automated discovery feature which can dramatically improve the efficiency of an information audit by going out into the organisation's network and classifying information asses.

Automate as much as possible: If at all possible, don't send out Spreadsheets asking the business to fill them out. The most likely scenario will be an Intern or junior member of staff will be 'volunteered' to carry out this prestigious task and will likely have little or no contextual information to guide them. At best you will get about 20% of what you need, and that is likely to be inaccurate. In most organisations Personal Data is likely to be in the following locations:

1. Internal Server-Based Databases (e.g. MS SQL, Oracle, MongoDB)
2. External 'Cloud' Databases (e.g. DynamoDB, SalesForce)
3. External Third Party Datasets
4. MS Access Databases {hopefully there aren't too many of these in your organisation}
5. Spreadsheets and Static Files

For bullet points 1, there should be documentation detailing the supporting applications available from your Project Management Office (PMO) or where these systems are managed by IT there should be operational documentation (e.g. Service Level data). For bullet points 2 and 3, there should be a contract in place or records of payment relating to third parties providing 'Cloud' services. For bullet points 4 and 5, there are network audit tools which have file discovery capabilities and can also generate reports from searches.

When auditing for accuracy, there are data quality tools which can look inside these databases and static files to confirm whether personal data exists and the completeness of the datasets. In both cases, the reports generated can form the basis of discussions with the business as to how compliant (or not) their processing activities are with the GDPR requirements. Readers may wonder why there are no recommendations for specific tools. This is deliberate. The Practitioners reading this book should identify tools appropriate for their organisations' needs. There are freeware tools which may be appropriate for small to medium enterprises (SMEs) which would be wholly inappropriate for a large multinational – and vice versa.

Gather and train your team: Those who will be assigned the task of seeking out personal data will need training. At the very least they should be trained on the definitions of Personal and Sensitive Data and what constitutes Processing. Leverage your Information Security resources as they understand the context and have access to tools.

---

[75] Article 5(1).d
[76] Article 5(1).f
[77] CMDB definition adapted from ITIL

Compile your findings: the final step in the audit process, once data on processing activities has been collected is to compile a Processing Register. Each Processing activity should contain the following information:

1. Process Name
2. Process Owner (Role)
3. Personal Data Processed
    a. Fields
    b. Volume
    c. Users
4. Sensitive Data Processed
    a. Fields
    b. Volume
    c. Users
5. Children's Data Processed
    a. Fields
    b. Volume
    c. Users
6. Automated Processing
    a. Description
    b. Link to Manual Process
7. Purpose(s) of processing activities
8. Lawful Basis for Processing[78]
9. Third Party Processor Involvement (See Chapter 14)
    a. Names
    b. Links to Contracts
10. Transfers to Third Countries or International Organisations (See Chapter 15)
    a. Names
    b. Safeguards
11. Process Map
12. Link to Data Protection Impact Assessment (DPIA) (See Chapter 09)
13. Link to Information Security Assessment (See Chapter 10)

Record Keeping

Those of you who have held the role of Data Protection Officer under the 1995 Directive, A Data Controller was required to provide their Supervisor Authority with a set of 'registrable particulars'. Under GDPR you are no longer required to notify the Supervisory Authority. Don't delete that registrable particulars document just yet as Controllers are required to maintain similar information which must be made available to the Supervisory Authority on request. Article 30 requires that the controller must maintain the following information:

1. Name and contact details of the controller
2. Purpose(s) of processing activities
3. Description of the categories of data subjects and of the categories of personal data;
4. Categories of recipients to whom the personal data have been or will be disclosed including recipients in

---

[78] Article 6: Lawfulness of Processing

third countries or international organisations;

5. Names of Third Countries and International Organisations where data is transferred and associated safeguards.
6. Retention Periods
7. General description of technical and organisational security controls

As will be apparent to existing DPOs, with the exception of describing technical and organisational security controls, the list above is very similar to the information contained in the registrable particulars.

GDPR now includes requirements for Processors to maintain records too. Processors must keep records of the following:

1. A list of Controllers to which the Processor processes personal data
2. Categories of processing carried out on behalf of each of the above Controllers
3. Names of Third Countries and International Organisations where data is transferred and associated safeguards.
4. General description of technical and organisational security controls

Process Mapping

When a process is first established a process map should be documented. If Business Analysts were involved in the underlying project, then you should have process maps documented...should being the operative word. Often at the end of projects, and even more so in AGILE projects, documentation can often be kicked into the long grass at the expense of getting the system over the line. Where process improvements are organic (i.e. the business make incremental changes outside a project) existing documentation may not be updated, or documentation may not be created at all. This isn't the business' fault per se, it usually because there isn't adequate knowledge of process mapping techniques within most businesses. In this section, we will look briefly at a business process modelling technique which can be used to map a process. Mapping processes has a number of benefits in itself in terms of understanding the process and aiding new employees to get up and running efficiently but in terms of data protection process mapping has the following benefits:

1. Provides a simple visual representation of the processing activity
2. Aids the reader to understand how Personal Data enters the process
3. Aids the reader to identify who interacts with the Personal Data
4. Aids the reader to identify controls and control gaps
5. Aids the reader to understand how Personal Data leaves the process
6. Gives Internal Audit a framework to conduct their testing activities
7. Demonstrates to the Supervisory Authority an organisation is managing its Data Protection Risk

Business Process Model & Notation (BPMN): Business Process Model & Notation as a concept was created to enable Business Analysts to document processes in a manner that supported interoperability between different internal departments with the same organisation and different organisations working together on different aspects of the same process or different processes which interact with each other. BPMN provides a very simple yet powerful notation which encompasses the following concepts:

1. Flow Objects – what causes data to move from one process to another?
   a. Events
   b. Activities
   c. Gateways

THE ULTIMATE GDPR PRACTITIONER GUIDE

2. Data – what data is used within the process?
    a. Objects
    b. Inputs
    c. Outputs
    d. Stores
3. Connecting Objects – how does data move around the process?
    a. Sequence Flows
    b. Message Flows
    c. Associations
    d. Data Associations
4. Swim-lanes – who are the processors?
    a. Pools
    b. Lanes
5. Artefacts – what additional information would make the process better understood?
    a. Group
    b. Text Annotation

With just the above components any manual or automated process can be mapped out. A full specification for the latest version of the BPMN standard can be found from the Object Management Group (OMG)[79]. In the example on the next page, BPMN is used to map out the process for a Candidate Filtering Process described below.

The process actors are identified by their pools and swim-lanes The HR Administrator, and Hiring Manager are in separate swim lanes but a single pool to denote they are part of the same organisation. The Candidate is in a separated swim lane because at this stage; the candidates are not part of the organisation. The process starts when candidates initiate the Send CV process and uploads a CV to a Data Store, the Human Resources Information System (HRIS) owned by the HR Administrator. Readers should be aware that within most process modelling methodologies; processes are described using *Verb-Noun* pairs (e.g. Send CV). Whenever data transfers between different pools this is depicted by a dotted line known as a 'message flow'. Once the CV hits the hiring organisation, a timer ticks down until the application deadline is reached. The HR Administrator carries out the first CV filter. This is where the process arrives at a logic gate, an exclusive gateway. An exclusive gateway requires only one path can be taken. Within BPMN there are a number of other logic gates (e.g. inclusive, parallel, event and complex). In this process, the gateway requires the HR admin filter candidate CVs into yes and no piles and then forwards the yes pile on to the hiring manager. After the second filtering process, a second exclusive gateway occurs. This time, the hiring manager filters the CVs into new yes and no piles. Those CVs in the yes pile are then contacted by HR to arrange an interview. Those candidates who aren't successful at either stage are then informed their application has been unsuccessful. In parallel with the candidate filtering process, there is also a trigger which recurs every 90 days to remove candidates details from the HRIS is they have been unsuccessful.

Practitioners can use this type of process map to identify potential data protection issues. For example, does the candidate receive privacy information when a CV is submitted? What fields are collected from the candidate when they register? Is there any automatic processing within the HRIS before the data is presented to the HR Administrator or the Hiring Manager? Is the candidate informed they could have their data removed from the HRIS earlier than 90 days and how they would go about making such a request...and so on.

Other Modelling Languages: BPMN is a great starting point for those who are new to modelling processes as the notation and logic is accessible. Practitioners should also familiarise themselves as appropriate, with other methodologies used such as Unified Modelling Language (UML), Flowcharting and Role Activity Diagrams (RAD).

---

[79] Object Management Group Business Process Model and Notation (http://www.bpmn.org/)

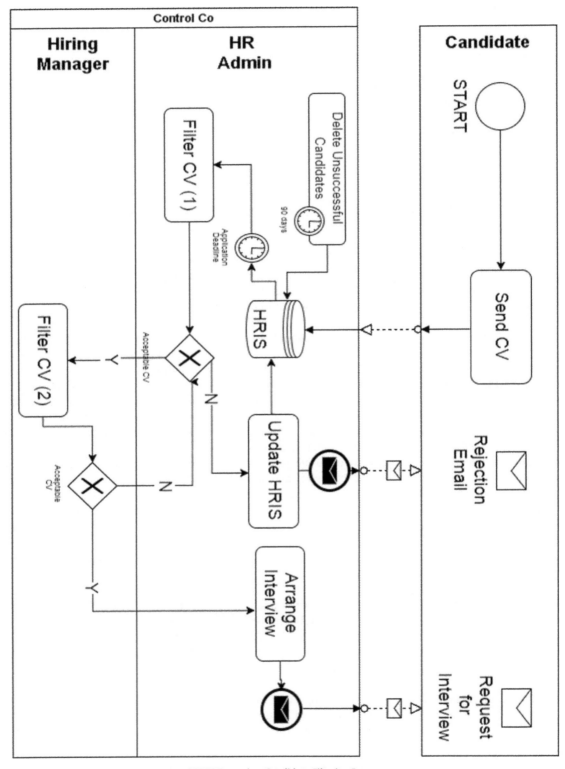

BPMN Example – Candidate Filtering Process

9. DATA PROTECTION IMPACT ASSESSMENT

Under GDPR, a Data Protection Impact Assessment (DPIA) will now form a vital part of new projects and proposals and can be used to help organisations identify the potential risks arising from their collection, use or handling of personal or sensitive data, and to find out if they are meeting their legal obligations. DPIAs focus on identifying the ways a new data processing project or changes to an existing processing activity may affect the rights and freedoms of data subjects and also aids organisations in making more informed decisions and better management of data protection risks. It is important to decide whether to do a DPIA early in the project life-cycle. If you fail to identify how your project is likely to affect the rights and freedoms of data subjects whose information you are processing, there are real risks for your organisation and for the success of your project. In this chapter, we will focus on the Data Protection Impact Assessment as described in Article 35 of GDPR. We will discuss the minimum requirements a DPIA must meet. We will discuss when to conduct a DPIA and whether it may be appropriate to incorporate the DPIA requirements into existing processes (e.g. Procurement, Project Management or Enterprise Risk Management). We will then walk through the steps required to complete a DPIA, culminating in an example of an initial and complete DPIA at the end of the chapter.

Data Protection Impact Assessments are not a new concept. Around the world, many countries require organisations to conduct and publish similar assessments known as Privacy Impact Assessments (PIA). In reality, compared to PIAs, the DPIA is relatively light touch and is a narrower in scope focusing predominantly on the protection of data, as opposed to broader aspects of privacy such as privacy of the person, the privacy of personal behaviour, and privacy of personal communications. While the DPIA doesn't formally require consideration of these extended privacy dimensions, Practitioners should, of course, bear them in mind.

What are the minimum requirements for a DPIA?

GDPR sets out that a DPIA must[80] contain at least:

1. Systematic description, purpose and lawful grounds of the envisaged processing operations
2. An assessment of the necessity and proportionality of the processing operations
3. An assessment of the risks to the rights and freedoms of data subjects

---

[80] Article 35(7) - Data Protection Impact Assessment expands on these requirements

4. the measures envisaged to address the risks, including safeguards, security measures and mechanisms to ensure the protection of personal data and to demonstrate compliance with GDPR.

When is a DPIA Required?

There are certain times when a Data Protection Impact Assessment is mandatory[81]. The more categories a processing activity falls into, the more likely a DPIA will be required. The following are processing activities which require a DPIA to be completed:

1. When the processing is likely to result in a high risk to the rights and freedoms of Data Subjects
2. When processing using new technologies
3. Processing involving profiling and automated decision making, of which either will produce legal effects
4. Processing on a large scale of special categories of data
5. A systematic monitoring of a publicly accessible area on a large scale
6. Evaluation or Scoring
7. Datasets that have been matched of combined
8. Data concerning vulnerable data subjects
9. Innovative use or applying technological or organisational solutions
10. Data transfer across borders outside the European Union
11. The organisational or societal context for the processing activity has changed
12. For existing processing that involved one or more of the items described from 1-11

> **EXAMPLE: A HR Director wishes to migrate a number of separate datasets held within an organisation, to a single database managed by a Third Party and hosted on Amazon Web Services (AWS). The new solution would automatically sift through candidate applications replacing a manual sifting process.**
>
> **This change in processing would require a DPIA as the processing would involve the use of new technologies, combined datasets and**

Exceptions

Article 35 does lay out certain conditions whereby a DPIA is not required. Supervisory Authorities have the option to list the kinds of processing activities which do not require a Data Protection Impact Assessment. At the time of going to print, there was no such list available with the UK or Irish Supervisory Authority, but it is expected these lists will be published within 2018. The other times a DPIA is not required are; where the processing is necessary for compliance with a legal obligation to which the controller is subject or; where processing is necessary for the performance of a task carried out in the public interest or in the exercise of official authority vested in the controller. GDPR[82] does, however, caveat the exceptions above will not apply if the Member States decrees a DPIA must be completed.

---

[81] Guidelines on Data Protection Impact Assessment (DPIA) and determining whether processing is "likely to result in a high risk" for the purposes of Regulation 2016/679, Adopted 04 April 2017
[82] Article 35(5) & (10): Data protection impact assessment

It is also worth noting GDPR requires an organisation to maintain records of all processing, including an assessment of risk and details of mitigating technical and organisational controls – so even if you decide not to do a DPIA, you are pretty much required to document the contents anyway. The key thing to be aware of, in respect to the DPIA is that, with the exception of existing processing activities, the DPIA must be conducted and concluded **prior** to processing commencing. As we will go on to discuss in Chapter 12 (Incident Management), should a Personal Data Breach occur, it is likely the Supervisory Authority will want to see the DPIA.

Consultation

When conducting a DPIA, GDPR[83] requires those who own the processing activity to seek the input from those who will be impacted by the affected processing activity as part of the Impact Assessment process. If the processing affects employees, local employment legislation may also require consultation with unions or works councils. Those operating in countries where such employment legislation doesn't apply but are likely to roll out a process internationally should be especially mindful of seeking consultation early to avoid costly redevelopment further down the line. In addition to consulting with employees and other interested parties, the Data Protection Officer must be involved, properly and in a timely manner, in all issues which relate to the protection of personal data. What this means in practice that whoever is commissioning this new (or changed) processing activity must tell the DPO about it as early in the process as possible. The DPO is required to ensure the DPIA process is implemented effectively and can also provide advice as requested. It would be wise to take full advantage of the DPO's expertise!

Codes of Conduct

Where an organisation is subject to a particular code of conduct, the person carrying out the DPIA must take into account the impact processing may have on adherence to the code.

> **EXAMPLE: A Telesales Organisation signed up to the DMA Code of Conduct, in addition to the requirements of GDPR would need to consider the five principles of put your customer first, RESPECT PRIVACY, be honest and fair, be diligent with data and, take responsibility.**

Standalone or Integrated?

It may be the case in your organisation that there already exists a process to assess the risks relating to new processes or changes to existing processes. Practitioners should consider whether an integrated approach may be an efficient way to reduce the overall burden and manageability relating to completing the DPIA. For example, if there already exists an Operational Risk Assessment or an Information Security Assessment process then consider whether the components of the DPIA could be incorporated. Incorporating other Risk Assessments into the DPIA process is not recommended as not all processes requiring Risk Assessment will require a DPIA and therefore additional complexity could be added to projects unnecessarily.

---

[83] Article 35(9)

The DPIA Process

At a high level, the following process diagram lays out the steps a person carrying out a Data Protection Impact Assessment must follow. The Practitioner must first assess whether a DPIA is required (I.e. where the processing falls into one or more of the categories described in the previous section). Once it is confirmed there are no exceptions which would negate the requirement for a DPIA, the Practitioner then completes the DPIA. The DPIA, taking into account any relevant codes of conduct, views of Data Subjects and other interested parties including the Data Protection Officer, is then reviewed by the controller and actions implemented. Where there are still considered to be high residual risks to the rights and freedoms of affected Data Subjects, there must be prior consultation with the Supervisory Authority.

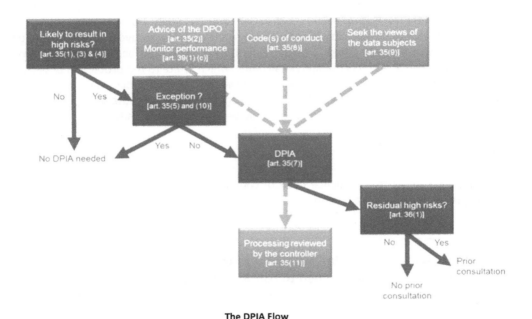

The DPIA Flow

In the proceeding paragraphs, we shall look at the DPIA component in more detail. There are a number of different methodologies across Europe such as CNIL's[84] Privacy Impact Assessment (PIA) and the AEPD's[85] Guía para una Evaluación de Impacto en la de Protección Datos Personales. The UK ICO also produces guidance on how to conduct a DPIA too. Outside the EU, there are also methodologies issued by Data Protection Regulators such as those produced by the Office of the Privacy Commissioner, New Zealand and the Office of the Australian Information Commissioner (OAIC). Whilst the guidance in this chapter focuses on meeting the requirements of GDPR Article 35; good practice has been drawn from these methodologies and guidance provided by the Article 29 Working Party[86]. For every stage described, there will be a pointer to an example DPIA. As with other examples within the book, it is there for informational purposes and is likely not to reflect any specific processing activity within a reader's organisation.

---

[84] Commission nationale de l'informatique et des libertés (DP Supervisory Authority, France)

[85] Agencia Española de Protección de Datos, (DP Supervisory Authority, Spain)

[86] Guidelines on Data Protection Impact Assessment (DPIA) and determining whether processing is "likely to result in a high risk" for the purposes of Regulation 2016/679, Adopted 04 April 2017

Scoping: As with many other activities, it is extremely useful to make sure everyone is on the same page as to what the Data Protection Impact Assessment will cover. In the example DPIA you will see there are items in the scope of the DPIA and also items not in scope. The items not in scope should also include a brief explanation as to why they won't be covered in the DPIA and, ideally, where they will be covered (e.g. in a separate document).

Scoping should always consider whether a full DPIA will be required and a checkpoint should be established to make this decision. The primary method used to determine whether a full DPIA is required is to carry out a screening process. This could be considered DPIA 'lite', and an example is included after this section. In some methodologies, it is recommended to include timelines, checkpoints and milestones relating to the DPIA in the scope section. If the DPIA is part of a project, consider incorporating timings into the project timeline (e.g. on the project's Gantt chart) rather than maintaining this timing information within the DPIA as minimising such temporary information should make the DPIA easier to maintain.

Information Gathering: In order to effectively complete a DPIA, the Practitioner will require various pieces of information. The following people will be key to getting the information required to document a DPIA effectively:

1. The Data Protection Officer – this person will be your Data Protection Subject Matter Expert!
2. Information Security Department – they are likely to be familiar with what you're trying to achieve and will be able to recommend best practice in terms of information security controls and to achieve compliance with Article 32
3. Business analysts and other project staff – they will understand the business aims, what's being put in place, and when various steps need to be taken
4. IT Developers and Engineers – they will be able to provide information on the systems being used and how the personal information will flow through the system (including how it will be stored and processed).
5. Marketing and communications advisers – they will help in understanding how the organisation uses information and can help coordinate any consultation needed for the DPIA
6. Risk and assurance people – they can help you identify risks, controls and other actions
7. Specialist staff groups who are affected by any proposals for handling personal information, such as call centre staff, information management staff, or human resources – they can give you the best information about how things will work on the ground
8. Customer or consumer groups – they can provide you information about how customers/consumers are likely to react to the proposed processing activities

Processing description: a key principle of GDPR is transparency. Those reading the DPIA need to know what the proposed processing activity consists. At a minimum the processing description should include the following information:

1. Describe the project – specifically, the purpose of changing what happens with personal information
2. Describe the personal Data involved and what will happen with it
3. Describe the Sensitive Data involved and what will happen with it
4. Describe the lawful grounds for collecting information
5. Assess the proportionality of the processing activities

Data Flow: the next step in the DPIA process is to describe the data flow. The old adage that a picture paints a thousand words applies to Data Flow. In the example, there are two diagrams. The first shows the current state which is useful to people reading the DPIA so they know how things look now and can help sell the proposed change –especially if it demonstrates improved compliance with Data Protection legislation. The second shows the future state. Diagrams must be an aid the understanding, therefore try to keep things as simple as possible. In addition to the diagrams, it is useful to add contextual information to aid understanding. See 'Changes to the Data Flow' in the example DPIA.

Review Principles & Rights: in this section, the Practitioner must review the 6 GDPR principles and 8 fundamental rights and ensure there are appropriate technical and organisational controls in place to minimise the risk to Data Subjects to an acceptable level. A great resource for those who would like examples of suitable data protection controls is Gérer les risques sur les libertés et la vie privée, la méthode issued by CNIL. Examples can also be found in the "Required Data Protection Controls" section of the example DPIA.

Identify Data Protection Risks: whilst the previous section should include appropriate controls to mitigate a lot of inherent risk, there may be aspects of the processing activity that still pose a high risk to the rights and freedoms of Data Subject. GDPR requires an assessment of such risks and adequate mitigation to be established and agreed.

> **EXAMPLE: A Controller wishes to use a third party to carry out processing activities on their behalf. When assessing the Data Protection Risks, it is identified the third party processor has not currently achieved any independent information security certification. This is assessed as a high inherent risk because the Controller will not have any ongoing independent assurance that the Processor is maintaining adequate technical and organisational controls.**
>
> **On the advice of the Data Protection Officer (DPO) and the Chief Information Security Officer (CISO), the Process Owner agrees to ensure the vendor provides information security metrics within their monthly service review pack. The Process Owner also agrees to fund an annual Information Security Vendor Assessment which will include in its scope verification of the vendor reported metrics.**

As mentioned in other sections, this book does not aim to replicate the plethora or risk management methodologies available, but it would be remiss not to include some discussion on the topic. Practitioners responsible for compiling the DPIA should first consider using the organisation's preferred risk management methodology before attempting to create something unilaterally. Risks identified during the DPIA must not sit in isolation but should be incorporated into the wider risk register of the affected department(s).

Where the organisation does not mandate a particular methodology the next port of call Practitioners should consider are the ISO standards. ISO 31000:2009 Risk management -- Principles and guidelines, is a very good place to start for organisations with no risk management in place.

Produce Report: once the relevant stakeholders have been consulted, information compiled, principles and rights of Data Subject review and data protection risks identified and treated – all that just described must be documented in a report. The key items the report must include are:

1. Characteristics of the project to enable an assessment of the risks to take place
2. Data protection and related risks
3. Identifying data protection solutions to reduce or eliminate the risks
4. Signing off on the outcomes of the DPIA
5. Integrating data protection solutions into the project

There is currently no prescribed format for a DPIA report; the critical aspect is ensuring the report meets the criteria as described in Article 35(7). An example initial and full DPIA report are included at the end of this chapter.

Prior Consultation: as is often the case, when assessing the residual risk of a project and after mitigating controls have been agreed, the residual risk may still be deemed outside the tolerance of an organisation's risk appetite. Normally in these cases, the senior management of an organisation may choose to accept the additional residual risk if it deems there is a commercial benefit to taking on the additional risk. When it comes to Data Protection, in such cases, where a DPIA concludes the proposed processing would result in a high risk, the Controller's senior management cannot unilaterally accept the risk and must consult[87] the Supervisory Authority prior to processing.

When consulting with the Supervisory Authority, the following information must be provided in addition to the DPIA where the information is not already included within the DPIA:

1. The respective responsibilities of the controller, joint controllers and processors involved in the processing, in particular for processing within a group of undertakings;
2. Contact details of the data protection officer;
3. any other information requested by the supervisory authority.

The most important aspect of prior consultation for organisations is that the process can take up to 14 weeks – 8 weeks for most situations but the consultation can be extended by a further 6 weeks where the intended processing is considered to be more complex. At the end of this period, the Supervisory Authority will provide written advice to the Controller which could include additional mandatory[88] controls to mitigate the additional residual risk. If an organisation is in the midst of a major transformation involving Personal or Sensitive data or needs to meet a specific deadline, those involved in running any related projects/programmes must be aware of the possibility prior consultation may be required. Organisations may need to consider ensuring the appropriate budget is available to implement additional controls to negate the requirement for prior consultation.

Review, Sign-Off and Manage: once the report has been completed, it should be reviewed by the relevant stakeholders and then signed-off by the accountable Process Owner. Sign-off is not the final step as the actions detailed in the DPIA must be managed until completion. In addition to confirming mitigating controls have been implemented and are operating effectively, GDPR requires the DPIA be reviewed whenever there is a change of risk which essentially means risks associated with processing must be incorporated into the organisation's wider risk management framework and monitored accordingly. There is additional guidance provided by the Article 29 Working Party which recommends, as a backstop, that the DPIA should be reviewed at least every three years.

Implement Recommendations: bearing in mind prior consultation considerations, the Process Owner must ensure any agreed control requirements to mitigate the risk to rights and freedoms of Data Subject are implemented. If controls are not implemented adequately the requirement to seek prior consultation still stands where the risk is still deemed to be high. In addition to other project risks, those involved in the implementation of such proposed processing might consider including the risk of the requirement to seek prior consultation on their RAID[89] logs to ensure the intended Process Owner remains engaged in ensuring appropriate resources are brought to bear.

Publish DPIA: to support the principle of transparency; an organisation may wish to publish a sanitised version of some or all their DPIAs. This concept is more prevalent in public organisations outside of the European Union however for organisations who want to demonstrate they respect their customers' rights, publishing sanitised DPIAs could be seen as a differentiator. There is, however, no mandatory requirement to publish a DPIA and organisations must weigh up whether publication could increase the risk to the rights and freedoms of Data Subjects.

---

[87] Article 36: Prior Consultation
[88] Article 58: Powers
[89] RAID – Risks, Assumptions, Issues, Dependencies

Example Data Protection Impact Assessment (DPIA) – Initial and Full Reports

Example Initial DPIA

NB: This example initial DPIA is for example only and will not be suitable for any particular organisation.

1. Project Details:

Project Name: RED FOX

Summary: Human Resources wish to migrate the existing Human Resources Information System (HRIS) based on PeopleSoft to a cloud-based managed service based on Microsoft SQL Server. The purpose of this migration is to increase automation of HR processes, improve compliance with current HR legislation and reduce costs.

The main stakeholders are Director of Human Resources, Chief Information Officer (CIO), Chief Risk Officer (CRO), Chief Information Security Officer (CISO), Employee Representative, and the Head of Procurement.

2. Personal information that the project will involve:

The table below describes the personal information that the project will involve:

Personal Data Types	Data Source	Purpose
(Potential) Employee personal details	Current HRIS & Onboarding Form	Fulfilling legal obligations under UK Employment Act
Next of Kin personal details	Current HRIS & Onboarding Form	Emergency Notification
(Potential) Employee employment details	Current HRIS & Onboarding Form & Contracts Database	Fulfilling legal obligations under UK Employment Act
Employee financial details	Current HRIS & Onboarding Form, Expenses System	Payroll Processing
(Potential) Employee education details	Current HRIS & Onboarding Form & References, Training Records from Learning Management System (LMS)	Maintaining accurate training and development records
(Potential) Employee Sensitive Data	Current HRIS, Diversity Questionnaire, interview notes. annual appraisal notes.	Fulfilling legal obligations under UK Employment Act
Health Information	Current HRIS, Sickness Records, Maternity Records	Benefits processing and fulfilling legal obligations under UK Employment Act
Behavioural Data	Company Owner Mobile Devices	Enhanced User Authentication for Remote Access

3. Initial Data Protection Screening:

Ser.	Data Protection Question	Yes / No	Description (if required)
DP1	Will this process involve the collection of new personal data?	Yes	As the new system can be accessed via the Internet data such as IP address and browser fingerprinting information will be collected.
DP2	Will there be a change in the way personal information is stored or secured?	Yes	Data will be stored on Third Party infrastructure outside the Controller's direct control.
DP3	Will there be a change to how sensitive information is managed?	Yes	Sensitive data will be processed on Third Party infrastructure outside the Controller's direct control.
DP4	Will Data Subjects be compelled to provide information about themselves	Yes	Data Subjects will be required to provide information as described in Section 2
DP5	Will personal information be processed outside the European Economic Area?	No	All processing will be carried out on infrastructure located in the UK and the Netherlands.
DP6	Will there be a requirement to retain data longer than statutory periods as laid down in relevant Member State law?	No	
DP7	Will the personal or sensitive information be shared in a new way?	Yes	Data will now be shared with a Third Party who will then share data with a number of existing and new third-party Processors.
DP8	Will Data Subjects have less access to their data than currently?	No	Data Subjects will have more access to their data within the proposed system.
DP9	Will the new processing involve automatic decision making / profiling?	Yes	The new system will automate aspects of the recruitment process (e.g. CV sifting)
DP10	Will the new processing create a new way of identifying Data Subjects?	Yes	Data Subjects' personal data will be available in a new database
DP11	Will the new processing allow surveillance, tracking or monitoring or movements behaviour or communications?	Yes	Part of the system involves authenticating remote access by geotagging the user to their office or home.
DP12	Will the new system involve direct or indirect communication with Data Subjects?	Yes	Employees will receive communication in relation to employee matters and emergency notifications

4. Initial Risk Assessment

Criteria	Score (L,M,H)
Level of information handling	
L – Minimal personal information will be handled M – A moderate amount of personal information (or information that could become personal information) will be handled H – A significant amount of personal information (or information that could become personal information) will be handled	**H**
Sensitivity of the information (e.g. health, financial, race)	
L – The information will not be sensitive M – The information may be considered to be sensitive H – The information will be highly sensitive	**H**
Significance of the changes	
L – Only minor change to existing functions/activities M – Substantial change to existing functions/activities; or a new initiative H – Major overhaul of existing functions/activities; or a new initiative that's significantly different	**M**
Interaction with others	
L – No interaction with other agencies M – Interaction with one or two other agencies H – Extensive cross-agency (that is, government) interaction or cross-sectional (non-government and government) interaction	**M**
Public impact	
L – Minimal impact on the organisation and clients M – Some impact on clients is likely due to changes to the handling of personal information, or the changes may raise public concern H – High impact on clients and the wider public, and concerns over aspects of project; or negative media is likely	**L**

Summary of Data Protection Risk Assessment

The Data Protection Risk Assessment for this project is rated as **HIGH**. This is because Sensitive personal information is involved, and several medium to high risks have been identified. As a result of this initial data protection risk assessment, it is recommended a full Data Protection Impact Assessment (DPIA) is conducted.

Sign-Off

I, the undersigned, certify, I have executed my duties as per the Data Protection Policy (v1.2, 2018) in respect to this Initial Data Protection Impact Assessment.

Name	Role	Signature	Date
J. Blogg	IT Project Manager	J Bloggs	25-05-18
A. Smith	HR Director	A Smith	25-05-18
S. Allardyce	Data Protection Officer	S Allardyce	25-05-18

Example Full DPIA

NB: This Full DPIA is for example only and will not be suitable for any particular organisation.

Version Control:

The current official copy of this DPIA shall be located on the Data Protection portal. If this document was found in any other location, the reader should check the Data Protection portal to confirm they are reading the current DPIA. The following version information is as follows:

Ver.	Description	Date	Author	Reviewer
0.1	Initial Draft	01/12/17	Business Analyst	DPO
0.9	Final Draft	05/01/18	Business Analyst	HR Director
1.0	Approved for Issue	20/03/18	Business Analyst	HR Director

Project Details:

Project Name: RED FOX

Summary: Human Resources wish to migrate the existing Human Resources Information System (HRIS) based on PeopleSoft to a cloud-based managed HRIS based on Microsoft SQL Server. The full description of the project can be found in the Business Case, Project Initiation Document (PID) and Business Requirements Document (BRD) located at https://companyintranet.com/projects/REDFOX/projectartifacts. The purpose of this migration is to increase automation of HR processes, improve compliance with current HR legislation and reduce costs. The purpose of this Data Protection Impact Assessment is to document the identification, assessment and treatment of data protection risks which may impact the rights and freedoms of in-scope data subjects.

The main contributors to this Data Protection Impact Assessment are:

1. Director of Human Resources
2. Data Protection Officer
3. Employee (Data Subject) Representative
4. HR Project Manager
5. HR Business Analyst
6. Information Security Analyst
7. Business Continuity Manager
8. Internal Legal Counsel

Scope

In-Scope: The following items are considered in the scope of this data protection impact assessment:

1. Lawful uses of data collected by / provided to the Third Party
2. Third Party HRIS Solution including mobile app

3. Third Party Provider's Technical and Organisational Controls
4. Interfaces with other third-party providers (e.g. Payroll)
5. Interfaces with Internal Human Resources Team
6. Interfaces with Employees
7. Processing of Next of Kin Information
8. Interfaces with internal systems

Out-of-Scope: The following items are considered out-of-scope of this data protection impact assessment:

1. Development activities related to initial customisation of new HRIS
2. Migration of Data from existing HRIS to Third Party Provider
3. Decommissioning of existing HRIS

Data Protection issues relating to Development, Migration and Decommissioning activities will be managed under the scope of the Data Protection Policy (Link Here)*90

Consultation

Consultation for this proposed processing activity has taken multiple forms. An employee representative has been actively engaged in the creation of this DPIA and provided inputs into the assessment of lawful grounds, proportionality and the risk assessment process. In addition, employees have been asked to complete a survey coordinated by marketing. The key item identified as of concern was the use of geo-location, most users believe this feature would be a disproportionate infringement on their right to privacy in their own homes. Some users expressed they would want assurance appropriate security control were in place and that the controls were tested regularly to ensure the controls remained effective.

Specified Purpose & Lawful Grounds for Processing

The table below documents the specific purpose data is collected and the lawful grounds for processing.

Personal Data Types	Data Source	Purpose	Lawful Grounds	Proportionality
Behavioural Data	Company Owner Mobile Devices	Enhanced User Authentication for Remote Access	Consent / Legitimate Interests	**Not proportional to the risk it seeks to mitigate.**
(Potential) Employee personal details	Current HRIS & Onboarding Form	Fulfilling legal obligations under UK Employment Act	Contractual obligation	Proportional when data is minimised
Next of Kin personal details	Current HRIS & Onboarding Form	Emergency Notification	Vital Interests	Proportional when data is minimised, and data subject is informed

---

90 This link would take the reader to the organisation's Data Protection Policy – See Chapter 07 for an example

(Potential) Employee employment details	Current HRIS & Onboarding Form & Contracts Database	Fulfilling legal obligations under UK Employment Act	Contractual obligation	Proportional when data is minimised
Employee financial details	Current HRIS & Onboarding Form, Expenses System	Payroll Processing	Contractual obligation	Proportional when data is minimised
(Potential) Employee education details	Current HRIS & Onboarding Form & References, Training Records from Learning Management System (LMS)	Maintaining accurate training and development records	Consent / Legitimate Interests	Proportional when data is minimised
(Potential) Employee Sensitive Data	Current HRIS, Diversity Questionnaire, interview notes. annual appraisal notes.	Fulfilling legal obligations under UK Employment Act	Vital Interests / Consent	Proportional when data is minimised, consent is provided and data retention limited
Health Information	Current HRIS, Sickness Records, Maternity Records	Benefits processing and fulfilling legal obligations under UK Employment Act	Contractual obligation	Proportional when data is minimised

Data Flow (Current State):

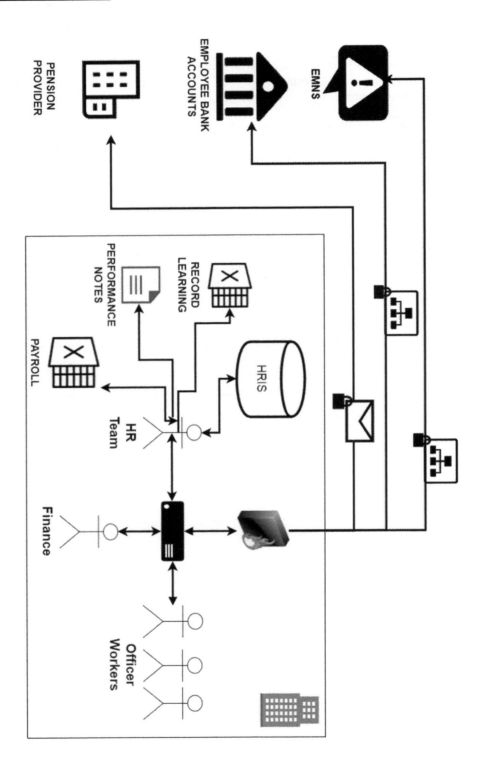

Data Flow (Future State):

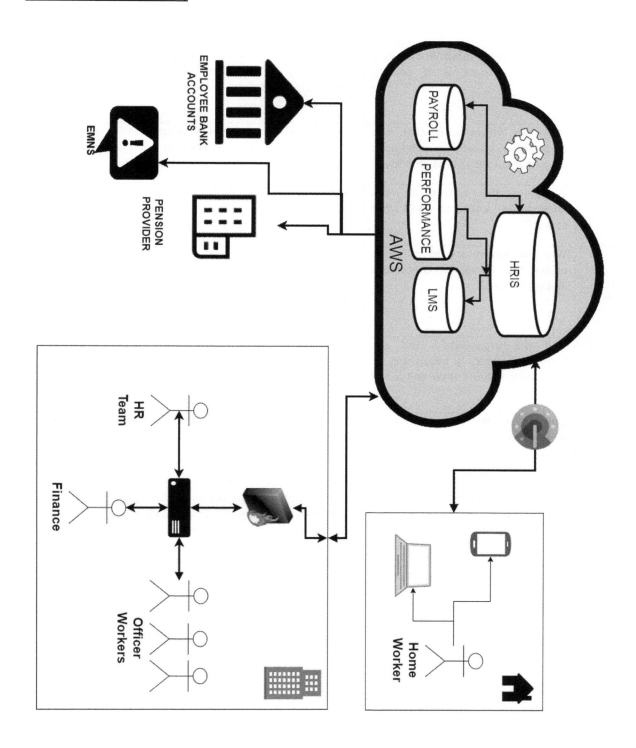

Changes to the Data Flow:

Ser.	Data Flow Question	Response
DF1	Is new personal information being collected? Where is it coming from?	Personal Data will flow over the Internet via a self-service portal. Personal Data will no longer flow directly from in-house systems but from a cloud platform maintained by a Third Party Processor.
DF2	Will the information that the organisation already holds be used for a new purpose? Why and how?	Personal Data currently held in disparate HR systems and spreadsheets will be migrated into a single cloud-based HRIS. The reason for this change is to e
DF3	What is the nature of the information collected and the source?	Please see initial Data Protection Impact Assessment
DF4	What measures are in place to ensure the information is accurate and up to date?	Employees will be periodically reminded (at least annually) to check the information stored within the system is accurate. Those nominated as next of kin will be periodically reminded (at least annually) to confirm the Personal Data held is accurate.
DF5	Will the organisation tell the individuals what is happening to their information? How will it tell them?	Candidates will be informed what is happening to their data via just-in-time privacy notices and a more detailed Data Protection Notice.
DF6	How is the information managed, handled or protected?	The Personal and Sensitive Data will be managed in part by the Third Party and in part by the organisation's HR Department.
DF7	Who will have access to the information (whether inside or outside the organisation)?	Third Party Employees and the organisation's HR department will have access to the full suite of data contained within the HRIS and supporting databases. Employees, Managers and the Finance Dept. will also have access to the information on a limited basis. Limited Information will also be shared with employee banks and the organisation's approved pension provider.
DF8	How long will the information be retained and how will it be disposed of?	Data will be stored no longer than statutory periods as laid down in relevant Member State law? Where no statutory periods exist, data shall be stored no longer than the retention periods stated in the organisations Records Management Policy.

Required Data Protection Controls:

Ser.	Right / Principle	Control	Accountable	Responsible	Due Date
CTL001	P1	Where consent is a condition for processing, consent shall be obtained prior to processing	HR Director	Legal	25-05-18
CTL002	P1	A contract shall exist between the Controller and the Processor	HR Director	Legal	25-05-18
CTL003	P2	A Data Protection Notice shall be published on the home page and on the section of the site.	HR Director	HR Project Manager	25-05-18
CTL004	P3	Data processed shall be limited to no more than that required to carry out processing activities	HR Director	HR Business Analyst	25-05-18
CTL005	P4	There shall be a process established to ensure accuracy of data and a process to correct inaccurate data	HR Director	HR Business Analyst	25-05-18
CTL006	P5	Personal data retention periods that are time-limited and appropriate to the purpose of the processing shall be defined.	HR Director	Legal	25-05-18
CTL007	P6	The project shall go through a separate Information Security and Business Continuity Risk Assessment process and implement the recommendations and requirements as agreed and commensurate with the risks to rights and freedoms of data Subjects	HR Director	Information Security Analyst	25-05-18
CTL008	R1	Statutory Information shall be provided to the Data Subjects regarding how data will be processed prior to processing activities commence. Data Subjects, in addition to employees, shall also include nominated NOK & potential candidates.	HR Director	HR Business Analyst	25-05-18
CTL009	R2	There shall be a process to support Subject Access Requests and ensure relevant personal data is made available within the statutory timeframe of 30 days. Where possible, this should be made available on a self-service basis.	HR Director	HR Business Analyst	25-05-18

CTL010	R3	There shall be a process to permit the reporting of inaccurate personal data and ensure inaccuracies are corrected as soon as practicable. Where possible, and with appropriate review, rectification should be available on a self-service basis.	HR Director	HR Business Analyst	25-05-18
CTL011	R4	There shall be a process to support the right to erasure where requested. The process must take into account the legal obligations of the Controller to retain data for statutory periods.	HR Director	HR Business Analyst	25-05-18
CTL012	R5	There shall be a process to support the right to restrict processing where requested. The process must take into account the legal obligations of the Controller and where the lawful basis for processing is a contract, the Data Subject must be informed of the implications restricting processing may have (e.g. They may not get paid).	HR Director	HR Business Analyst	25-05-18
CTL013	R6	There shall be functionality built into the system to support Data Subjects port their data. The data must be securely provided to the Data Subject in a CSV format.	HR Director	HR Business Analyst	25-05-18
CTL014	R7	There shall be a process to support the right to object.	HR Director	HR Business Analyst	25-05-18
CTL015	R8	There shall be a process to support the right to object to automated decision making. This process must include a human workaround for all automated decision-making which produces a legal or similarly significant effect on the data subject (e.g. removes them from a CV sift).	HR Director	HR Business Analyst	25-05-18
CTL016	R8	Processes involving automated decision-making must be reviewed to ensure processing is fair and transparent, and effective technical and organisational measure are implemented to minimise the risk of errors and correct inaccuracies.	HR Director	HR Business Analyst	25-05-18

Data Protection Risk Assessment:

The following risks have been identified during this Data Protection Impact Assessment:

Ser.	Risk Description	Principle / Right[91]	I	L	Risk
RSK001	Personal information is collected without a clear purpose or without clear legal authority	P1	H	H	VH
RSK002	The organisation doesn't comply with basic standards and expectations for information security and records management	P6	H	H	VH
RSK003	Poor-quality information may lead to decisions that impact negatively on individuals (e.g. Information on ex-employees transferred into Emergency Mass Notification System (EMNS)	P4, R3, R8	H	M	H
RSK004	Collection methods may be unjustifiably intrusive	P2	M	M	M
RSK005	The system can't trace who has accessed a file – so you can't tell whether there are problems with unauthorised access	P6	H	L	M
RSK006	Individuals (e.g. Next of Kin) may not be aware that information is being collected, who will use it or what it's being used for. If they become aware only later, they may be surprised and upset	P2, R1 R4, R5, R7	M	L	L

Data Protection Recommendations / Requirements:

Based on the DPIA Risk Assessment, the following requirements and recommendations have been identified:

Ser.	Ref.	Description	Recommendation / Requirement
REC001	RSK001	Have a clear privacy statement saying where you get personal information from.	Requirement
REC002	RSK001	Behavioural Data relating to geo-locating Data Subjects is not proportionate to the risk it seeks to mitigate, and therefore its collection is prohibited	Requirement
REC003	RSK001	Provide people with a way to see the information you hold about them (like a dashboard) and give them the opportunity to correct it if it's wrong	Recommendation

---

[91] This section refers to the 6 principles (CARPPA) and 8 rights (PREPAROI) of GDPR – See Chapter 04

REC004	RSK002	Ensure that service providers are contractually bound to comply with specific data protection safeguards	Requirement
REC005	RSK002	Ensure there is a process to periodically (no less than annually) assess the Service Providers technical and organisational controls	Requirement
REC006	RSK003	Ensure there's a clearly defined process by which an individual can discuss or dispute the accuracy of the personal information you hold about them	Requirement

Data Protection Action Plan:

Based on the risks, recommendations and requirements, the following actions have been agreed with Action Owners and deadlines assigned.

Ser.	Ref.	Action	Accountable	Responsible	Due Date
ACT001	REC001	Document and Publish clear privacy statement	HR Director	Legal	25-05-18
ACT002	REC002	Ensure any functionality to collect location data of data subjects is disabled	HR Director	HR Project Manager	25-05-18
ACT003	REC004	Put in place contractual safeguards	HR Director	Legal	25-05-18
ACT004	REC005	Design, document and implement a process to periodically (no less than annually) assess the Service Providers technical and organisational controls	HR Director	Information Security Analyst	25-05-18
ACT005	REC006	Design, document and implement a process by which an individual can discuss or dispute the accuracy of the personal information you hold about them	HR Director	HR Business Analyst	25-05-18

Prior Consultation

The residual risk to rights and freedoms of Data Subjects for this project is rated as **MEDIUM** and therefore prior consultation is **NOT REQUIRED**.

The justification for the risk rating is due to the existing mitigating technical and organisation controls built into the new solution, and the agreed actions agreed as identified during the Risk Assessment process. As a result of these combined actions, it is not assessed the new solution will, currently, pose a high risk to the rights and freedoms of Data Subjects.

Sign-Off

I, the undersigned, certify, I have executed my duties as per the Data Protection Policy (v1.2, 2018) in respect to this Initial Data Protection Impact Assessment.

Name	Role	Signature	Date
J. Blogg	IT Project Manager	J Bloggs	25-05-18
A. Smith	HR Director	A Smith	25-05-18
S. Allardyce	Data Protection Officer	S Allardyce	25-05-18

End of DPIA

10. INFORMATION SECURITY

This book and thus this chapter, does not intend to be an information security reference. However, GDPR makes it abundantly clear; organisations must ensure personal data processing is conducted securely. It would be therefore remiss to omit a chapter dedicated to Information Security. I have aimed this chapter at the level of those Practitioners who are not from an information security background but does assume some knowledge so apologies to those of you who are from a security background (you may even want to skip this chapter!). Whilst there are terms and concepts I mention to encourage further reading, I am not going to discuss any single control expansively as they often represent whole books of knowledge in themselves. In essence, this chapter aims to give you a very basic knowledge of corporate information security.

If you're interested in learning more about information security, I recommend enrolling in the BCS[92] Information Security Management Principles (ISMP) or an ISO 27001 Lead Implementer courses - with a reputable provider. These courses are fairly basic and don't have an experience component but will give you a good foundation knowledge.

What is Information Security?

Information Security can be defined as: "The protection of information and information systems from unauthorized access, use, disclosure, disruption, modification, or destruction in order to provide confidentiality, integrity, and availability."[93] The term information security is often interchanged with Information Risk, Information Security risk and sometimes Cyber Security. In some organisations, it is common to hear people talk of Cyber Security as a discipline focussing on technical controls such as Intrusion Detection Systems (IDS) and Security Information & Event Management (SIEM) and Firewalls with Information Security focussing on administrative controls such as Information Classification, Access Management, Awareness and Risk Assessment. In other organisations, there is a different approach following a 'Lines of Defence' model which delineates risk across the Business, Risk & Compliance functions and Internal Audit. The Lines of Defence approach is often seen in Financial Services. In some organisations, Information Security is split in two with a Security Operations and an Advisory function (Sec Ops & Advisory. This model would align with the Lines of Defence model with Sec Ops often sitting in the IT department, and would be highly process driven. The Advisory function would typically sit in the Risk Department and be more consultative in nature, dealing with novel issues or exceptions to standards.

---

[92] BCS: British Computing Society
[93] NIST 800-53 (Revision 4): Security and Privacy Controls for Federal Information Systems and Organisations

Line	Typical Tasks
1 (Business)	Directly involved in business activities Writes & Follows Procedures Implements Controls Collects metrics Own Risk
2 (Governance)	Not involved in business activities Designs Controls Authors & Issues policies Provides Consultation & Advice Provide Risk Management Framework Runs Exercises
3 (Audit)	Independent Tests Controls Provides Assurance

Lines of Defence Model

Another, and sadly far too common, approach is for Information Security to sit wholly within IT and seen as a purely IT issue. If your organisation has this final structure, I would strongly advise using your influence and persuasion skills to change the structure as soon as you can as it can often lead to conflicts of interest. Can the information security team be objective when they report to the CIO – I would suggest it is highly unlikely. Whichever structure you have, it's useful to understand the structure, so you know whom to talk to about a particular issue.

Know your Environment

There is absolutely no point putting in place shiny security appliances if you do not understand the environment you are protecting. Similarly, there is no way an organisation can claim they are compliant with GDPR if they don't know where personal data is processed and on what systems. The naïve approach is to ask the business. I have seen this happen in many organisations and the information security or data protection Practitioner who relies on such information is going to end up being blindsided by a nasty security breach. The most important takeaway from this book in terms of information security is TRUST but VERIFY! Sure, take what the business and IT department tell you as what they believe is a true account (they most likely believe it is) Then go and confirm, either with a secondary source or with evidence. The same applies when assessing the security of a third party or outsourced service provider. If it cannot be evidenced, no matter what an interviewee is telling you – it isn't happening! So how do you find out the truth about what is happening in your organisation?

CMDB: Firstly, if you're organisation has a Configuration Management Database (CMDB) then get someone to give you read access and walk you through how to interpret the information. Someone in the InfoSec team should be able to help you. If your organisation has a Database Administrator (DBA), sit down with them and get them to run you through the databases they support. Ask the DBA to provide the database schemas. Schemas show the tables and fields in the database and can be a good way of identifying potential sources of personal and sensitive data.

ITIL Service Management Catalogue: If your organisation is aligned with ITIL,[94] they will follow a service management approach which requires the maintenance of certain documentation. The Service Catalogue is such an ITIL document, and it will contain information on all the operational services. This is a good starting point for identifying the current batch of data-driven apps, but you should also look in the Service Portfolio as this will show the retired services and also the pipeline. Knowing about the retired services will be incredibly useful as they tend to be archived off and no longer maintained – which means no longer maintained for security too! In addition to the security element, it's important to ensure they still remain in scope for subject access requests and data is removed when the appropriate retention date is reached. The pipeline is incredibly useful because – and this may be a surprise – sometimes people don't tell information security / data protection they are developing some new application. Remember you will not always be told what is going on, so you must be proactive

Project Portfolio: Another good place to find information is the Project Management Office (PMO). In a similar way to ITIL based organisations, those who follow a project management methodology will usually have a list of the pipeline, current and completed projects. Reviewing these lists will be invaluable in helping a DPO determine where data may be lurking across an organisation.

Financial Records: The CMDB, ITIL and Project methods are useful when organisations have mature processes, but they are still only as good as the information recorded. One part of an organisation which is usually very good at record keeping is finance – if someone has spent, or is intending to spend, money, Finance will have a record. Interpreting financial information may be a bit more complicated but can yield lots of useful information. Ask finance for a list of IT vendors before going to IT, and you can then ask questions such as I see you had an increase in Amazon Web Services last month, what was the reason for that? Or, I see you engaged a SharePoint contractor last month, what project are they working on? Obviously, it's important not to come across like you're interrogating the person, but it's never a bad thing to have a good idea of the answer before you ask a probing question.

Legal Records: Similar to Finance, Legal is a wealth of information. Typically for big-ticket items or items above a certain threshold, legal will be involved to review contractual documents. By reviewing such documentation, it may be possible to find information relating to Processors who are processing personal or sensitive information.

Incidents & Near Misses: Finally, and not the greatest method, is to identify data sources through near misses. Usually, this occurs through the tuning of an organisation's security tools. For example, an organisation may be looking at improving the uptake of email encryption and so generates a list of most (and least) frequently used domains (e.g. @foxredrisk.com) where users are sending (and receiving) emails. So as to focus on high-risk transfers, the security team filter those transfers where files are attached. For further granularity, the may filter files containing personal or sensitive data. During this study, the security team identify a department sharing personal data with a third party. On further investigation, it turns out a member of the department used a corporate credit card and so there was no formal project, no finance involvement and no contract. With the advent of commoditised cloud technology, this kind of scenario is all too common that it has its own name – shadow IT. While the above example looked at email, security teams could equally help identify personal data through file-system scans, anomalous internet activity (e.g. use of a Cloud Application Security Broker CASB) or rogue File Transfer Protocol (FTP) activity. As should be apparent, there is no one way to gain a full picture of your environment. The DPO will have to rely on multiple techniques and multiple sources of information. The key though is to TRUST but VERIFY!

---

[94] ITIL: Information Technology Infrastructure Library

The CIRAN Paradigm

As mentioned earlier in this chapter, information security is about providing confidentiality, integrity and availability (CIA) to information and information systems. Some information security professionals use expanded definitions to include Resiliency and Non-Repudiation to form the mnemonic CIRAN (pronounced *'Key-Ran'* like the Olympic Cycling event). What these tenets do is provide a straw man for those assessing the security risks for an information system or data set. By looking at each of these areas separately and then holistically, appropriate technical and organisational controls can be put in place. Let's look at each in a little more detail focussing on how they relate to Data Protection:

Confidentiality: ensuring only those with the need to know can access information or information systems. In terms of privacy, this is ensuring that a Data Subject's personal data is secured so it cannot be accessed by unauthorised persons. Typical confidentiality controls include Identity & Access Management (IAM), Encryption, Information Classification and Data Leakage Prevention (DLP).

Integrity: ensuring the information processed within an information system is accurate, but also the methods used to process information are not flawed. This is of particular relevance to GDPR in terms of the Right to Rectification[95] and Rights pertaining to Profiling[96] and the principle that data must be accurate and maintained[97]. Typical controls used to provide integrity are Hashing, Reconciliations, Segregation of Duties and Input Validation.

Resilience: ensuring systems are designed in a way so they can continue to run given likely operational issues. This is not to be confused with Availability which we shall discuss later in this section. The analogy of a boxer always comes to mind when discussing resilience. A bad boxer will get hit, fall down and stay down. A good boxer will get hit from time to time but when they fall down, they may take some of the count but will get back up and continue. A resilient boxer is one who can avoid most of the punches and absorb the ones that actually make contact – they don't fall down. Resilience is key to data protection across all aspects of upholding a Data Subjects rights. Typical Resilience controls include Patching & Upgrades (i.e. System Maintenance), Environmental Separation (i.e. People in Offices, Systems in Data Centres), Elastic Computing, Parallel Processing Operational Structures separated by geography, Data Striping and Virtualisation.

Availability: ensuring information is available to those that need it, as and when they need it. Data Subjects have a Right to Access[98] and in certain cases the Right to Portability[99]. In many cases, Data Subjects also have a Right to Withdraw Consent[100], a Right to Restrict Processing[101] and a Right to Erasure[102]. As you can see, it is not simply a case of ensuring data is available, but also ensuring there are processes in place to rescind availability. Typical Availability controls include Backups, Archiving and Restoration, Service Continuity Programmes, Denial of Service (DoS) protection and secure Application Programme Interfaces (APIs). eDiscovery tools may also be considered as an availability tool in terms of Data Protection to ensure an organisation can comply with subject access requests.

---

[95] Article 16: Right to Rectification
[96] Article 22: Automated individual decision-making, including profiling
[97] Article 5: Principles relating to processing of personal data
[98] Article 15: Right of Access by the Data Subject
[99] Article 20: Right to Data Portability
[100] Article 7: Conditions for Consent
[101] Article 18: Right to restriction of processing
[102] Article 17: Right to erasure ('right to be forgotten')

Non-Repudiation: ensuring the source of information cannot be repudiated, ideally without alteration or corruption. Essentially Non-Repudiation is trust. For example, how can a Controller prove a Data Subject gave informed, explicit consent to a Data Processing activity.

As an example, in the pre-digital era, a person would receive a contract and then sign two copies, one being kept by themselves and the other kept by the other party. In order to prevent either side stating they didn't sign the contract, a witness signature would also be included. In the digital era, two parties can electronically sign a contract using separate private encryption keys known only to each party, with what is known as a Trusted Third Party (TTP) acting as the 'witness' to the electronic signatures. The entire process relies heavily on cryptographic techniques. A challenge, however, does exist in the digital scenario in that either party could potentially repudiate a digital signature by stating their private encryption key had been compromised which the TTP, unlike a human witness, could neither confirm nor deny. For the most part, this trust model works and is the cornerstone of how most secure websites (e.g. When we pay for goods or access online banking) work.

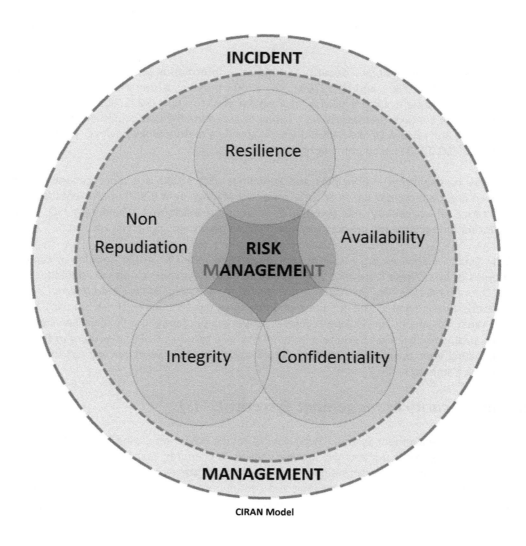

CIRAN Model

Information Risk Management (IRM)

As anyone who has managed information security will tell you (at least with a straight face), there are very few systems in the interconnected world we live in that can be effectively used and totally secure. As such there will always be a trade-off between usability and security and so sitting in the centre of the CIRAN wheel is information risk management (IRM). This book is not a risk management book, so I am not going to labour the topic, except to say there are a number of useful standards and methodologies one can leverage:

Factor Analysis of Information Risk (FAIR): FAIR is a framework for assessing information risk by putting information risk in context. FAIR includes a value component as, quite logically posits, it doesn't matter what the risk is to an asset if the asset has limited value.

Operationally Critical Threat, Asset and Vulnerability Evaluation (OCTAVE): Originally OCTAVE, OCTAVE Allegro is the current evolution of a risk management framework for Information Security from the Software Engineering Institute. In contrast to FAIR which is predominantly quantitative in approach, OCTAVE Allegro is qualitative in approach.

ISO 27005:2011 Information technology -- Security techniques -- Information security risk management: Typically used in conjunction with ISO 27001 and ISO 27002, ISO 27005 provides a framework to manage risk within an information security management system (ISMS). In a similar way to FAIR, ISO 27005 suggests going through a process of establishing the context, then assessing, treating or accepting the risk, communicating risk outcomes and a process of monitoring and review. Unlike FAIR it does not specify a methodology however FAIR could be used as a methodology within an ISO 27000 based framework.

ISO 31000:2009 Risk management – Principles and guidelines: ISO 31000 is a more general risk management framework which an organisation may use in an Enterprise Risk Management (ERM) implementation. ISO 27005 has been aligned in terms of vocabulary and techniques. If your organisation is aligned to ISO 31000 for ERM, encompassing information security and privacy risks into this framework would be well advised.

Operational Risk: Financial Services organisations are required to retain a certain amount of capital to mitigate against certain types of loss. These losses are split into three main risk types: credit risk, liquidity/market risk and operational risk. Operational risk[103] is *"the risk of loss resulting from inadequate or failed internal processes, people and systems or from external events."* The definition of operational risk includes legal risk but excludes strategic and reputational risk. What this means for data protection Practitioners operating in a financial services environment is that privacy / data protection will now become a material risk as a result of GDPR. If you are in financial services, I would advise contacting your operational risk team and discuss how they want privacy risk managed within the wider operational risk framework.

Information Security Management Systems(ISMS)

An Information Security Management System (ISMS) is a systematic way of managing information security within an organisation. Typical management systems will include policies, procedures, standards and guidelines that set out the implementation of technical and organisational controls within an organisation. A good ISMS framework will also include some form of risk management, monitoring and continuous improvement methodology. As this is not an information security book and there are countless resources dedicated to the topic we shall not be going into depth. Needless to say, the most common standard organisations can be certified to is ISO 27001.

---

[103] Principles for the Sound Management of Operational Risk, Bank of International Settlements, Jun 2011

It's important to note ISO 27001 is a standard aimed at demonstrating an organisation has a framework in place for managing information security risk. It does not certify that the certificate holder is secure, nor does it confirm the holder's appetite for risk. It's therefore still important to carry out additional due-diligence as per that described in Chapter 14 to ensure a Processor is a good cultural fit.

EXAMPLE: The Board of Dover-Locke PLC holds ISO 27001. It has an effective, enterprise risk management framework, including a Risk Appetite statement. The Board's appetite for information risk is set as HIGH. In a number of projects, information risks assessed as HIGH risk have been accepted by an accountable senior manager on the executive management team. One such risk is not enabling system logging; therefore, means they won't be able to identify unauthorised access to systems processing personal data.

This action would not be considered incompatible with ISO 27001 certification as the organisation can demonstrate the information risk has been formally managed. Not having system logging in this scenario would not be raised as even a minor non-compliance.

Where the primary benefit to achieving certification to ISO 27001 lies, is that it provides a means of demonstrating information security competency which has been independently assessed by a third party. The other benefit to third parties and the public is the scope of the certification can be independently verified through a register maintained by the certification body.

Defence Detect Manage (DDM)

(Good) Information Security Professionals accept it's not going to be a case of if an organisation will be compromised but when – and how bad! The way this is represented in the CIRAN wheel is the dotted edges depicting the porous nature of most corporate networks That's not to say we should abandon all attempts to secure data, because a breach is inevitable but that we must redefine information security strategies to ensure the focus is not solely on putting up rings of fire around systems and then living in denial that they will ever get breached – or worse still have no way of knowing if systems have been breached.

My philosophy for a long time has been to try and prevent as much as possible but be able to detect malevolent behaviour very quickly. Once detected, manage the situation to minimise the impact to as low as possible. The approach I favour is DDM – Defend, Detect, Manage.

Defend: attempt through various technical and organisational controls to mitigate 99% of the threats to your organisation. Sounds simple, doesn't it! OK, if it were that simple we probably wouldn't need to Detect or Manage. There are some straightforward principles you can employ that often get overlooked. If you're too busy to do them all or you meet resistance from business units (or IT) then prioritise in the order below:

0. Design Security from the ground up (obviously!)
1. Be amazing at Change Control!

Whilst IT Change Control is not in itself an Information Security Control; system change is where so many things go wrong. Organisations are more likely to suffer material impact because of a poorly implemented change than from an external hacker or malicious insider. I challenge anyone to prove me wrong! If the Information Security team is not all over the Change Control processes, then something is awry. OK, on we go...

2. Harden & Patch Operating Systems using golden images (e.g. such as those provided by CIS[104])
3. Patch Internet-facing applications
4. Patch or remove common desktop applications (e.g. Flash and Java). If it's not needed, get rid.
5. Implement Firewalls, IDS, Antivirus and Web Filtering
6. Use separate firewall rules for each business application - don't just send all traffic through a proxy.
7. Tune web filtering but flag all uncategorised sites, so users are warned before proceeding. This should significantly reduce chances of successful phishing attempts.
8. Implement a Data Leakage Prevention (DLP) solution across endpoints and tune it properly. Don't just use it to detect that the horse has already bolted!
9. Implement a Backup and Restoration regimen – and test it regularly!
10. Standardise and virtualise the Desktop Environment – this should significantly reduce the maintenance and recovery burden.
11. Implement Attribute-Based Application Control (ABAC) and reduce access privileges to an absolute minimum. Whatever they say, they don't need Admin privileges on all domains!
12. Implement Multi-Factor Authentication (MFA) combined with Single Sign-On (SSO) – Reduce the password burden for your employees.

There are many more things an information security function can do in collaboration with the technology function but, if done well, these 12 measures should make an attacker think twice about breaking into your organisation and hopefully try someone else instead.

Detect: attempt through technical and organisational controls to detect the 1% of successful attacks on your organisation. The trick is to have a process whereby you can identify the absence of the normal (e.g. A system is no longer doing what it normally does) or the presence of the abnormal (e.g. A system which has no reason to access a site on the Internet is suddenly sending transmitting gigabytes of data into the Tor network). Again simple to state, but clearly a lot more challenging to implement. Organisations can reduce complexity somewhat by splitting the detection task into detecting the external threats and detecting the internal threats.

The most common method to detect external threats is through tools such as Anti-Virus (AV), Intrusion Detection Systems (IDS), Network Health Monitors or trawling through system logs when something goes wrong. For a more holistic approach, the organisation can look to take information from all these systems, combining security data with application, operating system and network logs in a Security Information & Event Management (SIEM) System. SIEMs can take millions of events and, if set up properly, can significantly automate the process of detecting a security breach. A highly tuned SIEM system can also help the security team spot weaknesses in security controls – allowing them to be fixed before they get breached.

The internal threat can be detected by monitoring access patterns, and data flows (often referred to as Data Leakage Prevention) for anomalous activity (discussed further in Chapter 12 – Incident Management). Such monitoring will require turning on certain logging functionality within systems which require monitoring and some form of methodology to identify the anomalous behaviour. Some of the more developed SIEMs have artificial intelligence capabilities which can identify when a user does something out of the ordinary and, if a security team has permitted, can temporarily suspend access until a situation is investigated.

---

[104] CIS: Centre for Internet Security

When it comes to detection, it is important to understand there will be a performance hit when system logging is enabled, and as such, SIEM programmes may be met with resistance from network engineers who are trying to eke out every last bit of performance. The other aspect of an effective detection strategy is to include any cloud services supporting data processing activities. Amazon's AWS and Microsoft's Azure cloud offerings both have logging features, so make sure these are in scope for your detection activities. Finally, breach notification must be included in a contractual agreement between Controller and Processor. Such an agreement should also include a requirement upon the Processor to have effective technical measures to quickly detect a security breach so that its impact can be minimised.

Manage: attempt through technical and organisational controls to minimise the impact of a security event. While there is a whole chapter of this book dedicated to Incident Management and Breach Notification as it relates to Data Protection, the management of information component goes wider than simply reacting to an event. The management component includes the measures put in place well before an incident which can be quickly brought to bear should a security event occur. For example, if an organisation is detecting it is being subjected to a Distributed Denial of Service (DDoS) attack by a group of hacktivists, having an appropriate architecture in place or a technical solution to mitigate the attack will significantly reduce the impact to Data Subjects trying to access their data. Both, however, are not something that can be put in place at the time of an attack and a technical solution is not going to be effective unless it is maintained and the process for using the tool is well practised.

Information Security teams and the business must work collaboratively to identify, through the risk management process, what the likely CIRAN risks are and have plans in place to deal with associated incidents. These plans must be tested regularly and, more importantly, robustly. The most common reason plans fail is because testing was either a tick box exercise or filled with naïve, over-optimistic assumption about the risks or value of an information system.

Security Assessment

Solid assessment of an organisation's information security capability is fundamental to a capability's effectiveness. In the following section, we will look at the types of assessments which should exist within your organisation's information security programme.

Internal Assessment: Internal Information Security Teams must be carrying out periodic assessments of the technical and organisational controls to confirm the controls (i.e. as documented in policy) are well designed, effectively operating and efficient. In addition to controls assessments, Information Security must perform risk-based security assessments on all projects involving information systems. Information Security must also perform risk-based security assessments on all vendors whereby the vendor will interact with the organisation's data or information systems – not just personal data and systems processing personal data.

External Assessment: From time-to-time organisations should seek external verification of their security programmes effectiveness. If an organisation is certified to ISO 27001, this external assessment will be baked in. First at the beginning and then ongoing assessments will be required in the form of six-monthly surveillance visits. The external assessment provides a fresh set of eyes into an organisation, who are not blinkered by a certain way of doing things. Assessors can bring specialist expertise and provide new perspectives which internal information security teams may not have considered.

The external assessment shows a heightened level of maturity. An external assessment carried out by competent and qualified third parties, demonstrates that an organisation is comfortable opening their doors to an independent third party and have that third party scrutinise their security controls. I would be very cautious about engaging with a Processor who is unwilling to be completely transparent regarding their information security capability. I would be equally concerned if a Processor's CISO (or Head of Information Security) was unhelpful during assessments or cited confidentiality as a reason not to provide the requested information.

Vulnerability Scanning: vulnerability scanning is a process whereby an organisation's systems are scanned against vulnerabilities known to the scanning tool. Typically, the scanning tool will highlight whether a security patch is available to close the vulnerability (and for how long the patch has been available). In addition to 'patchable' vulnerabilities, there are also vulnerabilities due to poor configuration, and in these cases, the scanning tool will usually provide a recommendation for a more secure configuration. Given the maturity of vulnerability scanning tools, it is feasible to have real-time vulnerability data across an organisation's entire infrastructure. Unfortunately knowing what the vulnerabilities are is only a small component of a broader patch and vulnerability management programme. The area where managing vulnerabilities fall down is the resource and effort required to plan, test and implement patches into operational systems when implementation requires periods of downtime. Whatever resource is deployed into vulnerability scanning, at least 10 times more should be deployed into remediation activities.

Penetration Testing: penetration testing is a focused type of system testing involving a greater element of manual testing, typically against high-risk systems or, more commonly, Internet-facing systems. There are a number of methodologies available: CBEST, Penetration Testing Execution Standard (PTES), NIST 800-115 and the Open Source Security Testing Methodology Manual (OSSTMM) to name a few. Each operates a staged approach which looks something like this:

1. Scoping (and de-scoping)
2. Reconnaissance
3. Vulnerability Identification
4. Vulnerability Exploitation (often only hypothetical)
5. Risk Assessment of Exploitable Vulnerabilities
6. Recommendations for remediation
7. Re-Assessment

At a minimum, organisations processing personal data on any system exposed to the Internet should be engaging a competent and qualified third-party penetration tester, to test the system's security rigorously. The frequency of penetration testing must be commensurate with the level of risk, but no less than annually. It is common for cautious IT folks to want to provide a standalone system for penetration testing purposes as they are worried the penetration testers may break an operational system. Business Units may also be worried about testing on Production systems due to confidentiality, integrity and availability concerns and may request a light-touch approach to testing. Internal Information Security teams should resist such suggestions and question why the operational system would break if it has appropriate security controls in place. That said, penetration testing should be conducted with the full support of the IT team managing the system and at a time where disruption to users is kept to the absolute minimum. Resources must also be available during the test window to deal with any unexpected activity resulting from the test. For those information security professionals who are perhaps have an enhanced operational cynicism; penetration tests can be supported by pre and post-test vulnerability scans and the enabling of verbose logging – just in case rogue IT engineers attempt to 'enhance' security temporarily for the testing period.

Audits: internal audit is the third and final internal line of defence. Risk-based audits can be an invaluable means of focussing attention on business units or teams who are less engaged than a Practitioner would perhaps wish. There are three common types of audit in commercial environments: the department level audit covering all controls in operation and thus a component of information security; the themed audit which would encompass a deep dive into a particular topic and; the governance audit where the second line control function is audited to determine the operation and effectiveness of oversight controls.

It is common for people to feel anxious about audits given findings are often reported at the highest level within the organisation. The key is to know what the issues are likely to be, before an audit. Where something cannot be fixed prior to the audit, it must not be covered up but a plan (and approved budget/resources) put in place to remediate the issue within a reasonable timeframe.

Security Metrics

The final topic I wish to cover in this chapter on Information Security is security metrics. This won't be a deep dive however the topic warrants some discussion as there is a requirement under GDPR to demonstrate processing activities are secure. It would be unrealistic to state activities are secure without evidence, and one of the most concise ways to monitor security compliance is the collection, analysis and reporting of security metrics. Your organisation's Information Security team should already be collecting security metrics, and the Data Protection Officer must be one of the recipients of these metrics. Metrics can vary in quality from organisation to organisation but at a minimum should include the following:

1. Name of the Metric
2. Purpose of the Metric
3. Method of calculation
4. Thresholds (Red, Amber, Green)
5. Recommended Action when hitting Amber threshold
6. Frequency of collection
7. Data Cut-off Point
8. Frequency of reporting & Audience
9. Owner

EXAMPLE:
1. NAME: % of Out of Support Operating Systems
2. PURPOSE: To identify systems with no support and no further security which could lead to increased system instability and a greater likelihood of a successful security breach.
3. METHOD: (Out of Support OS / Total OS) * 100
4. THRESHOLDS: G < 1%, A < 1%, R < 2% (for more than 3 months)
5. RECOMMENDED ACTION: Immediately upgrade affected systems
6. COLLECTION FREQUENCY: Weekly
7. CUT-OFF: Last Friday of month
8. REPORTING FREQUENCY: Monthly to IT Committee, Qtrly to Board
9. METRIC OWNER: Head of Infrastructure

When reporting metrics, it is critical to include a qualitative assessment of trends, even if the metrics are improving. It's also important to ensure improvements aren't solely as a result of the metric owner de-scoping resources which are too difficult to remediate. Finally, reporting should, where appropriate, include trend information collected for interim periods and not just from the last report for a particular audience. (e.g. If the IT committee meet monthly and the Board only meet quarterly, the Board report should show trend data at monthly intervals). Security metrics are only as useful as the action they drive. If your organisation's metrics are not driving the right behaviour, the metrics are either; not fully understood, or you are using the wrong metrics. When deciding to use a particular metric always ask 'What action do I want to drive?" For those who wish to develop their understanding of security metrics consider reviewing ISO/IEC 27004:2016 Information technology — Security techniques — Information security management — Monitoring, measurement, analysis and evaluation. This international standard provides an excellent specification for creating and implementing effective security metrics in any size of organisation and can be easily applied to developing broader data protection metrics.

11. DATA PROTECTION BY DESIGN & BY DEFAULT

For those of us who have operated within technology environments, it will be pretty obvious how much easier it is to bake capability into a system, at the beginning of the system's life, than bolting it on part way through – even more so when it will materially affect the way users interact with the system. This challenge goes to the crux of what the drafters of GDPR are trying to achieve by including requirements[105] for organisations to ensure systems (and broader processes) are designed with data protection controls and are configured with those controls to the highest level of data protection by default.

In this chapter, we will review the information life-cycle to highlight where data protection controls are likely to be required to uphold data subjects' rights. We will then break down some of the more common controls an organisation should put in place to ensure Data Protection is a core component of any system's (or process's) design. It is essential to read this chapter with an understanding that a system is not required to have every single one of the controls mentioned, but appropriate controls commensurate with the risks identified. At the end of this Chapter is included a Data Protection Design Specification which can be used to document system requirements.

Information Life-Cycle & Records Management

You may recall GDPR defines processing as: 'any operation or set of operations which is performed on personal data or on sets of personal data, whether or not by automated means, such as collection, recording, organisation, structuring, storage, adaptation or alteration, retrieval, consultation, use, disclosure by transmission, dissemination or otherwise making available, alignment or combination, restriction, erasure or destruction.' This definition, while explicit in ensuring organisations are in no doubt what activities constitute processing activities, may be less helpful in creating a clear system design. A more straightforward framework for designing data protection controls into a system or process is the Information Life-Cycle (ILC). The ILC follows data from its Collection, all the way through its life until destruction. The stages of the ILC are

Collection: how does data enter the organisation. Does it involve manual intervention from a Data Subject or does it get collected automatically? Is the information already in a machine-readable form or has the information been 'scraped' from different publicly available sources? A system or process must have in place technical and procedural steps to capture records and then apply metadata to support classification and indexing so that information can be easily retrieved at a later time.

---

[105] Article 25: Data protection by design and by default

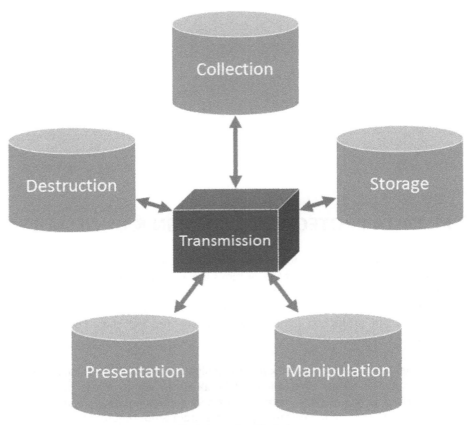

The Information Life-Cycle

Storage: where will the data be stored (including archiving & Backups). Determining these factors will aid in ensuring data doesn't accidentally end up in a location it shouldn't be. If part of the system design includes offsite backups, it is critical to know what physical locations the backups will be stored – especially if the location is in a third country[106]. In addition to knowing where data is located, organisations must be able to control who has access to Personal and Sensitive Data.

Manipulation: what will the organisation do to the data (e.g. turn data into a credit score). Processing must be lawful. When designing a system, care must be taken to ensure Personal and Sensitive data cannot be manipulated in a manner which does not have a legal foundation. In addition to lawfulness care must be taken to ensure any manipulation techniques are controlled to ensure high levels of information integrity.

Presentation: how will the data be presented to its intended audience (e.g. in a report). When considering how data is to be presented, the Practitioner must consider how data will be accurately presented, who will have access to the presented material and what are the possible follow-on uses of the presented materials (e.g. will there be further internal / external processing activities).

Destruction: how will the data be destroyed at the end of its useful life. Data destruction doesn't just happen at the end of a system's life because data will be created and destroyed at frequent intervals throughout a system's life.

---

[106] Chapter 5 - Transfers of personal data to third countries or international organisations

When considering data protection, it's important to understand whether data is truly destroyed or simply rendered inactive in a different table in the database (e.g. like the recycle bin on your desktop).

The central (or axle) of the cycle is **Transmission**: how does the data move through the different stages of its life. In addition to considering transmission as part of a closed system, Practitioner must also consider how data will be transmitted to new systems (e.g. system migrations).

By segmenting the ILC in the above manner, it becomes a lot easier to manage than working with the 18 processing activities described in the GDPR definition of processing. Using the ILC will also simplify the process of documenting system requirements so that at each stage of processing, the rights of the Data Subject are upheld (See DP Design Specification at the end of this chapter). While the topic is out of the scope of this book, if you are familiar with the Business Analysis technique of process mapping (e.g. using UML[107] or BPMN[108]), the above six stages of the ILC can be easily translated into a process swimlanes for easy visualisation. In addition to taking an Information Life-Cycle approach, consider if not already in place, adopting the framework specified in ISO 15489:2016 Information and documentation — Records management. In 2016, the standard was updated after 15 years and contains a structured approach to implementing records management holistically, above and beyond that required for GDPR compliance. The ILC approach in this book has similar characteristics so don't worry, you don't necessarily need to buy the standard!

Information Classification

A key component of designing an information system is to understand the value of the information assets which are processed within the system. To understand information assets, it is recommended organisations implement an information classification and handling regime, underpinned by an information classification policy. The policy can be standalone, or often it is included in an Information Security or Data Protection Policy. An Information Classification policy should, at a minimum, codify:

1. The information classification labels & descriptions
2. Labelling requirements
3. Descriptors & Codewords
4. Minimum Handling requirements
5. Appendix providing classification examples

What Information Classification serves to achieve is ensuring everyone in the organisation knows how to handle information appropriately, for example when information must be encrypted, how it must be stored, and what information can and cannot be shared. Information Classification, implemented well, can save organisations money by ensuring employees apply a sliding scale of controls dependent on the information's classification. Information classification labels and their associated descriptions must be universally understood across the organisation.

Labels and Descriptions: these are the tags which will be used to classify information within your organisation. At a minimum, organisations should have no less than four classifications. The four classifications should include a classification for information which is permitted to be published to the general public, a classification for information for internal consumption, a classification for sensitive information, and a classification for very sensitive information. Each classification must also include a description, so end users have some context.

---

[107] UML: Unified Modelling Language
[108] BPMN: Business Process Modelling Notation

> **EXAMPLE: Information marked as TOP SECRET[109] is that whose release is liable to cause considerable loss of life, international diplomatic incidents, or severely impact ongoing intelligence operations. Disclosure of such information is assumed to be above the threshold for Official Secrets Act prosecution.**

Labelling requirements: so that end users can identify classified information it is essential to set clear guidelines on how information must be labelled. Labelling could be placing the classification in the header and footer of a document. In some cases, where you may wish to distribute information in a document to multiple audiences, it is common to see individual paragraphs classified. When it comes to systems, the label should be included on the login page, and any outputs generated from the system should also be appropriately classified.

There will be occasions when it is not possible to label a system or document (e.g. information systems maintained by a Third Party). In these cases, a statement must be included in the Information classification policy explaining the default classification of any information which does not contain a label.

> **EXAMPLE: It is important when operating in a multilingual environment to ensure chosen labels will work across all the countries your organisation operates. If a person in one country directly translates a classification label, would there be any ambiguity in how they handled a document?**

Descriptors & Code words: a descriptor is an additional label which can be added to an organisation's standard classifications. These descriptors service to compartmentalise information further than the primary classifications. In most cases, this will signify to the end user additional handling instructions are required. Often, the handling instructions related to limiting the distribution of particular content to a more specific audience but could also infer other additional handling requirements. The following are common descriptors:

1. PUBLIC – POLICY
2. INTERNAL – BUDGET
3. CONFIDENTIAL – COMMERCIAL
4. SECRET – MEDICAL

Code words offer organisations an opportunity to control handling further. Two common codewords are ORCON (ORiginator CONtrolled) which is used to alert an end user that they must seek explicit permission from the information owner before sharing the information, and LOCSEN (LOCation SENsitive) which is used to alert the end user that information may be sensitive in specific locations. Another frequent use of descriptors is to support sharing information with a third party. The organisations in which the information can be shared would be listed with the originating organisation list first.

---

[109] UK Government Security Classifications Policy (GSCP) introduced in 2014

EXAMPLE: NDH enters into a commercial agreement with Gluhwein Traumhaft. The two organisations share intellectual property classified in the following way:

'SECRET – ORCON – NDH / GLUHWEIN TRAUMHAFT'

In this example, GT must handle the information a per NDH handling instructions and must not distribute the information without first seeking permission from NDH

Minimum Handling Requirements: for information classification to work a policy must state how information, classified at a certain level, must be handled. Handling controls must link back to the information life-cycle stages and must be understood by end users as the absolute minimum measures required to protect the information.

EXAMPLE:

Information marked as SECRET must be:

- Labelled as SECRET in the Header and Footer of every page in the document

- Encrypted as per Encryption Standard during collection, in storage, and during transmission

- Securely destroyed as per Destruction Standard at the end of its life

Information Systems marked as SECRET or containing SECRET information must be:

- Subject to a security review every TWELVE months

- Subject to access recertification every THREE months

- Subject to activity logging

Classification of information marked as SECRET must be reviewed every SIX months with a view to declassify or destroy.

Examples Appendix: while the label description should enable an end user to classify a document, which isn't currently labelled independently, it is useful to provide examples of common documents which are in use across your organisation. You may have noticed there hasn't been a suggestion to have a classification, descriptor or code word called 'PERSONAL DATA'. Adding such a classification may seem like a good idea, but I would caution against such an approach, and instead, place information or information systems containing personal data into a broader classification (e.g. CONFIDENTIAL – ORCON).

Systems Development Life Cycle (SDLC)

Ensuring data protection forms part of a system's design requires a Practitioner to have an understanding of the Systems[110] Development Life Cycle (SDLC).

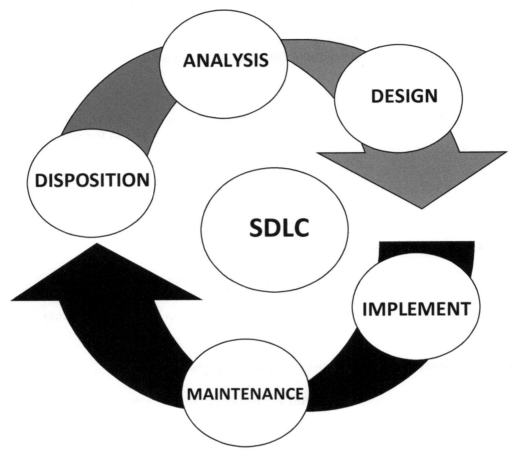

Systems Development Life Cycle (SDLC)

For Data Protection to be truly included in a system's design (and by default), the Practitioner must understand development is a cycle and not a point in time activity. There is no point just going through a Data Protection Impact Assessment (DPIA) at the beginning of a system's life and then expecting those controls to remain untouched. Maintaining data protection controls will require ongoing involvement by the Data Protection Officer (or a properly delegated authority). The different stages of the lifecycle are:

Analysis: at this stage, the system should go through Data Protection Impact Assessment (DPIA) as described in Chapter 09. In order to ensure the DPIA is completed correctly, the Project Sponsor, accountable for delivery, will need to ensure the Project Manager, who is coordinating the analysis activity, is actively engaging with the Data Protection Officer. Both the Project Sponsor and the DPO should sign off on the DPIA.

---

[110] The words Secure, System and Software are often interchanged in the SDLC acronym

Design: once it is understood what the system needs to do, the next stage is to design the system. The stage will include developing functionality and the user experience (UX). In this stage, the Practitioner must provide appropriate input on issues such as interface design, business rules and database structures.

EXAMPLE: When designing a customer registration form, is only the absolute minimum personal data collected to perform the task? Are all other fields set to optional? Are marketing preferences set to Opt-In?

Implement: during the implementation phase of development, the system is built, tested and deployed. The Practitioner will need to increase their engagement throughout this phase as things can change significantly from what was agreed at the design phase. This uncertainty is partly due to a popular development methodology in operation across the private sector called AGILE. AGILE is a methodology whereby not all the capability is agreed up front, and so UX and functionality will change (sometimes beyond all recognition) right up until the last minute of deployment.

Before final deployment, systems will typically go through some interim deployment phases. The most common deployment phases are:

1. Deployed into a Development (DEV) environment
2. Deployed into a Quality Assurance (QA) environment
3. Deployed into a User Acceptance Testing (UAT) environment
4. Deployed into a Production (PROD) environment
5. Deployed into a Disaster Recovery (DR) environment

In deployment phases 1 & 2 there should be no requirement to process live personal data however many organisations take a shortcut by using live data instead of generating test data. What this means for the Practitioner is, where these environments contain live data, the environments must be brought into scope of data protection technical and organisational controls. At each phase of deployment, the Data Protection Officer should sign-off they are comfortable the agreed data protection controls have been implemented.

Maintenance: once a system is deployed into a Production (PROD) environment, the system is considered to be operational. Deployment is not the end of the Practitioner's involvement in the system. System development will continue in the form of changes, fixes (correcting problems identified after deployment) and new features. The Practitioner will, therefore, need to assess these changes, fixes and features to understand their impact on Data Subject's rights.

Disposition: sometimes called the decommissioning phase, this is when the system has reached the end of its life. Ending the life of a system is not as simple as just turning it off and then deleting the data – if only! Data held within a system may require retaining for legal reasons and as such data will need migrating to a brand new system or possibly a Data Warehouse. Systems dependencies must be reviewed to ensure there are no unexpected consequences after the system is decoupled from the wider environment. Just as in the previous stages, the Practitioner will need to be involved to ensure rights are protected.

As should now be apparent there are lots of aspects to consider when it comes to ensuring systems and processes are designed with data protection in mind. If you are not a particularly technical Practitioner, it may be wise to partner with the information security function and ensure data protection controls form part of their broader information security assessment process. While these previous sections have discussed the governance activities to facilitate Data Protection by Design and Default, the following sections will consider the primary data protection controls that Practitioners should be recommending.

End User Computing Applications (EUCA)

As mentioned briefly in the Information Security Chapter, there is a phenomenon called 'Shadow IT' that relates predominantly to end users procuring IT services independently of the governance and control of a central IT function. In addition to Shadow IT there is another concept Practitioners must be aware of – End User Computing Applications (EUCA). End User Computing is where an End User uses commonly available productivity software, such as spreadsheet software, and creates an application which either, replaces in part or, replace in full the functionality of a formally managed system or application. 99.99999%[111] of organisations have EUC. EUCA is not necessarily a bad thing and can actually help identify future system requirements but when EUCA are used as part of a processing activity, EUCA must be secured.

Picture the scene: A department has a requirement to build an IT system to automate a task. The department head makes a request to IT for development resources, stating the solution must be ready in the next 30 days (for reasons unbeknownst to anyone!). IT respond, saying they will be able to support the request but with their current workload and available resources it will take at least six months before they can even look at the department's development needs. At that point, the department will need to engage in a formal project to ensure the development work is properly governed. Frustrated with this response the department head goes back to his business and complains to his team during a meeting the project will have to be shelved as IT does not have the time. During this meeting, a young and ambitious member of the department raises her hand and says she could create a similar solution to the problem in a spreadsheet. The department head, keen to see the benefits of the project as soon as possible tell her to get it done.

After six months, the solution has grown and developed and is now fundamental to the operations of the department. The spreadsheet contains significant volumes of personal data extracted from a secure database when the spreadsheet was developed. The solution is working so well for the department; the department head ends a support contract for their original IT-managed system and now relies solely on the spreadsheet. Six more months' pass, and as a result of poor results, the department is forced to make some of its employees redundant. One of these employees, in retaliation, makes some subtle changes to some of the macros coded into the spreadsheet and alters some customer records. Three months after they leave all the customers are sent an automated email containing a tirade of abuse, and then another macro randomises each customer's Personal Data with the personal data of other customers. The whole incident caused the organisation inordinate amounts of reputational damage.

The above is not a particularly extreme example, organisations have lost $millions[112] as a result of spreadsheet errors, suffered significant reputational damage[113], and in some cases, the lack of appropriate control has led to major fraud[114] events. Personal data is not immune from such compromises. On the 8 February 2017 the Deputy Chief Privacy Officer of Boeing notified the Office of the US Attorney General that a member of staff emailed his spouse 36,000 employee records, not realising personal data was included in columns hidden from view. What is particularly interesting about the Boeing case is the organisation sells Data Leakage Prevention (DLP) software which should have prevented the leak occurring!

---

[111] I want to say 100% but there just may be one or two organisations that do not have any EUCA

[112] How The London Whale Debacle Is Partly the Result of an Error Using Excel: Reported in the Business Insider on 12 October 2013

[113] M&S takes back shop-soiled figures: Reported in the FT on 7 July 2016

[114] The AIB Scandal: Reported in the Guardian on 20 February 2002

Defining EUCA: it is important to differentiate between static files used by an individual and a true EUCA which will be within the scope of GDPR. To classify an EUCA, a Practitioner can ask the following questions. If the answer to question 1 and any other questions is yes, then the EUCA must be put in the scope of data protection by design and default:

1. Does the EUCA include personal data?
2. Will the EUCA update a system of record?
3. Does the EUCA significantly impact business operations?
4. Will the EUCA materially inform management decisions?
5. Does the EUCA have multiple users?
6. Does the EUCA impact a significant volume of customers, employees or transactions?

Identifying EUCA: the first step to identifying EUC is to use the discovery tools built into most file management systems. Searching for common spreadsheet (e.g. *.csv, *.xls, *.wks, *.ods) and database (*.sql, *.sqlite, *.accdb, *.dbs, *.frm, *.jet, *.nsf) file extensions across network file shares is a really good place to start if you don't have anything currently in place. The hierarchy of the file structure, the name of the file and the size will also give clues as to the content. If you have some budget to spend, there are dedicated EUCA discovery tools which will be able to search the files and identify whether a file contains personal data.

Securing or migrating: by their very nature, it is a lot more challenging to secure EUCA than a managed IT system. That said, there are some controls which can be put in place to secure EUCA[115]. The following are controls which should be in place for EUCA processing personal data:

1. Information Classification & Handling
2. Access Management
3. Segregation of Duties
4. Change Control
5. Pseudonymisation
6. Input / Output Validation
7. Recovery & Archiving
8. Documentation

The identification of EUCA can form the basis of formal development work. Organisations may wish to analyse which processing activities are heavily reliant on EUCA to prioritise the development of the same functionality into managed IT systems.

Consent Mechanisms

While there are a number of ways processing can be deemed as lawful[116], consent is a common mechanism. When designing systems where the lawful basis for processing relies upon consent, there are a number of things to consider. The first is to ensure any requirement to provide consent is explained in clear English. Consent must be explicit and by default consent must be set to opt-out – you cannot automatically tick a box or combine a tick box with confusing language which influences a person to provide consent.

---

[115] European Spreadsheet Risk Interest Group Best Practice: http://www.eusprig.org/best-practice.htm
[116] Article 6: Lawfulness of Processing

EXAMPLE: Both choices opt out by default but the first consent statement would not be acceptable?

☑ From time to time, we may wish to provide you information about our products and services. If you do not wish to withdraw from this processing activity, remove the tick from the box.

☐ Tick the box if you consent to ABC Ltd providing you information about our products and services via a weekly email.

In addition to the mechanism used to provide consent, there must be a mechanism to withdraw consent. GDPR makes is explicitly clear this must be as easy as it was to provide consent. What this means in practice is not simply making the actual action of providing consent is the same tick box, but that the Data Subject can find where that withdraw consent tick box resides in a menu system. It would not be acceptable to bury the withdrawal tick box in layers of menus and then in the middle of a lot of other obscure settings. When creating consent interfaces, developers must ensure there is enough granularity in the design to cope with the requirement to provide specific and explicit consent. Systems must not be designed to force a user to consent to multiple processing activities.

EXAMPLE: The first example would not be permitted under GPDR.

☐ Tick the box if you consent to ABC Ltd processing your data to support your use of this website, to enable us to market our products to you via a weekly email, and to send your data to our network of third parties.

The second examples would be acceptable:

☐ Tick the box if you consent to ABC Ltd processing your data to support your use of this website.

☐ Tick the box if you consent to ABC Ltd providing you information about our products and services via a weekly email.

☐ Tick the box if you consent to ABC Ltd providing your information to third parties.

Whenever you need to obtain consent, the system must be able to record the consent decision and ensure consent choices are linked to both internal processes and those which are processed by third parties.

Data Minimisation

Every item of personal data collected must be justified. Practitioners must make it clear to those responsible for system design that only the absolute minimum of personal or sensitive data is to be collected. Personal or sensitive data and personal data collected for other purposes must be not be flagged on physical or electronic input forms as mandatory[117]. The same applies to information collected from the user automatically and potentially without their knowledge (e.g. IP address or Geolocation).

> **DID YOU KNOW: One really simple way to minimise data in an organisation is to stop attaching files to emails. Instead, include a link to access controlled file locations. That way if the email is accidentally sent to the wrong recipient, they will not be able to access the files. If a person in the list changes departments, when their access is revoked again, they will no longer have access to the files.**
>
> **The other benefits of this organisational change will be reduced email storage costs, improved security, reduced eDiscovery burden and improved version control. Not only that but solutions such as SharePoint can also provide usage data so if your system is pumping out reports, which no one is actually reading, they can be turned off – minimising data even further!**

Privacy Dashboards

Social Media Privacy Dashboard

A Privacy Dashboard is a set of controls whereby the End User can control their own privacy settings. Privacy Dashboards are common on social media platforms where an End User will share considerable amounts of personal

---
[117] Article 7: Conditions for Consent

data. Privacy Dashboards are a very useful way to automate the administration of privacy rights by giving the Data Subject more granular control over how their data is processed. Privacy Dashboards must be supported by a 'back-end' which ensures any changes made by a Data Subject are promulgated through all relevant processing activities.

> **EXAMPLE: George unticks a box in the privacy dashboard on Monty-Axel LLC's website withdrawing his consent to have third parties contact him with details of their new products. Monty-Axel LLC must have a process for communicating this withdrawal of consent to any third party in possession of George's details.**
>
> **Those third parties must also have processes in place to restrict any processing activity which relates to George and, if appropriate, processes to remove George's data from their systems.**

Just-in-time Privacy Notices

As you will recall from chapter 04 personal data must not only be processed in a fair and transparent manner but collected only for a specified, explicit and legitimate purpose. The drafters of the Regulation also make it clear the information presented to the Data Subject must be easily accessible, easy to understand and that clear and plain language be used. One method in which plain language communication can be achieved is through the use of just-in-time privacy notices, placed next to an input field on an online form.

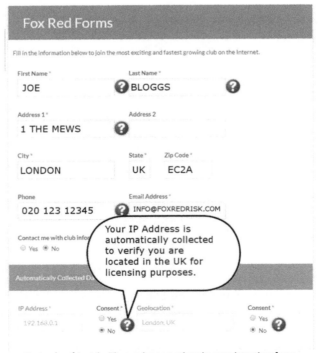

Example of Just-in-Time privacy notices in a registration form

The Data Subject would hover over the question mark and be provided with a clear plain language explanation why the data must be collected. A further recommendation would be to include a link to the full privacy notice should the Data Subject require further information. Practitioners and UX designers may also wish to consider how they alert a Data Subject about data which is automatically collected and how they gain consent to collect the data. One option (see below) would be to populate fields at the bottom of an online form and show the user what is being automatically collected. Just-in-time privacy notices and a radio button which could be used to provide informed active consent.

Pseudonymisation

Pseudonymisation is a process whereby personal data is stripped out of a dataset and replaced with an anonymous identifier. This identifier could still be married back to the original data subject if one has access to the key. Pseudonymisation could be used in scenarios such as Service Desk systems where the nature of the query and resolution are stored in the Service Desk with a unique identifier relating to the person making the service request. The identifier could be stored within a linked Access Management System, HR Information System (HRIS) or in the case of customers, a Customer Relationship Management (CRM) system.

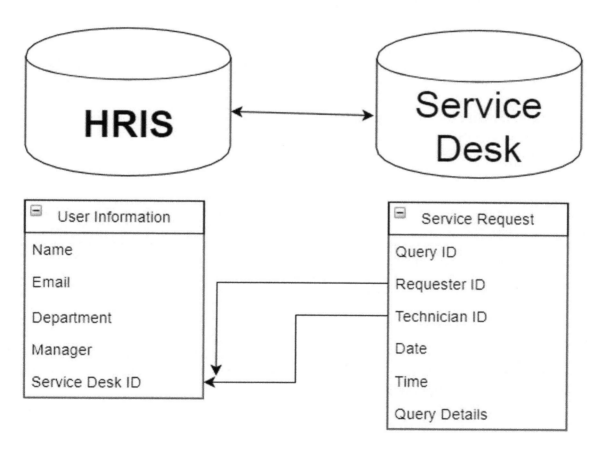

Pseudonymisation in operation within two databases

Let's expand on the Service Desk Example. Should the Service Desk system become compromised, it would be much more difficult for an unauthorised actor to gain access to supporting personal information as the personal data would not be stored in the Service Desk System - only the unique pseudonymised identifier. Pseudonymisation can also be applied to data held outside a database infrastructure such as End User Computing Applications (EUCA) and static data reports.

Wherever data is used for statistical purposes, personal data could be stripped out and replaced with a unique identifier. Where personal data is required, consideration should be considered in relation to whether reducing granularity would be appropriate.

> **EXAMPLE: A Marketing Manager at NDH Ltd wishes to understand the effectiveness of a marketing campaign for a new drone. The campaign targeted a particular demographic (18-25-year-olds based in London). The Marketing Manager requests an extract from the purchasing system with the name, DoB, Date of Purchase and full address of all customers who purchased the drone. This is so she can slice and dice the information by home location, age etc.**
>
> **Under GDPR this may not be appropriate when the objectives of the marketing manager could be achieved with pseudonymised data. For example, a spreadsheet could be generated whereby:**
>
> **A unique ID replaces the customer name**
> **Only the year of birth is supplied**
> **Only the City component of the address is supplied**

Ideally, data extracted from secure systems into spreadsheets for further analysis should be kept to the absolute minimum[118]. Instead, common reports should be generated which meet the End Users' information requirements without exposing the underlying personal data. Where more granular analysis is required, the user should be provided with tools which facilitate secure, limited, read-only access to official systems of record. Whether within a managed system or within an EUCA, data is not pseudonymised if there is enough data (i.e. within separate fields) which can be combined to identify a Data Subject.

> **EXAMPLE: A table containing the name, gender, DOB and address would not be pseudonymised by removing the name alone because the other information would be enough to identify the Data Subject.**

---

[118] Missing child benefit CDs: what went wrong, and why it would have carried on regardless as reported in Computer Weekly. 21 November 2007.

Encryption & other Cryptographic Techniques

Encryption is a vast topic, the subject of hundreds of books. As such I am not going to go into significant detail on the topic. What I will do is cover the topic at a high level and in particular, how it can be used in the context of data protection. It's useful to understand different cryptographic techniques exist but not all are considered to fall under the subset of encryption. For the purposes of this book encryption relies on a key (or keys) which are used to encrypt and decrypt data. Encoding and one way cryptographic techniques such as Hashing will be discussed but these methods in themselves are not encryption techniques in themselves. Here are the definitions:

Cryptography: Cryptography is the science and art of coding and decoding secret messages, information or data

Encryption: encryption is the method by which messages, information or data is converted from a readable form to an encoded version that can only be decoded by another entity if they have access to a decryption key

Encoding: Encoding is the process of converting data into a format required for a number of information processing needs (e.g. Encryption)

Hashing: Hashing is the process of generating a value or values from a string of text using a mathematical function. In its cryptographic application, hashing is usually always a one-way process whereby it should not be possible to derive the original value from the hashed value.

DID YOU KNOW: An encoding technique officially known as steganography is widely used in Film & TV under a different name: Easter Egg. Film-makers hide Easter eggs throughout their films in the hope fans will detect them. In the 1999 film Fight Club, Director David Fincher placed a Starbucks[119] cup in every scene of the film. This related back to his time in Los Angeles where he couldn't find a good cup of coffee. Then Starbucks arrived and were now on every corner. Fincher said the [inclusion of a] Starbuck cup signified sometimes you could have too much of a good thing. I would expand more about other Easter Eggs in the film, but I've already broken the first rule.

Background to encryption: encryption[120], a component of cryptography, is the process of encoding information in a manner that hides the true meaning of the original information. Historically, this would involve using one or more techniques to jumble up or transpose text into an unintelligible string of characters using a secret key, known only to sender and recipient. For encryption to be effective, the time required to break encryption must be longer than the useful life of the encrypted information. As computing power increased, historical encryption methods became obsolete; as the information encrypted could be decrypted while the information was still useful.

---

[119] 11 Easter Eggs You Never Noticed in your Favourite Movies: Reported in the Huffington Post on 17 October 2014

[120] Cryptography: An Introductory Crash Course on the Science and Art of Coding and Decoding of Messages, Ciphers, Cryptograms and Encryption. Bull G., 2016

EXAMPLE: During WWII the Allies were able to intercept German Naval communications, encrypted using a machine codenamed ENIGMA[121]. The encryption method used was changed every day at Midnight. Allied Forces were not able to decrypt the information fast enough for it to be historically useful (i.e. analyse what has already happened).

Alan Turing, a British mathematician and crypto-analyst, working with others and building on the work of Polish Mathematicians, designed and built the Turing Bombe machine. This machine, when provided with certain information (i.e. a known, unchanging fragment of the encrypted message), was able to quickly identify the encryption key so all messages for the day could be deciphered at will.

The machine was so successful; the Allies had to ensure the Germans did not find out Enigma code had been broken, often leading to the difficult decision of ignoring life-saving intelligence to avoid suspicion.

In the information age, mathematics has provided a significantly increased level of complexity in the form of encryption algorithms which cannot, using current computing power, be decrypted for hundreds of years. Unfortunately, as encryption technology moves forward, so to do the tools used to break the ciphers. The next evolution in cryptography and crypto-analysis will be the advent of Quantum Computing where it is possible current encryption methods could become obsolete. For now, though, we are ok, and you can still use your online banking – relatively – securely.

Types of Encryption: the two main types of encryption used today are symmetric and asymmetric encryption. Both methods involve the use of secret keys. In symmetric encryption, the secret key used to encrypt and decrypt the message is the same. This means once the key is compromised, communication to any recipient using the key can be decrypted. This presents three main problems, firstly the key must be shared and so is vulnerable to interception. Secondly, the more it is used, the more it is vulnerable to being broken using crypto-analysis techniques. Thirdly, the sender and recipient cannot authenticate each other.

EXAMPLE: DDH Ltd. Share a symmetric key (via a USB memory stick through the post once a quarter) with all its suppliers to facilitate secure communications over the Internet. While DDH Ltd is communicating with its suppliers, a hacker is intercepting the encrypted communications. Due to the high volumes of traffic and the infrequent key change, the hacker is able to use crypto-analysis to decode previous and future messages between DDH Ltd and all their suppliers – until the next key change.

Once the key has been deciphered, not only can the hacker intercept messages, they can also pretend to be DDH Ltd or one of the suppliers and either alter legitimate messages or falsify new messages.

---

[121] Enigma: The Battle for the Code: Sebag-Montefiore H., 2004

Now the above example is *highly* simplified, but hopefully, it highlights the flaws in the use of symmetric encryption. Some of these weaknesses can be mitigated by frequent key exchange and the use protocols such as Message Authentication Code (MAC), but there are better alternatives, as will go on to discuss. So when should one use symmetric key encryption? Symmetric encryption is most effectively used for data whilst in the Information Life-Cycle storage state as it is unlikely keys or data will be compromised through regular transmission over insecure channels. When it comes to data in the transmission stage of the Information Life-Cycle, symmetric key encryption could be used where either the sender or recipient does not have the infrastructure to support asymmetric encryption methods and communication is either infrequent or one time. If, however symmetric key encryption in the transmission stage can be avoided; it should be avoided.'

EXAMPLE: DDH Ltd. Wishes to make a one-time personal data transfer to the FCA to support an investigation. In the restricted timeframe it would not be feasible to implement an asymmetric encryption mechanism. DDH Ltd encrypts the data using AES-256 (a symmetric algorithm) and sends via email. The Sender then contacts the FCA recipient via a different method (e.g. Phone) and provides a 16-character key. Once the file is stored in a secure, access controlled file-system, the encrypted file is then removed from both the sender and recipient inboxes, and the FCA recipient then emails confirmation of destruction.

Asymmetric encryption not only relies on secret keys but a combination of secret keys and public keys. In asymmetric encryption both the sender and recipient have mathematically linked private and public keys. The sequence is as follows:

1. Sender retrieves Recipient Public Key
2. Sender encrypts message using combination of Sender Private Key and Recipient Public Key
3. Message is then sent from Sender to Recipient
4. Recipient retrieves Sender Public Key
5. Sender decrypts message using combination of Recipient Private Key and Sender Public Key

As should be apparent from the process flow described above, the Sender and Recipient Private keys are never sent across the communication channel (e.g. the Internet) and so this method is considerably more secure than symmetric encryption. Not only is it more secure, the combination of private and public keys also provides a mechanism for authentication and non-repudiation. Where possible, when it comes to the data transmission stage of the Information Life-Cycle, asymmetric encryption should be the preferred choice.

Digital Certificates: most people, albeit unconsciously, will have come across certificates as they are the fabric of eCommerce. Digital certificates are what makes the padlock appear in web browsers on the payment pages of retail sites and (hopefully) all eBanking sites. As mentioned earlier in asymmetric encryption senders and recipients share public keys but how does one side know the public key of the other is legitimate. The answer is that a third party known as a Certificate Authority (CA) 'vouches' that the public key is legitimately owned by an organisation by issuing a digital certificate.

> **EXAMPLE: When you access an eBanking site, your web browser attempts to establish a secure connection. Before it uses the public key provided by the eBanking site, it checks with a Certificate Authority to confirm if the public key is legitimate. If it is not, then the site will warn the user that trust has not been established and the connection cannot be considered secure.**

Key Security: encryption is reliant on the security of encryption keys. Organisations must ensure any system design incorporates robust key management. Where encryption relies on a third party such as a Certificate Authority (CA), appropriate due diligence must be conducted to confirm there is a high level of trust and that the CA isn't compromised[122].

Hashing: in simple terms, hashing is a one-way cryptographic technique, that is to say, whatever you hash cannot be reversed. Sounds a strange thing to do, but as we will go on to explain, it is an incredibly useful tool from a data protection perspective. Hashing can be used to create a digital fingerprint and can also be used to protect certain types of data at rest as an extra step prior to transmission. In the former case, if the sender of a file wanted to provide proof to a recipient the file hadn't been compromised in transit, the sender could send the file's corresponding hash in a separate channel. The recipient could rehash the file on receipt, and if the hashes are the same, the recipient would have a reasonable assurance the file has not been compromised. From a data protection perspective, this could be used (alongside other cryptographic techniques) in the Subject Access Request process, when sending data electronically, to provide assurance to a Data Subject their data hasn't been compromised in transit.

In the latter use of hashing, the technique is commonly used to obfuscate login passwords for websites and online portals. Instead of sending or storing the password, the password is hashed, and then the hash is stored - instead of the password. Each time the user then enters their password to log in, it is the hash which is then compared to a database entry rather than comparing a clear text password. In reality, hashing alone is no longer sufficient as a means of securely storing passwords. This is because humans don't always make great choices when it comes to choosing their passwords and hackers have built tables of hash values based on a commonly used password. When mitigating against this vulnerability, password hashes are 'salted' before hashing. Salting is the appending of a cryptographically strong random number to a password and then hashing the combination.

The use of salted passwords has a number of benefits. If there are two users with the same password, there would not be two identical hashes. It increases the effort the hacker has to go through to crack the underlying password and, the people administrating the database containing the salted password hash value will not be able to work out your actual password – great control against the insider threat! Sadly, even as late as 2017, there are organisations ignoring this extremely basic control and are still storing passwords in clear text[123] - absolutely bonkers!

---

[122] DigiNotar SSL certificate hack amounts to cyberwar, says expert: Reported in the Guardian on 5 September 2011.
[123] Hetzner hack: Top South African web host hit with mega-breach, every client may be exposed: Reported in International Business Times on 2 November 2017

EXAMPLE:

Passphrase: Nat Lofthouse was born in Bolton in 1925!
Password: NLwbiBi1925

Salt 1: 1581357865
SHA-256 Hash = Salt 1 + Password =
05af163fe7815f425dba0de10921d3404fbdf7bfcdf74bca01be5a642150dd96

Salt 2: 1658136578
SHA-256 Hash = Salt 2 + Password =
f4db847353d4e7e668c962c41266ac9a1d145d0444c5d068128f23ff9f14d59d

Encryption and the Right to be Forgotten: when considering the specification for storing information, an organisation could consider using Data Subject level encryption keys. What this means in practice is that each Data Subject would be assigned an encryption key. All personal data related to the Data Subject would be encrypted using the encryption key. Should the Data Subject make a legitimate request to be forgotten, the keys could be securely deleted and thus render the encrypted data irretrievable.

A feature of both encryption keys and digital certificates is an expiry component. Keys and certificates can be set to expire after a certain period. This feature could be useful in enforcing data retention periods. I recommend proceeding with extreme caution in designing in such a feature as many a system outage has been caused by someone forgetting to remember to do something about an expiring encryption key!

The ugly side of encryption: a discussion on encryption in the context of data protection would not be complete without discussing ransomware. Ransomware is a form of malicious software which can be used to encrypt an organisation's data, making it unusable, unless the organisation pays a ransom. The hacker who introduces the ransomware would hold the encryption key and typically requests payment through a currency called Bitcoin (which also uses encryption to avoid leaving a paper trail back to the hacker) before providing the key back to the organisation. Organisations must take measures to protect the personal data and supporting processes from ransomware. Useful controls to Defend, Detect and Manage the spectre of ransomware are:

1. Segregated Backups
2. Training & Awareness
3. Anti-Malware Protection
4. Patch & Vulnerability Management
5. SIEM solutions
6. Identity & Access Management
7. Centrally Managed Virtualisation

In summary, encryption can be used to support data protection by encrypting stored data and data in transit; Encryption can also support the authentication of a third party and support the right to be forgotten. Encryption can, however, be used against an organisation, so it's important to put controls in place to defend against the malevolent uses of encryption.

Identity and Access Management (IAM)

Identity & Access Management (IAM) is a fundamental control required for ensuring, only those people who have a valid business need to access data, regardless of position or seniority, get access – and no one else. IAM is probably joint top with patch management for the title "Security control that organisations do the worst". Before we go on to a good practice IAM model, it's useful to discuss some of the key components of good IAM.

The principle of Least Privilege: giving end users (and IT Admins/Database Admins) the lowest level of access required to do their work. If they do not need the access, then it must be removed. If the person is not using (or never has used) access credentials, there must be a mechanism to suspend/revoke the unneeded access. This is to defend against both rogue insiders doing activities beyond that which they're authorised (whether maliciously or accidentally), as well as limiting the damage that a hacker could do if they ever managed to compromise a user's credentials.

> **EXAMPLE: No End User should have access rights which give them the capability to delete an entire database single-handedly.**

Segregation of Duties: separating conflicting access to avoid unauthorised activities. There are certain tasks which include control steps (e.g. Review or Approve) to aid in the prevention of unauthorised activity such as Fraud. While it should be clear to most that a person must not approve their own work, some systems still permit such activity. When designing a new system for processing personal data, segregation of duties controls must be built in and a segregation of duties matrix must be documented and maintained.

> **EXAMPLE: No End User should be able to edit the address and Bank details of a Customer and then be able to approve the change themselves.**

Starters, Transferees, Leavers STL (also known as Joiners, Movers, Leavers JML): every application / system must have a process to set up new users, to revoke access when a person changes department and to remove access when a person leaves the organisation. A good practice is to treat a user transferring from one department to another as a quasi-leaver. This would mean, all system access is reduced to nothing and then system access is re-provisioned based on their needs in their new department. This prevents 'Access Creep' where a person who moves from one department to another or gets promoted, builds up significantly more access than required. Access Creep has been attributed to a number of major fraud[124] cases.

Justification, Approval and Recertification: before access is provided, there must be a justification which includes an explicit reason why access is required. Access must then be approved by a competent supervisor who can attest to the justification and will supervise the End User's activities. As access requirements can change periodically (e.g. due to promotion or change of role) access must also be periodically recertified against the original justification and the

---

[124] How Kerviel exposed lax controls at Société Générale: Reported in the Financial Times on 7 February 2008.

system's segregation of duties matrix. If access is no longer required, the access must be removed or adjusted. If there is new justification, this must be recorded and subsequently approved. The frequency of recertification must be risk-based with high-risk employees or systems assessed more frequently. It is not uncommon when designing in IAM processes that a member of Information Security is also involved in the access approval chain.

EXAMPLE: Tom works in Marketing. He wishes to gain Admin access to the Human Resources Information System (HRIS). Tom's justification is he needs the access to do his job.

Tom's manager, Jane, denies Tom's request because the business justification is too vague and inadequate and in any case, the access is too high, and to a system, Tom has no legitimate right to access.

The Information Security Analyst/Manager is not approving whether access is appropriate but confirming the governance steps required to approve access have been conducted properly. In the above example, had Jane approved the request, Information Security would step in and halt provisioning until the appropriate information had been provided. Information Security would, in parallel, provide training to Jane to avoid a repeat event.

Big Brother should be watching: monitoring of normal users (and IT users with elevated privileges) activity must be in place. Monitoring must be sufficient to identify suspicious activity in a timely manner in order that corrective action can be taken quickly. Common items to monitor are:

1. System access while User is: travelling, sick, no longer employed
2. Failed password attempts
3. Admin accounts created and removed in short period (e.g. less than 24 hours)
4. File access by users in a different department
5. Out-of-hours Internet Access
6. Remote Access
7. Firewall changes
8. Data Leakage (Email, USB, Internet, Instant Messaging)
9. Social Media
10. Installation of Desktop Software
11. Access to Cloud Services
12. Direct Access to Databases (e.g. ODBC, OLEDB, SOAP)

It is highly likely user activity monitoring will be untenable if conducted using manual processes. Organisations must incorporate this monitoring into a Security Information and Event Management (SIEM) system. Many SIEMs are now able to provide sophisticated user behaviour analytics (UBA/UEBA) capabilities which automate the process of identifying suspicious activity. It's important to ensure monitoring tools are not considered a replacement for information analysts but a tool which makes them more efficient. There have been cases[125] where unauthorised activity had been identified by automated systems, but no action was taken.

---

[125] Kweku Adoboli: a rogue trader's tale: Reported in Financial Times on 22 October 2015

Attribute-Based Access Control (ABAC): organisations must have technical and organisational controls in place to provision and enforce access. Organisations typically go on a journey with access control. In low-maturity organisations, system owners simply shoehorn users into the out-of-the-box access profiles created by the software vendor. Managers usually have little or no knowledge of what access their employees and have relied heavily on vendor recommendations. As organisations move into the next level of maturity, system owners begin to customise role profiles to company needs at the beginning of the system's life. At some point in the system's life, that initial knowledge becomes decayed due to poor change control. Users are no longer assigned profiles, but instead Managers request system administrators copy access from one user to another user. This becomes a problem when the current user has been given extra privileges (e.g. to cover someone's leave). This access is then copied. The next person gains additional privileges, and so on and so forth until the role profile of the fifth person bears no resemblance to the original locked down role. This is another type of the Access Creep described earlier. The next level of maturity is Role-Based Access Control (RBAC). In RBAC an employee's business role is assigned access privileges for all relevant systems across the organisation. When a new employee starts, access is provisioned based on a change controlled template. The same applies when a user changes department – their access is reduced to zero and then built up again based on their new employee business role. In organisations which employ RBAC, the copying of access permissions from one user to another is prohibited. For systems with highly granular permissions, it is not uncommon for change controlled 'dummy' accounts to be used to improve the efficiency of provisioning. The most modern access control model is known as Attribute Based Access Control (ABAC). ABAC is defined[126] as *"an access control method where subject requests to perform operations on objects are granted or denied based on assigned attributes of the subject, assigned attributes of the object, environmental conditions, and a set of policies that are specified in terms of those attributes and conditions."*

> **EXAMPLE: An ABAC policy could be defined whereby: HR Managers with TOP SECRET clearance would be able to see all HR information up to and including TOP SECRET wherever it existed in the organisation.**

In an ABAC organisation, every employee (a Subject) would be assigned certain attributes (e.g. Department="HR", Management Level="8", Clearance="TOP SECRET"). Every object would also be assigned attributes (e.g. Classification="SECRET", Type="HR"). Governing the relationship between Subjects and Objects are access policies which contain the rules determining how subject and objects can interact. ABAC offers a lot more control over access, as long as subjects and objects have accurate attributes. ABAC can make Starters, Transferees and Leavers processes highly efficient. As soon as an employee changes department, the department attribute would change in their profile. As soon as this configuration change is made, previous access is immediately revoked, and new access rights are immediately live. The fourth core component of ABAC is the concept of environmental conditions. Environmental conditions are items such as time of day or physical location. Other conditions could include threat-level or Change Freezes. What this allows an ABAC organisation to do, is to set up conditions whereby current subject-object policy defined relationships can be dynamically changed due to changes in environmental conditions. As soon as those environmental conditions return to normal, normal access would resume. ABAC is an access management model to which organisations should aspire. ABAC implemented well should considerably improve security and significantly reduce the administrative burden associated with managing user access. For organisations wishing to implement ABAC, review the supporting documentation for the XACML[127] standard maintained by OASIS.

---

[126] NIST Special Publication 800-162: Guide to Attribute Based Access Control (ABAC) Definition and Considerations, January 2014.
[127] eXtensible Access Control Markup Language (XACML) Version 3.0 Plus Errata 01, January 2017.

> **EXAMPLE: During a cyber-attack, an organisation's threat level is set to DEFCON2. This triggers an environmental condition whereby remote access to all databases containing personal data is revoked.**
>
> **Shortly afterwards, it is determined the organisation has been infected by ransomware increasing the threat level to DEFCON1. This triggers an environmental condition whereby all access to all databases containing personal data is revoked - with the exception of the incident management team.**

Data Protection and APIs

A Data Protection by Design and Default chapter would not be complete without a discussion on the topic of Application Programming Interfaces (API). APIs are pretty much what they say they are, a programming interface between applications. A good way to think about how an API operates is in terms of how restaurant customers interact with a chef through a waiter. A customer (the Client) provides information in the form of an order (the request) to the waiter (the API). Prior to going to the Chef (the Server), the waiter performs some initial confirmation the order is correct (input validation). The waiter then goes to the chef and informs the chef of one or more customers orders, and the chef will give the waiter a number of responses. Responses could be the menu option is not available (400 Bad Request[128]), the food will be served in 40 minutes (202 Accepted), or the chef could provide the waiter with the food immediately (201 Created). The waiter would then come back to the customer with the chef's response.

APIs are ubiquitous. APIs power weather apps on your phone, help people search for books on Amazon or help sales teams interact with their customers in Salesforce. I'd be surprised if at some point in the last 24 hours you hadn't used an API to interact with a website in some shape or form. So now we know what an API is and how it works, what are the Data Protection issues which require consideration[129]?

Use RESTful APIs: REST APIs are a type of Application Programming Interface which introduces design constraints in order to improve interoperability. The constraints are:

1. Uniform Interface – simplify and decouple architecture
2. Stateless – the state is contained in the request
3. Cacheable – common requests-responses are cached
4. Client-Server – Client and Server are separated
5. Layered System – Client can't see beyond the API

Implementing RESTful APIs would be a very efficient way of providing a Data Subject with the Right to Portability.

Use an API description language: one of the key components of GDPR is transparency and documentation will be key to demonstrating this principle. Using an API description language will aid in ensuring the functionality of APIs is understood. Common API description languages which are both human and machine readable are Swagger (OpenAPI) and RESTful API Markup Language (RAML).

---

[128] HTTP Return Codes in RESTful APIs
[129] RESTful API Design: Best Practices in API Design with REST. Biehl M., 2016

CORS: stands for Cross-Origin Resource Sharing. This is a control to prevent Cross Site Scripting (XSS) or Cross-Site Request Forgery (CSRF) attacks however its implementation can also catch legitimate API calls. When designing an API, consider the use of a pre-flight request which collects security configuration information (i.e. in the Access-Control-Allow-Header).

Support both JSON and XML: JavaScript Object Notation (JSON) and eXtensible Markup Language (XML) are ways of structuring text in a self-describing, hierarchical way. JSON and XML can usually be understood by both human and machine and because they are both structured, the data held within can be manipulated, formatted or stored as per the end users' requirements.

```
EXAMPLE: JSON Response:
{"alumni":[
  { "firstName":"Stephen", "lastName":"Massey" },
  { "firstName":"Kate", "lastName":"Massey" },
  { "firstName":"Cooper", "lastName":"Dog" }
]}
```

If both JSON and XML are supported, any data connected to the API could be easily ported to any other system supporting one of these two standards. Being able to access data in a structured form such as JSON or XML is going to make data portability and eDiscovery a lot more straightforward too. If you absolutely must choose just one, I prefer JSON over XML. It is shorter, quicker to read and write; it can use arrays and, as became apparent in creating these examples, requires a lot less knowledge of Latin grammar!

```
EXAMPLE: XML Response:
<alumni>
  <alumnus>
    <firstName>Stephen</firstName> <lastName>Massey</lastName>
  </alumnus>
  <alumna>
    <firstName>Kate</firstName> <lastName>Massey</lastName>
  </alumna>
  <alumnus>
    <firstName>Cooper</firstName> <lastName>Dog</lastName>
  </alumnus>
</alumnuss>
```

Implement API Keys: an API key is a unique identifier which facilitates lightweight authentication and authorisation to make an API call. API keys can support monitoring activities but cannot be relied upon for non-repudiation as keys can be compromised. In addition to keys, authentication can be further enhanced by using the HTTP Basic and HTTP Digest mechanisms. If there is no delegated authorisation consider using OAuth

API over TLS: in order to protect API keys, and the data sent to/received from the API, the API traffic must only be sent over a secure communication channel (e.g. TLS). To ensure this is enforced the API must be set up to reject insecure requests.

Don't expose Personal or Sensitive data over public APIs: when setting up APIs to share data over the Internet with the general public, it must not be possible for personal or sensitive data to be exposed to anyone other than the data subject via a legitimate, authenticated request.

Input/Output Validation: as will be described a little further on, a common method of gaining unauthorised access to systems is to inject code into legitimate API requests. This injected code can be used to gain unauthorised system access. Before an API request is processed, there must be input validation at the server level (not on the client side where it can be easily bypassed!). Input validation should identify and throw out errors if anything but a legitimate request is made. The same validation concepts apply to output too. A simple way to implement output validation is to check whether the JSON or XML data conforms to the serialisation rules for their respective schema. Output which fails these validation tests must be logged as a 500 Server Error and flagged to the development team for urgent investigation.

Traffic Shaping: restricting requests and responses dependent on policies and environmental conditions can massively improve the security and availability of your API. Consider restricting who can access data (e.g. by IP range or by the time of day or perhaps geographic location. Consider restricting the amount of data any one requestor can request in one go. Have a plan in place to revoke access (e.g. by invalidating a compromised API key) if a requestor is abusing the API.

APIs are a great way of making the process of sharing data between people and systems simple and straightforward. Because of this simplicity, APIs can also be abused to extract significant volumes of data. Following the above design principles for APIs which share personal data will go a long way to reducing data protection risk.

OWASP Top 10

Practitioners should be aware good practice is for modern data-driven applications to be accessed through an Internet browser (e.g. Firefox, Chrome or Internet Explorer/Edge) with the data sitting in a database on a server in a data centre. The ideal scenario is that the 'web' application is browser agnostic and will, therefore, work no matter which browser is used (however a lot of corporate applications still tend to favour Internet Explorer). In the next two sections, we will look at the current good security practices for developing the web application and securing the backend database.

Whilst the responsibility for security sits with the CISO; the DPO must have a high-level understanding of what should be in place. When it comes to developing applications, internally or through the use of a third party, an organisation should ensure applications involved in the processing of personal data are developed using a mature, secure systems development lifecycle (SDLC) and – ideally - do not contain any of the vulnerabilities contained in the OWASP[130] Top 10.

---

[130] OWASP: Open Web Application Security Project

This list, which is periodically updated, contains what are currently considered the ten most critical web application security risks. The 2017[131] top 10 security risks are:

Injection: Injection flaws, such as SQL, OS, and LDAP injection occur when untrusted data is sent to an interpreter as part of a command or query. The attacker's hostile data can trick the interpreter into executing unintended commands or accessing data without proper authorization. To prevent keep data separate from commands and queries.

Broken Authentication: Application functions related to authentication and session management are often implemented incorrectly, allowing attackers to compromise passwords, keys, or session tokens, or to exploit other implementation flaws to assume other users' identities (temporarily or permanently). To prevent, do not ship or deploy with any default credentials, particularly for admin users.

Sensitive Data Exposure: Many web applications and APIs do not properly protect sensitive data, such as financial, healthcare, and PII. Attackers may steal or modify such weakly protected data to conduct credit card fraud, identity theft, or other crimes. Sensitive data deserves extra protection such as encryption at rest or in transit, as well as special precautions when exchanged with the browser. To prevent, classify data, review the privacy laws or regulations applicable to sensitive data, and protect as per regulatory requirements. Don't store data unnecessarily and encrypt data at rest.

XML External Entity: Many older or poorly configured XML Processors evaluate external entity references within XML documents. External entities can be used to disclose internal files using the file URI handler, internal SMB file shares on unpatched Windows servers, internal port scanning, remote code execution, and denial of service attacks, such as the Billion Laughs attack. To prevent, disable XML external entity and DTD processing in all XML parsers in your application, implement positive ("whitelisting") input validation, filtering, or sanitisation and patch or upgrade all the latest XML Processors and libraries.

Broken Access Control: Restrictions on what authenticated users are allowed to do are not properly enforced. Attackers can exploit these flaws to access unauthorized functionality and/or data, such as access other users' accounts, view sensitive files, modify other users' data, change access rights, etc. To prevent, default access to deny, implement access control mechanisms once and re-use them throughout the application. Log access control failures, alert admins when appropriate. Rate limit API and Controller access to minimise the harm from automated attack tooling.

Security Misconfiguration: Security misconfiguration is the most common issue which exposes data. It can be due in part to manual or ad hoc configuration (or not configuring at all), insecure default configurations, open Amazon AWS S3 buckets, misconfigured HTTP headers, error messages containing sensitive information, not patching or upgrading systems, frameworks, dependencies, and components in a timely fashion (or at all). To prevent, implement a repeatable hardening process that makes it fast and easy to deploy environments that are properly locked down. Remove or do not install any unnecessary features, components, documentation and samples. Remove unused dependencies and frameworks. Implement a process to triage and deploy all updates and patches in a timely manner to each deployed environment. This process needs to include all dependencies, components, and libraries.

Cross Site Scripting (XSS): XSS flaws occur whenever an application includes untrusted data in a new web page without proper validation or escaping, or updates an existing web page with user-supplied data using a browser API that can create JavaScript. XSS allows attackers to execute scripts in the victim's browser which can hijack user

---

[131] OWASP Foundation (https://www.owasp.org). ShareAlike 4.0 (CC BY-SA 4.0)

sessions, deface web sites, or redirect the user to malicious sites. To prevent, separate untrusted data from active browser content.

Insecure Deserialization: Insecure deserialization flaws occur when an application receives hostile serialized objects. Insecure deserialization leads to remote code execution. Even if deserialization flaws do not result in remote code execution, serialized objects can be replayed, tampered or deleted to spoof users, conduct injection attacks, and elevate privileges. To prevent, do not accept serialized objects from untrusted sources or to use serialization mediums that only permit primitive data types.

Using components with known vulnerabilities: Components, such as libraries, frameworks, and other software modules, run with the same privileges as the application. If a vulnerable component is exploited, such an attack can facilitate serious data loss or server takeover. Applications and APIs using components with known vulnerabilities may undermine application defences and enable various attacks and impacts. To prevent, remove unused dependencies, unnecessary features, components, files, and documentation. Only obtain your components from official sources and, when possible, prefer signed packages to reduce the chance of getting a modified, malicious component.

Insufficient Logging and Monitoring: Insufficient logging and monitoring, coupled with missing or ineffective integration with incident response, allows attackers to further attack systems, maintain persistence, pivot to more systems, and tamper, extract, or destroy data. To prevent, ensure all login, access control failures, input validation failures can be logged with sufficient user context to identify suspicious or malicious accounts, and held for sufficient time to allow delayed forensic analysis. Ensure high-value transactions have an audit trail with integrity controls to prevent tampering or deletion, such as append-only database tables or similar.

While the above section details the OWASP Top 10, the OWASP site contains a wealth of information. If your developers are not aware of the OWASP material – bring it to their attention and work with the information security team to get the concepts and controls embedded in your organisation's development lifecycle.

DID YOU KNOW: If your organisation is developing mobile applications (e.g. for Android or iPhone), OWASP also produces a Top 10 mobile application security risks too.

Data Protection and Database Design

While OWASP covers web application development, it doesn't really provide answers to the backend database(s). This section looks at the common database data protection issues and effective controls which can be implemented to mitigate the risk to the personal data stored in your organisation's databases. There are many different types of database and many different vendors, as such, this section will remain as generic as possible. If your organisation develops using a particular database technology, I would recommend augmenting the advice produced here, with the recommendations provided by the vendor in their product documentation.

Ensure all tables in the database are normalised to third normal form: poorly designed data structures can lead to modification, insertion and deletion issues[132]. What this means from a data protection perspective, is that personal data could become inconsistent over time or, if certain records are deleted, other linked data could also be lost. Practitioners must ensure those designing database structures (or schemas) normalise to at least third normal form, 3NF (or ideally Boyce-Codd normal form) so that referential integrity is enforced and duplication of data is minimised. Such an approach will be essential in terms of managing the rights of access, the right to data portability and the right to be forgotten.

Data(base) minimisation: if you have adopted the third normal form principle (which I really hope you have) then the data within your database should already be technically minimised. There are however some other things which should be considered. Firstly, could the amount of personal data be minimised in one database by linking to the same data stored elsewhere. This is commonly achieved via an Application Programming Interface (API). This approach is not uncommon. In the commercial world, many organisations' user data is stored in a repository such as Microsoft Active Directory (AD) and then accessed by other systems such as SharePoint. Similarly, HRIS (e.g. PeopleSoft) could also be used as a central repository for employee data for internal applications. It is important to establish in the design phase that this data from the CRM or HRIS is not just simply extracted from one system and then uploaded into the new system but linked. If the data is to simply copied (instead of linking), then you are now increasing the amounts of personal data which needs to be secured and the likelihood of a problem in one system causing problems elsewhere!

No Personal Data in Primary / Foreign Keys: primary and foreign keys are used to establish relationships between sets of data, stored in different tables of a database. The keys enforce referential integrity and therefore need to be unique within a table. Often, and more commonly in migration projects, personal data is used as a primary key (as a lazy shortcut!). This key could be something known to be unique such as a person's email address or worse, a combination of personal data items concatenated together (e.g. UID = FNAME+SNAME+DOB+PCODE). The problem with using this approach is that referential integrity now relies on personal data. The most common issue with this approach is when development teams want to use live PROD data in a pseudonymised or randomised form to test functionality in DEV, QA and UAT environments but face problems as removal of fields containing personal data also serving as primary keys will destroy referential integrity and cause the database to function in unexpected ways.

Database Hardening: as with servers and applications, databases can also be hardened. Practitioners involved in the design stage of a database should confirm the security configuration of the database is commensurate with the value of the data stored and the level of risk to which the data is exposed. The Centre for Internet Security maintains hardening standards for common enterprise database solutions including MS SQL and Oracle DB. CIS also includes hardening standards for NoSQL databases such as MongoDB. If you're using it (which is not recommended in an enterprise environment), CIS also has a hardening standard for MySQL so there really is no excuse not to put basic database security controls in place as the heavy lifting has already been done!

---

[132] Beginning Database Design. Churcher C., 2012

Access Management: while we have discussed access management models earlier in this chapter, it is still worth reinforcing the importance of robust access control at the database level. Where it is possible administrative access to the backend database should be minimised and segregated so that the least amount of people can access, modify or change the data stored in the database. Consider implementing access management models which prevent IT support staff from accessing data when working through user issues unless absolutely necessary.

When it comes to end users, access must be provided through a front-end application which enforces access management policies. It is all too common for Database Administrators to provide direct access to a backend database (e.g. through ODBC, OLEDB or SOAP). Providing such direct connections must be avoided at all costs as these types of connection are very often totally uncontrolled. Two risks which these connections present, is data can be extracted from a database and then shared with those who don't have permission to access the information legitimately. Data could also be taken outside the organisation's secure environment (e.g. on a USB drive or even just printed out). Data can also be manipulated and then reintroduced into the same (or other) system with errors causing integrity issues. To avoid the situation whereby a direct access connection must be made, organisations must ensure appropriate capability is developed in the managed environment to avoid the need for direct connections.

Extracts and Reports: there is no point securing a database to the level of Fort Knox if users can extract all the personal and sensitive data in the form of a CSV file and then walk off with the file. A good practice is to build the reports required by end users in as close to the end result as possible. It is common for people in marketing, finance and HR to ask for system extracts and when they are asked what they need them for, they nonchalantly say 'so I can use it to create a chart in Excel for my monthly reporting'. End Users are so often unaware the end product they require can be built and automated without their intermediate Excel shenanigans. If End Users do need extra control over the end results, they should be provided with appropriate tools such as Business Objects or Tableau (or their equivalents) where access to data can be more effectively controlled.

Audit Trails: I am not going to labour this point as we have already discussed throughout the chapter. Suffice it to say; database activity must be in the scope of monitoring. All attempts to create, modify, extract data from the system (including unsuccessful) must be logged. Remember when it comes to logging of Database activity logs may also include personal data, and so affected logs fall in the scope of GDPR too.

EXAMPLE: An employee in the Sales Department attempts to create a report of all customers and their contact details. The week before the same employee had submitted their resignation. The systems would not permit the user to download the report.

Whilst the access control policy functioned as intended; such an action should also be flagged in the Security Information and Event Management (SIEM) system as it could be indicative of other unauthorised activity.

Artificial Intelligence / Big Data / Analytics

Organisations now have access to massive datasets which can tell them about pretty much any aspect of how their organisation functions or how both potential and actual customers interact (or don't interact) with their business. Organisations can target customers using information provided on social media and can also use such data to tailor their products and services at the invididual level. Up until recently a lot of the grunt work analysis has been based upon human designed and implemented algorithms. These algorithms can profile a Data Subject and using that profile make inferences about the Data Subject (Profiling) and also support automated decision-making processes (e.g. Score a person on a specific set of criteria in order to determine their eligibility for a loan). What is changing the landscape is the use of Artificial Intelligence (AI). Artificial Intelligence can look at large volumes of data and make its own judgements and then design its own algorithms to categorise the data – all without human intervention. This has led to some amazing innovations[133] but can also be a significant data protection and privacy risk.

The primary reasons AI or Analytics can pose a greater data protection risk – more so than other forms of processing – is due to the significantly higher volumes of data, the data collected without Data Subject knowledge (e.g. identifiers collected from their devices or tracking cookies collected when visiting websites) and the potential for mistakes when creating inferred datasets (e.g. inferring from a purchase of a One Direction album that the purchaser has female children in the 7-13 age range).

In any circumstance where artificial intelligence, big data or analytics are used to process personal data or make inferences about Data Subjects, the processing is absolutely covered by the General Data Protection Regulation[134]. All the things we have discussed in this chapter must be considered when implementing such systems but in particular Practitioners must consider the following when implementing any system that will include Artificial Intelligence or Analytics:

1. How will Data Subjects be informed of this activity, in particular where data is inferred or unconsciously collected?
2. How will Data Subjects provide / withdraw their consent?
3. How will the Controller ensure the AI system is free from legal discrimination (e.g. Discriminatory Racial Profiling)?
4. How will the Controller ensure the AI system is free from unjustified results (e.g. Promoting a fake news story because it has been already shared by a lot of people)?
5. How will you provide access to Data Subjects in relation to inferred and unconsciously collected data?
6. Where a system makes incorrect inferences about a data subject, how can these be identified and rectified?
7. Where an AI system makes a decision about a Data Subject that has a legal effect, what measures are in place to provide an alternative manual process.
8. How will the Process Owner ensure the processing is both lawful and proportional?
9. How will the Controller facilitate the Data Subject's Right to be Forgotten?

As you can see, there are quite a few additional things to think about. These additional requirements shouldn't discourage the use of Artificial Intelligence or Analytics but organisations must ensure the rights and freedoms of Data Subjects are upheld – as the more Data Subjects involved, the greater the impact would be should a Controller or Processor get it wrong!

[133] Alphabet's DeepMind Is Trying to Transform Health Care — But Should an AI Company Have Your Health Records? As reported on Bloomberg Business Week (online), dated 28 November.
[134] Article 22: Automated individual decision-making, including profiling

Computer Vision & CCTV

Computer vision is where images captured via CCTV or other videos are processed via computers. Many readers may have modern cameras or camera phones which show a circle round a subject's face just before you take a picture – this is computer vision. Readers may also be aware of enhanced facial recognition in casinos to identify potential cheats or Automatic Number Plate Recognition (ANPR) which can detect the location of a stolen vehicle. It is now possible on Facebook, when you upload a photo, to automatically identify your friends' faces and suggests a tag. Whilst CCTV has been pervasive across major cities, predominantly to support crime prevention, computer vision is becoming more and more pervasive. Computer vision and its use in marketing, in particular, has increased significantly.

> **EXAMPLE 1: Computer Vision could be used by a major sporting brand to identify the logos of competitor brands in photos on your social media accounts (e.g. Facebook, Instagram and Twitter) and then target specific advertising about to you and your friends about their brand. The brand may also choose to target negative advertising about a competitor to those it identifies as wearing a competitors' logo.**

> **EXAMPLE 2: Computer Vision could be used by a shop to identify a shopper's image from their social media account and then using additional data about your likes, preferences and spending power, to tailor signage and pricing to increase the likelihood of you making a purchase.**

In any circumstance where basic CCTV or Computer Vision systems are used, their use, and associated processing, are covered by the General Data Protection Regulation. All the things we have discussed in this chapter must be considered when implementing such systems but in particular Practitioners must consider:

10. How will Data Subjects be informed of this activity?
11. How will Data Subjects provide / withdraw their consent?
12. How will collection of CCTV or Computer Vision footage be limited to prevent inadvertent collection of Data Subjects who have not provided consent? (e.g. Data Subjects profiled when passing by a shop but not entering).
13. How will video footage and metadata be secured? Who will have access to the data?
14. How will the Controller facilitate a Data Subject's Right of Access to the footage?
15. How long will footage and metadata be retained
16. How will the Controller facilitate the Data Subject's Right to be Forgotten?

When it comes to Data Protection by Design and Default, there is quite a lot to think about. There is a lot of technical discussions that will be required. The aim of this chapter is not to intimidate a non-technical practitioner, but to highlight that they should seek support from Information Security who should be well equipped to lend a hand. Fundamentally from a design perspective, the key is to use what is technically possible to manage the risks associated with a set of personal data all the way through the Information Life-Cycle. If you can do that, you're doing an amazing job!

Data Protection Design Specification Template

Data Protection Design Requirements (version X.X)		
Project Name: [System Name]		
Project Sponsor: [Insert Name]		
Project Manager: [Insert Name]		
System Owner: [Insert Name]		
Link to Project Documentation: [Insert Link]		
ILC Stage / Rights	**Requirement**	**Owner**
1. COLLECTION		
Rectification		
Profiling		
Object		
Informed		
2. STORAGE		
Portability		
Rectification		
Erasure		
Profiling		
Access		
Restriction		
Object		
Informed		
3. MANIPULATION		
Rectification		
Erasure		
Profiling		
Access		
Restriction		
Object		
Informed		

Data Protection Design Requirements (Continued)		
ILC Stage / Rights	**Requirement**	**Owner**
4. PRESENTATION		
Rectification		
Erasure		
Access		
Restriction		
Object		
Informed		
5. TRANSMISSION		
Portability		
Restriction		
Object		
Informed		
6. DESTRUCTION		
Erasure		
Informed		
Sign-Off		
Project Sponsor		
System Owner		
Data Protection Officer		

NB: This specification must be included in the wider system specification / requirements document. All data protection requirements shall be classified as mandatory.

12. INCIDENT MANAGEMENT & BREACH NOTIFICATION

There is a growing belief amongst information security professionals, security breaches are inevitable. It's no longer a case 'if' an organisation will be breached but 'when'. There are so many high profile incidents, in 2017, organisations such as Equifax, Bupa, Uber and ABTA[135] all reported significant data breaches involving the compromise of personal data. When personal data is compromised by criminals, Data Subjects are exposed to an increased risk of identity theft or fraud. A data subject could find they have become a victim at a time when they themselves are looking to take out a loan to buy a car, or applying for a mortgage, only to be informed their [loan] application is declined because of suspicious credit activity. Imagine that car is needed to get to work or that house sale falls through and you can quickly start to see the impact a Personal Data breach could have on a data subject.

Data Protection legislators of the preceding 95/46/EC Directive understood security breaches would clearly have an impact on the rights and freedoms of Data Subjects as the 1995 directive states[136]:

"Member States shall provide that the controller must implement appropriate technical and organizational measures to protect personal data against accidental or unlawful destruction or accidental loss, alteration, unauthorized disclosure or access, in particular where the processing involves the transmission of data over a network, and against all other unlawful forms of processing. Having regard to state of the art and the cost of their implementation, such measures shall ensure a level of security appropriate to the risks represented by the processing and the nature of the data to be protected.

The Member States shall provide that the controller must, where processing is carried out on his behalf, choose a processor providing sufficient guarantees in respect of the technical security measures and organizational measures governing the processing to be carried out, and must ensure compliance with those measures."

While the 1995 Directive required Data Controllers and Processors to keep data secure, it did not place any requirement on Controllers of Processors to inform a Supervisory Authority or the Data Subjects themselves. A Data Subject may first come to learn of a Personal Data breach when they become a victim of fraud or if the breach is high profile and hits the 24-hour news cycle. GDPR now includes a requirement to notify the Supervisory Authority and in some instances the Data Subjects. This chapter will discuss what constitutes a 'notifiable' breach; the incident management processes an organisation should put in place and how to notify the Supervisory Authority and Data Subjects.

---

[135] Association of British Travel Agents
[136] Directive 95/46/EC - Article 17: Security of Processing

What is a Data Breach?

Organisations will have varying ideas as to what is considered a reportable data breach, so it is first important to understand what is considered a breach under GDPR. GDPR defines a Personal Data Breach as:

"a breach of security leading to the accidental or unlawful destruction, loss, alteration, unauthorised disclosure of, or access to, personal data transmitted, stored or otherwise processed;"

A lot of organisations will currently work to a narrower definition of a security breach which only includes breaches of confidentiality such as the following example:

> **EXAMPLE: A hacker attacks a system via a poorly configured web server and is able to use SQL injection to force a database to display the entire customer records table in the hacker's browser. This event would be considered a breach because personal data was unlawfully accessed.**

Not only does the definition include data theft or accidental disclosure, but the definition also covers scenarios whereby data is deliberately or accidentally destroyed.

> **EXAMPLE: A disgruntled employee logs into an organisation's Customer Relationship Management (CRM) system and deletes the PRODUCTION database. The deleted database contained the personal data of all the organisation's customers. This event would be considered a breach because Personal Data has been unlawfully destroyed.**

The definition also includes reference to alteration of data too. Alteration could occur in a number of ways. A manual error, a coding error or a configuration error are the most likely ways data could be accidentally or unlawfully altered.

> **EXAMPLE: EdgeCat Ltd hires a third party software developer to integrate an Emergency Mass Notification System (EMNS) with their Human Resources Information System (HRIS). A developer accidentally maps the relationship the wrong way round resulting in the contact information of all employees to be updated with sample data in the EMNS. This event would be considered a breach because Personal Data has been accidentally altered.**

The Incident Response Life-Cycle

I apologise in advance for subjecting the reader to yet another life-cycle, but the Incident Response Life-Cycle is an incredibly useful tool to support the management of incidents. Hopefully, Practitioners won't need to wheel around this life-cycle too many times, however, from experience, it is more likely than one thinks. Incidents are not always malicious, a poorly implemented change, or an end-user accidentally pressing delete when they mean to press copy, can often have a more detrimental effect on operations than a malicious attacker. Now that GDPR makes reporting certain types of incidents mandatory, however, it will be absolutely critical for organisations to have an effective incident response process in place.

Before we work through the incident response life-cycle, when responding to Personal Data Breach Events Practitioners should first seek to integrate incident response into an organisation's wider incident management framework. Where an already established incident management system is not available, practitioners should seek to establish a system covering the incident response life-cycle below. In this section, we will look at each step at a high level so that a practitioner knows what should be in place.

Incident Response Life-Cycle

Preparation: effective incident response must start long before an incident happens to have a good chance of minimising the impact of a personal data breach. The following preparatory steps are recommended[137]:

1. <u>Establish a formal incident response capability</u> – the most common approach is the formation of an Incident Management Team (IMT), often borne out of a Business Continuity Management System (BCMS). In mature organisations with a business model heavily reliant on high availability technology, a Computer Security Incident Response Team (CSIRT) may be in place. When establishing an IMT or a CSIRT, as a Controller ensure relevant Processors form part of the team and, as a Processor, ensure the Controller forms part of the team too. Smaller organisations may not have the capability to deal with complex incidents so ensure specialist expertise gaps are identified and planned for (e.g. IT Forensics, Legal, PR) and whether any of these services need to be retained. Depending on the nature of the incident, a typical CSIRT would likely comprise some or all of the following people/roles:

   1. (Major) Incident Manager
   2. Information Security Representative
   3. Data Protection Officer (as appropriate)
   4. Risk Management Representative
   5. Legal Counsel (as appropriate)
   6. Network / Server / Database Engineers (as required)
   7. Systems Vendors (as required)
   8. Data Processors (as required)
   9. Human Resources (as required)
   10. Public Relations (as required)

2. <u>Create an Incident Response Policy</u> – policy will be the cornerstone of the incident response program. It defines when an event is considered incidents, establishes the organisational context for incident response, defines roles and responsibilities, and lists the requirements for reporting incidents. Observant practitioners who have already read the chapter on Data Protection policy may have noted the Incident Response policy is included in the 'Related Policies' section.

3. <u>Develop an incident response plan and procedures based on the incident response policy</u> – once you have buy-in from a policy perspective and your team is in place, it is now time to create your plan. The plan will detail the procedural elements of the incident response life-cycle, those within the IMT/CSIRT should go through. More important than the plan itself is regular and robust testing of the plan. The more robust plan testing becomes, the easier dealing with live incidents will become – or as the British Army says "train hard, fight easy".

4. <u>Establish notifications procedures</u> – while notification may form part of your incident response plan, it is worth calling these procedures out separately. When organisations typically think about notification, communication is focussed on letting internal stakeholders know what is happening. GDPR has specific requirements in relation to notifying the Supervisory Authority and notifying data subjects which will be discussed later in this chapter.

5. <u>Synchronise Watches</u> – OK, maybe I got a little carried away with the military references for a second! What this means is make sure every network device, server, and desktop are all running off the same time source. Synchronisation can be achieved using Network Time Protocol (NTP). When devices use NTP, they all take their time from a reference clock and then promulgates the time throughout a network. Ensuring all

---

[137] Adapted from NIST 800-61 (Revision 2), Computer Security Incident Handling Guide, NIST, August 2012

infrastructure uses the same time means events will be recorded in logs using the same time. Ensuring all log sources are recording events using the same time source will make detection and analysis significantly more accurate and effective.

Detection: as GDPR places a deadline upon Controllers and Processors to report incidents within 72 hours the date and time an organisation becomes aware of an incident is a key piece of information. What does aware actually mean? The guidance[138] states awareness begins when a Controller *"has a reasonable degree of certainty that a security incident has occurred that has led to personal data being compromised."* The guidance goes on to say that a Controller is not necessarily in an aware state until it has made an initial investigation into a reported incident to confirm whether there has indeed been a personal data breach. A word of caution in regards to timeliness of reporting. If an event has been reported and the report appears credible, the Supervisory Authority will have an expectation that investigations will be initiated and concluded promptly. Hopefully, that is clear so let's get back to discussing detection. Now detection was briefly discussed in Chapter 10 (Information Security) we will avoid repetition but cover some additional points. A key aspect of detection is to identify likely attack vectors. Incident Responders should already have a good idea of where attacks are likely to be initiated but for those of Practitioners who are not aware here are some common attack vectors used to infiltrate organisations:

1. External / Removable Media (e.g. USB Memory Sticks)
2. Internet (e.g. virus downloaded from a compromised website)
3. Email (e.g. virus in an email attachment or phishing link)
4. Social Engineering (e.g. someone pretending to be a senior manager)
5. Theft (e.g. someone stealing a laptop)
6. Malicious Insider (e.g. a disgruntled employee stealing data)
7. Compromised Third Party Processor (hackers first hack a Processor in order to get to a Controller[139])
8. Compromised Mobile App

The best places to look for suspicious activity are listed below. Remember, some of the systems below are only going to work if they are turned on and collecting the right kinds of data from an organisations technology infrastructure. Practitioners will need to work with their Information Security teams to ensure the following sources are operating optimally:

1. Intrusion Detection / Prevention Systems (IDPS)
2. Security Information and Event Management (SIEM)
3. Anti-Virus and Anti-Spam Software
4. File Integrity Monitoring
5. Operating System, Service and Application Logs
6. Network Device Logs
7. Network Flows
8. Open Source Threat Intelligence
9. Reporting from your employees
10. Reporting from other organisations and your network

Once an incident has been detected, a record should be created and communicated to an agreed set of stakeholders. For high maturity organisations, there are advance reporting methodologies such as the Incident Object Description Exchange Format (IODEF)[140] that provides a framework for sharing information commonly exchanged by CSIRTs

---

[138] Guidelines on Personal data breach notification under Regulation 2016/679. Article 29 WP, Adopted October 2017
[139] Target Hackers Broke in Via HVAC Company as reported in Krebs on Security, dated 05 Feb 2014.
[140] RFC 5070: The Incident Object Description Exchange Format (https://www.ietf.org/rfc/rfc5070.txt). Dec 2007

about computer security incidents. For organisations which are lower on the maturity curve, consider including the following information in your incident reports:

1. The current status of the incident (new, in progress, forwarded for investigation, resolved, etc.)
2. A summary of the incident
3. Indicators related to the incident
4. Other incidents related to this incident
5. Actions that were were taken by all incident handlers on this incident
6. Chain of custody, if applicable
7. Impact assessments related to the incident
8. Contact information for other involved parties (e.g., system owners, system administrators)
9. A list of evidence gathered during the incident investigation
10. Comments from incident handlers
11. Next steps to be taken (e.g., rebuild the host, interview witnesses)

Analysis: for those who are not aware, the volume of events emanating from the information sources described in the detection section can run into billions of events per day. If your organisation is running just a few servers and maybe 50-100 desktops, events can still run into the tens of millions per day. Analysing all this data is no easy task. While it is not likely the Data Practitioner carry out this analytical work, it is useful to know at a high level how security breaches are analysed.

1. Profiling – There is an old analyst idiom that says "Investigate where there is the absence of the normal or presence of the abnormal"[141]. If something stops happening which was expected, e.g. when a Server is pinged, it responds, this requires investigation. Where something is now happening that doesn't normally, e.g. an unexpectedly high volume of data is leaving the organisation via a Server which is not supposed to be connected to the Internet this also requires investigation. So how does one determine what is 'normal'? Profiling is the technique used to measure the expected characteristics of a network and server infrastructure so that those maintaining the infrastructure can quickly detect when something is wrong.

2. Noise Reduction – once the analyst has baselined a system, then it's important to filter out the noise. Remember there may be billions of events every day, and even with a SIEM, it will be a nigh on impossible task to make sense of all the events without some form of filtering. One approach to filtering is filtering at source (i.e. don't collect certain logs from lower risk systems). Such an approach will provide improved performance and reduce storage and processing costs, but the downside is if analysis can't be conducted if the data doesn't exist. It is recommended to collect as much data as is practical and filter within the SIEM than not collect data at all. Where there are considerable volumes, consider archiving historical data for a predefined retention period on less-expensive storage.

3. Event Correlation[142] – this technique looks at information from different sources and identifies unauthorised activity from seemingly innocuous behaviour, which on its own may seem benign, but when correlated it becomes clear the activity is malign. A good example would be correlating file access with user leave dates. If on a particular day, a user is recorded as being on holiday, however, while not in the office their user account is accessing files on an internal server, this should throw up a red flag. Another example would be If a user account is created and deleted within a small period of time (e.g. active for less than 24 hours) and that user account performs a number of actions across the network. The events across the network should be correlated and analysed further for malicious activity. The key to effective correlation is standardised

---

[141] Low Intensity Operations: Subversion, Insurgency, Peace-keeping. Kitson F., 2010
[142] Security Information and Event Management (SIEM) Implementation, Miller et Al., 2010

time stamps across all logs and automation. Security Information & Event Management (SIEM) system can do a great job when it comes to automating correlation. SIEMs can also trigger alerts or set certain actions into motion when they detect correlated activity.

4. Cause and Effect Analysis[143] – cause and effect can be a great technique to check detection tools are working as expected. The analyst posits a hypothesis that if X occurs on the network, we should see events P, Q and R. For example if a server is disconnected from the network, what should happen and what actually happened. Netflix has turned Cause and Effect Analysis into an art form. Netflix uses a set of tools called the Simian Army based on the principles of chaos[144] which deliberately cause systems outages in Productions systems to aid engineers to improve the overall system design. Organisations with the requirement to provide high availability should aspire to implement their own Simian Armies!

5. Linchpin[145] Analysis – this technique is where analyst tests a specific theory by sifting through event data to confirm or deny whether there is evidence of related activity within log event data. For example, an analyst may posit the hypothesis "there should be no connections from the organisation's infrastructure to the TOR[146] network". The analyst then uses information about the TOR network to confirm if there are any connections. If connections are then identified, further investigation should follow to identify what is happening.

6. Trend Analysis – trend analysis is a useful technique when analysing events chronologically. This analysis may be directly related to the raw event logs themselves or analysis of previously investigated incidents. For example, trend analysis could identify unusual spikes in activity such as in the chart below which would warrant further investigation.

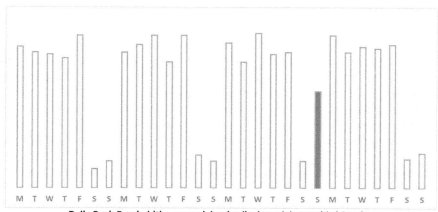

Daily Peak Bandwidth – unexplained spike in activity on third Sunday

The list of techniques described above are not exhaustive but a very good place to start. Security Analysts, at the very least, should have ensured systems are profiled, noise is reduced as much as possible but most importantly, ensured all event logs are synchronised.

---

[143] Structured Analytic Techniques for Intelligence Analysis, Pherson RH & Heuer R., 2014
[144] Principles of Chaos Engineer. (http://principlesofchaos.org/). April 2017
[145] Improving Intelligence Analysis at CIA: Dick Heuer's Contribution to Intelligence Analysis, Davis J., 1999
[146] TOR: The Onion Router. An anonymity network used to enhance privacy (https://www.torproject.org/)

Containment: one of the key areas a Supervisory Authority will want to get information on is how a personal data breach has affected the rights of data subjects and what the Controller has done to minimise / contain the incident. Supervisory Authorities will have an expectation Controllers and Processors have planned and tested strategies to cope with the most likely types of personal data breach facing their organisation. This book is not designed to be an exhaustive list of containment strategies, but needless to say, whichever strategy employed consideration must be given to the following issues:

1. Potential for further damage
2. Preservation of Evidence
3. Service availability
4. Time and resources needed to implement the strategy
5. Effectiveness of the strategy
6. Recovery Time / Point Objectives
7. Media Response

When dealing with an event where there is malicious involvement, containment must also include preventing further breaches as it would be foolhardy to move to recovery and then be breached again. The Incident Response team will want to confirm the identity of the attacker (or at least the origination IP(s) of the attack) and the mechanism of the attack and take appropriate action. In some cases, and in coordination with law enforcement, there may be scenarios whereby attackers are kept 'on-the-line' and redirected to a dummy server (sometimes known as a honey trap) to facilitate further intelligence gathering activities. Any continued exposure to an attacker must be weighed against the risk to further disruption and damage to an organisation's infrastructure and the impact a prolonged attack may have on the rights and freedoms of Data Subjects. Containment must also cover how your organisation deals with the media and the general public. Practitioners must ensure those dealing with media are provided with appropriate training. It is also worth considering who is put in front of the cameras as the CEO may not always be the best choice[147].

Recovery: as with incident response, recovery does not start when something is going wrong. IT Service Continuity or IT Disaster Recovery are programmes of work which must be embedded into business as usual (BAU) IT operations. There must be effective and robustly tested plans in place to recover with as minimum disruption as possible. For those interested in establishing an effective framework for recovery, consider ISO 27031:2011[148]. From experience, there can be a tendency to neglect actual testing and carry out hypothetical walkthroughs. For anyone who is faced with a team reluctant to properly test a system's resilience, be concerned – if IT does not have faith the recovery strategy contained in the plan will work in a test, it's definitely not going to work in a real-life event!

Post-Incident: once the dust has settled, there may be a desire to breathe a sigh of relief systems are back up and running and then get on with the day job – catching up on all the things you have not got done because of dealing with the incident. The Incident Response team must avoid this temptation and ensure a Post-Incident Lessons Learned process is completed after each incident. At a minimum this process should document answers to the following questions:

1. Contemporaneously, exactly what happened and to what?
2. What was the root cause of the incident?
3. How well did the Incident Responders perform? Could they have performed better?
4. Were the documented incident response procedures followed? Were they adequate?

---

[147] United Airlines CEO Oscar Munoz won't be promoted to chairman as reported on money.cnn.com 22 April 2017
[148] ISO/IEC 27031:2011 Information technology — Security techniques — Guidelines for information and communications technology readiness for business continuity

5. Were the documented recovery procedures followed? Were they adequate?
6. What were the information gaps?
7. How could information sharing with external organisation be improved?
8. Could the defence against a future incident be improved? How?
9. Could the detection and response to a future incident be improved? How?

The answers to these questions should be included in a Post-Incident Report, and any recommendations / follow-up actions are tracked (e.g. through individual service desk tickets or action log). In addition to the post-incident report, evidence must be preserved, maintaining the chain of custody should the evidence be required to support a prosecution. There are forensics specialists who can support this activity, and if there is not the capability in-house, I would recommend getting specialists in as soon as possible before the useful information is lost.

Calculating Data Breach Severity

One of the first things someone is going to ask when a breach is identified is likely to be "So how bad is it?". A Practitioner will, therefore, need to have a consistent methodology for calculating the severity of a data breach. The following methodology, developed by the European Union Agency for Network and Information Security (ENISA)[149] in conjunction with the bundesbeauftragte für den Datenschutz und die informationsfreiheit and the Hellenic data protection authority is a means of consistently calculating the potential severity of a Personal Data Breach. Practitioners may find it useful to use the methodology to proactively assess the impact of various breach scenarios as part of their incident management planning. The ENISA methodology incorporates three elements into a mathematical formula. The elements are as follows:

Data Processing Context (DPC): In this component, the type of data and the nature of the processing activities are categorised and scored.

Type	Description	Basic Score
Simple	Eg. biographical data, contact details, full name, data on education, family life, professional experience, etc.	1
Behavioural	Eg. location, traffic data, data on personal preferences and habits, etc.	2
Financial	Any type of financial data (e.g. income, financial transactions, bank statements, investments, credit cards, invoices, etc.). Includes social welfare data related to financial information.	3
Sensitive	Any type of sensitive data (e.g. health, political affiliation, sexual life)	4

Preliminary Basic Score Table

While each type of data is given a preliminary basic score, the score can be increased depending on the following factors:

---

[149] Recommendations for a methodology of the assessment of severity of personal data breaches, ENISA, Dec 2013

Type	Description	Score
Simple	when the volume of "simple data" and/or the characteristics of the controller are such that certain profiling of the individual can be enabled or assumptions about the individual's social/financial status can be made.	2
Simple	when the "simple data" and/or the characteristics of the controller can lead to assumptions about the individual's health status, sexual preferences, political or religious beliefs.	3
Simple	when due to certain characteristics of the individual (e.g. vulnerable groups, minors), the information can be critical for their personal safety or physical/psychological conditions.	4
Behavioural	when the volume of "behavioural data" and/or the characteristics of the controller are such that a profile of the individual can be created, exposing detailed information about his/her everyday life and habits.	3
Behavioural	when due to the nature and/or volume of the specific data set, full financial (e.g. credit card) information is disclosed that could enable fraud or a detailed social/financial profile is created.	4
Financial	when due to the nature and/or volume of the specific data set, full financial (e.g. credit card) information is disclosed that could enable fraud or a detailed social/financial profile is created.	4

DPC Increasing Factors

Conversely, the score can be decreased depending on the following factors:

Type	Description	Score
Behavioural	when the nature of the data set does not provide any substantial insight to the individual's behavioural information or the data can be collected easily (independently from the breach) through publicly available sources (e.g. a combination of information from web searches).	1
Financial	when the nature of the data set does not provide any substantial insight into the individual's financial information (e.g. the fact that a person is the customer of a certain bank without further details).	1
Financial	when the specific dataset includes some financial information but still does not provide any significant insight into the individual's financial status/situation (e.g. simple bank account numbers without further details).	2
Sensitive	when the nature of the data set does not provide any substantial insight to the individual's behavioural information or the data can be collected easily (independently from the breach) through publicly available sources (e.g. a combination of information from web searches).	1
Sensitive	when nature of data can lead to general assumptions.	2
Sensitive	when nature of data can lead to assumptions about sensitive information.	3

DPC decreasing Factors

For all data types, there is a final component to determining the Data Processing Context Score. This factor looks at the external factors to the type of data and should be used to either increase or decrease the DPC score to no more than 4 and no lower than 1. ENISA advise caution lowering the score to less than the preliminary basic score without solid justification (you have been warned!):

Increasing Factors	Decreasing Factors
Volume of Data Breached	Invalidity/inaccuracy of the data
Characteristics of Data Controller (e.g. Bank, Rehabilitation Clinic)	Public Availability
Characteristics of the individuals (e.g. Drug Addict)	Nature of Data

DPC contextual factors

Let's work through two examples to determine how we can establish the DPC score.

EXAMPLE 1: A Controller loses location data for 1,000 Data Subjects.

Preliminary Basic Score = 2 (Behavioural Data)

The locations data is for a period of 3 years. Increase from Basic Score (+1) = 3
The lost location data is over 10 years old (-1) = 2
The location data is pseudonymised (-1?) = 2

Final DPC Score = 2. While score could potentially be reduced to 1 formulaically, there is insufficient justification to reduce below the preliminary basic score.

EXAMPLE 2: A Controller loses 1,500 Data Subject Records relating to their trade union membership.

Preliminary Basic Score = 4 (Sensitive Data)

The data related to attendance at a Unison event (-1) = 3
The data was the attendance for a one-hour event during a 7-day conference (-1) = 2
The event was covered by multiple TV channels

Final DPC score = 2. While the final score is 2 lower than the preliminary basic score, it is less likely attendance at a trade union event would cause damage to the individual Data Subjects.

Ease in which the data subject can be identified (EI): When calculating this score, the Practitioner must consider both direct identification to a single unique Data Subject from the compromised data and indirect identification of a Data Subject by combining the compromised data with other sources. The scoring mechanism is as follows:

Level	Description	Score
Negligible	it is extremely difficult to match the data to a particular person, but still, it could be possible under certain conditions	0.25
Limited	it is to match the data to a particular person with access to additional data sources	0.50
Significant	identification is possible indirectly from the data breached with basic research needed to discover the individual's identity	0.75
Maximum	identification is possible directly from the data breached with no special research needed to discover the individual's identity	1.00

Ease of Identification Scoring Table

EXAMPLE 1: A pseudonymised table containing a unique identifier, gender, height, weight, postcode would have an ease of identification rating of negligible (0.25) because it would be extremely difficult to identify individual data subjects - unless you measured and weighed everyone in a particular postcode.

EXAMPLE 2: A database of Passport ID page images, first name, last name, postcode would have an ease of identification rating of Maximum (1.0) because individual data subjects would be directly identifiable.

Circumstances of the Breach (CB): the circumstances of the breach, unlike the first two components (DP & EI), which look purely at the inherent nature of the data, assess what actually happened during the breach. Scoring is based on the nature of the loss of confidentiality, integrity and availability. In addition, there are additional scoring considerations where the personal data breach is considered to be underpinned by malicious intent (i.e. the act was deliberate and not accidental). CB scoring is cumulative with a scoring mechanism as follows:

Loss	Description	Score
Confidentiality	Compromised to a number of known recipients (e.g. One customer's records sent to another unrelated customer)	0.25
Confidentiality	Compromised to an unknown number of unknown recipients (e.g. wrongly configured website makes data publically accessible on internet)	0.5

Integrity	data altered and possibly used in an incorrect or illegal way but with the possibility to recover	0.25
Integrity	data altered and possibly used in an incorrect or illegal way without the possibility to recover	0.5
Availability	temporal unavailability	0.25
Availability	data cannot be recovered from the controller or the individuals	0.5
Malicious	the breach was due to an intentional action in order to harm the data controller or individuals	0.5

Breach Circumstances Scoring Table

EXAMPLE 1: An incorrect setup mail merge emails single monthly statement to the incorrect customer. This would be a loss of confidentiality with the compromise limited to a number of known recipients. As the breach was as a result of an error, there is no requirement to add 0.5 for malicious intent.

The score would be 0.25.

EXAMPLE 2: An incorrectly configured web server makes data publically available on the Internet. A hacker identifies the web server and clears the database tables. The database administrator has made regular backups so the data can, theoretically, be restored. There are compound issues in this example. There was an error resulting in a loss of confidentiality to an unknown number of unknown individuals which was not malicious. There was a temporal loss of availability which was malicious.

The score would be 1.25 (0.5 + 0.25 + 0.5)

By inputting the three severity components, described in this section, into the following formula, a data breach severity score can be calculated:

$$Severity = (DPC \times EI) + CB$$

Once a severity score has been calculated, the score can be checked against the following table to determine the severity rating:

Severity Score	Rating	Description
SE < 2	LOW	Individuals either will not be affected or may encounter a few inconveniences, which they will overcome without any problem (time spent re-entering information, annoyances, irritations, etc.).
2 ≤ SE < 3	MEDIUM	Individuals may encounter significant inconveniences, which they will be able to overcome despite a few difficulties (extra costs, denial of access to business services, fear, lack of understanding, stress, minor physical ailments, etc.).
3 ≤ SE< 4	HIGH	Individuals may encounter significant consequences, which they should be able to overcome albeit with serious difficulties (misappropriation of funds, blacklisting by banks, property damage, loss of employment, subpoena, worsening of health, etc.).
4 ≤ SE	VERY HIGH	Individuals may encounter significant, or even irreversible, consequences, which they may not overcome (financial distress such as substantial debt or inability to work, long-term psychological or physical ailments, death, etc.).

Severity Scoring Taxonomy

Let's look a couple of examples where we take assess a breach and score for severity using all the scoring components:

EXAMPLE 1: 100 Data Subject Records relating to their membership of a Drug Rehabilitation Clinic are placed on a publicly accessible social media gossip site. The fields disclosed are fname, lname, address, postcode, email, phonenumber. The act was carried out deliberately by a disgruntled employee.

DPC = 3 Whilst simple data, the characteristics of the controller can lead to assumptions about the individual's health status (i.e. they may be a drug addict, could be infected with HIV or Hepatitis).

EI = 1.0 Identification is possible directly from the data breached with no special research needed to discover the individual's identity.

CB = 1.0 Data was compromised to an unknown number of unknown recipients on a publically accessible social media site (+0.5), and the act was malicious (+0.5).

Severity = (3 x 1.0) + 1.0 = 4 (HIGH) - Individuals may encounter significant consequences, which they should be able to overcome albeit with serious difficulties

---

EXAMPLE 2: 1,500 Data Subject Records relating to their trade union membership are accidentally deleted days before annual membership renewal. There was no backup, and the data is permanently lost. Data included: MembershipID, Membership Status, Renewal Date, Membership Level.

DPC = 1 Simple data

EI = 0.25 It is extremely difficult to match the data to a particular person, but still it could be possible under certain conditions (i.e. with other data in other parts of the organisation).

CD = 0.5 As the data was not backed up, manually restoring the data would only be partially successful.

Severity = (1.0 x 0.25) + 0.5 = 0.75 (LOW) Individuals either will not be affected or may encounter a few inconveniences, which they will overcome without any problem

---

Notification to the Supervisory Authority

A Supervisory Authority must be notified, in the case of a personal data breach. Not only that but the controller shall without undue delay and, where feasible, inform the Supervisory Authority no later than 72 hours after having become aware of the breach. The one exception is where the personal data breach is unlikely to result in a risk to the rights and freedoms of natural persons. So what does all that mean?

Firstly, a Controller and Processor must understand what a data breach under GDPR looks like which we have covered in the previous section, secondly they need to understand when a breach must be reported. Essentially, if the data is encrypted and the key remains secure, then a personal data breach would not require reporting. If a database was corrupted, but the Controller had a second live database which could be restored instantaneously, then the personal data breach would not require reporting. Pretty much everything else falls under the scope of reportable.

EXAMPLE 1: An National Health Service (NHS) Trust becomes victim to a ransomware attack which encrypts a whole database of customer records. Doctors are not able to access the records of patients who are undergoing treatment for critical illnesses. Whilst the records were temporarily unavailable; there was no breach of confidentiality.

This would be a reportable personal data breach.

EXAMPLE 2: Whilst at a Christmas function, an employee leaves their laptop, containing details of 20,000 home insurance policies, behind in a bar. The laptop is never handed in but was protected with 256-AES whole disk encryption – the encryption key was not compromise.

This would not be considered a reportable personal data breach.

When reporting an event to the Supervisory Authority, the following information must form part of the notification text:

1. describe the nature of the personal data breach including where possible, the categories and approximate number of data subjects concerned and the categories and approximate number of personal data records concerned;
2. communicate the name and contact details of the data protection officer or another contact point where more information can be obtained;
3. describe the likely consequences of the personal data breach;
4. describe the measures taken or proposed to be taken by the controller to address the personal data breach, including, where appropriate, measures to mitigate its possible adverse effects.

EXAMPLE NOTIFICATION:

NB: This notification is for example only; Supervisory Authorities may mandate personal data breaches are reported in a specific format. Always check with the Supervisory Authority for current guidance.

Controller:	**Eye-Osta LLC**
Processor:	**Global Operational Processing Ltd**
DPO Details:	**O. Coyle, o.coyle@lofthouse-RE.co.uk, 01204 777777**
Reference:	**LRE-INC003**
Date Reported:	**04-02-2018**
Date of Incident:	**02-02-2018**
Nature of Incident:	**Processor Server Hacked**
Records Lost:	**5,000 customer records**
Data Types Lost:	**Simple and Financial Data**
Severity Score/Rating:	**5 (VERY HIGH) (DPC 4 = 1 EI = 1.0 CB = 1.0)**
Malicious:	**Yes**

Details: On the 03-Feb-2018, our payments processor (Global Operational Processing Ltd) reported a server connected to the Internet was compromised by an as yet unknown Hacker. 5,000 customer records have been confirmed as compromised including the following financial data: Debit Card Primary Account Number (PAN), Expiry Date and Security Code.

Likely Consequences: due to the nature of the specific data set, full financial information has been disclosed that could enable fraud.

Measures Taken: The following initial actions have been taken:

1. Affected Virtual Server has been taken offline and preserved
2. New Virtual Server Image created, tested and put into PROD including all currently available OS and Application level security patches.
3. System and Network logs have been preserved for forensic analysis
4. Incident has been reported to Action Fraud and NCSC
5. *Management has taken a decision not to inform Data Subjects to avoid reputational damage as the fault was with the Processor's Infrastructure.*

Attachments:

1. Copy of email from Processor reporting the incident
2. Copy of Data Protection Impact Assessment (DPIA) for affected process

Notification to Data Subjects

When a personal data breach is likely to result in a high risk to Data Subjects' rights and freedoms, under GDPR, a Controller must not only notify the Supervisory Authority but communicate the personal data breach to the data subjects affected within a reasonable timeframe[150]. Such communication must adhere to the principle of transparency and be presented to each affected Data Subject in clear and intelligible language. Where breaches occur affecting Data Subjects in the different EU Member States, Controllers should ensure messages are clear and plain in the Data Subjects' primary language.

There are some exceptions where a Controller is not required to communicate a security breach and these exceptions are as follows:

1. The compromised data is unintelligible (i.e. it is encrypted, and the key remains secure)
2. The Controller has put in place mechanisms to prevent harm to the Data Subjects affected
3. There are too many people affected! In such cases, public communication (e.g. TV broadcast) or similar measure must be implemented whereby data subjects are informed in an equally effective manner.

> **EXAMPLE: In the case of the third TALKTALK breach in October 2016, TalkTalk's CEO, Dido Harding appeared on the BBC and explained what had happened and what TalkTalk where doing to protect those Data Subjects affected.**

In the example Supervisory Authority notification in the previous section, hawk-eyed Practitioners may have noticed the 5th measure taken by the Controller – a decision not to inform affected Data Subjects. In such cases, where the Controller has taken a decision not to inform Data Subjects, GDPR gives Supervisory Authorities the power to compel a Controller to inform Data Subjects where the Supervisory Authority believes there is a high residual risk to the affected Data Subjects. Given transparency is fundamental to GDPR, where the incident criteria warrants a report to the Supervisory Authority, organisations should set a higher bar for choosing not to report the breach to Data Subjects.

---

[150] Article 34: Communication of a personal data breach to the data subject

13. DATA SUBJECT ACCESS REQUESTS (DSAR)

One of the most commonly used Data Subject rights under the current data protection regulatory regime is the right to access. This is where the Data Subject can ask for information held about them by a Controller. The right to access[151] is a right which can enhance or severely damage an organisation's reputation but organisations often get upholding this right woefully wrong! Sadly, a lot of organisations treat the process as a hindrance for a broad range of reasons rather than as an opportunity for improved customer service. Some common reasons for seeing the Data Subject Access Request (DSAR) process negatively are; the feeling it will be a disproportionate effort to comply with the request and that providing the Data Subject access to their data may result in (or support) legal action against the Controller. Neither of these justifiable reasons for Controllers or Processors to be obstructive when responding to an access request and often serve to highlight there are other issues which need to be fixed! In this chapter we will discuss what a Data Subject Access Request now looks like under GDPR and how to deal with a DSAR in a manner which maintains (or improves) your organisation's reputation. We will look at the information an organisation must provide to the Data Subject and what tools an organisation may need to put in place to support the DSAR process. We will look at some common concerns raised by data subjects and the measures that can be put in place to minimise the chances of a complaint to the Supervisory Authority – and all that goes with such a complaint.

What is a Data Subject Access Request (DSAR)?

Under the General Data Protection Regulation an EU Data Subject has the right to ask a Controller for access to certain information held about them and the Controller must provide access to said information. The Data Subject can ask for the following:

1. The personal data the Controller holds
2. the reasons you are processing their data
3. the categories of personal data concerned;
4. information about the existence of profiling and automated decision making and also information about the logic and consequences of such activity.
5. Who the data will be shared with, including if the data is going to a third country (see Chapter 15) and the associated safeguards

---

[151] Article 15: Right of access by the data subject

6. How long the data will be stored and why it will be stored for that period
7. Where the data was provided by someone else, information about those information sources
8. Information about their rights to rectification, erasure, restrict or object to processing
9. Information about their right to lodge a complaint with the Supervisory Authority

So, quite a lot of information. It's worth noting that your organisation may also be covered by other legislation which requires your organisation to provide data to a Data Subject.

Key changes to Data Subject Access Requests

Aside from additional information, which we covered in the previous section, the following key changes have been incorporated into the Right to Access under GDPR:

1. Organisations can no longer charge an Administration Fee (except in certain limited circumstances)
2. Organisations have to respond as soon as possible and no later than 30 days (down from 40 days)
3. Organisations must provide the information, if requested, in electronic form (e.g. in PDFs instead of a print-out)

Whilst on the surface there doesn't appear to be many changes, these change could be significant if an organisations processes for supporting DSARs are poor or inefficient. A key dissuader under the current data protection legislation from opportunist subject access requests was the fee. Now this fee has been removed organisation could expect to see a lot more DSARS. Couple this with the reduced deadline, outsourcers holding the only source of data and ever increasing volumes of data, and life could become quite tricky for the unprepared Controller. In a later section we will discuss how to reduce some of the risk these changes could pose.

FOI or DSAR?

Most countries in Europe have additional legislation which covers the right of citizens to obtain information. Typically, these acts cover information that is not covered by the Data Protection Regulation but is processed by public services. These pieces of legislation are often referred to as Freedom of Information (FOI) Acts and are implemented to strengthen accountability and transparency by those spending public money to act in an appropriate and ethical manner. Additionally, there is a lot of information held by the government which, if were made accessible, could encourage innovation and improved public services.

> **EXAMPLE: Data held by Health Inspectors has been used to power an app which citizens can check to see what score their favourite takeaway has been given in their last inspection. Such an app could also alert customers when their favourite takeaway has failed their last inspection too!**

When planning how to deal with Data Subject Access Requests, the practitioner must be mindful that a Data Subject could make either and FOI or DSAR request and the request could be rejected because the request is valid (i.e. the subject is entitled to the information) but they individual has used the incorrect piece of legislation. Organisations should ensure, if those dealing with FOI requests and DSAR are not in the same team, they are cross-trained to recognise when the request should still be fulfilled.

Exemptions

There are certain situations in which an organisation is exempt from the requirement to provide access to the information they hold on a Data Subject. Prior to using one of these exemptions it is extremely useful to consult the Supervisory Authority to confirm if the exemption applies. The following are a common but not exhaustive list of exemptions. GDPR allows Member States to determine which exemptions (such as freedom of expression[152]) are permitted in their particular territory:

1. Journalistic purposes: Data Subjects cannot ascertain the source(s) behind an article published in the public interest.
2. Crime and Taxation: Data Subjects cannot ascertain if they are – or have been –subject to a criminal investigation
3. Management Planning Information: Data Subjects cannot request information such as whether they have been identified for redundancy
4. Negotiations with the Requestor: Data Subjects in negotiations with a Controller cannot seek details of the Controller's negotiating position
5. Information under which legal professional privilege applies: Data Subjects cannot use a DSAR to request information covered by legal privilege.

Common concerns raised by Data Subjects

A significant volume of cases which the Supervisory Authorities deal with relates to issues surrounding DSARs. The UK Supervisory Authority publishes data on their case work[153] and in the year between September 2016 to August 2017 approximately 27% of cases (650 of 2383) related to subject access or obtaining data as the primary focus of the case. Common reasons for making complaints are:

1. Delay - Requests taking too long or go over the deadline
2. Not an SAR - The Controller does not believe the request falls within the scope of a SAR and refuses to provide the requested information
3. Poor Searches - Data Subject believes information is incomplete
4. No Data Held - The Controller states they have no in-scope data and the Data Subject believes this not to be true
5. Disproportionate Effort - The Controller believes the request falls in to the scope of an exemption under disproportionate effort
6. Repeated Requests - A data subject is making repeated requests
7. Third Party Data - Where the Data Subject is requesting information relating to third parties (e.g. the source of a reference)

If a Practitioner or a DPO is faced with a situation where their organisation is considering not fulfilling a DSAR because of one of the above scenarios, they should contact the Supervisory Authority for advice and guidance. The Supervisory Authority[154] is there to help Controllers comply with GDPR not simply enforce the Regulation. In addition to contacting the Supervisory Authority, the following will aid in meeting your DSAR requirements:

---

[152] Article 85: Processing and freedom of expression and information

[153] Latest figures available at time of going to print - https://ico.org.uk/about-the-ico/our-information/complaints-and-concerns-data-sets/
[154] Article 57: Tasks

1. Tackle the underlying issues: DSARs often form part of wider complaints. Review complaints metrics and ensure underlying issues are resolved. Seeing the DSAR process as a means by which to continuously improve, should reduce DSAR effort and should also have the added benefit of improving customer (and employee) satisfaction.
2. Reduce the data held: organisations may be holding information that is no longer required for business purposes or legal retention purposes. In both these cases, securely delete the data. Organisations hoarding data 'just in case' significantly increase the effort required to support DSARs
3. Self-Service: where systems permit, make as much information available to the Data Subject on a self-service basis. Any data available self-service would be exempt from the scope of DSAR searches. When making any data available self-service ensure the system goes through the DPIA process to ensure Data Subjects' Personal Data is not being put under increased risk.
4. Information Classification: Marking documents and systems that contain personal data can significantly reduce the search effort – as long as information is correctly classified
5. Regular Training: Practitioners could periodically send front line employees DSARs and assess their response to a variety of different situations. Where responses fall short of expectations, provide under-performing employees with appropriate training and retest soon after.
6. Incorporate Processors into your DSAR process: Processors holding Personal Data must be integrated into the DSAR process. Consider including Service Level Agreements in contracts to ensure they provide data faster than the 30 day deadline so that you as the Controller can comply.

The Subject Access Request Process

Now we have discussed the background the DSARs let's look at the process itself. The following steps should be included in your Data Subject Access Request (DSAR) process:

1. Identify the SAR
2. Acknowledge a SAR has been made and respond to Data Subject
3. Verify Data Subject's Identity
4. Request scope of information required
5. Conduct Searches
6. Consider changes to the data during collection and reporting
7. Redaction
8. Compile and Review
9. Supporting information
10. Securely send the information

Identify the SAR: The first thing a Practitioner must ensure is clear across the organisation is that a Data Subject Access Request may not necessarily come with a bright flashing neon sign saying 'I am a Subject Access Request'. Often the request is rolled up in a wider complaint. Organisations are not permitted to make a Data Subject fill out a particular form and under GDPR the request can be made through any channel into the organisation and to any person (including the cleaner – albeit highly unlikely!). A DSAR may also come through a Processor too. In all these cases the person dealing with the customer is not permitted to redirect the user to someone else but must pass on the request to the appropriate team within the organisation or the Data Protection Officer (DPO).

Acknowledge an SAR has been made and respond to Data Subject: the DSAR process should be considered a customer service and like any good customer service process, the Data Subject making the request should be contacted as soon as possible with an acknowledgement of the request. The request at this stage can be a holding response to confirm receipt but could include other information relating to the process such as informing the Data Subjects of their rights under GDPR.

Verify Data Subject's Identity: because DSARs could be made over social media or by a member of the general public an organisation must take every reasonable step to verify the requestor's identity. What an organisation must not do is use this step to delay processing a request by asking a Data Subject with whom an existing relationship has been established and the identity of the requestor is known.

EXAMPLE: A former employee is involved in a grievance process and has made a DSAR to a member of the HR team. The Data Subject is known to the member of the HR Team and have been corresponding over email and over telephone. The context of the DSAR is such that it would not be reasonable for the HR Officer to state they did not know the identity of the person making the request.

In this case, it would not be reasonable for the HR Officer to request additional identification documentation such as certified copies of passports and proof of address.

There are times however where a Data Subject has been identified by the Controller but contact between Data Subject and Controller is infrequent. In such cases it would be reasonable for the Controller to re-verify the identity of the Data Subject. The fundamental principle to keep in mind is you must not uphold one right (Access) at the expense of a principle (Security) or vice versa. In terms of carrying out the rest of the DSAR process, there is little reason not to begin the searches at this time whilst waiting for verification of identity to ensure the 30-day deadline is met. Remember, verification of identity only affects the rights and freedoms of data subjects when the information is provided to the requestor – it is not meant to provide the Controller with extra time to do the work.

Request scope of information required: as with the current DSAR regime, it is absolutely reasonable for the Controller to ask for further information to support the request. Often the Data Subject has a specific reason for making the request and is willing to provide information to help expedite the DSAR process. The Data Subject however, does not have to provide additional information and could simply re-assert the original request.

EXAMPLE 1: A former Bank Customer receives emails about a Credit Card they believed they had cancelled. After repeatedly unsubscribing from the emails, they continue to be sent.

The Customer makes a DSAR for all information held by the Bank. The Bank's DPO asks the customer if they could let them know exactly what they are looking for. The Customer, who just wants the emails to stop, explains the situation to the DPO.

It turns out the reason why the emails keep coming is because there is a residual amount left on the credit card and so the Bank is required by law to keep providing statements. The issue is resolved by donating the residual amount to charity so the card can be closed.

EXAMPLE 2: A former employee is looking to take legal action against their former employee for constructive dismissal. To support their legal action, the former employee makes a DSAR to the HR Director. The HR Director suspects this may be a precursor to legal action, and writes to request the specific information the former employee is looking to receive. The former employee responds stating they want everything the company holds.

The company must now process the DSAR and provide all the information held to which the former employee is entitled to see. The company must provide the information even if they suspect (or know) the information will be used to support legal action. The company is not permitted to withhold information the Data Subject is entitled to just because it may increase the legal risk to the company.

Conduct Searches: once the Controller knows the scope of the DSAR it is now time to carry out the searches. This may involve physical searches of paper records in addition to electronic records. Physical records are considered in scope when they form part of a relevant filing system. What UK case law has determined a relevant filing system to be is a system where records could be searched for by means of the Data Subject's Name or other unique identifier stored in either a paper-based or electronic indexing system. For the most part the searches will be electronic and need to consider all systems where Personal or Sensitive Data is held on the Data Subject including at third parties and on systems such as CCTV. At this stage if you have conducted an Information Audit (See Chapter 08) and have Records Management (See Chapter 11) processes in place, conducting effective searches should be a straightforward task.

Consider changes to the data during collection and reporting: for certain types of data (e.g. Transactional), the information may change quite frequently. It is ok to update the data as those changes occur. What organisations are not permitted to do is update or change content because they feel it may be embarrassing or inaccurate.

EXAMPLE: An email within the scope of a DSAR has a comment from a Customer Service Representative stating the Data Subject is a 'whinging busy body who should get a life'.

The Controller would not be permitted to withhold this content or edit the content to remove the embarrassing content. The Controller may wish to consider how they are going to manage the potential fallout, consider disciplinary action for the Customer Service Representative and education for all their Customer Service Representatives on what is (and is not) permitted in official communication.

Compile and Review: now you have all the data, it is time to compile into one secure location and review the material. What you are reviewing the material for are the following:

6. Completeness: Do you have all the relevant information?
7. Exemptions: Is any information covered by one of the exemptions discussed in the last section?
8. Third Parties: does the material compiled contain other data subjects

Once you are comfortable you have the information required, removed information covered by any relevant exemptions and identified any other identifiable data subjects it is time to move onto the next stage.

Redaction: As highlighted earlier, one cannot uphold one right at the expense of another. The same applies to upholding the rights of one Data Subject at the expense of other Data Subjects. Where information is to be provided to a Data Subject under the Right of Access, information relating to other Data Subjects which could either identify them or adversely affect their rights and freedoms should be removed or redacted. The most common method to redact a document physically is to; print the document, use a black marker to remove content and then photocopy the document. The Data Subject would then be provided the photocopy. These days this process can be performed electronically and there are a number of solutions which can both search for potential sources of third party personal data and automatically redact the content wherever is appears. These solutions can then save the redacted content to a second PDF file for onward secure transmission to the requesting Data Subject. There may be cases where third parties can be identified. A common example is if the third party provides consent for their association with the information.

EXAMPLE: A manager was asked to provide a reference in confidence to another manager for a team member who wanted to move teams. When the team member wasn't ultimately selected for the role, they felt it was because of the reference and instead of just asking the manager to see the reference, submitted a DSAR to get a copy.

The manager was then asked if they would be happy for the content to be provided and the manager, having been fair to the Data Subject, consented to providing the reference stating had they asked directly, they would have been happy to provide, and also explain, the content.

Supporting information: now that all the information has been compiled, third parties' rights and freedoms have been appropriate safeguarded the penultimate step is to add supporting information, where appropriate, to explain the processing and in particular any terms, codes etc which may not be decipherable by a Data Subject who does not have working knowledge of the processing activities. In addition to providing such information, it is good practice to provide details about the Data Subject's rights. It may be some information needs correcting, it may be the Data Subject wants the information to be deleted or perhaps to invoke their right to restrict processing. By providing appropriate information up front about these rights should save time for both the Data Subject and the organisation in dealing with the fall out.

Securely send the information: GDPR requires information to be provided under the Right of Access must be sent securely. As previously mentioned a Data Subject can now make a DSAR electronically and also receive the information requested in an electronic format. This means the method in which the information is transmitted to the Data Subject, from the Controller, must be secure. The primary mechanism to secure information in transit (as discussed in Chapter 11) is encryption. Those Practitioners implementing DSAR processes must ensure there is a secure method of sending the data. If passwords are to be used in such a process the password must not be sent in the same channel as the content.

EXAMPLE: Content sent by encrypted email, password sent by SMS to Data Subject's phone

---

14. THIRD PARTIES & OUTSOURCING

For those working in organisations large and small, it is possible not all your data processing activities are conducted in-house. Whether it be a large organisation migrating their internal IT infrastructure to AWS or Azure or a Small to Medium Enterprise (SME) who use a cloud-based Human Resources Information System (HRIS), it is highly likely some form of data processing is performed by a third party Processor. "Not us", says one person at the back of the hall. "We do everything in-house". OK, maybe there are those that do everything in-house, but it is highly unlikely. Very few organisations do everything themselves. The drafters of GDPR understand this facet of how modern businesses works and have strengthened the requirements concerning how Data Controllers and Data Processors must operate. There are now requirements mandating contracts must be in place which contain appropriate safeguards, but under GDPR it will not be enough to simply rely on a contract, Controllers are required to monitor the Processing activity to ensure ongoing compliance with the requirements of GDPR too[155].

Some industries, such as financial services, already have requirements surrounding outsourcing[156]. The UK Financial Conduct Authority (FCA) has issued specific guidance in terms of technology outsourcing too which is reflected in the rules and regulations of other Member States across Europe and in many other countries across the world. The FCA defines cloud computing for example as *"encompassing a range of IT services provided in various formats over the internet. This includes, for example, private, public or hybrid cloud, as well as Infrastructure as a Service (IaaS), Platform as a Service (PaaS), and Software as a Service (SaaS)"*. Further on in the same guidance, the FCA confirms that *"where a third party delivers services on behalf of a regulated firm - including a cloud provider - this is considered outsourcing and firms need to consider the relevant regulatory obligations and how they comply with them."* The guidance goes on to say that the regulated firm must *"consider any additional legal or regulatory obligations and requirements that may arise such as through the [UK] Data Protection Act 1998 (DPA)"*. Now this guidance is a couple of years old, and it is likely updated guidance will be issued in 2018 after the publication of the UK Data Protection Bill 2018 but what it serves to demonstrate is that considering data protection when outsourcing services is not a new concept. What the new regulation puts in place is a stricter regime and tougher penalties, including for Processors, should they not uphold the rights and freedoms of Data Subjects. This additional governance activity may, initially at least, seem like a lot more work – and if your organisation is not actively monitoring its Third Party Processors it probably will involve more work but if approached in a positive way could offer a number of

---

[155] Article 28: Processor
[156] FCA Handbook SYSC 8.1: General outsourcing requirements

improvements to the service companies receive from their outsourced service providers and ultimately reduce costs. Controllers shouldn't feel to put out through because GDPR has provided Controllers with some improved protections. For example, under the current Data Protection Legislation liability was solely with the Controller, under GDPR, Processors are also liable for a failure to comply with GDPR[157]. These changes are not only positive for the Controller; they open additional ways a Data Subject can seek redress as Data Subjects can now seek a judicial remedy against a Processor[158] in addition to a Controller.

In this chapter, we will look at the relationship between Controller and Processor as they relate to outsourcing. We will look at the requirements of GDPR when it comes to engaging with a Third Party Processor, and we will look at the Data Protection considerations, those involved in the outsourcing process must consider, to ensure any outsourcing involving the processing of Personal or Sensitive Data is compliant with the requirements of GDPR. Practitioners should consider working through the information provided in this chapter with their respective Legal, Risk, Procurement, Business Continuity and Information Security Teams.

The Controller-Processor relationship

As previously described, the Controller is the natural or legal person, public authority, agency or other body which, alone or jointly with others, determines the purposes and means of the processing of personal data. The Controller will need to ensure Data Subjects' rights are upheld and this includes Third Party Processors (e.g. an Outsourced Service Provider). The Controller will be required to ensure personal and sensitive data is processed securely, how long data is to be retained and whether data can be disclosed to Third Party Processors. The Controller is ultimately accountable for upholding Data Subjects' rights as they apply to the data the Controller (and any Third Party Processors acting lawfully on their behalf) processes. There may be times when two or more organisations determine the purposes and means of processing. In these cases, the organisations are considered to be Joint Controllers[159]. Joint Controllers are responsible for ensuring their responsibilities for upholding the rights and freedoms of Data Subjects, and this will include processing activities conducted by Third Party Processors on behalf of one or more Joint Controllers, as it relates to joint processing activities.

EXAMPLE: Holling & Milne LLC and Davenport Wrensome LLC are Joint Controllers. Davenport Wrensome LLC outsource part of this processing to a third party Processor. While only one Controller has chosen to outsource; both Controllers are jointly responsible for ensuring the provisions of Article 28 are met.

Now a Processor, on the other hand, is a natural or legal person, public authority, agency or other body which processes personal data on behalf of the Controller. A Processor is not permitted to conduct any processing activity on personal data provided by a Controller without the Controller's express permission – and only when that processing is lawful. Processors must also uphold the rights of Data Subjects and in many cases may be both a Controller and a Processor. If you are a Processor, it is important to know you cannot absolve yourself of personal responsibility should a data breach occur which involves a Controller's data – especially if there are no penalties laid

---

[157] Article 82: Right to compensation and liability
[158] Article 79: Right to an effective judicial remedy against a controller or processor
[159] Article 26: Joint controllers

out in a Controller-Processor contract. Supervisory Authorities now have additional powers[160] to impose temporary or definitive limitations on processing including a ban on processing. GDPR now strengthens the requirements for Controllers to supervise Processors and now makes it mandatory for any Controller-Processor relationship to be governed by a legally binding contract.

What would happen in your organisation if one of your Processors was no temporarily banned from processing your customers' personal data?

What would happen in your organisation if one of your Processors was no PERMANENTLY banned from processing your customers' personal data?

Is this risk on your organisation's Risk Register?

Data Protection through the Procurement and Supply Life-Cycle

Whichever of your organisation's services you wish to outsource – Manufacturing, Data Centre, Applications Management, Call Centre, Business Process or Supply Chain – if Personal Data is involved then it must be factored into your outsourcing lifecycle. As with any significant change in your organisation, it is good practice to follow an established methodology. The Chartered Institute of Purchasing & Supply (CIPS) have such a methodology[161] which is split into 13 distinct phases:

1. Understand the need and develop a high-level specification
2. Market/Commodity and options (inc make or buy assessment)
3. Develop strategy/plan
4. Pre-procurement / market test and market engagement
5. Develop documentation, PPQ / detailed spec / combine with 1
6. Supplier selection to participate in Invitation to Tender (ITT) / Request for Quotation (RFQ) / negotiation
7. Issue ITT/RFQ
8. Bid/Tender Evaluation and validation
9. Contract award and implementation
10. Warehouse logistics and receipt
11. Contract performance review and continuous improvement
12. Supplier Relationship Management and Supply Chain management and development
13. Asset management/end of life and lessons learnt

In this section, we shall look at the data protection considerations during each phase of the procurement and supply life-cycle. If you are not familiar with the CIPS Procurement & Supply Life-Cycle, it is recommended reading the guidance below while also reviewing the wider methodology which can be accessed at the website in the footnote below. For clarity, we shall assume this processing involves Personal Data.

Understand the need and develop a high-level specification: at this stage of the procurement & supply life-cycle,

---

[160] Article 58(2).f: Powers
[161] Procurement and Supply Cycle (https://www.cips.org/en-gb/knowledge/procurement-cycle/). © CIPS (2014)

the business will be focussed on trying to solve a problem they feel they have in regards to their operational processes. The issue may be efficiency or cost-saving or a plethora of other reasons. At this stage, the business is probably not likely to be thinking of Data Protection but they must. When considering outsourcing a processing activity, a business unit should contact the Data Protection Officer (DPO) and ascertain whether they are required to conduct an initial Data Protection Impact Assessment (DPIA) as per Chapter 09. In addition to the initial DPIA, the business must incorporate data protection into the high-level specification which often contained in a Business Requirements Document (BRD).

The Business requirements document is a critical artefact of the procurement and supply life-cycle as it is the specifications contained in this document which will be used by the shortlisted vendors to provide their quotation. Often, when procurement is wrapped within a poorly implemented AGILE project, there is a tendency to gloss over the BRD as people misinterpret that in agile not everything needs to be ready on day one as not everything needs to be written down yet. Even in AGILE projects, the more you can define in your BRD, the more likely you will get the service or product you want. To aid the Practitioner, there is a detailed data protection requirement specification at the end of this chapter. Requirements can be then categorised using the MoSCoW method which expands to:

1. Must Have Requirements – These requirements are the absolute minimum requirement.
2. Should Have Requirements – It would be expected the service or system has these features to support the core requirements
3. Could Have Requirements – It would be beneficial for the service or system to have these features, but it would be still ok to proceed with the outsourcing arrangement.
4. Will **NOT** Have Requirements –These capabilities will not be features of the new system OR this category can also be used to define quality requirements (e.g. The system will **not** have any of the vulnerabilities listed in the 2017 OWASP Top 10[162])

Market/Commodity and options (inc make or buy assessment): now the business understands their need, and has developed a high-level specification, it is time to assess the options. GDPR rears its head again in the form of the following requirement[163]:

"Where processing is to be carried out on behalf of a controller, the controller shall use only processors providing sufficient guarantees to implement appropriate technical and organisational measures in such a manner that processing will meet the requirements of this Regulation and ensure the protection of the rights of the data subject. "

What this means is when scoping out the market and identifying potential suppliers, data protection competence must be a mandatory consideration. Many organisations rely on ISO 27001 as a useful measuring stick for information security. Practitioners must, however, be mindful this does not cover all aspects of data protection and until formal certification mechanisms are in place[164] the onus will be on the Controller to identify Processors who are demonstrating a positive approach to Data Protection – reference to their approach on their website is a good starting point but further down the procurement & supply life-cycle a deeper dive will be required.

Develop strategy/plan: it is at this stage when the Process Owner should initiate a full Data Protection Impact Assessment[165]. The output of the DPIA must then feed into the wider procurement strategy.

Pre-procurement / market test and market engagement: the DPIA continues to be developed during this phase as

---

162 See Chapter 11: Data Protection by Design and Default
163 Article 28(1)
164 Article 42: Certification
165 Article 35: Data protection impact assessment

the Process Owner seeks consultation with stakeholders including the Data Subjects.

Develop documentation, PPQ / detailed spec / combine with stage 1 spec: in this stage, the DPIA is concluded with the controls and action plan forming the basis for the detailed data protection requirements to be documented in the pre-purchase questionnaire (PPQ) and the detailed specification (which would be an enrichment of the BRD – Business Requirements Document created in stage 1). When populating a PPQ consider including some or all of the following questions:

1. Who has overall responsibility for data protection in your organisation?
2. Who is your Data Protection Supervisory Authority?
3. What are the contact details of your Data Protection Officer?
4. Do you hold any Data Protection Certifications?
5. Please attach a copy of your Data Protection Policy
6. How does your organisation identify and classify Personal and Sensitive Data?
7. Do you transfer Personal Data outside the EEA? If yes, what is the legal basis and what are the safeguards you have in place?
8. Is Data Protection referred to in employee contracts of employment?

Supplier selection to participate in Invitation to Tender (ITT) / Request for Quotation (RFQ) / negotiation: it is likely at this stage; a long list of potential Processors has been identified. A procurement manager should be working with the Process Owner at this stage to apply selection criteria to shortlist the vendors to around 3-4. Before the final shortlist is agreed, the Data Protection Officer should be at the very minimum consulted as to what should be included in the selection criteria in regards to data protection and where weighting is applied, how much weighting should be placed on data protection. Organisations should ideally consider seeking a formal opinion on the vendors from the Data Protection Officer or, involve them further by requesting the DPO validate the selection scoring process - as it relates to data protection. The Request for Quotation should now include more detailed questions surrounding data protection. Practitioners should consider including some or all of the following questions:

1. Describe your policy review and approval process.
2. When your organisation collects personal data from a subject do you clearly state what it is being collected for, how it will be processed and who will process it and does the data subject have to provide consent for this?
3. Where you collect data from children (subjects under 16 in the UK), do you actively seek parental consent?
4. Does your risk assessment cover the management of personal data or special category data?
5. Do you have a process for dealing with Subject Access or Data Portability requests within an appropriate timescale?
6. Describe your process for correcting inaccurate records, deleting records or suspending the processing of records?
7. Do you have documented data retention periods, do these cover contractual and legal requirements?
8. Do you have a data protection or data privacy statement compliant with the requirements of the General Data Protection Regulation (GDPR)? Who assessed the statement's compliance?
9. Do you have mechanisms in place which make it as easy for the data subject to remove consent for data processing and do you ensure it is as easy to remove consent as it was for them to give it?
10. For each piece of personal information held, how do you record the purpose for which it was obtained?
11. For each piece of personal information held, how do you record the justification for obtaining it?
12. For each piece of special category data held, how do you record the justification for obtaining it?
13. For each piece of personal information held, how do you record whether your organisation is the data processor or the data controller?
14. Where you disclose personal data to a supplier/provider does the contract explicitly impose the obligation to maintain appropriate technical and organisational measures to protect personal data in line with relevant

legislation?

15. Where criminal record checks are carried out, how do you ensure that explicit consent has been obtained from employees and that such checks are carried out for lawful purposes?

16. Do you ensure that a data protection impact assessment is carried out for all new systems and projects where personal data is in use, and there may be a risk to privacy? Please attach a copy of the DPIA for the proposed service.

17. What is your process for notifying personal data breaches to the Supervisory Authority and affected data subjects?

Issue ITT/RFQ: this stage is light touch from the Controller's perspective, but now the onus is on the Processor to demonstrate their data protection credentials. Processors will need to provide responses to questions in RFQ documents which satisfy the Controller making the request, bearing in mind that GDPR will increase the weight afforded to data protection related questions. Those responsible for completing RFQs in Processor organisations should consult with their Data Protection Officer and ensure responses demonstrate the Processor is capable of meeting the regulatory requirements as they relate to the Processing activity – inept responses may end up costing Processors valuable contracts!

Bid/Tender Evaluation and validation: similarly, to the supplier selection to participate in an Invitation to Tender, once RFQ responses are returned by shortlisted vendors, a more detailed evaluation and validation must now take place. Organisations can be very quick to outsource purely on cost, and this can end up being extremely costly for the organisation. Prior to making the final decision organisations should consider further due-diligence to confirm the content on the RFQs such as evidence collection or onsite audits.

An Organisation can outsource a service, but they can't outsource the risk!

Consider how much weighting is applied purely to cost and how much to risk

Ensure the cost of monitoring compliance is factored into the evaluation

---

Contract award and implementation: Whilst not the only consideration of a Processor contract, the GDPR requires Controllers put in place a written legally binding contract which contains the following:

1. The permitted processing activities
2. Confidentiality measures both at the organisational level and at the individual level
3. Technical and Organisational Security Controls
4. Conditions for engaging other Processors
5. Measures required to support the Controller uphold Data Subject's Rights (e.g. Right to Access)
6. Controls to support compliance monitoring, in particular security and where prior consultation is required
7. The treatment of data at the end of the provisioned service
8. Right to audit and the right to access to information to support the audit process

As will be mentioned again in Chapter 15, the European Commission has endorsed Standard Contractual Clauses

(SCC) [166] for transfers to Third Countries which organisations may find useful in the development of any of their Processor Contracts. In addition to the mandatory data protection contractual requirements, Controllers must establish Service Level Agreements (SLA), Key Performance Indicators (KPI) and associated periodic reporting requirements. These SLAs will support point 6 and point 11 in that they will be evidence the Controller is monitoring the Processors compliance with GDPR.

Warehouse logistics and receipt: whilst this may be more akin to a world of physical goods, the basic premise holds true when a Practitioner considers this as the transition phase, migrating the internal processing activity out to a Processor providing the same service on the Controller's behalf. It is usually at this stage an organisation has the last chance to check the appropriate controls are in place before a system goes live. If the Procurement and Supply process is wrapped within a project management methodology, there should be transition gateways in which each of the individual requirements contained in the Business Requirements Document (BRD). For each of the Data Protection requirements contained therein, as the DPO is required to monitor compliance, the DPO would, therefore, need to provide an opinion on whether the measure in place is appropriate. It would then be down to the appropriate level of management within the organisation whether the outsourcing arrangement can take place. Typically, this is ascertained through the organisation's risk management process. Whilst a decision may be taken at a lower managerial level, if the Data Protection Officer is not happy with the technical and organisational controls in place at the processor, the DPO has the authority to escalate the issue first to the most senior level of management and, where appropriate, to the Supervisory Authority. It is in the Process Owner's interest to ensure this part of the process goes smoothly from a data protection perspective so keep the DPO informed and involved as much as practicable!

Contract performance review and continuous improvement: at this stage of the procurement and supply life-cycle, the Processing will be in full swing. It will be incumbent on the Controller to monitor the supplier. The most common approach is a combination of the following:

1. Service Level / KPI Reporting
2. Service Review Meetings
3. Audits

Practitioners will want to ensure there are Data Protection KPIs and that these are reported on and discussed in the periodic Service Review meetings. As discussed in the Contract Aware and Implementation phase, the contract must include a Right to Audit. The right to audit should be exercised at least annually and be appropriate in scope to ensure the Processor is complying with the requirements of the contract. Those conducting the audit should review the service reporting and the data protection impact assessment as part of the audit to confirm what is documented reflects reality. Organisations who don't have the appropriate skills in-house to conduct data protection audits, may wish to consider engaging a third party to act on their behalf – not forgetting the auditor should have also been procured using the same life-cycle approach described here.

Supplier Relationship Management and Supply Chain management and development: this phase of procurement involves managing the portfolio of suppliers and determining how many resources should be devoted to any specific supplier. Suppliers will constantly be developing their products and services and introducing new products and services too. Practitioners will need to be keyed into strategic procurement decisions and be assessing how these decisions may affect the risk to the rights and freedoms of data subjects. There will also be cases where suppliers are performing well in the core service delivery but under-performing in terms of data protection compliance. The practitioner will need to ensure this information is fed into the strategic decision-making process as if the core

---

[166] Model Contracts for the transfer of personal data to third countries (http://ec.europa.eu/justice/data-protection/international-transfers/transfer/index_en.htm)

service offering grows in a non-compliant processor, so too may the likelihood of a serious personal data breach.

Asset management / end of life and lessons learnt: as the business grows, shrinks or changes direction, existing service providers may no longer be able to provide a compelling service offering. In other circumstances, a supplier may no longer be performing at the agreed level. In these circumstances, an organisation may determine a need to exit a supplier relationship either to cease carrying out a service altogether, bring the service back in-house or potentially migrate to a different supplier. In any of these circumstances, there will be data protection considerations to consider, and of course one of those will be to review the DPIA. For those eagle-eyed, you will note in the contract stage there are certain requirements which must be placed in a Processor contract. One of those items is how data will be treated at the end of the supplier relationship. The details wording is as follows: *"That contract or other legal act shall stipulate, in particular, that the processor at the choice of the controller, deletes or returns all the personal data to the controller after the end of the provision of services relating to processing, and deletes existing copies unless Union or Member State law requires storage of the personal data."* The Practitioner must ensure the data held by the processor for any legally required purpose is not used for any other purpose not agreed within the original Processor contract too.

EXAMPLE: A Processor is required to retain customer records for a period of 5 years to support an extended warranty. The Processor is given notice that one of their Controllers is to exit their current contract.

The Processor would not be able to use the affected Personal Data for other purposes (e.g. to market other products or to sell the data to another organisation) even after the contract with the Controller organisation ends.

As you can see, there is a lot of data protection considerations within the procurement and supply life-cycle. If your organisation relies heavily on outsourced service providers to support processing activities, you must ensure there are contracts and a DPIA in place and that the Processor is continually monitored for compliance. A failure to do so could result in enforcement action which could include, at the lower end, corrective action requirements but at the upper end of censure, a processing ban and administrative fines – *Caveat Emptor*[167]!

---

[167] Caveat Emptor (Latin): Buyer Beware

Example Data Protection Detailed Specification

NB: This specification is for example only and will not be suitable for any particular outsourcing arrangement.

Requirement Title:	**PROVISION OF CONSENT FOR MARKETING DURING WEBSITE ONBOARDING**				
Project Reference:	PRJ040513	**Name:**	MERCURY		
Requirement Reference:	NFRQ001	**Benefit:**	Upholding the rights and freedoms of Data Subjects	**Status:**	In Scope
Requirement Type:	Non-Functional (Mandatory)		**MoSCoW:**	Must Have	
Cross-reference to business process:	Onboarding process (FRQ003), Account Profile (FRQ012), API (FRQ023)				
Purpose:	Ensure those completing the website registration process, are able to provide their informed, explicit consent for their data to be used for direct marketing purposes.				
As is business requirement:	As this is a new system, there is currently no consent mechanism in place.				
To be business requirement:	The registration form will contain just-in-time privacy information next to each field which will be used to support marketing activities. The notice shall explain, in addition to any other purpose for data collection, the data collected may be used to support marketing activities if consent is provided. At the end of the registration form, there shall be an unticked tick box with the following copy next to the tick-box. "Tick the box if you consent to [insert company name] providing you information about our products and services via a weekly email." The tick box shall be linked to a database field, attributable to the user to record their consent preference. The user shall be provided with a mechanism within one menu level of their account profile (see FRQ012) to withdraw consent. There shall be a mechanism in which consent preference is promulgated to the marketing system to ensure users are not contacted whereby they have not provided consent or have withdrawn consent.				
Business rules:	The system must not allow Users to be contacted if they withdraw consent The system must not force Users (i.e. through required form fields) to provide information which will be solely used for marketing purposes Marketing consent must separate from all other forms of consent Users must not be automatically opted-in				
Quality Criteria:	The wording is free from typos There are no mandatory fields solely related to marketing activities The tick box is unticked by default When the tick box is ticked, the correct preference is recorded in the correct user's database record. When the tick box is unticked, the correct preference is recorded in the correct user's record.				

	The method to withdraw consent is easily navigable and within one level of the account profile The [load] time taken to access this menu is the same as to access any other menu item (i.e. not throttled). The [load] time taken to save the consent preference is the same as saving any other preference (i.e. not throttled).
Cross reference to existing document(s):	Project Business Case Data Protection Policy General Data Protection Regulation (GDPR) Privacy and Electronic Communications Regulation (PECR)
Issues:	The system may not be able to support multiple languages (e.g. the languages of the 28 Member States of the European Union.
Owner:	Director of Human Resources
Quality Assessor:	Data Protection Officer
Version:	1.0
Approved:	25-May-2018

15. THIRD COUNTRIES AND ORGANISATIONS OUTSIDE THE EU

The European Union takes data protection very seriously. However, this is not the case elsewhere across the globe. It may surprise those Practitioners who may not deal with international transfers of Personal Data that even the way the United States protects the rights and freedoms of its citizens in relation to data protection (and wider privacy rights and freedoms) has been called into question[168]. Some Practitioners may also wonder why it matters when their particular organisation only processes Personal or Sensitive Data in a single country within the EU. The reason why it's important is because your organisation may use cloud services to support your operations. Your website, your email servers, for example, may be sat in data centres in the United States or Canada or elsewhere across the globe. The organisations you partner with may be located in the UK, but again, their infrastructure may be in part located outside of the EU. Under both the current EU data protection legislation and under GDPR transfers to third countries are prohibited without certain safeguards. The regulation[169] states: *"Any transfer of personal data which are undergoing processing or are intended for processing after transfer to a third country or to an international organisation shall take place only if, subject to the other provisions of this Regulation, the conditions laid down in this Chapter are complied with by the controller and processor, including for onward transfers of personal data from the third country or an international organisation to another third country or to another international organisation. All provisions in Chapter 5 of the GDPR shall be applied in order to ensure that the level of protection of natural persons guaranteed by this Regulation is not undermined."*

What this basically means is an organisation must not transfer data to a third country, or parts of international organisation operating outside the EU, unless there are adequate safeguards in place which will protect the rights and freedoms of EU Data Subjects. In this chapter, we will discuss what safeguards must be put in place prior to transferring data outside the European Union.

> **EXAMPLE: Would an EU Data Subject be able to exercise their right to an effective judicial remedy against a Processor in Afghanistan should their Personal Data become compromised?**

---

[168] No Place to Hide: Edward Snowden, the NSA and the Surveillance State. Greenwald G., 2015.
[169] Article 44: General principle for transfers

Adequacy

Whilst there may be countries where the rights and freedoms of citizens are woefully poor (e.g. Syria, Eritrea and North Korea), there are many countries located outside the European Union (e.g. Canada, Australia and New Zealand) [170] which have an equivalent or greater regard to the rights and freedoms of their citizens. In such cases, the European Union recognises equivalency in the form of adequacy[171] decisions. These adequacy decisions look at a variety of areas of governance when determining adequacy and not solely relating to Data Protection with the key areas being:

1. The Rule of Law
2. Rules on the onward transfer of Data
3. The existence of a Data Protection Supervisory Authority
4. International commitments
5. Obligations arising from legally binding conventions or instruments
6. Participation in multilateral or regional systems

At the time of going to print, the European Commission has so far recognised Andorra, Argentina, Canada (Commercial Organisations), Faeroe Islands, Guernsey, Israel, Isle of Man, Jersey, New Zealand, Switzerland and Uruguay as providing adequate protection. For countries in the European Free Trade Area (EFTA)[172], with the exception of Switzerland which is mentioned above, is that Personal Data can flow between the 28 EU Member States and without any further safeguard being necessary. An adequacy decision may also be limited to specific sectors within a third country. For example, in the case of Canada, only certain types of Personal Data can be transferred to certain types of organisation. Practitioners must ensure they understand the limitations of an adequacy decision before relying on the decision as a lawful basis to transfer Personal Data.

Adequacy decisions are not fixed forever. The European Commission is required to monitor Third Countries and where the Commission determines a country is no longer providing adequate protections has the power to repeal, amend or suspend an adequacy decision. Where an organisation is relying on an adequacy decision as the basis for transferring Personal Data to a Third Country, the Practitioner or Data Protection Officer must maintain awareness in relation to whether any adequacy decision which is relied upon for the transfer of Personal Data to a Third Country remain valid[173].

---

[170] Freedom in the World 2017, Populists and Autocrats: The Dual Threat to Global Democracy. Freedom House. 2017

[171] Article 45: Transfers on the basis of an adequacy decision

[172] Norway, Liechtenstein and Iceland

173 COM(2015) 566 final: Transfer of Personal Data from the EU to the United States of America under Directive 95/46/EC following the Judgment by the Court of Justice in Case C-362/14 (Schrems). November 2015

Safeguards

In cases where there is not an adequacy decision as per Article 45 of GDPR, or the adequacy decision doesn't cover your organisation's specific processing needs, the Regulation requires safeguards be put in place to ensure Data Subjects' rights are enforceable and that Data Subjects have access to effective judicial remedies. This is achieved by having one or more of the following in place:

1. A legally binding and enforceable instrument between public authorities or bodies;
2. Binding Corporate Rules[174]
3. Standard Data Protection clauses
4. Approved Code of Conduct[175]
5. Approved Certification Mechanism[176]

In the cases of options 4 and 5, these cannot stand alone and must be combined with binding and enforceable commitments of the controller or processor in the third country to apply the appropriate safeguards, including as regards data subjects' rights.

Binding Corporate Rules: these are internal rules (such as a Code of Conduct) adopted by multinationals and define a global policy with regard to the international transfers of personal data within the same corporate group to entities located in countries which do not provide an adequate level of protection. BCR ensure that all transfers are made within a group, benefit from an adequate level of protection. This is an alternative to the company having to sign standard contractual clauses each time it needs to transfer data to a member of its group and may be preferable where it becomes too burdensome to sign contractual clauses for each transfer made within a group. It should be noted that Binding Corporate Rules do not provide a basis for transfers made outside the group.

EXAMPLE: A multinational operating in the EU with an operations centre in Manila may use Binding Corporate Rules to transfer data to the Manilla operations centre. The operations centre wishes to sub-contract some of their processing activities to a local company. This processing would involve the transfer of Personal Data relating to EU Data Subjects.

Because this local company is not part of the multinational, the Binding Corporate Rules used as the basis for lawful transfer to a Third Country (i.e. the Philippines) would not apply to the sub-contractor Processor but the BCR must contain requirements relating to how onward transfers are controlled.

BCR must contain in particular Privacy principles (transparency, data quality, security, etc.), Tools of effectiveness (audit, training, complaint handling system, etc.), and an element proving that BCR are binding.

Standard Contractual Clauses (SCC): we have discussed SCC already in the context of Outsourcing in Chapter 14, so we shall not repeat that content except to say that where an adequacy decision is not available SCC's may be used where those SCC's have been adopted by a Supervisory Authority and the European Commission. At the time of print, the European Commission has so far issued two sets of standard contractual clauses (also known as Model

---

[174] Article 47: Binding Corporate Rules
[175] Article 40: Codes of Conduct
[176] Article 42: Certification

Contract Clauses)[177] for transfers from data controllers to data controllers established outside the EU/EEA and one set for the transfer to processors established outside the EU/EEA.

Derogations

There are certain situations whereby, even without an adequacy decision or appropriate safeguards that Personal Data may be transferred to a Third Country. These are referred to as derogations[178] and are where the:

1. data subject has provided informed, explicit consent to the proposed transfer, and in particular, informed as to the risks associated with there being no adequacy decision or appropriate safeguards
2. transfer is necessary for the performance of a contract
3. transfer is necessary for the conclusion or performance of a contract
4. transfer is necessary for important reasons of public interest;
5. transfer is necessary for the establishment, exercise or defence of legal claims;
6. transfer is necessary in order to protect the vital interests of the data subject or of other persons, where the data subject is physically or legally incapable of giving consent;
7. transfer is made from a register which according to Union or Member State law

---

EXAMPLE: A company has just set up its first office outside the EU in China. Three employees, resident in Paris, are transferring to the new Branch in Beijing. The company does not yet have Binding Corporate Rules in place, and China does not have an adequacy decision, but the new office HR Manager requires Personal Data to process work visas and other local onboarding requirements.

In this case, the Controller may determine transfer is necessary for the performance of an (employment) contract between the data subject and the controller and the implementation of pre-contractual measures taken at the data subject's request.

The Controller may also seek to gain explicit, informed consent from the Data Subjects, explaining that there is no adequacy decision in place for China and no other appropriate safeguards in place.

There exists a further situation where data may be transferred to a Third Country whereby there is no adequacy decision, no appropriate safeguards and derogations exist. This is where the transfer is non-repetitive and where the number of data subjects are limited. In such cases – and I'll be honest I could not find an explicit example which was not potentially covered by legitimate interests – the Supervisory Authority and the Data Subject should[179] be informed.

---

[177] Model Contracts for the transfer of personal data to third countries (http://ec.europa.eu/justice/data-protection/international-transfers/transfer/index_en.htm)
[178] Article 49: Derogations for specific situations
[179] Recital 113

Designating a Representative

Whilst the rest of this chapter has looked at the flow of data from a Controller or Processor inside the EU, to those organisations established and located outside of the EU, it is an important final point to remind the Practitioner that GDPR has extra-territorial applicability. Organisations outside of the EU who are processing Personal or Sensitive Data relating to EU Data Subjects, or monitoring the behaviour or EU Data Subjects, must still comply with GDPR even though they are located outside of the EU for all intents and purposes at the time of interaction with an EU Data Subject.

> **EXAMPLE: An EU Data Subject books a flight with a Mexican Airline via their website hosted in the United States. Even though the airline is a Mexican company and the EU Data Subject is consciously providing data to their website, the Airline is still required to comply with the requirements of the EU General Data Protection Regulation.**

To support compliance activities, organisations established outside the EU must appoint a representative[180]. If your organisation already has a branch in the EU, there is no requirement to appoint a representative. The Article 27 Representative serves as a point of contact between your business, data subjects and EU Supervisory Authorities. In order to support the Controller or Processor, the Representative could, in addition to acting as a point of contact hold a copy of relevant data protection records[181].

A representative is not a replacement for a Controller or Processor outside the EU and shall not be held liable for the Controller or Processor failing to uphold the rights and freedoms of EU Data Subjects. Where your organisation requires a representative, consider the language barriers you may face when dealing with 28 different countries and choose a country which is best aligned with your language needs. If you're a South American company dealing primarily with Spanish Data Subjects, it may be more appropriate to appoint a representative in Spain. If you're a North African company, again it may be appropriate to appoint a representative in France. If your company is based in South Africa, you wish to consider a Representative in Holland. Whichever country is chosen, the requirement is that the Representative must be based in an EU Member State.

---

[180] Article 27: Representatives of controllers or processors not established in the Union
[181] Article 30: Records of processing activities

PART II: THE EU GENERAL DATA PROTECTION REGULATION[182]

---

[182] http://eur-lex.europa.eu, © European Union, 1998-2017

I: GENERAL PROVISIONS

Article 1: Subject-matter and objectives

1.   This Regulation lays down rules relating to the protection of Natural Persons with regard to the processing of personal data and rules relating to the free movement of personal data.

2.   This Regulation protects fundamental rights and freedoms of Natural Persons and in particular their right to the protection of personal data.

3.   The free movement of personal data within the Union shall be neither restricted nor prohibited for reasons connected with the protection of Natural Persons with regard to the processing of personal data.

Article 2: Material scope

1.   This Regulation applies to the processing of personal data wholly or partly by automated means and to the processing other than by automated means of personal data which form part of a filing system or are intended to form part of a filing system.

2.   This Regulation does not apply to the processing of personal data:

   1.   in the course of an activity which falls outside the scope of Union law;
   2.   by the Member States when carrying out activities which fall within the scope of Chapter 2 of Title V of the TEU;
   3.   by a Natural Person in the course of a purely personal or household activity;
   4.   by competent authorities for the purposes of the prevention, investigation, detection or prosecution of criminal offences or the execution of criminal penalties, including the safeguarding against and the prevention of threats to public security.

3.   For the processing of personal data by the Union institutions, bodies, offices and agencies, Regulation (EC) No 45/2001 applies. Regulation (EC) No 45/2001 and other Union legal acts applicable to such processing of personal data shall be adapted to the principles and rules of this Regulation in accordance with Article 98.

4.   This Regulation shall be without prejudice to the application of Directive 2000/31/EC, in particular of the liability rules of intermediary service providers in Articles 12 to 15 of that Directive.

Article 3: Territorial scope

1.   This Regulation applies to the processing of personal data in the context of the activities of an establishment of a Controller or a Processor in the Union, regardless of whether the processing takes place in the Union or not.

2.   This Regulation applies to the processing of personal data of Data Subjects who are in the Union by a Controller or Processor not established in the Union, where the processing activities are related to:

1.   the offering of goods or services, irrespective of whether a payment of the Data Subject is required, to such Data Subjects in the Union; or
2.   the monitoring of their behaviour as far as their behaviour takes place within the Union.

3.   This Regulation applies to the processing of personal data by a Controller not established in the Union, but in a place where Member State law applies by virtue of public international law.

Article 4: Definitions

For the purposes of this Regulation:

1.   'personal data' means any information relating to an identified or identifiable Natural Person ('Data Subject'); an identifiable Natural Person is one who can be identified, directly or indirectly, in particular by reference to an identifier such as a name, an identification number, location data, an online identifier or to one or more factors specific to the physical, physiological, genetic, mental, economic, cultural or social identity of that Natural Person;

2.   'processing' means any operation or set of operations which is performed on personal data or on sets of personal data, whether or not by automated means, such as collection, recording, organisation, structuring, storage, adaptation or alteration, retrieval, consultation, use, disclosure by transmission, dissemination or otherwise making available, alignment or combination, restriction, erasure or destruction;

3.   'restriction of processing' means the marking of stored personal data with the aim of limiting their processing in the future;

4.   'profiling' means any form of automated processing of personal data consisting of the use of personal data to evaluate certain personal aspects relating to a Natural Person, in particular to analyse or predict aspects concerning that Natural Person's performance at work, economic situation, health, personal preferences, interests, reliability, behaviour, location or movements;

5.   'pseudonymisation' means the processing of personal data in such a manner that the personal data can no longer be attributed to a specific Data Subject without the use of additional information, provided that such additional information is kept separately and is subject to technical and organisational measures to ensure that the personal data are not attributed to an identified or identifiable Natural Person;

6.   'filing system' means any structured set of personal data which are accessible according to specific criteria, whether centralised, decentralised or dispersed on a functional or geographical basis;

7.   'Controller' means the natural or legal person, public authority, agency or other body which, alone or jointly with others, determines the purposes and means of the processing of personal data; where the purposes and means of such processing are determined by Union or Member State law, the Controller or the specific criteria for its nomination may be provided for by Union or Member State law;

8.   'Processor' means a natural or legal person, public authority, agency or other body which processes personal data on behalf of the Controller;

9.   'recipient' means a natural or legal person, public authority, agency or another body, to which the personal data are disclosed, whether a third party or not. However, public authorities which may receive personal data in the framework of a particular inquiry in accordance with Union or Member State law shall not be regarded as recipients; the processing of those data by those public authorities shall be in compliance with the applicable data protection rules according to the purposes of the processing;

10.   'third party' means a natural or legal person, public authority, agency or body other than the Data Subject, Controller, Processor and persons who, under the direct authority of the Controller or Processor, are authorised to process personal data;

11.   'consent' of the Data Subject means any freely given, specific, informed and unambiguous indication of the Data Subject's wishes by which he or she, by a statement or by a clear affirmative action, signifies agreement to the processing of personal data relating to him or her;

12.   'personal data breach' means a breach of security leading to the accidental or unlawful destruction, loss, alteration, unauthorised disclosure of, or access to, personal data transmitted, stored or otherwise processed;

13.   'genetic data' means personal data relating to the inherited or acquired genetic characteristics of a Natural Person which give unique information about the physiology or the health of that Natural Person and which result, in particular, from an analysis of a biological sample from the Natural Person in question;

14.   'biometric data' means personal data resulting from specific technical processing relating to the physical, physiological or behavioural characteristics of a Natural Person, which allow or confirm the unique identification of that Natural Person, such as facial images or dactyloscopic data;

15.   'data concerning health' means personal data related to the physical or mental health of a Natural Person, including the provision of health care services, which reveal information about his or her health status;

16.   'main establishment' means:

   1.   as regards a Controller with establishments in more than one Member State, the place of its central administration in the Union, unless the decisions on the purposes and means of the processing of personal data are taken in another establishment of the Controller in the Union and the latter establishment has the power to have such decisions implemented, in which case the establishment having taken such decisions is to be considered to be the main establishment;
   2.   as regards a Processor with establishments in more than one Member State, the place of its central administration in the Union, or, if the Processor has no central administration in the Union, the establishment of the Processor in the Union where the main processing activities in the context of the activities of an establishment of the Processor take place to the extent that the Processor is subject to specific obligations under this Regulation;

17.   'representative' means a natural or legal person established in the Union who, designated by the Controller or Processor in writing pursuant to Article 27, represents the Controller or Processor with regard to their respective obligations under this Regulation;

18.   'enterprise' means a natural or legal person engaged in an economic activity, irrespective of its legal form, including partnerships or associations regularly engaged in an economic activity;

19. 'group of undertakings' means a controlling undertaking and its controlled undertakings;

20. 'binding corporate rules' means personal data protection policies which are adhered to by a Controller or Processor established on the territory of a Member State for transfers or a set of transfers of personal data to a Controller or Processor in one or more third countries within a group of undertakings, or group of enterprises engaged in a joint economic activity;

21. 'Supervisory Authority' means an independent public authority which is established by a Member State pursuant to Article 51;

22. 'Supervisory Authority concerned' means a Supervisory Authority which is concerned by the processing of personal data because:

1. the Controller or Processor is established on the territory of the Member State of that Supervisory Authority;
2. Data Subjects residing in the Member State of that Supervisory Authority are substantially affected or likely to be substantially affected by the processing; or
3. a complaint has been lodged with that Supervisory Authority;

23. 'cross-border processing' means either:

1. processing of personal data which takes place in the context of the activities of establishments in more than one Member State of a Controller or Processor in the Union where the Controller or Processor is established in more than one Member State; or
2. processing of personal data which takes place in the context of the activities of a single establishment of a Controller or Processor in the Union but which substantially affects or is likely to substantially affect Data Subjects in more than one Member State.

24. 'relevant and reasoned objection' means an objection to a draft decision as to whether there is an infringement of this Regulation, or whether envisaged action in relation to the Controller or Processor complies with this Regulation, which clearly demonstrates the significance of the risks posed by the draft decision as regards the fundamental rights and freedoms of Data Subjects and, where applicable, the free flow of personal data within the Union;

25. 'information society service' means a service as defined in point (b) of Article 1 of Directive (EU) 2015/1535 of the European Parliament and of the Council (¹);

26. 'international organisation' means an organisation and its subordinate bodies governed by public international law, or any other body which is set up by, or on the basis of, an agreement between two or more countries.

II: PRINCIPLES

Article 5: Principles relating to processing of personal data

1. Personal data shall be:

    1. processed lawfully, fairly and in a transparent manner in relation to the Data Subject ('lawfulness, fairness and transparency');
    2. collected for specified, explicit and legitimate purposes and not further processed in a manner that is incompatible with those purposes; further processing for archiving purposes in the public interest, scientific or historical research purposes or statistical purposes shall, in accordance with Article 89(1), not be considered to be incompatible with the initial purposes ('purpose limitation');
    3. adequate, relevant and limited to what is necessary in relation to the purposes for which they are processed ('data minimisation');
    4. accurate and, where necessary, kept up to date; every reasonable step must be taken to ensure that personal data that are inaccurate, having regard to the purposes for which they are processed, are erased or rectified without delay ('accuracy');
    5. kept in a form which permits identification of Data Subjects for no longer than is necessary for the purposes for which the personal data are processed; personal data may be stored for longer periods insofar as the personal data will be processed solely for archiving purposes in the public interest, scientific or historical research purposes or statistical purposes in accordance with Article 89(1) subject to implementation of the appropriate technical and organisational measures required by this Regulation in order to safeguard the rights and freedoms of the Data Subject ('storage limitation');
    6. processed in a manner that ensures appropriate security of the personal data, including protection against unauthorised or unlawful processing and against accidental loss, destruction or damage, using appropriate technical or organisational measures ('integrity and confidentiality').

2. The Controller shall be responsible for, and be able to demonstrate compliance with, paragraph 1 ('accountability').

Article 6: Lawfulness of processing

1. Processing shall be lawful only if and to the extent that at least one of the following applies:

    1. the Data Subject has given consent to the processing of his or her personal data for one or more specific purposes;
    2. processing is necessary for the performance of a contract to which the Data Subject is party or in order to take steps at the request of the Data Subject prior to entering into a contract;
    3. processing is necessary for compliance with a legal obligation to which the Controller is subject;
    4. processing is necessary in order to protect the vital interests of the Data Subject or of another Natural Person;
    5. processing is necessary for the performance of a task carried out in the public interest or in the exercise of official authority vested in the Controller;
    6. processing is necessary for the purposes of the legitimate interests pursued by the Controller or by a third party, except where such interests are overridden by the interests or fundamental rights and freedoms of the Data Subject which require protection of personal data, in particular where the Data Subject is a child.

Point (f) of the first subparagraph shall not apply to processing carried out by public authorities in the performance of their tasks.

2.   Member States may maintain or introduce more specific provisions to adapt the application of the rules of this Regulation with regard to processing for compliance with points (c) and (e) of paragraph 1 by determining more precisely specific requirements for the processing and other measures to ensure lawful and fair processing including for other specific processing situations as provided for in Chapter IX.

3.   The basis for the processing referred to in point (c) and (e) of paragraph 1 shall be laid down by:

1.   Union law; or
2.   Member State law to which the Controller is subject.

The purpose of the processing shall be determined in that legal basis or, as regards the processing referred to in point (e) of paragraph 1, shall be necessary for the performance of a task carried out in the public interest or in the exercise of official authority vested in the Controller. That legal basis may contain specific provisions to adapt the application of rules of this Regulation, inter alia: the general conditions governing the lawfulness of processing by the Controller; the types of data which are subject to the processing; the Data Subjects concerned; the entities to, and the purposes for which, the personal data may be disclosed; the purpose limitation; storage periods; and processing operations and processing procedures, including measures to ensure lawful and fair processing such as those for other specific processing situations as provided for in Chapter IX. The Union or the Member State law shall meet an objective of public interest and be proportionate to the legitimate aim pursued.

4.   Where the processing for a purpose other than that for which the personal data have been collected is not based on the Data Subject's consent or on a Union or Member State law which constitutes a necessary and proportionate measure in a democratic society to safeguard the objectives referred to in Article 23(1), the Controller shall, in order to ascertain whether processing for another purpose is compatible with the purpose for which the personal data are initially collected, take into account, inter alia:

1.   any link between the purposes for which the personal data have been collected and the purposes of the intended further processing;
2.   the context in which the personal data have been collected, in particular regarding the relationship between Data Subjects and the Controller;
3.   the nature of the personal data, in particular whether special categories of personal data are processed, pursuant to Article 9, or whether personal data related to criminal convictions and offences are processed, pursuant to Article 10;
4.   the possible consequences of the intended further processing for Data Subjects;
5.   the existence of appropriate safeguards, which may include encryption or pseudonymisation.

Article 7: Conditions for consent

1.   Where processing is based on consent, the Controller shall be able to demonstrate that the Data Subject has consented to processing of his or her personal data.

2.   If the Data Subject's consent is given in the context of a written declaration which also concerns other matters, the request for consent shall be presented in a manner which is clearly distinguishable from the other matters, in an intelligible and easily accessible form, using clear and plain language. Any part of such a declaration which constitutes an infringement of this Regulation shall not be binding.

3.   The Data Subject shall have the right to withdraw his or her consent at any time. The withdrawal of consent shall not affect the lawfulness of processing based on consent before its withdrawal. Prior to giving consent, the Data Subject shall be informed thereof. It shall be as easy to withdraw as to give consent.

4.   When assessing whether consent is freely given, utmost account shall be taken of whether, inter alia, the performance of a contract, including the provision of a service, is conditional on consent to the processing of personal data that is not necessary for the performance of that contract.

Article 8: Conditions applicable to child's consent in relation to information society services

1.   Where point (a) of Article 6 applies, in relation to the offer of information society services directly to a child, the processing of the personal data of a child shall be lawful where the child is at least 16 years old. Where the child is below the age of 16 years, such processing shall be lawful only if and to the extent that consent is given or authorised by the holder of parental responsibility over the child. Member States may provide by law for a lower age for those purposes provided that such lower age is not below 13 years.

2.   The Controller shall make reasonable efforts to verify in such cases that consent is given or authorised by the holder of parental responsibility over the child, taking into consideration available technology.

3.   Paragraph 1 shall not affect the general contract law of Member States such as the rules on the validity, formation or effect of a contract in relation to a child.

Article. 9: Processing of special categories of personal data

1.   Processing of personal data revealing racial or ethnic origin, political opinions, religious or philosophical beliefs, or trade union membership, and the processing of genetic data, biometric data for the purpose of uniquely identifying a Natural Person, data concerning health or data concerning a Natural Person's sex life or sexual orientation shall be prohibited.

2.   Paragraph 1 shall not apply if one of the following applies:

1. the Data Subject has given explicit consent to the processing of those personal data for one or more specified purposes, except where Union or Member State law provide that the prohibition referred to in paragraph 1 may not be lifted by the Data Subject;
2. processing is necessary for the purposes of carrying out the obligations and exercising specific rights of the Controller or of the Data Subject in the field of employment and social security and social protection law in so far as it is authorised by Union or Member State law or a collective agreement pursuant to Member State law providing for appropriate safeguards for the fundamental rights and the interests of the Data Subject;
3. processing is necessary to protect the vital interests of the Data Subject or of another Natural Person where the Data Subject is physically or legally incapable of giving consent;
4. processing is carried out in the course of its legitimate activities with appropriate safeguards by a foundation, association or any other not-for-profit body with a political, philosophical, religious or trade union aim and on condition that the processing relates solely to the members or to former members of the body or to persons who have regular contact with it in connection with its purposes and that the personal data are not disclosed outside that body without the consent of the Data Subjects;
5. processing relates to personal data which are manifestly made public by the Data Subject;
6. processing is necessary for the establishment, exercise or defence of legal claims or whenever courts are acting in their judicial capacity;
7. processing is necessary for reasons of substantial public interest, on the basis of Union or Member State law which shall be proportionate to the aim pursued, respect the essence of the right to data protection and provide for suitable and specific measures to safeguard the fundamental rights and the interests of the Data Subject;
8. processing is necessary for the purposes of preventive or occupational medicine, for the assessment of the

working capacity of the employee, medical diagnosis, the provision of health or social care or treatment or the management of health or social care systems and services on the basis of Union or Member State law or pursuant to contract with a health professional and subject to the conditions and safeguards referred to in paragraph 3;

9. processing is necessary for reasons of public interest in the area of public health, such as protecting against serious cross-border threats to health or ensuring high standards of quality and safety of health care and of medicinal products or medical devices, on the basis of Union or Member State law which provides for suitable and specific measures to safeguard the rights and freedoms of the Data Subject, in particular professional secrecy;

10. processing is necessary for archiving purposes in the public interest, scientific or historical research purposes or statistical purposes in accordance with Article 89(1) based on Union or Member State law which shall be proportionate to the aim pursued, respect the essence of the right to data protection and provide for suitable and specific measures to safeguard the fundamental rights and the interests of the Data Subject.

3. Personal data referred to in paragraph 1 may be processed for the purposes referred to in point (h) of paragraph 2 when those data are processed by or under the responsibility of a professional subject to the obligation of professional secrecy under Union or Member State law or rules established by national competent bodies or by another person also subject to an obligation of secrecy under Union or Member State law or rules established by national competent bodies.

4. Member States may maintain or introduce further conditions, including limitations, with regard to the processing of genetic data, biometric data or data concerning health.

Article. 10: Processing of personal data relating to criminal convictions and offences

Processing of personal data relating to criminal convictions and offences or related security measures based on Article 6(1) shall be carried out only under the control of official authority or when the processing is authorised by Union or Member State law providing for appropriate safeguards for the rights and freedoms of Data Subjects. Any comprehensive register of criminal convictions shall be kept only under the control of official authority.

Article 11: Processing which does not require identification

1. If the purposes for which a Controller processes personal data do not or do no longer require the identification of a Data Subject by the Controller, the Controller shall not be obliged to maintain, acquire or process additional information in order to identify the Data Subject for the sole purpose of complying with this Regulation.

2. Where, in cases referred to in paragraph 1 of this Article, the Controller is able to demonstrate that it is not in a position to identify the Data Subject, the Controller shall inform the Data Subject accordingly, if possible. In such cases, Articles 15 to 20 shall not apply except where the Data Subject, for the purpose of exercising his or her rights under those articles, provides additional information enabling his or her identification.

III: RIGHTS OF THE DATA SUBJECT

Article 12: Transparent information, communication and modalities for the exercise of the rights of the Data Subject

1.   The Controller shall take appropriate measures to provide any information referred to in Articles 13 and 14 and any communication under Articles 15 to 22 and 34 relating to processing to the Data Subject in a concise, transparent, intelligible and easily accessible form, using clear and plain language, in particular for any information addressed specifically to a child. The information shall be provided in writing, or by other means, including, where appropriate, by electronic means. When requested by the Data Subject, the information may be provided orally, provided that the identity of the Data Subject is proven by other means.

2.   The Controller shall facilitate the exercise of Data Subject rights under Articles 15 to 22. In the cases referred to in Article 11, the Controller shall not refuse to act on the request of the Data Subject for exercising his or her rights under Articles 15 to 22, unless the Controller demonstrates that it is not in a position to identify the Data Subject.

3.   The Controller shall provide information on action taken on a request under Articles 15 to 22 to the Data Subject without undue delay and in any event within one month of receipt of the request. That period may be extended by two further months where necessary, taking into account the complexity and number of the requests. The Controller shall inform the Data Subject of any such extension within one month of receipt of the request, together with the reasons for the delay. Where the Data Subject makes the request by electronic form means, the information shall be provided by electronic means where possible, unless otherwise requested by the Data Subject.

4.   If the Controller does not take action on the request of the Data Subject, the Controller shall inform the Data Subject without delay and at the latest within one month of receipt of the request of the reasons for not taking action and on the possibility of lodging a complaint with a Supervisory Authority and seeking a judicial remedy.

5.   Information provided under Articles 13 and 14 and any communication and any actions taken under Articles 15 to 22 and 34 shall be provided free of charge. Where requests from a Data Subject are manifestly unfounded or excessive, in particular because of their repetitive character, the Controller may either:

    1.   charge a reasonable fee taking into account the administrative costs of providing the information or communication or taking the action requested; or
    2.   refuse to act on the request.

The Controller shall bear the burden of demonstrating the manifestly unfounded or excessive character of the request.

6.   Without prejudice to Article 11, where the Controller has reasonable doubts concerning the identity of the Natural Person making the request referred to in Articles 15 to 21, the Controller may request the provision of additional information necessary to confirm the identity of the Data Subject.

7.   The information to be provided to Data Subjects pursuant to Articles 13 and 14 may be provided in combination with standardised icons in order to give in an easily visible, intelligible and clearly legible manner a meaningful overview of the intended processing. Where the icons are presented electronically they shall be machine-readable.

8.   The Commission shall be empowered to adopt delegated acts in accordance with Article 92 for the purpose of determining the information to be presented by the icons and the procedures for providing standardised icons.

Article 13: Information to be provided where personal data are collected from the Data Subject

1.   Where personal data relating to a Data Subject are collected from the Data Subject, the Controller shall, at the time when personal data are obtained, provide the Data Subject with all of the following information:

   1. the identity and the contact details of the Controller and, where applicable, of the Controller's representative;
   2. the contact details of the data protection officer, where applicable;
   3. the purposes of the processing for which the personal data are intended as well as the legal basis for the processing;
   4. where the processing is based on point (f) of Article 6, the legitimate interests pursued by the Controller or by a third party;
   5. the recipients or categories of recipients of the personal data, if any;
   6. where applicable, the fact that the Controller intends to transfer personal data to a third country or international organisation and the existence or absence of an adequacy decision by the Commission, or in the case of transfers referred to in Article 46 or 47, or the second subparagraph of Article 49, reference to the appropriate or suitable safeguards and the means by which to obtain a copy of them or where they have been made available.

2.   In addition to the information referred to in paragraph 1, the Controller shall, at the time when personal data are obtained, provide the Data Subject with the following further information necessary to ensure fair and transparent processing:

   1. the period for which the personal data will be stored, or if that is not possible, the criteria used to determine that period;
   2. the existence of the right to request from the Controller access to and rectification or erasure of personal data or restriction of processing concerning the Data Subject or to object to processing as well as the right to data portability;
   3. where the processing is based on point (a) of Article 6 or point (a) of Article 9, the existence of the right to withdraw consent at any time, without affecting the lawfulness of processing based on consent before its withdrawal;
   4. the right to lodge a complaint with a Supervisory Authority;
   5. whether the provision of personal data is a statutory or contractual requirement, or a requirement necessary to enter into a contract, as well as whether the Data Subject is obliged to provide the personal data and of the possible consequences of failure to provide such data;
   6. the existence of automated decision-making, including profiling, referred to in Article 22 and (4) and, at least in those cases, meaningful information about the logic involved, as well as the significance and the envisaged consequences of such processing for the Data Subject.

3.   Where the Controller intends to further process the personal data for a purpose other than that for which the personal data were collected, the Controller shall provide the Data Subject prior to that further processing with information on that other purpose and with any relevant further information as referred to in paragraph 2.

4.   Paragraphs 1, 2 and 3 shall not apply where and insofar as the Data Subject already has the information.

Article 14: Information to be provided where personal data have not been obtained from the Data Subject

Where personal data have not been obtained from the Data Subject, the Controller shall provide the Data Subject with the following information:

1. the identity and the contact details of the Controller and, where applicable, of the Controller's representative;
2. the contact details of the data protection officer, where applicable;
3. the purposes of the processing for which the personal data are intended as well as the legal basis for the processing;
4. the categories of personal data concerned;
5. the recipients or categories of recipients of the personal data, if any;
6. where applicable, that the Controller intends to transfer personal data to a recipient in a third country or international organisation and the existence or absence of an adequacy decision by the Commission, or in the case of transfers referred to in Article 46 or 47, or the second subparagraph of Article 49, reference to the appropriate or suitable safeguards and the means to obtain a copy of them or where they have been made available.

2. In addition to the information referred to in paragraph 1, the Controller shall provide the Data Subject with the following information necessary to ensure fair and transparent processing in respect of the Data Subject:

1. the period for which the personal data will be stored, or if that is not possible, the criteria used to determine that period;
2. where the processing is based on point (f) of Article 6, the legitimate interests pursued by the Controller or by a third party;
3. the existence of the right to request from the Controller access to and rectification or erasure of personal data or restriction of processing concerning the Data Subject and to object to processing as well as the right to data portability;
4. where processing is based on point (a) of Article 6 or point (a) of Article 9, the existence of the right to withdraw consent at any time, without affecting the lawfulness of processing based on consent before its withdrawal;
5. the right to lodge a complaint with a Supervisory Authority;
6. from which source the personal data originate, and if applicable, whether it came from publicly accessible sources;
7. the existence of automated decision-making, including profiling, referred to in Article 22 and, at least in those cases, meaningful information about the logic involved, as well as the significance and the envisaged consequences of such processing for the Data Subject.

3. The Controller shall provide the information referred to in paragraphs 1 and 2:

1. within a reasonable period after obtaining the personal data, but at the latest within one month, having regard to the specific circumstances in which the personal data are processed;
2. if the personal data are to be used for communication with the Data Subject, at the latest at the time of the first communication to that Data Subject; or
3. if a disclosure to another recipient is envisaged, at the latest when the personal data are first disclosed.
4. Where the Controller intends to further process the personal data for a purpose other than that for which the personal data were obtained, the Controller shall provide the Data Subject prior to that further

processing with information on that other purpose and with any relevant further information as referred to in paragraph 2.

Paragraphs 1 to 4 shall not apply where and insofar as:

1. the Data Subject already has the information;
2. the provision of such information proves impossible or would involve a disproportionate effort, in particular for processing for archiving purposes in the public interest, scientific or historical research purposes or statistical purposes, subject to the conditions and safeguards referred to in Article 89 or in so far as the obligation referred to in paragraph 1 of this Article is likely to render impossible or seriously impair the achievement of the objectives of that processing. In such cases the Controller shall take appropriate measures to protect the Data Subject's rights and freedoms and legitimate interests, including making the information publicly available;
3. obtaining or disclosure is expressly laid down by Union or Member State law to which the Controller is subject and which provides appropriate measures to protect the Data Subject's legitimate interests; or
4. where the personal data must remain confidential subject to an obligation of professional secrecy regulated by Union or Member State law, including a statutory obligation of secrecy.

Article 15: Right of access by the Data Subject

1. The Data Subject shall have the right to obtain from the Controller confirmation as to whether or not personal data concerning him or her are being processed, and, where that is the case, access to the personal data and the following information:

   1. the purposes of the processing;
   2. the categories of personal data concerned;
   3. the recipients or categories of recipient to whom the personal data have been or will be disclosed, in particular recipients in third countries or international organisations;
   4. where possible, the envisaged period for which the personal data will be stored, or, if not possible, the criteria used to determine that period;
   5. the existence of the right to request from the Controller rectification or erasure of personal data or restriction of processing of personal data concerning the Data Subject or to object to such processing;
   6. the right to lodge a complaint with a Supervisory Authority;
   7. where the personal data are not collected from the Data Subject, any available information as to their source;
   8. the existence of automated decision-making, including profiling, referred to in Article 22 and, at least in those cases, meaningful information about the logic involved, as well as the significance and the envisaged consequences of such processing for the Data Subject.

2. Where personal data are transferred to a third country or to an international organisation, the Data Subject shall have the right to be informed of the appropriate safeguards pursuant to Article 46 relating to the transfer.

3. The Controller shall provide a copy of the personal data undergoing processing. For any further copies requested by the Data Subject, the Controller may charge a reasonable fee based on administrative costs. Where the Data Subject makes the request by electronic means, and unless otherwise requested by the Data Subject, the information shall be provided in a commonly used electronic form.

4. The right to obtain a copy referred to in paragraph 3 shall not adversely affect the rights and freedoms of others.

Article 16: Right to rectification

The Data Subject shall have the right to obtain from the Controller without undue delay the rectification of inaccurate personal data concerning him or her. Taking into account the purposes of the processing, the Data Subject shall have the right to have incomplete personal data completed, including by means of providing a supplementary statement.

Article 17: Right to erasure ('right to be forgotten')

1.   The Data Subject shall have the right to obtain from the Controller the erasure of personal data concerning him or her without undue delay and the Controller shall have the obligation to erase personal data without undue delay where one of the following grounds applies:

 1.   the personal data are no longer necessary in relation to the purposes for which they were collected or otherwise processed;
 2.   the Data Subject withdraws consent on which the processing is based according to point (a) of Article 6, or point (a) of Article 9, and where there is no other legal ground for the processing;
 3.   the Data Subject objects to the processing pursuant to Article 21 and there are no overriding legitimate grounds for the processing, or the Data Subject objects to the processing pursuant to Article 21;
 4.   the personal data have been unlawfully processed;
 5.   the personal data have to be erased for compliance with a legal obligation in Union or Member State law to which the Controller is subject;
 6.   the personal data have been collected in relation to the offer of information society services referred to in Article 8.

2.   Where the Controller has made the personal data public and is obliged pursuant to paragraph 1 to erase the personal data, the Controller, taking account of available technology and the cost of implementation, shall take reasonable steps, including technical measures, to inform Controllers which are processing the personal data that the Data Subject has requested the erasure by such Controllers of any links to, or copy or replication of, those personal data.

3.   Paragraphs 1 and 2 shall not apply to the extent that processing is necessary:

 1.   for exercising the right of freedom of expression and information;
 2.   for compliance with a legal obligation which requires processing by Union or Member State law to which the Controller is subject or for the performance of a task carried out in the public interest or in the exercise of official authority vested in the Controller;
 3.   for reasons of public interest in the area of public health in accordance with points (h) and (i) of Article 9;

 4.   for archiving purposes in the public interest, scientific or historical research purposes or statistical purposes in accordance with Article 89 in so far as the right referred to in paragraph 1 is likely to render impossible or seriously impair the achievement of the objectives of that processing; or
 5.   for the establishment, exercise or defence of legal claims.

Article 18: Right to restriction of processing

1.   The Data Subject shall have the right to obtain from the Controller restriction of processing where one of the following applies:

1. the accuracy of the personal data is contested by the Data Subject, for a period enabling the Controller to verify the accuracy of the personal data;
2. the processing is unlawful and the Data Subject opposes the erasure of the personal data and requests the restriction of their use instead;
3. the Controller no longer needs the personal data for the purposes of the processing, but they are required by the Data Subject for the establishment, exercise or defence of legal claims;
4. the Data Subject has objected to processing pursuant to Article 21 pending the verification whether the legitimate grounds of the Controller override those of the Data Subject.

2. Where processing has been restricted under paragraph 1, such personal data shall, with the exception of storage, only be processed with the Data Subject's consent or for the establishment, exercise or defence of legal claims or for the protection of the rights of another natural or legal person or for reasons of important public interest of the Union or of a Member State.

3. A Data Subject who has obtained restriction of processing pursuant to paragraph 1 shall be informed by the Controller before the restriction of processing is lifted.

Article 19: Notification obligation regarding rectification or erasure of personal data or restriction of processing

The Controller shall communicate any rectification or erasure of personal data or restriction of processing carried out in accordance with Article 16, Article 17 and Article 18 to each recipient to whom the personal data have been disclosed, unless this proves impossible or involves disproportionate effort. The Controller shall inform the Data Subject about those recipients if the Data Subject requests it.

Article 20: Right to data portability

1. The Data Subject shall have the right to receive the personal data concerning him or her, which he or she has provided to a Controller, in a structured, commonly used and machine-readable format and have the right to transmit those data to another Controller without hindrance from the Controller to which the personal data have been provided, where:

1. the processing is based on consent pursuant to point (a) of Article 6 or point (a) of Article 9(2) or on a contract pursuant to point (b) of Article 6; and
2. the processing is carried out by automated means.

2. In exercising his or her right to data portability pursuant to paragraph 1, the Data Subject shall have the right to have the personal data transmitted directly from one Controller to another, where technically feasible.

3. The exercise of the right referred to in paragraph 1 of this Article shall be without prejudice to Article 17. That right shall not apply to processing necessary for the performance of a task carried out in the public interest or in the exercise of official authority vested in the Controller.

4. The right referred to in paragraph 1 shall not adversely affect the rights and freedoms of others.

Article 21: Right to object

1.   The Data Subject shall have the right to object, on grounds relating to his or her particular situation, at any time to processing of personal data concerning him or her which is based on point (e) or (f) of Article 6(1), including profiling based on those provisions. The Controller shall no longer process the personal data unless the Controller demonstrates compelling legitimate grounds for the processing which override the interests, rights and freedoms of the Data Subject or for the establishment, exercise or defence of legal claims.

2.   Where personal data are processed for direct marketing purposes, the Data Subject shall have the right to object at any time to processing of personal data concerning him or her for such marketing, which includes profiling to the extent that it is related to such direct marketing.

3.   Where the Data Subject objects to processing for direct marketing purposes, the personal data shall no longer be processed for such purposes.

4.   At the latest at the time of the first communication with the Data Subject, the right referred to in paragraphs 1 and 2 shall be explicitly brought to the attention of the Data Subject and shall be presented clearly and separately from any other information.

5.   In the context of the use of information society services, and notwithstanding Directive 2002/58/EC, the Data Subject may exercise his or her right to object by automated means using technical specifications.

6.   Where personal data are processed for scientific or historical research purposes or statistical purposes pursuant to Article 89(1), the Data Subject, on grounds relating to his or her particular situation, shall have the right to object to processing of personal data concerning him or her, unless the processing is necessary for the performance of a task carried out for reasons of public interest.

Article 22: Automated individual decision-making, including profiling

1.   The Data Subject shall have the right not to be subject to a decision based solely on automated processing, including profiling, which produces legal effects concerning him or her or similarly significantly affects him or her.

2.   Paragraph 1 shall not apply if the decision:

    1.   is necessary for entering into, or performance of, a contract between the Data Subject and a data Controller;
    2.   is authorised by Union or Member State law to which the Controller is subject and which also lays down suitable measures to safeguard the Data Subject's rights and freedoms and legitimate interests; or
    3.   is based on the Data Subject's explicit consent.

3.   In the cases referred to in points (a) and (c) of paragraph 2, the data Controller shall implement suitable measures to safeguard the Data Subject's rights and freedoms and legitimate interests, at least the right to obtain human intervention on the part of the Controller, to express his or her point of view and to contest the decision.

4.   Decisions referred to in paragraph 2 shall not be based on special categories of personal data referred to in Article 9(2)1), unless point (a) or (g) of Article 9(2) applies and suitable measures to safeguard the Data Subject's rights and freedoms and legitimate interests are in place.

Article 23: Restrictions

1.   Union or Member State law to which the data Controller or Processor is subject may restrict by way of a legislative measure the scope of the obligations and rights provided for in Articles 12 to 22 and Article 34, as well as Article 5 in so far as its provisions correspond to the rights and obligations provided for in Articles 12 to 22, when such a restriction respects the essence of the fundamental rights and freedoms and is a necessary and proportionate measure in a democratic society to safeguard:

1.   national security;
2.   defence;
3.   public security;
4.   the prevention, investigation, detection or prosecution of criminal offences or the execution of criminal penalties, including the safeguarding against and the prevention of threats to public security;
5.   other important objectives of general public interest of the Union or of a Member State, in particular an important economic or financial interest of the Union or of a Member State, including monetary, budgetary and taxation a matters, public health and social security;
6.   the protection of judicial independence and judicial proceedings;
7.   the prevention, investigation, detection and prosecution of breaches of ethics for regulated professions;
8.   a monitoring, inspection or regulatory function connected, even occasionally, to the exercise of official authority in the cases referred to in points (a) to (e) and (g);
9.   the protection of the Data Subject or the rights and freedoms of others;
10.   the enforcement of civil law claims.

2.   In particular, any legislative measure referred to in paragraph 1 shall contain specific provisions at least, where relevant, as to:

1.   the purposes of the processing or categories of processing;
2.   he categories of personal data;
3.   the scope of the restrictions introduced;
4.   the safeguards to prevent abuse or unlawful access or transfer;
5.   the specification of the Controller or categories of Controllers;
6.   the storage periods and the applicable safeguards taking into account the nature, scope and purposes of the processing or categories of processing;
7.   the risks to the rights and freedoms of Data Subjects; and
8.   the right of Data Subjects to be informed about the restriction, unless that may be prejudicial to the purpose of the restriction.

IV: CONTROLLER AND PROCESSOR

Article 24: Responsibility of the Controller

1.   Taking into account the nature, scope, context and purposes of processing as well as the risks of varying likelihood and severity for the rights and freedoms of Natural Persons, the Controller shall implement appropriate technical and organisational measures to ensure and to be able to demonstrate that processing is performed in accordance with this Regulation. Those measures shall be reviewed and updated where necessary.

2.   Where proportionate in relation to processing activities, the measures referred to in paragraph 1 shall include the implementation of appropriate data protection policies by the Controller.

3.   Adherence to approved codes of conduct as referred to in Article 40 or approved certification mechanisms as referred to in Article 42 may be used as an element by which to demonstrate compliance with the obligations of the Controller.

Article 25: Data protection by design and by default

1.   Taking into account the state of the art, the cost of implementation and the nature, scope, context and purposes of processing as well as the risks of varying likelihood and severity for rights and freedoms of Natural Persons posed by the processing, the Controller shall, both at the time of the determination of the means for processing and at the time of the processing itself, implement appropriate technical and organisational measures, such as pseudonymisation, which are designed to implement data-protection principles, such as data minimisation, in an effective manner and to integrate the necessary safeguards into the processing in order to meet the requirements of this Regulation and protect the rights of Data Subjects.

2.   The Controller shall implement appropriate technical and organisational measures for ensuring that, by default, only personal data which are necessary for each specific purpose of the processing are processed. That obligation applies to the amount of personal data collected, the extent of their processing, the period of their storage and their accessibility. In particular, such measures shall ensure that by default personal data are not made accessible without the individual's intervention to an indefinite number of Natural Persons.

3.   An approved certification mechanism pursuant to Article 42 may be used as an element to demonstrate compliance with the requirements set out in paragraphs 1 and 2 of this Article.

Article 26: Joint Controllers

1.   Where two or more Controllers jointly determine the purposes and means of processing, they shall be joint Controllers. They shall in a transparent manner determine their respective responsibilities for compliance with the obligations under this Regulation, in particular as regards the exercising of the rights of the Data Subject and their respective duties to provide the information referred to in Articles 13 and 14, by means of an arrangement between them unless, and in so far as, the respective responsibilities of the Controllers are determined by Union or Member State law to which the Controllers are subject. The arrangement may designate a contact point for Data Subjects.

2.   The arrangement referred to in paragraph 1 shall duly reflect the respective roles and relationships of the joint Controllers vis-à-vis the Data Subjects. The essence of the arrangement shall be made available to the Data Subject.

3.   Irrespective of the terms of the arrangement referred to in paragraph 1, the Data Subject may exercise his or her rights under this Regulation in respect of and against each of the Controllers.

Article 27: Representatives of Controllers or Processors not established in the Union

1.   Where Article 3(2) applies, the Controller or the Processor shall designate in writing a representative in the Union.

2.   The obligation laid down in paragraph 1 of this Article shall not apply to:

   1.   processing which is occasional, does not include, on a large scale, processing of special categories of data as referred to in Article 9(1) or processing of personal data relating to criminal convictions and offences referred to in Article 10, and is unlikely to result in a risk to the rights and freedoms of Natural Persons, taking into account the nature, context, scope and purposes of the processing; or
   2.   a public authority or body.

3.   The representative shall be established in one of the Member States where the Data Subjects, whose personal data are processed in relation to the offering of goods or services to them, or whose behaviour is monitored, are.

4.   The representative shall be mandated by the Controller or Processor to be addressed in addition to or instead of the Controller or the Processor by, in particular, supervisory authorities and Data Subjects, on all issues related to processing, for the purposes of ensuring compliance with this Regulation.

5.   The designation of a representative by the Controller or Processor shall be without prejudice to legal actions which could be initiated against the Controller or the Processor themselves.

Article 28: Processor

1.   Where processing is to be carried out on behalf of a Controller, the Controller shall use only Processors providing sufficient guarantees to implement appropriate technical and organisational measures in such a manner that processing will meet the requirements of this Regulation and ensure the protection of the rights of the Data Subject.

2.   The Processor shall not engage another Processor without prior specific or general written authorisation of the Controller. In the case of general written authorisation, the Processor shall inform the Controller of any intended changes concerning the addition or replacement of other Processors, thereby giving the Controller the opportunity to object to such changes.

3.   Processing by a Processor shall be governed by a contract or other legal act under Union or Member State law, that is binding on the Processor with regard to the Controller and that sets out the subject-matter and duration of the processing, the nature and purpose of the processing, the type of personal data and categories of Data Subjects and the obligations and rights of the Controller. That contract or other legal act shall stipulate, in particular, that the Processor:

   1.   processes the personal data only on documented instructions from the Controller, including with regard to transfers of personal data to a third country or an international organisation, unless required to do so by Union or Member State law to which the Processor is subject; in such a case, the Processor shall inform the Controller of that legal requirement before processing, unless that law prohibits such information on important grounds of public interest;
   2.   ensures that persons authorised to process the personal data have committed themselves to confidentiality or are under an appropriate statutory obligation of confidentiality;
   3.   takes all measures required pursuant to Article 32;

4. respects the conditions referred to in paragraphs 2 and 4 for engaging another Processor;

5. taking into account the nature of the processing, assists the Controller by appropriate technical and organisational measures, insofar as this is possible, for the fulfilment of the Controller's obligation to respond to requests for exercising the Data Subject's rights laid down in Chapter III;

6. assists the Controller in ensuring compliance with the obligations pursuant to Articles 32 to 36 taking into account the nature of processing and the information available to the Processor;

7. at the choice of the Controller, deletes or returns all the personal data to the Controller after the end of the provision of services relating to processing, and deletes existing copies unless Union or Member State law requires storage of the personal data;

8. makes available to the Controller all information necessary to demonstrate compliance with the obligations laid down in this Article and allow for and contribute to audits, including inspections, conducted by the Controller or another auditor mandated by the Controller.

With regard to point (h) of the first subparagraph, the Processor shall immediately inform the Controller if, in its opinion, an instruction infringes this Regulation or other Union or Member State data protection provisions.

4. Where a Processor engages another Processor for carrying out specific processing activities on behalf of the Controller, the same data protection obligations as set out in the contract or other legal act between the Controller and the Processor as referred to in paragraph 3 shall be imposed on that other Processor by way of a contract or other legal act under Union or Member State law, in particular providing sufficient guarantees to implement appropriate technical and organisational measures in such a manner that the processing will meet the requirements of this Regulation. Where that other Processor fails to fulfil its data protection obligations, the initial Processor shall remain fully liable to the Controller for the performance of that other Processor's obligations.

5. Adherence of a Processor to an approved code of conduct as referred to in Article 40 or an approved certification mechanism as referred to in Article 42 may be used as an element by which to demonstrate sufficient guarantees as referred to in paragraphs 1 and 4 of this Article.

6. Without prejudice to an individual contract between the Controller and the Processor, the contract or the other legal act referred to in paragraphs 3 and 4 of this Article may be based, in whole or in part, on standard contractual clauses referred to in paragraphs 7 and 8 of this Article, including when they are part of a certification granted to the Controller or Processor pursuant to Articles 42 and 43.

7. The Commission may lay down standard contractual clauses for the matters referred to in paragraph 3 and 4 of this Article and in accordance with the examination procedure referred to in Article 93(2).

8. A Supervisory Authority may adopt standard contractual clauses for the matters referred to in paragraph 3 and 4 of this Article and in accordance with the consistency mechanism referred to in Article 63.

9. The contract or the other legal act referred to in paragraphs 3 and 4 shall be in writing, including in electronic form.

10. Without prejudice to Articles 82, 83 and 84, if a Processor infringes this Regulation by determining the purposes and means of processing, the Processor shall be considered to be a Controller in respect of that processing.

Article 29: Processing under the authority of the Controller or Processor

The Processor and any person acting under the authority of the Controller or of the Processor, who has access to personal data, shall not process those data except on instructions from the Controller, unless required to do so by

Union or Member State law.

Article 30: Records of processing activities

1.   Each Controller and, where applicable, the Controller's representative, shall maintain a record of processing activities under its responsibility. That record shall contain all of the following information:

   1.   the name and contact details of the Controller and, where applicable, the joint Controller, the Controller's representative and the data protection officer;
   2.   the purposes of the processing;
   3.   a description of the categories of Data Subjects and of the categories of personal data;
   4.   the categories of recipients to whom the personal data have been or will be disclosed including recipients in third countries or international organisations;
   5.   where applicable, transfers of personal data to a third country or an international organisation, including the identification of that third country or international organisation and, in the case of transfers referred to in the second subparagraph of Article 49(1), the documentation of suitable safeguards;
   6.   where possible, the envisaged time limits for erasure of the different categories of data;
   7.   where possible, a general description of the technical and organisational security measures referred to in Article 32(1).

2.   Each Processor and, where applicable, the Processor's representative shall maintain a record of all categories of processing activities carried out on behalf of a Controller, containing:

   1.   the name and contact details of the Processor or Processors and of each Controller on behalf of which the Processor is acting, and, where applicable, of the Controller's or the Processor's representative, and the data protection officer;
   2.   the categories of processing carried out on behalf of each Controller;
   3.   where applicable, transfers of personal data to a third country or an international organisation, including the identification of that third country or international organisation and, in the case of transfers referred to in the second subparagraph of Article 49(1), the documentation of suitable safeguards;
   4.   where possible, a general description of the technical and organisational security measures referred to in Article 32(1).
   5.   The records referred to in paragraphs 1 and 2 shall be in writing, including in electronic form.
   6.   The Controller or the Processor and, where applicable, the Controller's or the Processor's representative, shall make the record available to the Supervisory Authority on request.
   7.   The obligations referred to in paragraphs 1 and 2 shall not apply to an enterprise or an organisation employing fewer than 250 persons unless the processing it carries out is likely to result in a risk to the rights and freedoms of Data Subjects, the processing is not occasional, or the processing includes special categories of data as referred to in Article 9(1) or personal data relating to criminal convictions and offences referred to in Article 10.

Article 31: Cooperation with the Supervisory Authority

The Controller and the Processor and, where applicable, their representatives, shall cooperate, on request, with the Supervisory Authority in the performance of its tasks.

Article 32: Security of processing

1.   Taking into account the state of the art, the costs of implementation and the nature, scope, context and purposes of processing as well as the risk of varying likelihood and severity for the rights and freedoms of Natural Persons, the Controller and the Processor shall implement appropriate technical and organisational measures to ensure a level of security appropriate to the risk, including inter alia as appropriate:

1.   the pseudonymisation and encryption of personal data;
2.   the ability to ensure the ongoing confidentiality, integrity, availability and resilience of processing systems and services;
3.   the ability to restore the availability and access to personal data in a timely manner in the event of a physical or technical incident;
4.   a process for regularly testing, assessing and evaluating the effectiveness of technical and organisational measures for ensuring the security of the processing.

2.   In assessing the appropriate level of security account shall be taken in particular of the risks that are presented by processing, in particular from accidental or unlawful destruction, loss, alteration, unauthorised disclosure of, or access to personal data transmitted, stored or otherwise processed.

3.   Adherence to an approved code of conduct as referred to in Article 40 or an approved certification mechanism as referred to in Article 42 may be used as an element by which to demonstrate compliance with the requirements set out in paragraph 1 of this Article.

4.   The Controller and Processor shall take steps to ensure that any Natural Person acting under the authority of the Controller or the Processor who has access to personal data does not process them except on instructions from the Controller, unless he or she is required to do so by Union or Member State law.

Article 33: Notification of a personal data breach to the Supervisory Authority

1.   In the case of a personal data breach, the Controller shall without undue delay and, where feasible, not later than 72 hours after having become aware of it, notify the personal data breach to the Supervisory Authority competent in accordance with Article 55, unless the personal data breach is unlikely to result in a risk to the rights and freedoms of Natural Persons. Where the notification to the Supervisory Authority is not made within 72 hours, it shall be accompanied by reasons for the delay.

2.   The Processor shall notify the Controller without undue delay after becoming aware of a personal data breach.

3.   The notification referred to in paragraph 1 shall at least:

1.   describe the nature of the personal data breach including where possible, the categories and approximate number of Data Subjects concerned and the categories and approximate number of personal data records concerned;
2.   communicate the name and contact details of the data protection officer or other contact point where more information can be obtained;
3.   describe the likely consequences of the personal data breach;
4.   describe the measures taken or proposed to be taken by the Controller to address the personal data breach, including, where appropriate, measures to mitigate its possible adverse effects.
5.   Where, and in so far as, it is not possible to provide the information at the same time, the information may be provided in phases without undue further delay.

6. The Controller shall document any personal data breaches, comprising the facts relating to the personal data breach, its effects and the remedial action taken. That documentation shall enable the Supervisory Authority to verify compliance with this Article.

Article 34: Communication of a personal data breach to the Data Subject

1. When the personal data breach is likely to result in a high risk to the rights and freedoms of Natural Persons, the Controller shall communicate the personal data breach to the Data Subject without undue delay.

2. The communication to the Data Subject referred to in paragraph 1 of this Article shall describe in clear and plain language the nature of the personal data breach and contain at least the information and measures referred to in points (b), (c) and (d) of Article 33(3).

3. The communication to the Data Subject referred to in paragraph 1 shall not be required if any of the following conditions are met:

    1. the Controller has implemented appropriate technical and organisational protection measures, and those measures were applied to the personal data affected by the personal data breach, in particular those that render the personal data unintelligible to any person who is not authorised to access it, such as encryption;
    2. the Controller has taken subsequent measures which ensure that the high risk to the rights and freedoms of Data Subjects referred to in paragraph 1 is no longer likely to materialise;
    3. it would involve disproportionate effort. In such a case, there shall instead be a public communication or similar measure whereby the Data Subjects are informed in an equally effective manner.
    4. If the Controller has not already communicated the personal data breach to the Data Subject, the Supervisory Authority, having considered the likelihood of the personal data breach resulting in a high risk, may require it to do so or may decide that any of the conditions referred to in paragraph 3 are met.

Article 35: Data protection impact assessment

1. Where a type of processing in particular using new technologies, and taking into account the nature, scope, context and purposes of the processing, is likely to result in a high risk to the rights and freedoms of Natural Persons, the Controller shall, prior to the processing, carry out an assessment of the impact of the envisaged processing operations on the protection of personal data. A single assessment may address a set of similar processing operations that present similar high risks.

2. The Controller shall seek the advice of the data protection officer, where designated, when carrying out a data protection impact assessment.

3. A data protection impact assessment referred to in paragraph 1 shall in particular be required in the case of:

    1. a systematic and extensive evaluation of personal aspects relating to Natural Persons which is based on automated processing, including profiling, and on which decisions are based that produce legal effects concerning the Natural Person or similarly significantly affect the Natural Person;
    2. processing on a large scale of special categories of data referred to in Article 9(1), or of personal data relating to criminal convictions and offences referred to in Article 10; or
    3. a systematic monitoring of a publicly accessible area on a large scale.
    4. The Supervisory Authority shall establish and make public a list of the kind of processing operations which are subject to the requirement for a data protection impact assessment pursuant to paragraph 1. The Supervisory Authority shall communicate those lists to the Board referred to in Article 68.

5.   The Supervisory Authority may also establish and make public a list of the kind of processing operations for which no data protection impact assessment is required. The Supervisory Authority shall communicate those lists to the Board.

6.   Prior to the adoption of the lists referred to in paragraphs 4 and 5, the competent Supervisory Authority shall apply the consistency mechanism referred to in Article 63where such lists involve processing activities which are related to the offering of goods or services to Data Subjects or to the monitoring of their behaviour in several Member States, or may substantially affect the free movement of personal data within the Union.

7.   The assessment shall contain at least:

1.   a systematic description of the envisaged processing operations and the purposes of the processing, including, where applicable, the legitimate interest pursued by the Controller;

2.   an assessment of the necessity and proportionality of the processing operations in relation to the purposes;

3.   an assessment of the risks to the rights and freedoms of Data Subjects referred to in paragraph 1; and

4.   the measures envisaged to address the risks, including safeguards, security measures and mechanisms to ensure the protection of personal data and to demonstrate compliance with this Regulation taking into account the rights and legitimate interests of Data Subjects and other persons concerned.

8.   Compliance with approved codes of conduct referred to in Article 40 by the relevant Controllers or Processors shall be taken into due account in assessing the impact of the processing operations performed by such Controllers or Processors, in particular for the purposes of a data protection impact assessment.

9.   Where appropriate, the Controller shall seek the views of Data Subjects or their representatives on the intended processing, without prejudice to the protection of commercial or public interests or the security of processing operations.

10.   Where processing pursuant to point (c) or (e) of Article 6(1) has a legal basis in Union law or in the law of the Member State to which the Controller is subject, that law regulates the specific processing operation or set of operations in question, and a data protection impact assessment has already been carried out as part of a general impact assessment in the context of the adoption of that legal basis, paragraphs 1 to 7 shall not apply unless Member States deem it to be necessary to carry out such an assessment prior to processing activities.

11.   Where necessary, the Controller shall carry out a review to assess if processing is performed in accordance with the data protection impact assessment at least when there is a change of the risk represented by processing operations.

Article 36: Prior consultation

1.   The Controller shall consult the Supervisory Authority prior to processing where a data protection impact assessment under Article 35 indicates that the processing would result in a high risk in the absence of measures taken by the Controller to mitigate the risk.

2.   Where the Supervisory Authority is of the opinion that the intended processing referred to in paragraph 1 would infringe this Regulation, in particular where the Controller has insufficiently identified or mitigated the risk, the Supervisory Authority shall, within period of up to eight weeks of receipt of the request for consultation, provide written advice to the Controller and, where applicable to the Processor, and may use any of its powers referred to in Article 58. That period may be extended by six weeks, taking into account the complexity of the intended processing. The Supervisory Authority shall inform the Controller and, where applicable, the Processor, of any such extension within one month of receipt of the request for consultation together with the reasons for the delay. Those periods

may be suspended until the Supervisory Authority has obtained information it has requested for the purposes of the consultation.

3.   When consulting the Supervisory Authority pursuant to paragraph 1, the Controller shall provide the Supervisory Authority with:

1. where applicable, the respective responsibilities of the Controller, joint Controllers and Processors involved in the processing, in particular for processing within a group of undertakings;
2. the purposes and means of the intended processing;
3. the measures and safeguards provided to protect the rights and freedoms of Data Subjects pursuant to this Regulation;
4. where applicable, the contact details of the data protection officer;
5. the data protection impact assessment provided for in Article 35; and
6. any other information requested by the Supervisory Authority.

4.   Member States shall consult the Supervisory Authority during the preparation of a proposal for a legislative measure to be adopted by a national parliament, or of a regulatory measure based on such a legislative measure, which relates to processing.

5.   Notwithstanding paragraph 1, Member State law may require Controllers to consult with, and obtain prior authorisation from, the Supervisory Authority in relation to processing by a Controller for the performance of a task carried out by the Controller in the public interest, including processing in relation to social protection and public health.

Article 37: Designation of the data protection officer

1.   The Controller and the Processor shall designate a data protection officer in any case where:

1. the processing is carried out by a public authority or body, except for courts acting in their judicial capacity;
2. the core activities of the Controller or the Processor consist of processing operations which, by virtue of their nature, their scope and/or their purposes, require regular and systematic monitoring of Data Subjects on a large scale; or
3. the core activities of the Controller or the Processor consist of processing on a large scale of special categories of data pursuant to Article 9 and personal data relating to criminal convictions and offences referred to in Article 10.

2.   A group of undertakings may appoint a single data protection officer provided that a data protection officer is easily accessible from each establishment.

3.   Where the Controller or the Processor is a public authority or body, a single data protection officer may be designated for several such authorities or bodies, taking account of their organisational structure and size.

4.   In cases other than those referred to in paragraph 1, the Controller or Processor or associations and other bodies representing categories of Controllers or Processors may or, where required by Union or Member State law shall, designate a data protection officer. The data protection officer may act for such associations and other bodies representing Controllers or Processors.

5.   The data protection officer shall be designated on the basis of professional qualities and, in particular, expert knowledge of data protection law and practices and the ability to fulfil the tasks referred to in Article 39.

6.   The data protection officer may be a staff member of the Controller or Processor, or fulfil the tasks on the basis of a service contract.

7.   The Controller or the Processor shall publish the contact details of the data protection officer and communicate them to the Supervisory Authority.

Article 38: Position of the data protection officer

1.   The Controller and the Processor shall ensure that the data protection officer is involved, properly and in a timely manner, in all issues which relate to the protection of personal data.

2.   The Controller and Processor shall support the data protection officer in performing the tasks referred to in Article 39 by providing resources necessary to carry out those tasks and access to personal data and processing operations, and to maintain his or her expert knowledge.

3.   The Controller and Processor shall ensure that the data protection officer does not receive any instructions regarding the exercise of those tasks. He or she shall not be dismissed or penalised by the Controller or the Processor for performing his tasks. The data protection officer shall directly report to the highest management level of the Controller or the Processor.

4.   Data subjects may contact the data protection officer with regard to all issues related to processing of their personal data and to the exercise of their rights under this Regulation.

5.   The data protection officer shall be bound by secrecy or confidentiality concerning the performance of his or her tasks, in accordance with Union or Member State law.

6.   The data protection officer may fulfil other tasks and duties. The Controller or Processor shall ensure that any such tasks and duties do not result in a conflict of interests.

Article 39: Tasks of the data protection officer

1.   The data protection officer shall have at least the following tasks:

   1.   to inform and advise the Controller or the Processor and the employees who carry out processing of their obligations pursuant to this Regulation and to other Union or Member State data protection provisions;
   2.   to monitor compliance with this Regulation, with other Union or Member State data protection provisions and with the policies of the Controller or Processor in relation to the protection of personal data, including the assignment of responsibilities, awareness-raising and training of staff involved in processing operations, and the related audits;
   3.   to provide advice where requested as regards the data protection impact assessment and monitor its performance pursuant to Article 35;
   4.   to cooperate with the Supervisory Authority;
   5.   to act as the contact point for the Supervisory Authority on issues relating to processing, including the prior consultation referred to in Article 36, and to consult, where appropriate, with regard to any other matter.

2.   The data protection officer shall in the performance of his or her tasks have due regard to the risk associated with processing operations, taking into account the nature, scope, context and purposes of processing.

Article 40: Codes of conduct

1.   The Member States, the supervisory authorities, the Board and the Commission shall encourage the drawing up of codes of conduct intended to contribute to the proper application of this Regulation, taking account of the specific features of the various processing sectors and the specific needs of micro, small and medium-sized enterprises.

2.   Associations and other bodies representing categories of Controllers or Processors may prepare codes of conduct, or amend or extend such codes, for the purpose of specifying the application of this Regulation, such as with regard to:

1.   fair and transparent processing;
2.   the legitimate interests pursued by Controllers in specific contexts;
3.   the collection of personal data;
4.   the pseudonymisation of personal data;
5.   the information provided to the public and to Data Subjects;
6.   the exercise of the rights of Data Subjects;
7.   the information provided to, and the protection of, children, and the manner in which the consent of the holders of parental responsibility over children is to be obtained;
8.   the measures and procedures referred to in Articles 24 and 25 and the measures to ensure security of processing referred to in Article 32;
9.   the notification of personal data breaches to supervisory authorities and the communication of such personal data breaches to Data Subjects;
10.   the transfer of personal data to third countries or international organisations; or
11.   out-of-court proceedings and other dispute resolution procedures for resolving disputes between Controllers and Data Subjects with regard to processing, without prejudice to the rights of Data Subjects pursuant to Articles 77 and 79.

3.   In addition to adherence by Controllers or Processors subject to this Regulation, codes of conduct approved pursuant to paragraph 5 of this Article and having general validity pursuant to paragraph 9 of this Article may also be adhered to by Controllers or Processors that are not subject to this Regulation pursuant to Article 3 in order to provide appropriate safeguards within the framework of personal data transfers to third countries or international organisations under the terms referred to in point (e) of Article 46(2). Such Controllers or Processors shall make binding and enforceable commitments, via contractual or other legally binding instruments, to apply those appropriate safeguards including with regard to the rights of Data Subjects.

4.   A code of conduct referred to in paragraph 2 of this Article shall contain mechanisms which enable the body referred to in Article 41(1) to carry out the mandatory monitoring of compliance with its provisions by the Controllers or Processors which undertake to apply it, without prejudice to the tasks and powers of supervisory authorities competent pursuant to Article 55 or 56.

5.   Associations and other bodies referred to in paragraph 2 of this Article which intend to prepare a code of conduct or to amend or extend an existing code shall submit the draft code, amendment or extension to the Supervisory Authority which is competent pursuant to Article 55. The Supervisory Authority shall provide an opinion on whether the draft code, amendment or extension complies with this Regulation and shall approve that draft code, amendment or extension if it finds that it provides sufficient appropriate safeguards.

6.   Where the draft code, or amendment or extension is approved in accordance with paragraph 5, and where the code of conduct concerned does not relate to processing activities in several Member States, the Supervisory Authority shall register and publish the code.

7.   Where a draft code of conduct relates to processing activities in several Member States, the Supervisory Authority which is competent pursuant to Article 55 shall, before approving the draft code, amendment or extension, submit it in the procedure referred to in Article 63 to the Board which shall provide an opinion on whether the draft code, amendment or extension complies with this Regulation or, in the situation referred to in paragraph 3 of this Article, provides appropriate safeguards.

8.   Where the opinion referred to in paragraph 7 confirms that the draft code, amendment or extension complies with this Regulation, or, in the situation referred to in paragraph 3, provides appropriate safeguards, the Board shall submit its opinion to the Commission.

9.   The Commission may, by way of implementing acts, decide that the approved code of conduct, amendment or extension submitted to it pursuant to paragraph 8 of this Article have general validity within the Union. Those implementing acts shall be adopted in accordance with the examination procedure set out in Article 93(2).

10.   The Commission shall ensure appropriate publicity for the approved codes which have been decided as having general validity in accordance with paragraph 9.

11.   The Board shall collate all approved codes of conduct, amendments and extensions in a register and shall make them publicly available by way of appropriate means.

Article 41: *Monitoring of approved codes of conduct*

1.   Without prejudice to the tasks and powers of the competent Supervisory Authority under Articles 57 and 58, the monitoring of compliance with a code of conduct pursuant to Article 40 may be carried out by a body which has an appropriate level of expertise in relation to the subject-matter of the code and is accredited for that purpose by the competent Supervisory Authority.

2.   A body as referred to in paragraph 1 may be accredited to monitor compliance with a code of conduct where that body has:

   1. demonstrated its independence and expertise in relation to the subject-matter of the code to the satisfaction of the competent Supervisory Authority;
   2. established procedures which allow it to assess the eligibility of Controllers and Processors concerned to apply the code, to monitor their compliance with its provisions and to periodically review its operation;
   3. established procedures and structures to handle complaints about infringements of the code or the manner in which the code has been, or is being, implemented by a Controller or Processor, and to make those procedures and structures transparent to Data Subjects and the public; and
   4. demonstrated to the satisfaction of the competent Supervisory Authority that its tasks and duties do not result in a conflict of interests.

3.   The competent Supervisory Authority shall submit the draft criteria for accreditation of a body as referred to in paragraph 1 of this Article to the Board pursuant to the consistency mechanism referred to in Article 63.

4.   Without prejudice to the tasks and powers of the competent Supervisory Authority and the provisions of Chapter VIII, a body as referred to in paragraph 1 of this Article shall, subject to appropriate safeguards, take appropriate action in cases of infringement of the code by a Controller or Processor, including suspension or exclusion of the Controller or Processor concerned from the code. It shall inform the competent Supervisory Authority of such actions and the reasons for taking them.

5.   The competent Supervisory Authority shall revoke the accreditation of a body as referred to in paragraph 1 if

the conditions for accreditation are not, or are no longer, met or where actions taken by the body infringe this Regulation.

6.   This Article shall not apply to processing carried out by public authorities and bodies.

Article 42: Certification

1.   The Member States, the supervisory authorities, the Board and the Commission shall encourage, in particular at Union level, the establishment of data protection certification mechanisms and of data protection seals and marks, for the purpose of demonstrating compliance with this Regulation of processing operations by Controllers and Processors. The specific needs of micro, small and medium-sized enterprises shall be taken into account.

2.   In addition to adherence by Controllers or Processors subject to this Regulation, data protection certification mechanisms, seals or marks approved pursuant to paragraph 5 of this Article may be established for the purpose of demonstrating the existence of appropriate safeguards provided by Controllers or Processors that are not subject to this Regulation pursuant to Article 3 within the framework of personal data transfers to third countries or international organisations under the terms referred to in point (f) of Article 46(2). Such Controllers or Processors shall make binding and enforceable commitments, via contractual or other legally binding instruments, to apply those appropriate safeguards, including with regard to the rights of Data Subjects.

3.   The certification shall be voluntary and available via a process that is transparent.

4.   A certification pursuant to this Article does not reduce the responsibility of the Controller or the Processor for compliance with this Regulation and is without prejudice to the tasks and powers of the supervisory authorities which are competent pursuant to Article 55 or 56.

5.   A certification pursuant to this Article shall be issued by the certification bodies referred to in Article 43 or by the competent Supervisory Authority, on the basis of criteria approved by that competent Supervisory Authority pursuant to Article 58(3) or by the Board pursuant to Article 63. Where the criteria are approved by the Board, this may result in a common certification, the European Data Protection Seal.

6.   The Controller or Processor which submits its processing to the certification mechanism shall provide the certification body referred to in Article 43, or where applicable, the competent Supervisory Authority, with all information and access to its processing activities which are necessary to conduct the certification procedure.

7.   Certification shall be issued to a Controller or Processor for a maximum period of three years and may be renewed, under the same conditions, provided that the relevant requirements continue to be met. Certification shall be withdrawn, as applicable, by the certification bodies referred to in Article 43 or by the competent Supervisory Authority where the requirements for the certification are not or are no longer met.

8.   The Board shall collate all certification mechanisms and data protection seals and marks in a register and shall make them publicly available by any appropriate means.

Article 43: Certification bodies

1.   Without prejudice to the tasks and powers of the competent Supervisory Authority under Articles 57 and 58, certification bodies which have an appropriate level of expertise in relation to data protection shall, after informing the Supervisory Authority in order to allow it to exercise its powers pursuant to point (h) of Article 58(2) where necessary, issue and renew certification. Member States shall ensure that those certification bodies are accredited

by one or both of the following:

1. the Supervisory Authority which is competent pursuant to Article 55 or 56;
2. the national accreditation body named in accordance with Regulation (EC) No 765/2008 of the European Parliament and of the Council[1] in accordance with EN-ISO/IEC 17065/2012 and with the additional requirements established by the Supervisory Authority which is competent pursuant to Article 55 or 56.

2.   Certification bodies referred to in paragraph 1 shall be accredited in accordance with that paragraph only where they have:

1. demonstrated their independence and expertise in relation to the subject-matter of the certification to the satisfaction of the competent Supervisory Authority;
2. undertaken to respect the criteria referred to in Article 42(5) and approved by the Supervisory Authority which is competent pursuant to Article 55 or 56 or by the Board pursuant to Article 63;
3. established procedures for the issuing, periodic review and withdrawal of data protection certification, seals and marks;
4. established procedures and structures to handle complaints about infringements of the certification or the manner in which the certification has been, or is being, implemented by the Controller or Processor, and to make those procedures and structures transparent to Data Subjects and the public; and
5. demonstrated, to the satisfaction of the competent Supervisory Authority, that their tasks and duties do not result in a conflict of interests.

3.   The accreditation of certification bodies as referred to in paragraphs 1 and 2 of this Article shall take place on the basis of criteria approved by the Supervisory Authority which is competent pursuant to Article 55 or 56 or by the Board pursuant to Article 63. In the case of accreditation pursuant to point (b) of paragraph 1 of this Article, those requirements shall complement those envisaged in Regulation (EC) No 765/2008 and the technical rules that describe the methods and procedures of the certification bodies.

4.   The certification bodies referred to in paragraph 1 shall be responsible for the proper assessment leading to the certification or the withdrawal of such certification without prejudice to the responsibility of the Controller or Processor for compliance with this Regulation. The accreditation shall be issued for a maximum period of five years and may be renewed on the same conditions provided that the certification body meets the requirements set out in this Article.

5.   The certification bodies referred to in paragraph 1 shall provide the competent supervisory authorities with the reasons for granting or withdrawing the requested certification.

6.   The requirements referred to in paragraph 3 of this Article and the criteria referred to in Article 42(5) shall be made public by the Supervisory Authority in an easily accessible form. The supervisory authorities shall also transmit those requirements and criteria to the Board. The Board shall collate all certification mechanisms and data protection seals in a register and shall make them publicly available by any appropriate means.

7.   Without prejudice to Chapter VIII, the competent Supervisory Authority or the national accreditation body shall revoke an accreditation of a certification body pursuant to paragraph 1 of this Article where the conditions for the accreditation are not, or are no longer, met or where actions taken by a certification body infringe this Regulation.
8.   The Commission shall be empowered to adopt delegated acts in accordance with Article 92 for the purpose of specifying the requirements to be taken into account for the data protection certification mechanisms referred to in Article 42(1).

9.   The Commission may adopt implementing acts laying down technical standards for certification mechanisms

and data protection seals and marks, and mechanisms to promote and recognise those certification mechanisms, seals and marks. Those implementing acts shall be adopted in accordance with the examination procedure referred to in Article 93(2).

V: TRANSFERS OF PERSONAL DATA TO THIRD COUNTRIES OR INTERNATIONAL ORGANISATIONS

Article 44: General principle for transfers

Any transfer of personal data which are undergoing processing or are intended for processing after transfer to a third country or to an international organisation shall take place only if, subject to the other provisions of this Regulation, the conditions laid down in this Chapter are complied with by the Controller and Processor, including for onward transfers of personal data from the third country or an international organisation to another third country or to another international organisation. All provisions in this Chapter shall be applied in order to ensure that the level of protection of Natural Persons guaranteed by this Regulation is not undermined.

Article 45: Transfers on the basis of an adequacy decision

1.   A transfer of personal data to a third country or an international organisation may take place where the Commission has decided that the third country, a territory or one or more specified sectors within that third country, or the international organisation in question ensures an adequate level of protection. Such a transfer shall not require any specific authorisation.

2.   When assessing the adequacy of the level of protection, the Commission shall, in particular, take account of the following elements:

   1.   the rule of law, respect for human rights and fundamental freedoms, relevant legislation, both general and sectoral, including concerning public security, defence, national security and criminal law and the access of public authorities to personal data, as well as the implementation of such legislation, data protection rules, professional rules and security measures, including rules for the onward transfer of personal data to another third country or international organisation which are complied with in that country or international organisation, case-law, as well as effective and enforceable Data Subject rights and effective administrative and judicial redress for the Data Subjects whose personal data are being transferred;
   2.   the existence and effective functioning of one or more independent supervisory authorities in the third country or to which an international organisation is subject, with responsibility for ensuring and enforcing compliance with the data protection rules, including adequate enforcement powers, for assisting and advising the Data Subjects in exercising their rights and for cooperation with the supervisory authorities of the Member States; and
   3.   the international commitments the third country or international organisation concerned has entered into, or other obligations arising from legally binding conventions or instruments as well as from its participation in multilateral or regional systems, in particular in relation to the protection of personal data.

3.   The Commission, after assessing the adequacy of the level of protection, may decide, by means of implementing act, that a third country, a territory or one or more specified sectors within a third country, or an international organisation ensures an adequate level of protection within the meaning of paragraph 2 of this Article. The implementing act shall provide for a mechanism for a periodic review, at least every four years, which shall take into account all relevant developments in the third country or international organisation. The implementing act shall specify its territorial and sectoral application and, where applicable, identify the Supervisory Authority or authorities referred to in point (b) of paragraph 2 of this Article. The implementing act shall be adopted in accordance with the examination procedure referred to in Article 93(2).

4.   The Commission shall, on an ongoing basis, monitor developments in third countries and international

organisations that could affect the functioning of decisions adopted pursuant to paragraph 3 of this Article and decisions adopted on the basis of Article 25(6) of Directive 95/46/EC.

5.   The Commission shall, where available information reveals, in particular following the review referred to in paragraph 3 of this Article, that a third country, a territory or one or more specified sectors within a third country, or an international organisation no longer ensures an adequate level of protection within the meaning of paragraph 2 of this Article, to the extent necessary, repeal, amend or suspend the decision referred to in paragraph 3 of this Article by means of implementing acts without retro-active effect. Those implementing acts shall be adopted in accordance with the examination procedure referred to in Article 93(2).

On duly justified imperative grounds of urgency, the Commission shall adopt immediately applicable implementing acts in accordance with the procedure referred to in Article 93(3).

6.   The Commission shall enter into consultations with the third country or international organisation with a view to remedying the situation giving rise to the decision made pursuant to paragraph 5.

7.   A decision pursuant to paragraph 5 of this Article is without prejudice to transfers of personal data to the third country, a territory or one or more specified sectors within that third country, or the international organisation in question pursuant to Articles 46 to 49.

8.   The Commission shall publish in the Official Journal of the European Union and on its website a list of the third countries, territories and specified sectors within a third country and international organisations for which it has decided that an adequate level of protection is or is no longer ensured.

9.   Decisions adopted by the Commission on the basis of Article 25(6) of Directive 95/46/EC shall remain in force until amended, replaced or repealed by a Commission Decision adopted in accordance with paragraph 3 or 5 of this Article.

Article 46: Transfers subject to appropriate safeguards

1.   In the absence of a decision pursuant to Article 45(3), a Controller or Processor may transfer personal data to a third country or an international organisation only if the Controller or Processor has provided appropriate safeguards, and on condition that enforceable Data Subject rights and effective legal remedies for Data Subjects are available.

2.   The appropriate safeguards referred to in paragraph 1 may be provided for, without requiring any specific authorisation from a Supervisory Authority, by:

1.   a legally binding and enforceable instrument between public authorities or bodies;
2.   binding corporate rules in accordance with Article 47;
3.   standard data protection clauses adopted by the Commission in accordance with the examination procedure referred to in Article 93(2);
4.   standard data protection clauses adopted by a Supervisory Authority and approved by the Commission pursuant to the examination procedure referred to in Article 93(2);
5.   an approved code of conduct pursuant to Article 40 together with binding and enforceable commitments of the Controller or Processor in the third country to apply the appropriate safeguards, including as regards Data Subjects' rights; or
6.   an approved certification mechanism pursuant to Article 42 together with binding and enforceable commitments of the Controller or Processor in the third country to apply the appropriate safeguards, including as regards Data Subjects' rights.

3.   Subject to the authorisation from the competent Supervisory Authority, the appropriate safeguards referred to in paragraph 1 may also be provided for, in particular, by:

1.   contractual clauses between the Controller or Processor and the Controller, Processor or the recipient of the personal data in the third country or international organisation; or
2.   provisions to be inserted into administrative arrangements between public authorities or bodies which include enforceable and effective Data Subject rights.

4.   The Supervisory Authority shall apply the consistency mechanism referred to in Article 63 in the cases referred to in paragraph 3 of this Article.

5.   Authorisations by a Member State or Supervisory Authority on the basis of Article 26(2) of Directive 95/46/EC shall remain valid until amended, replaced or repealed, if necessary, by that Supervisory Authority. Decisions adopted by the Commission on the basis of Article 26(4) of Directive 95/46/EC shall remain in force until amended, replaced or repealed, if necessary, by a Commission Decision adopted in accordance with paragraph 2 of this Article.

Article 47: Binding corporate rules

1.   The competent Supervisory Authority shall approve binding corporate rules in accordance with the consistency mechanism set out in Article 63, provided that they:

1.   are legally binding and apply to and are enforced by every member concerned of the group of undertakings, or group of enterprises engaged in a joint economic activity, including their employees;
2.   expressly confer enforceable rights on Data Subjects with regard to the processing of their personal data; and
3.   fulfil the requirements laid down in paragraph 2.

2.   The binding corporate rules referred to in paragraph 1 shall specify at least:

1.   the structure and contact details of the group of undertakings, or group of enterprises engaged in a joint economic activity and of each of its members;
2.   the data transfers or set of transfers, including the categories of personal data, the type of processing and its purposes, the type of Data Subjects affected and the identification of the third country or countries in question;
3.   their legally binding nature, both internally and externally;
4.   the application of the general data protection principles, in particular purpose limitation, data minimisation, limited storage periods, data quality, data protection by design and by default, legal basis for processing, processing of special categories of personal data, measures to ensure data security, and the requirements in respect of onward transfers to bodies not bound by the binding corporate rules;
5.   the rights of Data Subjects in regard to processing and the means to exercise those rights, including the right not to be subject to decisions based solely on automated processing, including profiling in accordance with Article 22, the right to lodge a complaint with the competent Supervisory Authority and before the competent courts of the Member States in accordance with Article 79, and to obtain redress and, where appropriate, compensation for a breach of the binding corporate rules;
6.   the acceptance by the Controller or Processor established on the territory of a Member State of liability for any breaches of the binding corporate rules by any member concerned not established in the Union; the Controller or the Processor shall be exempt from that liability, in whole or in part, only if it proves that that member is not responsible for the event giving rise to the damage;
7.   how the information on the binding corporate rules, in particular on the provisions referred to in points (d), (e) and (f) of this paragraph is provided to the Data Subjects in addition to Articles 13 and 14;

8. the tasks of any data protection officer designated in accordance with Article 37 or any other person or entity in charge of the monitoring compliance with the binding corporate rules within the group of undertakings, or group of enterprises engaged in a joint economic activity, as well as monitoring training and complaint-handling;

9. the complaint procedures;

10. the mechanisms within the group of undertakings, or group of enterprises engaged in a joint economic activity for ensuring the verification of compliance with the binding corporate rules. Such mechanisms shall include data protection audits and methods for ensuring corrective actions to protect the rights of the Data Subject. Results of such verification should be communicated to the person or entity referred to in point (h) and to the board of the controlling undertaking of a group of undertakings, or of the group of enterprises engaged in a joint economic activity, and should be available upon request to the competent Supervisory Authority;

11. the mechanisms for reporting and recording changes to the rules and reporting those changes to the Supervisory Authority;

12. the cooperation mechanism with the Supervisory Authority to ensure compliance by any member of the group of undertakings, or group of enterprises engaged in a joint economic activity, in particular by making available to the Supervisory Authority the results of verifications of the measures referred to in point (j);

13. the mechanisms for reporting to the competent Supervisory Authority any legal requirements to which a member of the group of undertakings, or group of enterprises engaged in a joint economic activity is subject in a third country which are likely to have a substantial adverse effect on the guarantees provided by the binding corporate rules; and

14. the appropriate data protection training to personnel having permanent or regular access to personal data.

3.   The Commission may specify the format and procedures for the exchange of information between Controllers, Processors and supervisory authorities for binding corporate rules within the meaning of this Article. Those implementing acts shall be adopted in accordance with the examination procedure set out in Article 93(2).

Article 48: Transfers or disclosures not authorised by Union law

Any judgment of a court or tribunal and any decision of an administrative authority of a third country requiring a Controller or Processor to transfer or disclose personal data may only be recognised or enforceable in any manner if based on an international agreement, such as a mutual legal assistance treaty, in force between the requesting third country and the Union or a Member State, without prejudice to other grounds for transfer pursuant to this Chapter.

Article 49: Derogations for specific situations

1. In the absence of an adequacy decision pursuant to Article 45(3), or of appropriate safeguards pursuant to Article 46, including binding corporate rules, a transfer or a set of transfers of personal data to a third country or an international organisation shall take place only on one of the following conditions:

1. the Data Subject has explicitly consented to the proposed transfer, after having been informed of the possible risks of such transfers for the Data Subject due to the absence of an adequacy decision and appropriate safeguards;

2. the transfer is necessary for the performance of a contract between the Data Subject and the Controller or the implementation of pre-contractual measures taken at the Data Subject's request;

3. the transfer is necessary for the conclusion or performance of a contract concluded in the interest of the Data Subject between the Controller and another natural or legal person;

4. the transfer is necessary for important reasons of public interest;

5. the transfer is necessary for the establishment, exercise or defence of legal claims;

6. the transfer is necessary in order to protect the vital interests of the Data Subject or of other persons, where the Data Subject is physically or legally incapable of giving consent;

7. the transfer is made from a register which according to Union or Member State law is intended to provide information to the public and which is open to consultation either by the public in general or by any person who can demonstrate a legitimate interest, but only to the extent that the conditions laid down by Union or Member State law for consultation are fulfilled in the particular case.

Where a transfer could not be based on a provision in Article 45 or 46, including the provisions on binding corporate rules, and none of the derogations for a specific situation referred to in the first subparagraph of this paragraph is applicable, a transfer to a third country or an international organisation may take place only if the transfer is not repetitive, concerns only a limited number of Data Subjects, is necessary for the purposes of compelling legitimate interests pursued by the Controller which are not overridden by the interests or rights and freedoms of the Data Subject, and the Controller has assessed all the circumstances surrounding the data transfer and has on the basis of that assessment provided suitable safeguards with regard to the protection of personal data. The Controller shall inform the Supervisory Authority of the transfer. The Controller shall, in addition to providing the information referred to in Articles 13 and 14, inform the Data Subject of the transfer and on the compelling legitimate interests pursued.

2. A transfer pursuant to point (g) of the first subparagraph of paragraph 1 shall not involve the entirety of the personal data or entire categories of the personal data contained in the register. Where the register is intended for consultation by persons having a legitimate interest, the transfer shall be made only at the request of those persons or if they are to be the recipients.

3. Points (a), (b) and (c) of the first subparagraph of paragraph 1 and the second subparagraph thereof shall not apply to activities carried out by public authorities in the exercise of their public powers.

4. The public interest referred to in point (d) of the first subparagraph of paragraph 1 shall be recognised in Union law or in the law of the Member State to which the Controller is subject.

5. In the absence of an adequacy decision, Union or Member State law may, for important reasons of public interest, expressly set limits to the transfer of specific categories of personal data to a third country or an international organisation. Member States shall notify such provisions to the Commission.

6. The Controller or Processor shall document the assessment as well as the suitable safeguards referred to in the second subparagraph of paragraph 1 of this Article in the records referred to in Article 30.

Article 50: International cooperation for the protection of personal data

1. In relation to third countries and international organisations, the Commission and supervisory authorities shall take appropriate steps to:

1. develop international cooperation mechanisms to facilitate the effective enforcement of legislation for the protection of personal data;

2. provide international mutual assistance in the enforcement of legislation for the protection of personal data, including through notification, complaint referral, investigative assistance and information exchange, subject to appropriate safeguards for the protection of personal data and other fundamental rights and freedoms;

3. engage relevant stakeholders in discussion and activities aimed at furthering international cooperation in the enforcement of legislation for the protection of personal data;

4. promote the exchange and documentation of personal data protection legislation and practice, including on

jurisdictional conflicts with third countries

VI: INDEPENDENT SUPERVISORY AUTHORITIES

Article 51: Supervisory Authority

1.   Each Member State shall provide for one or more independent public authorities to be responsible for monitoring the application of this Regulation, in order to protect the fundamental rights and freedoms of Natural Persons in relation to processing and to facilitate the free flow of personal data within the Union ('Supervisory Authority').

2.   Each Supervisory Authority shall contribute to the consistent application of this Regulation throughout the Union. For that purpose, the supervisory authorities shall cooperate with each other and the Commission in accordance with Chapter VII.

3.   Where more than one Supervisory Authority is established in a Member State, that Member State shall designate the Supervisory Authority which is to represent those authorities in the Board and shall set out the mechanism to ensure compliance by the other authorities with the rules relating to the consistency mechanism referred to in Article 63.

4.   Each Member State shall notify to the Commission the provisions of its law which it adopts pursuant to this Chapter, by 25 May 2018 and, without delay, any subsequent amendment affecting them.

Article 52: Independence

1.   Each Supervisory Authority shall act with complete independence in performing its tasks and exercising its powers in accordance with this Regulation.

2.   The member or members of each Supervisory Authority shall, in the performance of their tasks and exercise of their powers in accordance with this Regulation, remain free from external influence, whether direct or indirect, and shall neither seek nor take instructions from anybody.

3.   Member or members of each Supervisory Authority shall refrain from any action incompatible with their duties and shall not, during their term of office, engage in any incompatible occupation, whether gainful or not.

4.   Each Member State shall ensure that each Supervisory Authority is provided with the human, technical and financial resources, premises and infrastructure necessary for the effective performance of its tasks and exercise of its powers, including those to be carried out in the context of mutual assistance, cooperation and participation in the Board.

5.   Each Member State shall ensure that each Supervisory Authority chooses and has its own staff which shall be subject to the exclusive direction of the member or members of the Supervisory Authority concerned.

6.   Each Member State shall ensure that each Supervisory Authority is subject to financial control which does not affect its independence and that it has separate, public annual budgets, which may be part of the overall state or national budge

Article 53: General conditions for members of Supervisory Authority

1.   Member States shall provide for each member of their supervisory authorities to be appointed by means of a transparent procedure by:

– their parliament;
– their government;
– their head of State; or
– an independent body entrusted with the appointment under Member State law.

2.   Each member shall have the qualifications, experience and skills, in particular in the area of the protection of personal data, required to perform its duties and exercise its powers.

3.   The duties of a member shall end in the event of the expiry of the term of office, resignation or compulsory retirement, in accordance with the law of the Member State concerned.

4.   A member shall be dismissed only in cases of serious misconduct or if the member no longer fulfils the conditions required for the performance of the duties.

Article 54: Rules on the establishment of the Supervisory Authority

1.   Each Member State shall provide by law for all of the following:

   1.   the establishment of each Supervisory Authority;
   2.   the qualifications and eligibility conditions required to be appointed as member of each Supervisory Authority;
   3.   the rules and procedures for the appointment of the member or members of each Supervisory Authority;
   4.   the duration of the term of the member or members of each Supervisory Authority of no less than four years, except for the first appointment after 24 May 2016, part of which may take place for a shorter period where that is necessary to protect the independence of the Supervisory Authority by means of a staggered appointment procedure;
   5.   whether and, if so, for how many terms the member or members of each Supervisory Authority is eligible for reappointment;
   6.   the conditions governing the obligations of the member or members and staff of each Supervisory Authority, prohibitions on actions, occupations and benefits incompatible therewith during and after the term of office and rules governing the cessation of employment.

2.   The member or members and the staff of each Supervisory Authority shall, in accordance with Union or Member State law, be subject to a duty of professional secrecy both during and after their term of office, with regard to any confidential information which has come to their knowledge in the course of the performance of their tasks or exercise of their powers. During their term of office, that duty of professional secrecy shall in particular apply to reporting by Natural Persons of infringements of this Regulation.

Article 55: Competence

1.   Each Supervisory Authority shall be competent for the performance of the tasks assigned to and the exercise of the powers conferred on it in accordance with this Regulation on the territory of its own Member State.

2.   Where processing is carried out by public authorities or private bodies acting on the basis of point (c) or (e) of Article 6(1), the Supervisory Authority of the Member State concerned shall be competent. In such cases Article 56 does not apply.

3.   Supervisory authorities shall not be competent to supervise processing operations of courts acting in their judicial capacity.

Article 56: Competence of the lead Supervisory Authority

1.   Without prejudice to Article 55, the Supervisory Authority of the main establishment or of the single establishment of the Controller or Processor shall be competent to act as lead Supervisory Authority for the cross-border processing carried out by that Controller or Processor in accordance with the procedure provided in Article 60.

2.   By derogation from paragraph 1, each Supervisory Authority shall be competent to handle a complaint lodged with it or a possible infringement of this Regulation, if the subject matter relates only to an establishment in its Member State or substantially affects Data Subjects only in its Member State.

3.   In the cases referred to in paragraph 2 of this Article, the Supervisory Authority shall inform the lead Supervisory Authority without delay on that matter. Within a period of three weeks after being informed the lead Supervisory Authority shall decide whether or not it will handle the case in accordance with the procedure provided in Article 60, taking into account whether or not there is an establishment of the Controller or Processor in the Member State of which the Supervisory Authority informed it.

4.   Where the lead Supervisory Authority decides to handle the case, the procedure provided in Article 60 shall apply. The Supervisory Authority which informed the lead Supervisory Authority may submit to the lead Supervisory Authority a draft for a decision. The lead Supervisory Authority shall take utmost account of that draft when preparing the draft decision referred to in Article 60(3).

5.   Where the lead Supervisory Authority decides not to handle the case, the Supervisory Authority which informed the lead Supervisory Authority shall handle it according to Articles 61 and 62.

6.   The lead Supervisory Authority shall be the sole interlocutor of the Controller or Processor for the cross-border processing carried out by that Controller or Processor.

Article 57: Tasks

1.   Without prejudice to other tasks set out under this Regulation, each Supervisory Authority shall on its territory:

   1.   monitor and enforce the application of this Regulation;
   2.   promote public awareness and understanding of the risks, rules, safeguards and rights in relation to processing. Activities addressed specifically to children shall receive specific attention;
   3.   advise, in accordance with Member State law, the national parliament, the government, and other institutions and bodies on legislative and administrative measures relating to the protection of Natural Persons' rights and freedoms with regard to processing;
   4.   promote the awareness of Controllers and Processors of their obligations under this Regulation;
   5.   upon request, provide information to any Data Subject concerning the exercise of their rights under this Regulation and, if appropriate, cooperate with the supervisory authorities in other Member States to that end;
   6.   handle complaints lodged by a Data Subject, or by a body, organisation or association in accordance with Article 80, and investigate, to the extent appropriate, the subject matter of the complaint and inform the complainant of the progress and the outcome of the investigation within a reasonable period, in particular if further investigation or coordination with another Supervisory Authority is necessary;
   7.   cooperate with, including sharing information and provide mutual assistance to, other supervisory authorities with a view to ensuring the consistency of application and enforcement of this Regulation;

8. conduct investigations on the application of this Regulation, including on the basis of information received from another Supervisory Authority or other public authority;

9. monitor relevant developments, insofar as they have an impact on the protection of personal data, in particular the development of information and communication technologies and commercial practices;

10. adopt standard contractual clauses referred to in Article 28(8) and in point (d) of Article 46(2);

11. establish and maintain a list in relation to the requirement for data protection impact assessment pursuant to Article 35(4);

12. give advice on the processing operations referred to in Article 36(2);

13. encourage the drawing up of codes of conduct pursuant to Article 40(1) and provide an opinion and approve such codes of conduct which provide sufficient safeguards, pursuant to Article 40(5);

14. encourage the establishment of data protection certification mechanisms and of data protection seals and marks pursuant to Article 42(1), and approve the criteria of certification pursuant to Article 42(5);

15. where applicable, carry out a periodic review of certifications issued in accordance with Article 42(7);

16. draft and publish the criteria for accreditation of a body for monitoring codes of conduct pursuant to Article 41 and of a certification body pursuant to Article 43;

17. conduct the accreditation of a body for monitoring codes of conduct pursuant to Article 41 and of a certification body pursuant to Article 43;

18. authorise contractual clauses and provisions referred to in Article 46(3);

19. approve binding corporate rules pursuant to Article 47;

20. contribute to the activities of the Board;

21. keep internal records of infringements of this Regulation and of measures taken in accordance with Article 58(2); and

22. fulfil any other tasks related to the protection of personal data.

2. Each Supervisory Authority shall facilitate the submission of complaints referred to in point (f) of paragraph 1 by measures such as a complaint submission form which can also be completed electronically, without excluding other means of communication.

3. The performance of the tasks of each Supervisory Authority shall be free of charge for the Data Subject and, where applicable, for the data protection officer.

4. Where requests are manifestly unfounded or excessive, in particular because of their repetitive character, the Supervisory Authority may charge a reasonable fee based on administrative costs, or refuse to act on the request. The Supervisory Authority shall bear the burden of demonstrating the manifestly unfounded or excessive character of the request.

Article 58: Powers

1. Each Supervisory Authority shall have all of the following investigative powers:

    1. to order the Controller and the Processor, and, where applicable, the Controller's or the Processor's representative to provide any information it requires for the performance of its tasks;

    2. to carry out investigations in the form of data protection audits;

    3. to carry out a review on certifications issued pursuant to Article 42(7);

    4. to notify the Controller or the Processor of an alleged infringement of this Regulation;

    5. to obtain, from the Controller and the Processor, access to all personal data and to all information necessary for the performance of its tasks;

    6. to obtain access to any premises of the Controller and the Processor, including to any data processing equipment and means, in accordance with Union or Member State procedural law.

2.   Each Supervisory Authority shall have all of the following corrective powers:

1.   to issue warnings to a Controller or Processor that intended processing operations are likely to infringe provisions of this Regulation;
2.   to issue reprimands to a Controller or a Processor where processing operations have infringed provisions of this Regulation;
3.   to order the Controller or the Processor to comply with the Data Subject's requests to exercise his or her rights pursuant to this Regulation;
4.   to order the Controller or Processor to bring processing operations into compliance with the provisions of this Regulation, where appropriate, in a specified manner and within a specified period;
5.   to order the Controller to communicate a personal data breach to the Data Subject;
6.   to impose a temporary or definitive limitation including a ban on processing;
7.   to order the rectification or erasure of personal data or restriction of processing pursuant to Articles 16, 17 and 18 and the notification of such actions to recipients to whom the personal data have been disclosed pursuant to Article 17(2) and Article 19;
8.   to withdraw a certification or to order the certification body to withdraw a certification issued pursuant to Articles 42 and 43, or to order the certification body not to issue certification if the requirements for the certification are not or are no longer met;
9.   to impose an administrative fine pursuant to Article 83, in addition to, or instead of measures referred to in this paragraph, depending on the circumstances of each individual case;
10. to order the suspension of data flows to a recipient in a third country or to an international organisation.

3.   Each Supervisory Authority shall have all of the following authorisation and advisory powers:

1.   to advise the Controller in accordance with the prior consultation procedure referred to in Article 36;
2.   to issue, on its own initiative or on request, opinions to the national parliament, the Member State government or, in accordance with Member State law, to other institutions and bodies as well as to the public on any issue related to the protection of personal data;
3.   to authorise processing referred to in Article 36(5), if the law of the Member State requires such prior authorisation;
4.   to issue an opinion and approve draft codes of conduct pursuant to Article 40(5);
5.   to accredit certification bodies pursuant to Article 43
6.   to issue certifications and approve criteria of certification in accordance with Article 42(5);
7.   to adopt standard data protection clauses referred to in Article 28(8) and in point (d) of Article 46(2);
8.   to authorise contractual clauses referred to in point (a) of Article 46(3);
9.   to authorise administrative arrangements referred to in point (b) of Article 46(3);
10. to approve binding corporate rules pursuant to Article 47.

4.   The exercise of the powers conferred on the Supervisory Authority pursuant to this Article shall be subject to appropriate safeguards, including effective judicial remedy and due process, set out in Union and Member State law in accordance with the Charter.

5.   Each Member State shall provide by law that its Supervisory Authority shall have the power to bring infringements of this Regulation to the attention of the judicial authorities and where appropriate, to commence or engage otherwise in legal proceedings, in order to enforce the provisions of this Regulation.

6.   Each Member State may provide by law that its Supervisory Authority shall have additional powers to those referred to in paragraphs 1, 2 and 3. The exercise of those powers shall not impair the effective operation of Chapter VII.

Article 59: Activity reports

Each Supervisory Authority shall draw up an annual report on its activities, which may include a list of types of infringement notified and types of measures taken in accordance with Article 58(2). Those reports shall be transmitted to the national parliament, the government and other authorities as designated by Member State law. They shall be made available to the public, to the Commission and to the Board.

VII: COOPERATION AND CONSISTENCY

Article 60: Cooperation between the lead Supervisory Authority and the other supervisory authorities concerned

1.   The lead Supervisory Authority shall cooperate with the other supervisory authorities concerned in accordance with this Article in an endeavour to reach consensus. The lead Supervisory Authority and the supervisory authorities concerned shall exchange all relevant information with each other.

2.   The lead Supervisory Authority may request at any time other supervisory authorities concerned to provide mutual assistance pursuant to Article 61 and may conduct joint operations pursuant to Article 62, in particular for carrying out investigations or for monitoring the implementation of a measure concerning a Controller or Processor established in another Member State.

3.   The lead Supervisory Authority shall, without delay, communicate the relevant information on the matter to the other supervisory authorities concerned. It shall without delay submit a draft decision to the other supervisory authorities concerned for their opinion and take due account of their views.

4.   Where any of the other supervisory authorities concerned within a period of four weeks after having been consulted in accordance with paragraph 3 of this Article, expresses a relevant and reasoned objection to the draft decision, the lead Supervisory Authority shall, if it does not follow the relevant and reasoned objection or is of the opinion that the objection is not relevant or reasoned, submit the matter to the consistency mechanism referred to in Article 63.

5.   Where the lead Supervisory Authority intends to follow the relevant and reasoned objection made, it shall submit to the other supervisory authorities concerned a revised draft decision for their opinion. That revised draft decision shall be subject to the procedure referred to in paragraph 4 within a period of two weeks.

6.   Where none of the other supervisory authorities concerned has objected to the draft decision submitted by the lead Supervisory Authority within the period referred to in paragraphs 4 and 5, the lead Supervisory Authority and the supervisory authorities concerned shall be deemed to be in agreement with that draft decision and shall be bound by it.

7.   The lead Supervisory Authority shall adopt and notify the decision to the main establishment or single establishment of the Controller or Processor, as the case may be and inform the other supervisory authorities concerned and the Board of the decision in question, including a summary of the relevant facts and grounds. The Supervisory Authority with which a complaint has been lodged shall inform the complainant on the decision.

8.   By derogation from paragraph 7, where a complaint is dismissed or rejected, the Supervisory Authority with which the complaint was lodged shall adopt the decision and notify it to the complainant and shall inform the Controller thereof.

9.   Where the lead Supervisory Authority and the supervisory authorities concerned agree to dismiss or reject parts of a complaint and to act on other parts of that complaint, a separate decision shall be adopted for each of those parts of the matter. The lead Supervisory Authority shall adopt the decision for the part concerning actions in relation to the Controller, shall notify it to the main establishment or single establishment of the Controller or Processor on the territory of its Member State and shall inform the complainant thereof, while the Supervisory Authority of the complainant shall adopt the decision for the part concerning dismissal or rejection of that complaint, and shall notify it to that complainant and shall inform the Controller or Processor thereof.

10. After being notified of the decision of the lead Supervisory Authority pursuant to paragraphs 7 and 9, the Controller or Processor shall take the necessary measures to ensure compliance with the decision as regards processing activities in the context of all its establishments in the Union. The Controller or Processor shall notify the measures taken for complying with the decision to the lead Supervisory Authority, which shall inform the other supervisory authorities concerned.

11. Where, in exceptional circumstances, a Supervisory Authority concerned has reasons to consider that there is an urgent need to act in order to protect the interests of Data Subjects, the urgency procedure referred to in Article 66 shall apply.

12. The lead Supervisory Authority and the other supervisory authorities concerned shall supply the information required under this Article to each other by electronic means, using a standardised format.

Article 61: Mutual assistance

1. Supervisory authorities shall provide each other with relevant information and mutual assistance in order to implement and apply this Regulation in a consistent manner, and shall put in place measures for effective cooperation with one another. Mutual assistance shall cover, in particular, information requests and supervisory measures, such as requests to carry out prior authorisations and consultations, inspections and investigations.

2. Each Supervisory Authority shall take all appropriate measures required to reply to a request of another Supervisory Authority without undue delay and no later than one month after receiving the request. Such measures may include, in particular, the transmission of relevant information on the conduct of an investigation.

3. Requests for assistance shall contain all the necessary information, including the purpose of and reasons for the request. Information exchanged shall be used only for the purpose for which it was requested.

4. The requested Supervisory Authority shall not refuse to comply with the request unless:

    1. it is not competent for the subject-matter of the request or for the measures it is requested to execute; or
    2. compliance with the request would infringe this Regulation or Union or Member State law to which the Supervisory Authority receiving the request is subject.

5. The requested Supervisory Authority shall inform the requesting Supervisory Authority of the results or, as the case may be, of the progress of the measures taken in order to respond to the request. The requested Supervisory Authority shall provide reasons for any refusal to comply with a request pursuant to paragraph 4.

6. Requested supervisory authorities shall, as a rule, supply the information requested by other supervisory authorities by electronic means, using a standardised format.

7. Requested supervisory authorities shall not charge a fee for any action taken by them pursuant to a request for mutual assistance. Supervisory authorities may agree on rules to indemnify each other for specific expenditure arising from the provision of mutual assistance in exceptional circumstances.

8. Where a Supervisory Authority does not provide the information referred to in paragraph 5 of this Article within one month of receiving the request of another Supervisory Authority, the requesting Supervisory Authority may adopt a provisional measure on the territory of its Member State in accordance with Article 55(1). In that case, the urgent need to act under Article 66(1) shall be presumed to be met and require an urgent binding decision from the Board pursuant to Article 66(2).

9.   The Commission may, by means of implementing acts, specify the format and procedures for mutual assistance referred to in this Article and the arrangements for the exchange of information by electronic means between supervisory authorities, and between supervisory authorities and the Board, in particular the standardised format referred to in paragraph 6 of this Article. Those implementing acts shall be adopted in accordance with the examination procedure referred to in Article 93(2).

Article 62: Joint operations of supervisory authorities

1.   The supervisory authorities shall, where appropriate, conduct joint operations including joint investigations and joint enforcement measures in which members or staff of the supervisory authorities of other Member States are involved.

2.   Where the Controller or Processor has establishments in several Member States or where a significant number of Data Subjects in more than one Member State are likely to be substantially affected by processing operations, a Supervisory Authority of each of those Member States shall have the right to participate in joint operations. The Supervisory Authority which is competent pursuant to Article 56(1) or (4) shall invite the Supervisory Authority of each of those Member States to take part in the joint operations and shall respond without delay to the request of a Supervisory Authority to participate.

3.   A Supervisory Authority may, in accordance with Member State law, and with the seconding Supervisory Authority's authorisation, confer powers, including investigative powers on the seconding Supervisory Authority's members or staff involved in joint operations or, in so far as the law of the Member State of the host Supervisory Authority permits, allow the seconding Supervisory Authority's members or staff to exercise their investigative powers in accordance with the law of the Member State of the seconding Supervisory Authority. Such investigative powers may be exercised only under the guidance and in the presence of members or staff of the host Supervisory Authority. The seconding Supervisory Authority's members or staff shall be subject to the Member State law of the host Supervisory Authority.

4.   Where, in accordance with paragraph 1, staff of a seconding Supervisory Authority operate in another Member State, the Member State of the host Supervisory Authority shall assume responsibility for their actions, including liability, for any damage caused by them during their operations, in accordance with the law of the Member State in whose territory they are operating.

5.   The Member State in whose territory the damage was caused shall make good such damage under the conditions applicable to damage caused by its own staff. The Member State of the seconding Supervisory Authority whose staff has caused damage to any person in the territory of another Member State shall reimburse that other Member State in full any sums it has paid to the persons entitled on their behalf.

6.   Without prejudice to the exercise of its rights vis-à-vis third parties and with the exception of paragraph 5, each Member State shall refrain, in the case provided for in paragraph 1, from requesting reimbursement from another Member State in relation to damage referred to in paragraph 4.

7.   Where a joint operation is intended and a Supervisory Authority does not, within one month, comply with the obligation laid down in the second sentence of paragraph 2 of this Article, the other supervisory authorities may adopt a provisional measure on the territory of its Member State in accordance with Article 55. In that case, the urgent need to act under Article 66(1) shall be presumed to be met and require an opinion or an urgent binding decision from the Board pursuant to Article 66(2).

Article 63: Consistency mechanism

In order to contribute to the consistent application of this Regulation throughout the Union, the supervisory authorities shall cooperate with each other and, where relevant, with the Commission, through the consistency mechanism as set out in this Section.

Article 64: Opinion of the Board

1.   The Board shall issue an opinion where a competent Supervisory Authority intends to adopt any of the measures below. To that end, the competent Supervisory Authority shall communicate the draft decision to the Board, when it:

    1.   aims to adopt a list of the processing operations subject to the requirement for a data protection impact assessment pursuant to Article 35(4);
    2.   concerns a matter pursuant to Article 40(7) whether a draft code of conduct or an amendment or extension to a code of conduct complies with this Regulation;
    3.   aims to approve the criteria for accreditation of a body pursuant to Article 41(3) or a certification body pursuant to Article 43(3);
    4.   aims to determine standard data protection clauses referred to in point (d) of Article 46(2) and in Article 28(8);
    5.   aims to authorise contractual clauses referred to in point (a) of Article 46(3); or
    6.   aims to approve binding corporate rules within the meaning of Article 47.

2.   Any Supervisory Authority, the Chair of the Board or the Commission may request that any matter of general application or producing effects in more than one Member State be examined by the Board with a view to obtaining an opinion, in particular where a competent Supervisory Authority does not comply with the obligations for mutual assistance in accordance with Article 61 or for joint operations in accordance with Article 62.

3.   In the cases referred to in paragraphs 1 and 2, the Board shall issue an opinion on the matter submitted to it provided that it has not already issued an opinion on the same matter. That opinion shall be adopted within eight weeks by simple majority of the members of the Board. That period may be extended by a further six weeks, taking into account the complexity of the subject matter. Regarding the draft decision referred to in paragraph 1 circulated to the members of the Board in accordance with paragraph 5, a member which has not objected within a reasonable period indicated by the Chair, shall be deemed to be in agreement with the draft decision.

4.   Supervisory authorities and the Commission shall, without undue delay, communicate by electronic means to the Board, using a standardised format any relevant information, including as the case may be a summary of the facts, the draft decision, the grounds which make the enactment of such measure necessary, and the views of other supervisory authorities concerned.

5.   The Chair of the Board shall, without undue, delay inform by electronic means:

    1.   the members of the Board and the Commission of any relevant information which has been communicated to it using a standardised format. The secretariat of the Board shall, where necessary, provide translations of relevant information; and
    2.   the Supervisory Authority referred to, as the case may be, in paragraphs 1 and 2, and the Commission of the opinion and make it public.

6.   The competent Supervisory Authority shall not adopt its draft decision referred to in paragraph 1 within the

period referred to in paragraph 3.

7.   The Supervisory Authority referred to in paragraph 1 shall take utmost account of the opinion of the Board and shall, within two weeks after receiving the opinion, communicate to the Chair of the Board by electronic means whether it will maintain or amend its draft decision and, if any, the amended draft decision, using a standardised format.

8.   Where the Supervisory Authority concerned informs the Chair of the Board within the period referred to in paragraph 7 of this Article that it does not intend to follow the opinion of the Board, in whole or in part, providing the relevant grounds, Article 65(1) shall apply.

Article 65: Dispute resolution by the Board

1.   In order to ensure the correct and consistent application of this Regulation in individual cases, the Board shall adopt a binding decision in the following cases:

   1.   where, in a case referred to in Article 60(4), a Supervisory Authority concerned has raised a relevant and reasoned objection to a draft decision of the lead authority or the lead authority has rejected such an objection as being not relevant or reasoned. The binding decision shall concern all the matters which are the subject of the relevant and reasoned objection, in particular whether there is an infringement of this Regulation;
   2.   where there are conflicting views on which of the supervisory authorities concerned is competent for the main establishment;
   3.   where a competent Supervisory Authority does not request the opinion of the Board in the cases referred to in Article 64(1), or does not follow the opinion of the Board issued under Article 64. In that case, any Supervisory Authority concerned or the Commission may communicate the matter to the Board.

2.   The decision referred to in paragraph 1 shall be adopted within one month from the referral of the subject-matter by a two-thirds majority of the members of the Board. That period may be extended by a further month on account of the complexity of the subject-matter. The decision referred to in paragraph 1 shall be reasoned and addressed to the lead Supervisory Authority and all the supervisory authorities concerned and binding on them.

3.   Where the Board has been unable to adopt a decision within the periods referred to in paragraph 2, it shall adopt its decision within two weeks following the expiration of the second month referred to in paragraph 2 by a simple majority of the members of the Board. Where the members of the Board are split, the decision shall by adopted by the vote of its Chair.

4.   The supervisory authorities concerned shall not adopt a decision on the subject matter submitted to the Board under paragraph 1 during the periods referred to in paragraphs 2 and 3.

5.   The Chair of the Board shall notify, without undue delay, the decision referred to in paragraph 1 to the supervisory authorities concerned. It shall inform the Commission thereof. The decision shall be published on the website of the Board without delay after the Supervisory Authority has notified the final decision referred to in paragraph 6.

6.   The lead Supervisory Authority or, as the case may be, the Supervisory Authority with which the complaint has been lodged shall adopt its final decision on the basis of the decision referred to in paragraph 1 of this Article, without undue delay and at the latest by one month after the Board has notified its decision. The lead Supervisory Authority or, as the case may be, the Supervisory Authority with which the complaint has been lodged, shall inform the Board of the date when its final decision is notified respectively to the Controller or the Processor and to the

Data Subject. The final decision of the supervisory authorities concerned shall be adopted under the terms of Article 60(7), (8) and (9). The final decision shall refer to the decision referred to in paragraph 1 of this Article and shall specify that the decision referred to in that paragraph will be published on the website of the Board in accordance with paragraph 5 of this Article. The final decision shall attach the decision referred to in paragraph 1 of this Article.

Article 66: Urgency procedure

1.   In exceptional circumstances, where a Supervisory Authority concerned considers that there is an urgent need to act in order to protect the rights and freedoms of Data Subjects, it may, by way of derogation from the consistency mechanism referred to in Articles 63, 64 and 65 or the procedure referred to in Article 60, immediately adopt provisional measures intended to produce legal effects on its own territory with a specified period of validity which shall not exceed three months. The Supervisory Authority shall, without delay, communicate those measures and the reasons for adopting them to the other supervisory authorities concerned, to the Board and to the Commission.

2.   Where a Supervisory Authority has taken a measure pursuant to paragraph 1 and considers that final measures need urgently be adopted, it may request an urgent opinion or an urgent binding decision from the Board, giving reasons for requesting such opinion or decision.

3.   Any Supervisory Authority may request an urgent opinion or an urgent binding decision, as the case may be, from the Board where a competent Supervisory Authority has not taken an appropriate measure in a situation where there is an urgent need to act, in order to protect the rights and freedoms of Data Subjects, giving reasons for requesting such opinion or decision, including for the urgent need to act.

4.   By derogation from Article 64(3) and Article 65(2), an urgent opinion or an urgent binding decision referred to in paragraphs 2 and 3 of this Article shall be adopted within two weeks by simple majority of the members of the Board.

Article 67: Exchange of information

1.   The Commission may adopt implementing acts of general scope in order to specify the arrangements for the exchange of information by electronic means between supervisory authorities, and between supervisory authorities and the Board, in particular the standardised format referred to in Article 64.

2.   Those implementing acts shall be adopted in accordance with the examination procedure referred to in Article 93(2).

Article 68: European Data Protection Board

1.   The European Data Protection Board (the 'Board') is hereby established as a body of the Union and shall have legal personality.

2.   The Board shall be represented by its Chair.

3.   The Board shall be composed of the head of one Supervisory Authority of each Member State and of the European Data Protection Supervisor, or their respective representatives.

4.   Where in a Member State more than one Supervisory Authority is responsible for monitoring the application of the provisions pursuant to this Regulation, a joint representative shall be appointed in accordance with that Member State's law.

5.   The Commission shall have the right to participate in the activities and meetings of the Board without voting right. The Commission shall designate a representative. The Chair of the Board shall communicate to the Commission the activities of the Board.

6.   In the cases referred to in Article 65, the European Data Protection Supervisor shall have voting rights only on decisions which concern principles and rules applicable to the Union institutions, bodies, offices and agencies which correspond in substance to those of this Regulation.

Article 69: Independence

1.   The Board shall act independently when performing its tasks or exercising its powers pursuant to Articles 70 and 71.

2.   Without prejudice to requests by the Commission referred to in point (b) of Article 70(1) and in Article 70(2), the Board shall, in the performance of its tasks or the exercise of its powers, neither seek nor take instructions from anybody.

Article 70: Tasks of the Board

1.   The Board shall ensure the consistent application of this Regulation. To that end, the Board shall, on its own initiative or, where relevant, at the request of the Commission, in particular:

1.   monitor and ensure the correct application of this Regulation in the cases provided for in Articles 64 and 65 without prejudice to the tasks of national supervisory authorities;
2.   advise the Commission on any issue related to the protection of personal data in the Union, including on any proposed amendment of this Regulation;
3.   advise the Commission on the format and procedures for the exchange of information between Controllers, Processors and supervisory authorities for binding corporate rules;
4.   issue guidelines, recommendations, and best practices on procedures for erasing links, copies or replications of personal data from publicly available communication services as referred to in Article 17(2);
5.   examine, on its own initiative, on request of one of its members or on request of the Commission, any question covering the application of this Regulation and issue guidelines, recommendations and best practices in order to encourage consistent application of this Regulation;
6.   issue guidelines, recommendations and best practices in accordance with point (e) of this paragraph for further specifying the criteria and conditions for decisions based on profiling pursuant to Article 22(2);
7.   issue guidelines, recommendations and best practices in accordance with point (e) of this paragraph for establishing the personal data breaches and determining the undue delay referred to in Article 33(1) and (2) and for the particular circumstances in which a Controller or a Processor is required to notify the personal data breach;
8.   issue guidelines, recommendations and best practices in accordance with point (e) of this paragraph as to the circumstances in which a personal data breach is likely to result in a high risk to the rights and freedoms of the Natural Persons referred to in Article 34(1).
9.   issue guidelines, recommendations and best practices in accordance with point (e) of this paragraph for the purpose of further specifying the criteria and requirements for personal data transfers based on binding corporate rules adhered to by Controllers and binding corporate rules adhered to by Processors and on further necessary requirements to ensure the protection of personal data of the Data Subjects concerned referred to in Article 47;
10.   issue guidelines, recommendations and best practices in accordance with point (e) of this paragraph for the

purpose of further specifying the criteria and requirements for the personal data transfers on the basis of Article 49(1);

11. draw up guidelines for supervisory authorities concerning the application of measures referred to in Article 58(1), (2) and (3) and the setting of administrative fines pursuant to Article 83;

12. review the practical application of the guidelines, recommendations and best practices referred to in points (e) and (f);

13. issue guidelines, recommendations and best practices in accordance with point (e) of this paragraph for establishing common procedures for reporting by Natural Persons of infringements of this Regulation pursuant to Article 54(2);

14. encourage the drawing-up of codes of conduct and the establishment of data protection certification mechanisms and data protection seals and marks pursuant to Articles 40 and 42;

15. carry out the accreditation of certification bodies and its periodic review pursuant to Article 43 and maintain a public register of accredited bodies pursuant to Article 43(6) and of the accredited Controllers or Processors established in third countries pursuant to Article 42(7);

16. specify the requirements referred to in Article 43(3) with a view to the accreditation of certification bodies under Article 42;

17. provide the Commission with an opinion on the certification requirements referred to in Article 43(8);

18. provide the Commission with an opinion on the icons referred to in Article 12(7);

19. provide the Commission with an opinion for the assessment of the adequacy of the level of protection in a third country or international organisation, including for the assessment whether a third country, a territory or one or more specified sectors within that third country, or an international organisation no longer ensures an adequate level of protection. To that end, the Commission shall provide the Board with all necessary documentation, including correspondence with the government of the third country, with regard to that third country, territory or specified sector, or with the international organisation.

20. issue opinions on draft decisions of supervisory authorities pursuant to the consistency mechanism referred to in Article 64(1), on matters submitted pursuant to Article 64(2) and to issue binding decisions pursuant to Article 65, including in cases referred to in Article 66;

21. promote the cooperation and the effective bilateral and multilateral exchange of information and best practices between the supervisory authorities;

22. promote common training programmes and facilitate personnel exchanges between the supervisory authorities and, where appropriate, with the supervisory authorities of third countries or with international organisations;

23. promote the exchange of knowledge and documentation on data protection legislation and practice with data protection supervisory authorities worldwide.

24. issue opinions on codes of conduct drawn up at Union level pursuant to Article 40(9); and

25. maintain a publicly accessible electronic register of decisions taken by supervisory authorities and courts on issues handled in the consistency mechanism.

2. Where the Commission requests advice from the Board, it may indicate a time limit, taking into account the urgency of the matter.

3. The Board shall forward its opinions, guidelines, recommendations, and best practices to the Commission and to the committee referred to in Article 93 and make them public.

4. The Board shall, where appropriate, consult interested parties and give them the opportunity to comment within a reasonable period. The Board shall, without prejudice to Article 76, make the results of the consultation procedure publicly available.

Article 71: Reports

1.   The Board shall draw up an annual report regarding the protection of Natural Persons with regard to processing in the Union and, where relevant, in third countries and international organisations. The report shall be made public and be transmitted to the European Parliament, to the Council and to the Commission.

2.   The annual report shall include a review of the practical application of the guidelines, recommendations and best practices referred to in point (l) of Article 70(1) as well as of the binding decisions referred to in Article 65.

Article 72: Procedure

1.   The Board shall take decisions by a simple majority of its members, unless otherwise provided for in this Regulation.

2.   The Board shall adopt its own rules of procedure by a two-thirds majority of its members and organise its own operational arrangements.

Article 73: Chair

1.   The Board shall elect a chair and two deputy chairs from amongst its members by simple majority.

2.   The term of office of the Chair and of the deputy chairs shall be five years and be renewable once.

Article 74: Tasks of the Chair

1.   The Chair shall have the following tasks:

    1.   to convene the meetings of the Board and prepare its agenda;
    2.   to notify decisions adopted by the Board pursuant to Article 65 to the lead Supervisory Authority and the supervisory authorities concerned;
    3.   to ensure the timely performance of the tasks of the Board, in particular in relation to the consistency mechanism referred to in Article 63.

2.   The Board shall lay down the allocation of tasks between the Chair and the deputy chairs in its rules of procedure.

Article 75: Secretariat

1.   The Board shall have a secretariat, which shall be provided by the European Data Protection Supervisor.

2.   The secretariat shall perform its tasks exclusively under the instructions of the Chair of the Board.

3.   The staff of the European Data Protection Supervisor involved in carrying out the tasks conferred on the Board by this Regulation shall be subject to separate reporting lines from the staff involved in carrying out tasks conferred on the European Data Protection Supervisor.

4.   Where appropriate, the Board and the European Data Protection Supervisor shall establish and publish a Memorandum of Understanding implementing this Article, determining the terms of their cooperation, and applicable to the staff of the European Data Protection Supervisor involved in carrying out the tasks conferred on the

Board by this Regulation.

5.   The secretariat shall provide analytical, administrative and logistical support to the Board.

6.   The secretariat shall be responsible in particular for:

1. the day-to-day business of the Board;
2. communication between the members of the Board, its Chair and the Commission;
3. communication with other institutions and the public;
4. the use of electronic means for the internal and external communication;
5. the translation of relevant information;
6. the preparation and follow-up of the meetings of the Board;
7. the preparation, drafting and publication of opinions, decisions on the settlement of disputes between supervisory authorities and other texts adopted by the Board.

Article 76: Confidentiality

1.   The discussions of the Board shall be confidential where the Board deems it necessary, as provided for in its rules of procedure.

2.   Access to documents submitted to members of the Board, experts and representatives of third parties shall be governed by Regulation (EC) No 1049/2001 of the European Parliament and of the Council[1].

VIII: REMEDIES, LIABILITY AND PENALTIES

Article 77: Right to lodge a complaint with a Supervisory Authority

1.   Without prejudice to any other administrative or judicial remedy, every Data Subject shall have the right to lodge a complaint with a Supervisory Authority, in particular in the Member State of his or her habitual residence, place of work or place of the alleged infringement if the Data Subject considers that the processing of personal data relating to him or her infringes this Regulation.

2.   The Supervisory Authority with which the complaint has been lodged shall inform the complainant on the progress and the outcome of the complaint including the possibility of a judicial remedy pursuant to Article 78.

Article 78: Right to an effective judicial remedy against a Supervisory Authority

1.   Without prejudice to any other administrative or non-judicial remedy, each natural or legal person shall have the right to an effective judicial remedy against a legally binding decision of a Supervisory Authority concerning them.

2.   Without prejudice to any other administrative or non-judicial remedy, each Data Subject shall have the right to an effective judicial remedy where the Supervisory Authority which is competent pursuant to Articles 55 and 56 does not handle a complaint or does not inform the Data Subject within three months on the progress or outcome of the complaint lodged pursuant to Article 77.

3.   Proceedings against a Supervisory Authority shall be brought before the courts of the Member State where the Supervisory Authority is established.

4.   Where proceedings are brought against a decision of a Supervisory Authority which was preceded by an opinion or a decision of the Board in the consistency mechanism, the Supervisory Authority shall forward that opinion or decision to the court.

Article 79: Right to an effective judicial remedy against a Controller or Processor

1.   Without prejudice to any available administrative or non-judicial remedy, including the right to lodge a complaint with a Supervisory Authority pursuant to Article 77, each Data Subject shall have the right to an effective judicial remedy where he or she considers that his or her rights under this Regulation have been infringed as a result of the processing of his or her personal data in non-compliance with this Regulation.

2.   Proceedings against a Controller or a Processor shall be brought before the courts of the Member State where the Controller or Processor has an establishment. Alternatively, such proceedings may be brought before the courts of the Member State where the Data Subject has his or her habitual residence, unless the Controller or Processor is a public authority of a Member State acting in the exercise of its public powers.

Article 80: Representation of Data Subjects

1.   The Data Subject shall have the right to mandate a not-for-profit body, organisation or association which has been properly constituted in accordance with the law of a Member State, has statutory objectives which are in the public interest, and is active in the field of the protection of Data Subjects' rights and freedoms with regard to the protection of their personal data to lodge the complaint on his or her behalf, to exercise the rights referred to in Articles 77, 78 and 79 on his or her behalf, and to exercise the right to receive compensation referred to in Article 82

on his or her behalf where provided for by Member State law

2.   Member States may provide that any body, organisation or association referred to in paragraph 1 of this Article, independently of a Data Subject's mandate, has the right to lodge, in that Member State, a complaint with the Supervisory Authority which is competent pursuant to Article 77 and to exercise the rights referred to in Articles 78 and 79 if it considers that the rights of a Data Subject under this Regulation have been infringed as a result of the processing.

Article 81: Suspension of proceedings

1.   Where a competent court of a Member State has information on proceedings, concerning the same subject matter as regards processing by the same Controller or Processor, that are pending in a court in another Member State, it shall contact that court in the other Member State to confirm the existence of such proceedings.

2.   Where proceedings concerning the same subject matter as regards processing of the same Controller or Processor are pending in a court in another Member State, any competent court other than the court first seized may suspend its proceedings.
3.   Where those proceedings are pending at first instance, any court other than the court first seized may also, on the application of one of the parties, decline jurisdiction if the court first seized has jurisdiction over the actions in question and its law permits the consolidation thereof.

Article 82: Right to compensation and liability

1.   Any person who has suffered material or non-material damage as a result of an infringement of this Regulation shall have the right to receive compensation from the Controller or Processor for the damage suffered.

2.   Any Controller involved in processing shall be liable for the damage caused by processing which infringes this Regulation. A Processor shall be liable for the damage caused by processing only where it has not complied with obligations of this Regulation specifically directed to Processors or where it has acted outside or contrary to lawful instructions of the Controller.

3.   A Controller or Processor shall be exempt from liability under paragraph 2 if it proves that it is not in any way responsible for the event giving rise to the damage.

4.   Where more than one Controller or Processor, or both a Controller and a Processor, are involved in the same processing and where they are, under paragraphs 2 and 3, responsible for any damage caused by processing, each Controller or Processor shall be held liable for the entire damage in order to ensure effective compensation of the Data Subject.

5.   Where a Controller or Processor has, in accordance with paragraph 4, paid full compensation for the damage suffered, that Controller or Processor shall be entitled to claim back from the other Controllers or Processors involved in the same processing that part of the compensation corresponding to their part of responsibility for the damage, in accordance with the conditions set out in paragraph 2.

6.   Court proceedings for exercising the right to receive compensation shall be brought before the courts competent under the law of the Member State referred to in Article 79(2).

Article 83: General conditions for imposing administrative fines

1.   Each Supervisory Authority shall ensure that the imposition of administrative fines pursuant to this Article in respect of infringements of this Regulation referred to in paragraphs 4, 5 and 6 shall in each individual case be effective, proportionate and dissuasive.

2.   Administrative fines shall, depending on the circumstances of each individual case, be imposed in addition to, or instead of, measures referred to in points (a) to (h) and (j) of Article 58(2). When deciding whether to impose an administrative fine and deciding on the amount of the administrative fine in each individual case due regard shall be given to the following:

1.   the nature, gravity and duration of the infringement taking into account the nature scope or purpose of the processing concerned as well as the number of Data Subjects affected and the level of damage suffered by them;
2.   the intentional or negligent character of the infringement;
3.   any action taken by the Controller or Processor to mitigate the damage suffered by Data Subjects;
4.   the degree of responsibility of the Controller or Processor taking into account technical and organisational measures implemented by them pursuant to Articles 25 and 32;
5.   any relevant previous infringements by the Controller or Processor;
6.   the degree of cooperation with the Supervisory Authority, in order to remedy the infringement and mitigate the possible adverse effects of the infringement;
7.   the categories of personal data affected by the infringement;
8.   the manner in which the infringement became known to the Supervisory Authority, in particular whether, and if so to what extent, the Controller or Processor notified the infringement;
9.   where measures referred to in Article 58(2) have previously been ordered against the Controller or Processor concerned with regard to the same subject-matter, compliance with those measures;
10. adherence to approved codes of conduct pursuant to Article 40 or approved certification mechanisms pursuant to Article 42; and
11. any other aggravating or mitigating factor applicable to the circumstances of the case, such as financial benefits gained, or losses avoided, directly or indirectly, from the infringement.

3.   If a Controller or Processor intentionally or negligently, for the same or linked processing operations, infringes several provisions of this Regulation, the total amount of the administrative fine shall not exceed the amount specified for the gravest infringement.

4.   Infringements of the following provisions shall, in accordance with paragraph 2, be subject to administrative fines up to 10 000 000 EUR, or in the case of an undertaking, up to 2 % of the total worldwide annual turnover of the preceding financial year, whichever is higher:
1.   the obligations of the Controller and the Processor pursuant to Articles 8, 11, 25 to 39 and 42 and 43;
2.   the obligations of the certification body pursuant to Articles 42 and 43;
3.   the obligations of the monitoring body pursuant to Article 41(4).

5.   Infringements of the following provisions shall, in accordance with paragraph 2, be subject to administrative fines up to 20 000 000 EUR, or in the case of an undertaking, up to 4 % of the total worldwide annual turnover of the preceding financial year, whichever is higher:
1.   the basic principles for processing, including conditions for consent, pursuant to Articles 5, 6, 7 and 9;
2.   the Data Subjects' rights pursuant to Articles 12 to 22;
3.   the transfers of personal data to a recipient in a third country or an international organisation pursuant to Articles 44 to 49;

4. any obligations pursuant to Member State law adopted under Chapter IX;

5. non-compliance with an order or a temporary or definitive limitation on processing or the suspension of data flows by the Supervisory Authority pursuant to Article 58(2) or failure to provide access in violation of Article 58(1).

6. Non-compliance with an order by the Supervisory Authority as referred to in Article 58(2) shall, in accordance with paragraph 2 of this Article, be subject to administrative fines up to 20 000 000 EUR, or in the case of an undertaking, up to 4 % of the total worldwide annual turnover of the preceding financial year, whichever is higher.

7. Without prejudice to the corrective powers of supervisory authorities pursuant to Article 58(2), each Member State may lay down the rules on whether and to what extent administrative fines may be imposed on public authorities and bodies established in that Member State.

8. The exercise by the Supervisory Authority of its powers under this Article shall be subject to appropriate procedural safeguards in accordance with Union and Member State law, including effective judicial remedy and due process.

9. Where the legal system of the Member State does not provide for administrative fines, this Article may be applied in such a manner that the fine is initiated by the competent Supervisory Authority and imposed by competent national courts, while ensuring that those legal remedies are effective and have an equivalent effect to the administrative fines imposed by supervisory authorities. In any event, the fines imposed shall be effective, proportionate and dissuasive. Those Member States shall notify to the Commission the provisions of their laws which they adopt pursuant to this paragraph by 25 May 2018 and, without delay, any subsequent amendment law or amendment affecting them.

Article 84: Penalties

1. Member States shall lay down the rules on other penalties applicable to infringements of this Regulation in particular for infringements which are not subject to administrative fines pursuant to Article 83, and shall take all measures necessary to ensure that they are implemented. Such penalties shall be effective, proportionate and dissuasive.

2. Each Member State shall notify to the Commission the provisions of its law which it adopts pursuant to paragraph 1, by 25 May 2018 and, without delay, any subsequent amendment affecting them.

IX: PROVISIONS RELATING TO SPECIFIC PROCESSING SITUATIONS

Article 85: Processing and freedom of expression and information

1. Member States shall by law reconcile the right to the protection of personal data pursuant to this Regulation with the right to freedom of expression and information, including processing for journalistic purposes and the purposes of academic, artistic or literary expression.

2. For processing carried out for journalistic purposes or the purpose of academic artistic or literary expression, Member States shall provide for exemptions or derogations from Chapter II (principles), Chapter III (rights of the Data Subject), Chapter IV (Controller and Processor), Chapter V (transfer of personal data to third countries or international organisations), Chapter VI (independent supervisory authorities), Chapter VII (cooperation and consistency) and Chapter IX (specific data processing situations) if they are necessary to reconcile the right to the protection of personal data with the freedom of expression and information.

3. Each Member State shall notify to the Commission the provisions of its law which it has adopted pursuant to paragraph 2 and, without delay, any subsequent amendment law or amendment affecting them.

Article 86: Processing and public access to official documents

Personal data in official documents held by a public authority or a public body or a private body for the performance of a task carried out in the public interest may be disclosed by the authority or body in accordance with Union or Member State law to which the public authority or body is subject in order to reconcile public access to official documents with the right to the protection of personal data pursuant to this Regulation.

Article 87: Processing of the national identification number

Member States may further determine the specific conditions for the processing of a national identification number or any other identifier of general application. In that case the national identification number or any other identifier of general application shall be used only under appropriate safeguards for the rights and freedoms of the Data Subject pursuant to this Regulation.

Article 88: Processing in the context of employment

1. Member States may, by law or by collective agreements, provide for more specific rules to ensure the protection of the rights and freedoms in respect of the processing of employees' personal data in the employment context, in particular for the purposes of the recruitment, the performance of the contract of employment, including discharge of obligations laid down by law or by collective agreements, management, planning and organisation of work, equality and diversity in the workplace, health and safety at work, protection of employer's or customer's property and for the purposes of the exercise and enjoyment, on an individual or collective basis, of rights and benefits related to employment, and for the purpose of the termination of the employment relationship.

2. Those rules shall include suitable and specific measures to safeguard the Data Subject's human dignity, legitimate interests and fundamental rights, with particular regard to the transparency of processing, the transfer of personal data within a group of undertakings, or a group of enterprises engaged in a joint economic activity and monitoring systems at the work place.

3. Each Member State shall notify to the Commission those provisions of its law which it adopts pursuant to paragraph 1, by 25 May 2018 and, without delay, any subsequent amendment affecting them.

Article 89: Safeguards and derogations relating to processing for archiving purposes in the public interest, scientific or historical research purposes or statistical purposes

1. Processing for archiving purposes in the public interest, scientific or historical research purposes or statistical purposes, shall be subject to appropriate safeguards, in accordance with this Regulation, for the rights and freedoms of the Data Subject. Those safeguards shall ensure that technical and organisational measures are in place in particular in order to ensure respect for the principle of data minimisation. Those measures may include pseudonymisation provided that those purposes can be fulfilled in that manner. Where those purposes can be fulfilled by further processing which does not permit or no longer permits the identification of Data Subjects, those purposes shall be fulfilled in that manner.
2. Where personal data are processed for scientific or historical research purposes or statistical purposes, Union or Member State law may provide for derogations from the rights referred to in Articles 15, 16, 18 and 21 subject to the conditions and safeguards referred to in paragraph 1 of this Article in so far as such rights are likely to render impossible or seriously impair the achievement of the specific purposes, and such derogations are necessary for the fulfilment of those purposes.
3. Where personal data are processed for archiving purposes in the public interest, Union or Member State law may provide for derogations from the rights referred to in Articles 15, 16, 18, 19, 20 and 21 subject to the conditions and safeguards referred to in paragraph 1 of this Article in so far as such rights are likely to render impossible or seriously impair the achievement of the specific purposes, and such derogations are necessary for the fulfilment of those purposes.
4. Where processing referred to in paragraphs 2 and 3 serves at the same time another purpose, the derogations shall apply only to processing for the purposes referred to in those paragraphs.

Article 90: Obligations of secrecy

1.   Member States may adopt specific rules to set out the powers of the supervisory authorities laid down in points (e) and (f) of Article 58(1) in relation to Controllers or Processors that are subject, under Union or Member State law or rules established by national competent bodies, to an obligation of professional secrecy or other equivalent obligations of secrecy where this is necessary and proportionate to reconcile the right of the protection of personal data with the obligation of secrecy. Those rules shall apply only with regard to personal data which the Controller or Processor has received as a result of or has obtained in an activity covered by that obligation of secrecy.

2.   Each Member State shall notify to the Commission the rules adopted pursuant to paragraph 1, by 25 May 2018 and, without delay, any subsequent amendment affecting them.

Article 91: Existing data protection rules of churches and religious associations

1.   Where in a Member State, churches and religious associations or communities apply, at the time of entry into force of this Regulation, comprehensive rules relating to the protection of Natural Persons with regard to processing, such rules may continue to apply, provided that they are brought into line with this Regulation.

2.   Churches and religious associations which apply comprehensive rules in accordance with paragraph 1 of this Article shall be subject to the supervision of an independent Supervisory Authority, which may be specific, provided that it fulfils the conditions laid down in Chapter VI of this Regulation.

X: DELEGATED ACTS AND IMPLEMENTING ACTS

Article 92: Exercise of the delegation

1.   The power to adopt delegated acts is conferred on the Commission subject to the conditions laid down in this Article.

2.   The delegation of power referred to in Article 12(8) and Article 43(8) shall be conferred on the Commission for an indeterminate period of time from 24 May 2016.

3.   The delegation of power referred to in Article 12(8) and Article 43(8) may be revoked at any time by the European Parliament or by the Council. A decision of revocation shall put an end to the delegation of power specified in that decision. It shall take effect the day following that of its publication in the Official Journal of the European Union or at a later date specified therein. It shall not affect the validity of any delegated acts already in force.

4.   As soon as it adopts a delegated act, the Commission shall notify it simultaneously to the European Parliament and to the Council.

5.   A delegated act adopted pursuant to Article 12(8) and Article 43(8) shall enter into force only if no objection has been expressed by either the European Parliament or the Council within a period of three months of notification of that act to the European Parliament and the Council or if, before the expiry of that period, the European Parliament and the Council have both informed the Commission that they will not object. That period shall be extended by three months at the initiative of the European Parliament or of the Council.

Article 93: Committee procedure

1.   The Commission shall be assisted by a committee. That committee shall be a committee within the meaning of Regulation (EU) No 182/2011.

2.   Where reference is made to this paragraph, Article 5 of Regulation (EU) No 182/2011shall apply.

3.   Where reference is made to this paragraph, Article 8 of Regulation ((EU) No 182/2011, in conjunction with Article 5 thereof, shall apply.

XI: FINAL PROVISIONS

Article 94: Repeal of Directive 95/46/EC

1. Directive 95/46/EC is repealed with effect from 25 May 2018.

2. References to the repealed Directive shall be construed as references to this Regulation. References to the Working Party on the Protection of Individuals with regard to the Processing of Personal Data established by Article 29 of Directive 95/46/EC shall be construed as references to the European Data Protection Board established by this Regulation.

Article 95: Relationship with Directive 2002/58/EC

This Regulation shall not impose additional obligations on natural or legal persons in relation to processing in connection with the provision of publicly available electronic communications services in public communication networks in the Union in relation to matters for which they are subject to specific obligations with the same objective set out in Directive 2002/58/EC

Article 96: Relationship with previously concluded Agreements

International agreements involving the transfer of personal data to third countries or international organisations which were concluded by Member States prior to 24 May 2016, and which comply with Union law as applicable prior to that date, shall remain in force until amended, replaced or revoked.

Article 97: Commission reports

1. By 25 May 2020 and every four years thereafter, the Commission shall submit a report on the evaluation and review of this Regulation to the European Parliament and to the Council. The reports shall be made public.

2. In the context of the evaluations and reviews referred to in paragraph 1, the Commission shall examine, in particular, the application and functioning of:

    1. Chapter V on the transfer of personal data to third countries or international organisations with particular regard to decisions adopted pursuant to Article 45(3) of this Regulation and decisions adopted on the basis of Article 25(6) of Directive 95/46/EC;
    2. Chapter VII on cooperation and consistency.
    3. For the purpose of paragraph 1, the Commission may request information from Member States and supervisory authorities.
    4. In carrying out the evaluations and reviews referred to in paragraphs 1 and 2, the Commission shall take into account the positions and findings of the European Parliament, of the Council, and of other relevant bodies or sources.
    5. The Commission shall, if necessary, submit appropriate proposals to amend this Regulation, in particular taking into account of developments in information technology and in the light of the state of progress in the information society.

Article 98: Review of other Union legal acts on data protection

The Commission shall, if appropriate, submit legislative proposals with a view to amending other Union legal acts on the protection of personal data, in order to ensure uniform and consistent protection of Natural Persons with regard to processing. This shall in particular concern the rules relating to the protection of Natural Persons with regard to processing by Union institutions, bodies, offices and agencies and on the free movement of such data

Article 99: Entry into force and application

1.   This Regulation shall enter into force on the twentieth day following that of its publication in the Official Journal of the European Union.

2.   It shall apply from 25 May 2018.

-End of GDPR Text -

PART III: THE RECITALS

THE RECITALS

1:37 - General Provisions

Recital 1: The protection of Natural Persons in relation to the processing of personal data is a fundamental right. Article 8(1) of the Charter of Fundamental Rights of the European Union (the 'Charter') and Article 16(1) of the Treaty on the Functioning of the European Union (TFEU) provide that everyone has the right to the protection of personal data concerning him or her.

Recital 2: The principles of, and rules on the protection of Natural Persons with regard to the processing of their personal data should, whatever their nationality or residence, respect their fundamental rights and freedoms, in particular their right to the protection of personal data. This Regulation is intended to contribute to the accomplishment of an area of freedom, security and justice and of an economic union, to economic and social progress, to the strengthening and the convergence of the economies within the internal market, and to the well-being of Natural Persons.

Recital 3: Directive 95/46/EC of the European Parliament and of the Council seeks to harmonise the protection of fundamental rights and freedoms of Natural Persons in respect of processing activities and to ensure the free flow of personal data between Member States.

Recital 4: The processing of personal data should be designed to serve mankind. The right to the protection of personal data is not an absolute right; it must be considered in relation to its function in society and be balanced against other fundamental rights, in accordance with the principle of proportionality. This Regulation respects all fundamental rights and observes the freedoms and principles recognised in the Charter as enshrined in the Treaties, in particular the respect for private and family life, home and communications, the protection of personal data, freedom of thought, conscience and religion, freedom of expression and information, freedom to conduct a business, the right to an effective remedy and to a fair trial, and cultural, religious and linguistic diversity.

Recital 5: The economic and social integration resulting from the functioning of the internal market has led to a substantial increase in cross-border flows of personal data. The exchange of personal data between public and private actors, including Natural Persons, associations and undertakings across the Union has increased. National authorities in the Member States are being called upon by Union law to cooperate and exchange personal data so as to be able to perform their duties or carry out tasks on behalf of an authority in another Member State.

Recital 6: Rapid technological developments and globalisation have brought new challenges for the protection of personal data. The scale of the collection and sharing of personal data has increased significantly. Technology allows both private companies and public authorities to make use of personal data on an unprecedented scale in order to pursue their activities. Natural persons increasingly make personal information available publicly and globally. Technology has transformed both the economy and social life, and should further facilitate the free flow of personal data within the Union and the transfer to third countries and international organisations, while ensuring a high level of the protection of personal data.

Recital 7: Those developments require a strong and more coherent data protection framework in the Union, backed by strong enforcement, given the importance of creating the trust that will allow the digital economy to develop across the internal market. Natural persons should have control of their own personal data. Legal and practical certainty for Natural Persons, economic operators and public authorities should be enhanced.

Recital 8: Where this Regulation provides for specifications or restrictions of its rules by Member State law, Member States may, as far as necessary for coherence and for making the national provisions comprehensible to the persons to whom they apply, incorporate elements of this Regulation into their national law.

Recital 9: The objectives and principles of Directive 95/46/EC remain sound, but it has not prevented fragmentation in the implementation of data protection across the Union, legal uncertainty or a widespread public perception that there are significant risks to the protection of Natural Persons, in particular with regard to online activity. Differences in the level of protection of the rights and freedoms of Natural Persons, in particular the right to the protection of personal data, with regard to the processing of personal data in the Member States may prevent the free flow of personal data throughout the Union. Those differences may therefore constitute an obstacle to the pursuit of economic activities at the level of the Union, distort competition and impede authorities in the discharge of their responsibilities under Union law. Such a difference in levels of protection is due to the existence of differences in the implementation and application of Directive 95/46/EC.

Recital 10: In order to ensure a consistent and high level of protection of Natural Persons and to remove the obstacles to flows of personal data within the Union, the level of protection of the rights and freedoms of Natural Persons with regard to the processing of such data should be equivalent in all Member States. Consistent and homogenous application of the rules for the protection of the fundamental rights and freedoms of Natural Persons with regard to the processing of personal data should be ensured throughout the Union. Regarding the processing of personal data for compliance with a legal obligation, for the performance of a task carried out in the public interest or in the exercise of official authority vested in the Controller, Member States should be allowed to maintain or introduce national provisions to further specify the application of the rules of this Regulation. In conjunction with the general and horizontal law on data protection implementing Directive 95/46/EC, Member States have several sector-specific laws in areas that need more specific provisions. This Regulation also provides a margin of manoeuvre for Member States to specify its rules, including for the processing of special categories of personal data ('sensitive data'). To that extent, this Regulation does not exclude Member State law that sets out the circumstances for specific processing situations, including determining more precisely the conditions under which the processing of personal data is lawful.

Recital 11: Effective protection of personal data throughout the Union requires the strengthening and setting out in detail of the rights of Data Subjects and the obligations of those who process and determine the processing of personal data, as well as equivalent powers for monitoring and ensuring compliance with the rules for the protection of personal data and equivalent sanctions for infringements in the Member States.

Recital 12: Article 16(2) TFEU mandates the European Parliament and the Council to lay down the rules relating to the protection of Natural Persons with regard to the processing of personal data and the rules relating to the free movement of personal data.

Recital 13: In order to ensure a consistent level of protection for Natural Persons throughout the Union and to prevent divergences hampering the free movement of personal data within the internal market, a Regulation is necessary to provide legal certainty and transparency for economic operators, including micro, small and medium-sized enterprises, and to provide Natural Persons in all Member States with the same level of legally enforceable rights and obligations and responsibilities for Controllers and Processors, to ensure consistent monitoring of the processing of personal data, and equivalent sanctions in all Member States as well as effective cooperation between the supervisory authorities of different Member States. The proper functioning of the internal market requires that the free movement of personal data within the Union is not restricted or prohibited for reasons connected with the protection of Natural Persons with regard to the processing of personal data. To take account of the specific situation of micro, small and medium-sized enterprises, this Regulation includes a derogation for organisations with fewer than 250 employees with regard to record-keeping. In addition, the Union institutions and bodies, and Member States and their supervisory authorities, are encouraged to take account of the specific needs of micro, small and medium-sized enterprises in the application of this Regulation. The notion of micro, small and medium-sized enterprises should draw from Article 2 of the Annex to Commission Recommendation 2003/361/EC

Recital 14: The protection afforded by this Regulation should apply to Natural Persons, whatever their nationality or place of residence, in relation to the processing of their personal data. This Regulation does not cover the processing of personal data which concerns legal persons and in particular undertakings established as legal persons, including the name and the form of the legal person and the contact details of the legal person.

Recital 15: In order to prevent creating a serious risk of circumvention, the protection of Natural Persons should be technologically neutral and should not depend on the techniques used. The protection of Natural Persons should apply to the processing of personal data by automated means, as well as to manual processing, if the personal data are contained or are intended to be contained in a filing system. Files or sets of files, as well as their cover pages, which are not structured according to specific criteria should not fall within the scope of this Regulation.

Recital 16: This Regulation does not apply to issues of protection of fundamental rights and freedoms or the free flow of personal data related to activities which fall outside the scope of Union law, such as activities concerning national security. This Regulation does not apply to the processing of personal data by the Member States when carrying out activities in relation to the common foreign and security policy of the Union.

Recital 17: Regulation (EC) No 45/2001 of the European Parliament and of the Council applies to the processing of personal data by the Union institutions, bodies, offices and agencies. Regulation (EC) No 45/2001 and other Union legal acts applicable to such processing of personal data should be adapted to the principles and rules established in this Regulation and applied in the light of this Regulation. In order to provide a strong and coherent data protection framework in the Union, the necessary adaptations of Regulation (EC) No 45/2001 should follow after the adoption of this Regulation, in order to allow application at the same time as this Regulation.

Recital 18: This Regulation does not apply to the processing of personal data by a Natural Person in the course of a purely personal or household activity and thus with no connection to a professional or commercial activity. Personal or household activities could include correspondence and the holding of addresses, or social networking and online activity undertaken within the context of such activities. However, this Regulation applies to Controllers or Processors which provide the means for processing personal data for such personal or household activities.

Recital 19: The protection of Natural Persons with regard to the processing of personal data by competent authorities for the purposes of the prevention, investigation, detection or prosecution of criminal offences or the execution of criminal penalties, including the safeguarding against and the prevention of threats to public security and the free movement of such data, is the subject of a specific Union legal act. This Regulation should not, therefore, apply to processing activities for those purposes. However, personal data processed by public authorities under this Regulation should, when used for those purposes, be governed by a more specific Union legal act, namely Directive (EU) 2016/680 of the European Parliament and of the Council (7). Member States may entrust competent authorities within the meaning of Directive (EU) 2016/680 with tasks which are not necessarily carried out for the purposes of the prevention, investigation, detection or prosecution of criminal offences or the execution of criminal penalties, including the safeguarding against and prevention of threats to public security, so that the processing of personal data for those other purposes, in so far as it is within the scope of Union law, falls within the scope of this Regulation.

With regard to the processing of personal data by those competent authorities for purposes falling within scope of this Regulation, Member States should be able to maintain or introduce more specific provisions to adapt the application of the rules of this Regulation. Such provisions may determine more precisely specific requirements for the processing of personal data by those competent authorities for those other purposes, taking into account the constitutional, organisational and administrative structure of the respective Member State. When the processing of personal data by private bodies falls within the scope of this Regulation, this Regulation should provide for the possibility for Member States under specific conditions to restrict by law certain obligations and rights when such a restriction constitutes a necessary and proportionate measure in a democratic society to safeguard specific important interests including public security and the prevention, investigation, detection or prosecution of criminal offences or the execution of criminal penalties, including the safeguarding against and the prevention of threats to public security. This is relevant for instance in the framework of anti-money laundering or the activities of forensic laboratories.

Recital 20: While this Regulation applies, inter alia, to the activities of courts and other judicial authorities, Union or Member State law could specify the processing operations and processing procedures in relation to the processing of personal data by courts and other judicial authorities. The competence of the supervisory authorities should not cover the processing of personal data when courts are acting in their judicial capacity, in order to safeguard the independence of the judiciary in the performance of its judicial tasks, including decision-making. It should be possible to entrust supervision of such data processing operations to specific bodies within the judicial system of the Member State, which should, in particular ensure compliance with the rules of this Regulation, enhance awareness among members of the judiciary of their obligations under this Regulation and handle complaints in relation to such data processing operations.

Recital 21: This Regulation is without prejudice to the application of Directive 2000/31/EC of the European Parliament and of the Council[1], in particular of the liability rules of intermediary service providers in Articles 12 to 15 of that Directive. That Directive seeks to contribute to the proper functioning of the internal market by ensuring the free movement of information society services between Member States.

Recital 22: Any processing of personal data in the context of the activities of an establishment of a Controller or a Processor in the Union should be carried out in accordance with this Regulation, regardless of whether the processing itself takes place within the Union. Establishment implies the effective and real exercise of activity through stable arrangements. The legal form of such arrangements, whether through a branch or a subsidiary with a legal personality, is not the determining factor in that respect.

Recital 23: In order to ensure that Natural Persons are not deprived of the protection to which they are entitled under this Regulation, the processing of personal data of Data Subjects who are in the Union by a Controller or a Processor not established in the Union should be subject to this Regulation where the processing activities are related to offering goods or services to such Data Subjects irrespective of whether connected to a payment. In order to determine whether such a Controller or Processor is offering goods or services to Data Subjects who are in the Union, it should be ascertained whether it is apparent that the Controller or Processor envisages offering services to Data Subjects in one or more Member States in the Union. Whereas the mere accessibility of the Controller's, Processor's or an intermediary's website in the Union, of an email address or of other contact details, or the use of a language generally used in the third country where the Controller is established, is insufficient to ascertain such intention, factors such as the use of a language or a currency generally used in one or more Member States with the possibility of ordering goods and services in that other language, or the mentioning of customers or users who are in the Union, may make it apparent that the Controller envisages offering goods or services to Data Subjects in the Union.

Recital 24: The processing of personal data of Data Subjects who are in the Union by a Controller or Processor not established in the Union should also be subject to this Regulation when it is related to the monitoring of the behaviour of such Data Subjects in so far as their behaviour takes place within the Union. In order to determine whether a processing activity can be considered to monitor the behaviour of Data Subjects, it should be ascertained whether Natural Persons are tracked on the internet including potential subsequent use of personal data processing techniques which consist of profiling a Natural Person, particularly in order to take decisions concerning her or him or for analysing or predicting her or his personal preferences, behaviours and attitudes.

Recital 25: Where Member State law applies by virtue of public international law, this Regulation should also apply to a Controller not established in the Union, such as in a Member State's diplomatic mission or consular post.

Recital 26: The principles of data protection should apply to any information concerning an identified or identifiable Natural Person. Personal data which have undergone pseudonymisation, which could be attributed to a Natural Person by the use of additional information should be considered to be information on an identifiable Natural Person. To determine whether a Natural Person is identifiable, account should be taken of all the means reasonably likely to be used, such as singling out, either by the Controller or by another person to identify the Natural Person directly or indirectly. To ascertain whether means are reasonably likely to be used to identify the Natural Person, account should be taken of all objective factors, such as the costs of and the amount of time required for identification, taking into consideration the available technology at the time of the processing and technological developments. The principles of data protection should therefore not apply to anonymous information, namely information which does not relate to an identified or identifiable Natural Person or to personal data rendered anonymous in such a manner that the Data Subject is not or no longer identifiable. This Regulation does not therefore concern the processing of such anonymous information, including for statistical or research purposes.

Recital 27: This Regulation does not apply to the personal data of deceased persons. Member States may provide for rules regarding the processing of personal data of deceased persons.

Recital 28: The application of pseudonymisation to personal data can reduce the risks to the Data Subjects concerned and help Controllers and Processors to meet their data-protection obligations. The explicit introduction of 'pseudonymisation' in this Regulation is not intended to preclude any other measures of data protection.

Recital 29: In order to create incentives to apply pseudonymisation when processing personal data, measures of pseudonymisation should, whilst allowing general analysis, be possible within the same Controller when that Controller has taken technical and organisational measures necessary to ensure, for the processing concerned, that this Regulation is implemented, and that additional information for attributing the personal data to a specific Data Subject is kept separately. The Controller processing the personal data should indicate the authorised persons within the same Controller.

Recital 30: Natural persons may be associated with online identifiers provided by their devices, applications, tools and protocols, such as internet protocol addresses, cookie identifiers or other identifiers such as radio frequency identification tags. This may leave traces which, in particular when combined with unique identifiers and other information received by the servers, may be used to create profiles of the Natural Persons and identify them.

Recital 31: Public authorities to which personal data are disclosed in accordance with a legal obligation for the exercise of their official mission, such as tax and customs authorities, financial investigation units, independent administrative authorities, or financial market authorities responsible for the regulation and supervision of securities markets should not be regarded as recipients if they receive personal data which are necessary to carry out a particular inquiry in the general interest, in accordance with Union or Member State law. The requests for disclosure sent by the public authorities should always be in writing, reasoned and occasional and should not concern the entirety of a filing system or lead to the interconnection of filing systems. The processing of personal data by those public authorities should comply with the applicable data-protection rules according to the purposes of the processing.

Recital 32: Consent should be given by a clear affirmative act establishing a freely given, specific, informed and unambiguous indication of the Data Subject's agreement to the processing of personal data relating to him or her, such as by a written statement, including by electronic means, or an oral statement. This could include ticking a box when visiting an internet website, choosing technical settings for information society services or another statement or conduct which clearly indicates in this context the Data Subject's acceptance of the proposed processing of his or her personal data. Silence, pre-ticked boxes or inactivity should not therefore constitute consent. Consent should cover all processing activities carried out for the same purpose or purposes. When the processing has multiple purposes, consent should be given for all of them. If the Data Subject's consent is to be given following a request by electronic means, the request must be clear, concise and not unnecessarily disruptive to the use of the service for which it is provided.

Recital 33: It is often not possible to fully identify the purpose of personal data processing for scientific research purposes at the time of data collection. Therefore, Data Subjects should be allowed to give their consent to certain areas of scientific research when in keeping with recognised ethical standards for scientific research. Data subjects should have the opportunity to give their consent only to certain areas of research or parts of research projects to the extent allowed by the intended purpose.

Recital 34: Genetic data should be defined as personal data relating to the inherited or acquired genetic characteristics of a Natural Person which result from the analysis of a biological sample from the Natural Person in question, in particular chromosomal, deoxyribonucleic acid (DNA) or ribonucleic acid (RNA) analysis, or from the analysis of another element enabling equivalent information to be obtained.

Recital 35: Personal data concerning health should include all data pertaining to the health status of a Data Subject which reveal information relating to the past, current or future physical or mental health status of the Data Subject. This includes information about the Natural Person collected in the course of the registration for, or the provision of, health care services as referred to in Directive 2011/24/EU of the European Parliament and of the Council to that Natural Person; a number, symbol or particular assigned to a Natural Person to uniquely identify the Natural Person for health purposes; information derived from the testing or examination of a body part or bodily substance, including from genetic data and biological samples; and any information on, for example, a disease, disability, disease risk, medical history, clinical treatment or the physiological or biomedical state of the Data Subject independent of its source, for example from a physician or other health professional, a hospital, a medical device or an in vitro diagnostic test.

Recital 36: The main establishment of a Controller in the Union should be the place of its central administration in the Union, unless the decisions on the purposes and means of the processing of personal data are taken in another establishment of the Controller in the Union, in which case that other establishment should be considered to be the main establishment. The main establishment of a Controller in the Union should be determined according to objective criteria and should imply the effective and real exercise of management activities determining the main decisions as to the purposes and means of processing through stable arrangements. That criterion should not depend on whether the processing of personal data is carried out at that location. The presence and use of technical means and technologies for processing personal data or processing activities do not, in themselves, constitute a main establishment and are therefore not determining criteria for a main establishment. The main establishment of the Processor should be the place of its central administration in the Union or, if it has no central administration in the Union, the place where the main processing activities take place in the Union. In cases involving both the Controller and the Processor, the competent lead Supervisory Authority should remain the Supervisory Authority of the Member State where the Controller has its main establishment, but the Supervisory Authority of the Processor should be considered to be a Supervisory Authority concerned and that Supervisory Authority should participate in the cooperation procedure provided for by this Regulation. In any case, the supervisory authorities of the Member State or Member States where the Processor has one or more establishments should not be considered to be supervisory authorities concerned where the draft decision concerns only the Controller. Where the processing is carried out by a group of undertakings, the main establishment of the controlling undertaking should be considered to be the main establishment of the group of undertakings, except where the purposes and means of processing are determined by another undertaking.

38:57 - Principles (38:57)

Recital 37: A group of undertakings should cover a controlling undertaking and its controlled undertakings, whereby the controlling undertaking should be the undertaking which can exert a dominant influence over the other undertakings by virtue, for example, of ownership, financial participation or the rules which govern it or the power to have personal data protection rules implemented. An undertaking which controls the processing of personal data in undertakings affiliated to it should be regarded, together with those undertakings, as a group of undertakings.

Recital 38: Children merit specific protection with regard to their personal data, as they may be less aware of the risks, consequences and safeguards concerned and their rights in relation to the processing of personal data. Such specific protection should, in particular, apply to the use of personal data of children for the purposes of marketing or creating personality or user profiles and the collection of personal data with regard to children when using services offered directly to a child. The consent of the holder of parental responsibility should not be necessary in the context of preventive or counselling services offered directly to a child.

Recital 39: Any processing of personal data should be lawful and fair. It should be transparent to Natural Persons that personal data concerning them are collected, used, consulted or otherwise processed and to what extent the personal data are or will be processed. The principle of transparency requires that any information and communication relating to the processing of those personal data be easily accessible and easy to understand, and that clear and plain language be used. That principle concerns, in particular, information to the Data Subjects on the identity of the Controller and the purposes of the processing and further information to ensure fair and transparent processing in respect of the Natural Persons concerned and their right to obtain confirmation and communication of personal data concerning them which are being processed. Natural persons should be made aware of risks, rules, safeguards and rights in relation to the processing of personal data and how to exercise their rights in relation to such processing. In particular, the specific purposes for which personal data are processed should be explicit and legitimate and determined at the time of the collection of the personal data. The personal data should be adequate, relevant and limited to what is necessary for the purposes for which they are processed. This requires, in particular, ensuring that the period for which the personal data are stored is limited to a strict minimum. Personal data should be processed only if the purpose of the processing could not reasonably be fulfilled by other means. In order to ensure that the personal data are not kept longer than necessary, time limits should be established by the Controller for erasure or for a periodic review. Every reasonable step should be taken to ensure that personal data which are inaccurate are rectified or deleted. Personal data should be processed in a manner that ensures appropriate security and confidentiality of the personal data, including for preventing unauthorised access to or use of personal data and the equipment used for the processing.

Recital 40: In order for processing to be lawful, personal data should be processed on the basis of the consent of the Data Subject concerned or some other legitimate basis, laid down by law, either in this Regulation or in other Union or Member State law as referred to in this Regulation, including the necessity for compliance with the legal obligation to which the Controller is subject or the necessity for the performance of a contract to which the Data Subject is party or in order to take steps at the request of the Data Subject prior to entering into a contract.

Recital 41: Where this Regulation refers to a legal basis or a legislative measure, this does not necessarily require a legislative act adopted by a parliament, without prejudice to requirements pursuant to the constitutional order of the Member State concerned. However, such a legal basis or legislative measure should be clear and precise and its application should be foreseeable to persons subject to it, in accordance with the case-law of the Court of Justice of the European Union (the 'Court of Justice') and the European Court of Human Rights.

Recital 42: Where processing is based on the Data Subject's consent, the Controller should be able to demonstrate that the Data Subject has given consent to the processing operation. In particular, in the context of a written declaration on another matter, safeguards should ensure that the Data Subject is aware of the fact that and the extent to which consent is given. In accordance with Council Directive 93/13/EEC a declaration of consent pre-formulated by the Controller should be provided in an intelligible and easily accessible form, using clear and plain language and it should not contain unfair terms. For consent to be informed, the Data Subject should be aware at least of the identity of the Controller and the purposes of the processing for which the personal data are intended. Consent should not be regarded as freely given if the Data Subject has no genuine or free choice or is unable to refuse or withdraw consent without detriment.

Recital 43: In order to ensure that consent is freely given, consent should not provide a valid legal ground for the processing of personal data in a specific case where there is a clear imbalance between the Data Subject and the Controller, in particular where the Controller is a public authority and it is therefore unlikely that consent was freely given in all the circumstances of that specific situation. Consent is presumed not to be freely given if it does not allow separate consent to be given to different personal data processing operations despite it being appropriate in the individual case, or if the performance of a contract, including the provision of a service, is dependent on the consent despite such consent not being necessary for such performance.

Recital 44: Processing should be lawful where it is necessary in the context of a contract or the intention to enter into a contract.

Recital 45: Where processing is carried out in accordance with a legal obligation to which the Controller is subject or where processing is necessary for the performance of a task carried out in the public interest or in the exercise of official authority, the processing should have a basis in Union or Member State law. This Regulation does not require a specific law for each individual processing. A law as a basis for several processing operations based on a legal obligation to which the Controller is subject or where processing is necessary for the performance of a task carried out in the public interest or in the exercise of an official authority may be sufficient. It should also be for Union or Member State law to determine the purpose of processing. Furthermore, that law could specify the general conditions of this Regulation governing the lawfulness of personal data processing, establish specifications for determining the Controller, the type of personal data which are subject to the processing, the Data Subjects concerned, the entities to which the personal data may be disclosed, the purpose limitations, the storage period and other measures to ensure lawful and fair processing. It should also be for Union or Member State law to determine whether the Controller performing a task carried out in the public interest or in the exercise of official authority should be a public authority or another natural or legal person governed by public law, or, where it is in the public interest to do so, including for health purposes such as public health and social protection and the management of health care services, by private law, such as a professional association.

Recital 46: The processing of personal data should also be regarded to be lawful where it is necessary to protect an interest which is essential for the life of the Data Subject or that of another Natural Person. Processing of personal data based on the vital interest of another Natural Person should in principle take place only where the processing cannot be manifestly based on another legal basis. Some types of processing may serve both important grounds of public interest and the vital interests of the Data Subject as for instance when processing is necessary for humanitarian purposes, including for monitoring epidemics and their spread or in situations of humanitarian emergencies, in particular in situations of natural and man-made disasters.

Recital 47: The legitimate interests of a Controller, including those of a Controller to which the personal data may be disclosed, or of a third party, may provide a legal basis for processing, provided that the interests or the fundamental rights and freedoms of the Data Subject are not overriding, taking into consideration the reasonable expectations of Data Subjects based on their relationship with the Controller. Such legitimate interest could exist for example where there is a relevant and appropriate relationship between the Data Subject and the Controller in situations such as where the Data Subject is a client or in the service of the Controller. At any rate the existence of a legitimate interest would need careful assessment including whether a Data Subject can reasonably expect at the time and in the context of the collection of the personal data that processing for that purpose may take place. The interests and fundamental rights of the Data Subject could in particular override the interest of the data Controller where personal data are processed in circumstances where Data Subjects do not reasonably expect further processing. Given that it is for the legislator to provide by law for the legal basis for public authorities to process personal data, that legal basis should not apply to the processing by public authorities in the performance of their tasks. The processing of personal data strictly necessary for the purposes of preventing fraud also constitutes a legitimate interest of the data Controller concerned. The processing of personal data for direct marketing purposes may be regarded as carried out for a legitimate interest.

Recital 48: Controllers that are part of a group of undertakings or institutions affiliated to a central body may have a legitimate interest in transmitting personal data within the group of undertakings for internal administrative purposes, including the processing of clients' or employees' personal data. The general principles for the transfer of personal data, within a group of undertakings, to an undertaking located in a third country remain unaffected.

Recital 49: The processing of personal data to the extent strictly necessary and proportionate for the purposes of ensuring network and information security, i.e. the ability of a network or an information system to resist, at a given level of confidence, accidental events or unlawful or malicious actions that compromise the availability, authenticity, integrity and confidentiality of stored or transmitted personal data, and the security of the related services offered by, or accessible via, those networks and systems, by public authorities, by computer emergency response teams (CERTs), computer security incident response teams (CSIRTs), by providers of electronic communications networks and services and by providers of security technologies and services, constitutes a legitimate interest of the data Controller concerned. This could, for example, include preventing unauthorised access to electronic communications networks and malicious code distribution and stopping 'denial of service' attacks and damage to computer and electronic communication systems.

Recital 50: The processing of personal data for purposes other than those for which the personal data were initially collected should be allowed only where the processing is compatible with the purposes for which the personal data were initially collected. In such a case, no legal basis separate from that which allowed the collection of the personal data is required. If the processing is necessary for the performance of a task carried out in the public interest or in the exercise of official authority vested in the Controller, Union or Member State law may determine and specify the tasks and purposes for which the further processing should be regarded as compatible and lawful. Further processing for archiving purposes in the public interest, scientific or historical research purposes or statistical purposes should be considered to be compatible lawful processing operations. The legal basis provided by Union or Member State law for the processing of personal data may also provide a legal basis for further processing. In order to ascertain whether a purpose of further processing is compatible with the purpose for which the personal data are initially collected, the Controller, after having met all the requirements for the lawfulness of the original processing, should take into account, inter alia: any link between those purposes and the purposes of the intended further processing; the context in which the personal data have been collected, in particular the reasonable expectations of Data Subjects based on their relationship with the Controller as to their further use; the nature of the personal data; the consequences of the intended further processing for Data Subjects; and the existence of appropriate safeguards in both the original and intended further processing operations.

Where the Data Subject has given consent or the processing is based on Union or Member State law which constitutes a necessary and proportionate measure in a democratic society to safeguard, in particular, important objectives of general public interest, the Controller should be allowed to further process the personal data irrespective of the compatibility of the purposes. In any case, the application of the principles set out in this Regulation and in particular the information of the Data Subject on those other purposes and on his or her rights including the right to object, should be ensured. Indicating possible criminal acts or threats to public security by the Controller and transmitting the relevant personal data in individual cases or in several cases relating to the same criminal act or threats to public security to a competent authority should be regarded as being in the legitimate interest pursued by the Controller. However, such transmission in the legitimate interest of the Controller or further processing of personal data should be prohibited if the processing is not compatible with a legal, professional or other binding obligation of secrecy.

Recital 51: Personal data which are, by their nature, particularly sensitive in relation to fundamental rights and freedoms merit specific protection as the context of their processing could create significant risks to the fundamental rights and freedoms. Those personal data should include personal data revealing racial or ethnic origin, whereby the use of the term 'racial origin' in this Regulation does not imply an acceptance by the Union of theories which attempt to determine the existence of separate human races. The processing of photographs should not systematically be considered to be processing of special categories of personal data as they are covered by the definition of biometric data only when processed through a specific technical means allowing the unique identification or authentication of a Natural Person. Such personal data should not be processed, unless processing is allowed in specific cases set out in this Regulation, taking into account that Member States law may lay down specific provisions on data protection in order to adapt the application of the rules of this Regulation for compliance with a legal obligation or for the performance of a task carried out in the public interest or in the exercise of official authority vested in the Controller. In addition to the specific requirements for such processing, the general principles and other rules of this Regulation should apply, in particular as regards the conditions for lawful processing. Derogations from the general prohibition for processing such special categories of personal data should be explicitly provided, inter alia, where the Data Subject gives his or her explicit consent or in respect of specific needs in particular where the processing is carried out in the course of legitimate activities by certain associations or foundations the purpose of which is to permit the exercise of fundamental freedoms.

Recital 52: Derogating from the prohibition on processing special categories of personal data should also be allowed when provided for in Union or Member State law and subject to suitable safeguards, so as to protect personal data and other fundamental rights, where it is in the public interest to do so, in particular processing personal data in the field of employment law, social protection law including pensions and for health security, monitoring and alert purposes, the prevention or control of communicable diseases and other serious threats to health. Such a derogation may be made for health purposes, including public health and the management of health-care services, especially in order to ensure the quality and cost-effectiveness of the procedures used for settling claims for benefits and services in the health insurance system, or for archiving purposes in the public interest, scientific or historical research purposes or statistical purposes. A derogation should also allow the processing of such personal data where necessary for the establishment, exercise or defence of legal claims, whether in court proceedings or in an administrative or out-of-court procedure.

Recital 53: Special categories of personal data which merit higher protection should be processed for health-related purposes only where necessary to achieve those purposes for the benefit of Natural Persons and society as a whole, in particular in the context of the management of health or social care services and systems, including processing by the management and central national health authorities of such data for the purpose of quality control, management information and the general national and local supervision of the health or social care system, and ensuring continuity of health or social care and cross-border healthcare or health security, monitoring and alert purposes, or for archiving purposes in the public interest, scientific or historical research purposes or statistical purposes, based on Union or Member State law which has to meet an objective of public interest, as well as for studies conducted in the public interest in the area of public health. Therefore, this Regulation should provide for harmonised conditions for the processing of special categories of personal data concerning health, in respect of specific needs, in particular where the processing of such data is carried out for certain health-related purposes by persons subject to a legal obligation of professional secrecy. Union or Member State law should provide for specific and suitable measures so as to protect the fundamental rights and the personal data of Natural Persons. Member States should be allowed to maintain or introduce further conditions, including limitations, with regard to the processing of genetic data, biometric data or data concerning health. However, this should not hamper the free flow of personal data within the Union when those conditions apply to cross-border processing of such data.

Recital 54: The processing of special categories of personal data may be necessary for reasons of public interest in the areas of public health without consent of the Data Subject. Such processing should be subject to suitable and specific measures so as to protect the rights and freedoms of Natural Persons. In that context, 'public health' should be interpreted as defined in Regulation (EC) No 1338/2008 of the European Parliament and of the Council, namely all elements related to health, namely health status, including morbidity and disability, the determinants having an effect on that health status, health care needs, resources allocated to health care, the provision of, and universal access to, health care as well as health care expenditure and financing, and the causes of mortality. Such processing of data concerning health for reasons of public interest should not result in personal data being processed for other purposes by third parties such as employers or insurance and banking companies.

Recital 55: Moreover, the processing of personal data by official authorities for the purpose of achieving the aims, laid down by constitutional law or by international public law, of officially recognised religious associations, is carried out on grounds of public interest.

Recital 56: Where in the course of electoral activities, the operation of the democratic system in a Member State requires that political parties compile personal data on people's political opinions, the processing of such data may be permitted for reasons of public interest, provided that appropriate safeguards are established.

Recital 57: If the personal data processed by a Controller do not permit the Controller to identify a Natural Person, the data Controller should not be obliged to acquire additional information in order to identify the Data Subject for the sole purpose of complying with any provision of this Regulation. However, the Controller should not refuse to take additional information provided by the Data Subject in order to support the exercise of his or her rights. Identification should include the digital identification of a Data Subject, for example through authentication mechanism such as the same credentials, used by the Data Subject to log-in to the on-line service offered by the data Controller.

Recital 58: The principle of transparency requires that any information addressed to the public or to the Data Subject be concise, easily accessible and easy to understand, and that clear and plain language and, additionally, where appropriate, visualisation be used. Such information could be provided in electronic form, for example, when addressed to the public, through a website. This is of particular relevance in situations where the proliferation of actors and the technological complexity of practice make it difficult for the Data Subject to know and understand whether, by whom and for what purpose personal data relating to him or her are being collected, such as in the case of online advertising. Given that children merit specific protection, any information and communication, where processing is addressed to a child, should be in such a clear and plain language that the child can easily understand.

58:73 - Rights of the Data Subject

Recital 59: Modalities should be provided for facilitating the exercise of the Data Subject's rights under this Regulation, including mechanisms to request and, if applicable, obtain, free of charge, in particular, access to and rectification or erasure of personal data and the exercise of the right to object. The Controller should also provide means for requests to be made electronically, especially where personal data are processed by electronic means. The Controller should be obliged to respond to requests from the Data Subject without undue delay and at the latest within one month and to give reasons where the Controller does not intend to comply with any such requests.

Recital 60: The principles of fair and transparent processing require that the Data Subject be informed of the existence of the processing operation and its purposes. The Controller should provide the Data Subject with any further information necessary to ensure fair and transparent processing taking into account the specific circumstances and context in which the personal data are processed. Furthermore, the Data Subject should be informed of the existence of profiling and the consequences of such profiling. Where the personal data are collected from the Data Subject, the Data Subject should also be informed whether he or she is obliged to provide the personal data and of the consequences, where he or she does not provide such data. That information may be provided in combination with standardised icons in order to give in an easily visible, intelligible and clearly legible manner, a meaningful overview of the intended processing. Where the icons are presented electronically, they should be machine-readable.

Recital 61: The information in relation to the processing of personal data relating to the Data Subject should be given to him or her at the time of collection from the Data Subject, or, where the personal data are obtained from another source, within a reasonable period, depending on the circumstances of the case. Where personal data can be legitimately disclosed to another recipient, the Data Subject should be informed when the personal data are first disclosed to the recipient. Where the Controller intends to process the personal data for a purpose other than that for which they were collected, the Controller should provide the Data Subject prior to that further processing with information on that other purpose and other necessary information. Where the origin of the personal data cannot be provided to the Data Subject because various sources have been used, general information should be provided.

Recital 62: However, it is not necessary to impose the obligation to provide information where the Data Subject already possesses the information, where the recording or disclosure of the personal data is expressly laid down by law or where the provision of information to the Data Subject proves to be impossible or would involve a disproportionate effort. The latter could in particular be the case where processing is carried out for archiving purposes in the public interest, scientific or historical research purposes or statistical purposes. In that regard, the number of Data Subjects, the age of the data and any appropriate safeguards adopted should be taken into consideration.

Recital 63: A Data Subject should have the right of access to personal data which have been collected concerning him or her, and to exercise that right easily and at reasonable intervals, in order to be aware of, and verify, the lawfulness of the processing. This includes the right for Data Subjects to have access to data concerning their health, for example the data in their medical records containing information such as diagnoses, examination results, assessments by treating physicians and any treatment or interventions provided. Every Data Subject should therefore have the right to know and obtain communication in particular with regard to the purposes for which the personal data are processed, where possible the period for which the personal data are processed, the recipients of the personal data, the logic involved in any automatic personal data processing and, at least when based on profiling, the consequences of such processing. Where possible, the Controller should be able to provide remote access to a secure system which would provide the Data Subject with direct access to his or her personal data. That right should not adversely affect the rights or freedoms of others, including trade secrets or intellectual property and in particular the copyright protecting the software. However, the result of those considerations should not be a refusal to provide all information to the Data Subject. Where the Controller processes a large quantity of information concerning the Data Subject, the Controller should be able to request that, before the information is delivered, the Data Subject specify the information or processing activities to which the request relates.

Recital 64: The Controller should use all reasonable measures to verify the identity of a Data Subject who requests access, in particular in the context of online services and online identifiers. A Controller should not retain personal data for the sole purpose of being able to react to potential requests.

Recital 65: A Data Subject should have the right to have personal data concerning him or her rectified and a 'right to be forgotten' where the retention of such data infringes this Regulation or Union or Member State law to which the Controller is subject. In particular, a Data Subject should have the right to have his or her personal data erased and no longer processed where the personal data are no longer necessary in relation to the purposes for which they are collected or otherwise processed, where a Data Subject has withdrawn his or her consent or objects to the processing of personal data concerning him or her, or where the processing of his or her personal data does not otherwise comply with this Regulation. That right is relevant in particular where the Data Subject has given his or her consent as a child and is not fully aware of the risks involved by the processing, and later wants to remove such personal data, especially on the internet. The Data Subject should be able to exercise that right notwithstanding the fact that he or she is no longer a child. However, the further retention of the personal data should be lawful where it is necessary, for exercising the right of freedom of expression and information, for compliance with a legal obligation, for the performance of a task carried out in the public interest or in the exercise of official authority vested in the Controller, on the grounds of public interest in the area of public health, for archiving purposes in the public interest, scientific or historical research purposes or statistical purposes, or for the establishment, exercise or defence of legal claims.

Recital 66: To strengthen the right to be forgotten in the online environment, the right to erasure should also be extended in such a way that a Controller who has made the personal data public should be obliged to inform the Controllers which are processing such personal data to erase any links to, or copies or replications of those personal data. In doing so, that Controller should take reasonable steps, taking into account available technology and the means available to the Controller, including technical measures, to inform the Controllers which are processing the personal data of the Data Subject's request.

Recital 67: Methods by which to restrict the processing of personal data could include, inter alia, temporarily moving the selected data to another processing system, making the selected personal data unavailable to users, or temporarily removing published data from a website. In automated filing systems, the restriction of processing should in principle be ensured by technical means in such a manner that the personal data are not subject to further processing operations and cannot be changed. The fact that the processing of personal data is restricted should be clearly indicated in the system.

Recital 68: To further strengthen the control over his or her own data, where the processing of personal data is carried out by automated means, the Data Subject should also be allowed to receive personal data concerning him or her which he or she has provided to a Controller in a structured, commonly used, machine-readable and interoperable format, and to transmit it to another Controller. Data Controllers should be encouraged to develop interoperable formats that enable data portability. That right should apply where the Data Subject provided the personal data on the basis of his or her consent or the processing is necessary for the performance of a contract. It should not apply where processing is based on a legal ground other than consent or contract. By its very nature, that right should not be exercised against Controllers processing personal data in the exercise of their public duties. It should therefore not apply where the processing of the personal data is necessary for compliance with a legal obligation to which the Controller is subject or for the performance of a task carried out in the public interest or in the exercise of an official authority vested in the Controller. The Data Subject's right to transmit or receive personal data concerning him or her should not create an obligation for the Controllers to adopt or maintain processing systems which are technically compatible. Where, in a certain set of personal data, more than one Data Subject is concerned, the right to receive the personal data should be without prejudice to the rights and freedoms of other Data Subjects in accordance with this Regulation. Furthermore, that right should not prejudice the right of the Data Subject to obtain the erasure of personal data and the limitations of that right as set out in this Regulation and should, in particular, not imply the erasure of personal data concerning the Data Subject which have been provided by him or her for the performance of a contract to the extent that and for as long as the personal data are necessary for the performance of that contract. Where technically feasible, the Data Subject should have the right to have the personal data transmitted directly from one Controller to another.

Recital 69: Where personal data might lawfully be processed because processing is necessary for the performance of a task carried out in the public interest or in the exercise of official authority vested in the Controller, or on grounds of the legitimate interests of a Controller or a third party, a Data Subject should, nevertheless, be entitled to object to the processing of any personal data relating to his or her particular situation. It should be for the Controller to demonstrate that its compelling legitimate interest overrides the interests or the fundamental rights and freedoms of the Data Subject.

Recital 70: Where personal data are processed for the purposes of direct marketing, the Data Subject should have the right to object to such processing, including profiling to the extent that it is related to such direct marketing, whether with regard to initial or further processing, at any time and free of charge. That right should be explicitly brought to the attention of the Data Subject and presented clearly and separately from any other information.

Recital 71: The Data Subject should have the right not to be subject to a decision, which may include a measure, evaluating personal aspects relating to him or her which is based solely on automated processing and which produces legal effects concerning him or her or similarly significantly affects him or her, such as automatic refusal of an online credit application or e-recruiting practices without any human intervention. Such processing includes 'profiling' that consists of any form of automated processing of personal data evaluating the personal aspects relating to a Natural Person, in particular to analyse or predict aspects concerning the Data Subject's performance at work, economic situation, health, personal preferences or interests, reliability or behaviour, location or movements, where it produces legal effects concerning him or her or similarly significantly affects him or her. However, decision-making based on such processing, including profiling, should be allowed where expressly authorised by Union or Member State law to which the Controller is subject, including for fraud and tax-evasion monitoring and prevention purposes conducted in accordance with the regulations, standards and recommendations of Union institutions or national oversight bodies and to ensure the security and reliability of a service provided by the Controller, or necessary for the entering or performance of a contract between the Data Subject and a Controller, or when the Data Subject has given his or her explicit consent. In any case, such processing should be subject to suitable safeguards, which should include specific information to the Data Subject and the right to obtain human intervention, to express his or her point of view, to obtain an explanation of the decision reached after such assessment and to challenge the decision. Such measure should not concern a child.

In order to ensure fair and transparent processing in respect of the Data Subject, taking into account the specific circumstances and context in which the personal data are processed, the Controller should use appropriate mathematical or statistical procedures for the profiling, implement technical and organisational measures appropriate to ensure, in particular, that factors which result in inaccuracies in personal data are corrected and the risk of errors is minimised, secure personal data in a manner that takes account of the potential risks involved for the interests and rights of the Data Subject and that prevents, inter alia, discriminatory effects on Natural Persons on the basis of racial or ethnic origin, political opinion, religion or beliefs, trade union membership, genetic or health status or sexual orientation, or that result in measures having such an effect. Automated decision-making and profiling based on special categories of personal data should be allowed only under specific conditions.

Recital 72: Profiling is subject to the rules of this Regulation governing the processing of personal data, such as the legal grounds for processing or data protection principles. The European Data Protection Board established by this Regulation (the 'Board') should be able to issue guidance in that context.

Recital 73: Restrictions concerning specific principles and the rights of information, access to and rectification or erasure of personal data, the right to data portability, the right to object, decisions based on profiling, as well as the communication of a personal data breach to a Data Subject and certain related obligations of the Controllers may be imposed by Union or Member State law, as far as necessary and proportionate in a democratic society to safeguard public security, including the protection of human life especially in response to natural or manmade disasters, the prevention, investigation and prosecution of criminal offences or the execution of criminal penalties, including the safeguarding against and the prevention of threats to public security, or of breaches of ethics for regulated professions, other important objectives of general public interest of the Union or of a Member State, in particular an important economic or financial interest of the Union or of a Member State, the keeping of public registers kept for reasons of general public interest, further processing of archived personal data to provide specific information related to the political behaviour under former totalitarian state regimes or the protection of the Data Subject or the rights and freedoms of others, including social protection, public health and humanitarian purposes. Those restrictions should be in accordance with the requirements set out in the Charter and in the European Convention for the Protection of Human Rights and Fundamental Freedoms.

74:100 - Controller and Processor

Recital 74: The responsibility and liability of the Controller for any processing of personal data carried out by the Controller or on the Controller's behalf should be established. In particular, the Controller should be obliged to implement appropriate and effective measures and be able to demonstrate the compliance of processing activities with this Regulation, including the effectiveness of the measures. Those measures should take into account the nature, scope, context and purposes of the processing and the risk to the rights and freedoms of Natural Persons.

Recital 75: The risk to the rights and freedoms of Natural Persons, of varying likelihood and severity, may result from personal data processing which could lead to physical, material or non-material damage, in particular: where the processing may give rise to discrimination, identity theft or fraud, financial loss, damage to the reputation, loss of confidentiality of personal data protected by professional secrecy, unauthorised reversal of pseudonymisation, or any other significant economic or social disadvantage; where Data Subjects might be deprived of their rights and freedoms or prevented from exercising control over their personal data; where personal data are processed which reveal racial or ethnic origin, political opinions, religion or philosophical beliefs, trade union membership, and the processing of genetic data, data concerning health or data concerning sex life or criminal convictions and offences or related security measures; where personal aspects are evaluated, in particular analysing or predicting aspects concerning performance at work, economic situation, health, personal preferences or interests, reliability or behaviour, location or movements, in order to create or use personal profiles; where personal data of vulnerable Natural Persons, in particular of children, are processed; or where processing involves a large amount of personal data and affects a large number of Data Subjects.

Recital 76: The likelihood and severity of the risk to the rights and freedoms of the Data Subject should be determined by reference to the nature, scope, context and purposes of the processing. Risk should be evaluated on the basis of an objective assessment; by which it is established whether data processing operations involve a risk or a high risk.

Recital 77: Guidance on the implementation of appropriate measures and on the demonstration of compliance by the Controller or the Processor, especially as regards the identification of the risk related to the processing, their assessment in terms of origin, nature, likelihood and severity, and the identification of best practices to mitigate the risk, could be provided in particular by means of approved codes of conduct, approved certifications, guidelines provided by the Board or indications provided by a data protection officer. The Board may also issue guidelines on processing operations that are considered to be unlikely to result in a high risk to the rights and freedoms of Natural Persons and indicate what measures may be sufficient in such cases to address such risk.

Recital 78: The protection of the rights and freedoms of Natural Persons with regard to the processing of personal data require that appropriate technical and organisational measures be taken to ensure that the requirements of this Regulation are met. In order to be able to demonstrate compliance with this Regulation, the Controller should adopt internal policies and implement measures which meet in particular the principles of data protection by design and data protection by default. Such measures could consist, inter alia, of minimising the processing of personal data, pseudonymising personal data as soon as possible, transparency with regard to the functions and processing of personal data, enabling the Data Subject to monitor the data processing, enabling the Controller to create and improve security features. When developing, designing, selecting and using applications, services and products that are based on the processing of personal data or process personal data to fulfil their task, producers of the products, services and applications should be encouraged to take into account the right to data protection when developing and designing such products, services and applications and, with due regard to the state of the art, to make sure that Controllers and Processors are able to fulfil their data protection obligations. The principles of data protection by design and by default should also be taken into consideration in the context of public tenders.

Recital 79: The protection of the rights and freedoms of Data Subjects as well as the responsibility and liability of

Controllers and Processors, also in relation to the monitoring by and measures of supervisory authorities, requires a clear allocation of the responsibilities under this Regulation, including where a Controller determines the purposes and means of the processing jointly with other Controllers or where a processing operation is carried out on behalf of a Controller.

Recital 80: Where a Controller or a Processor not established in the Union is processing personal data of Data Subjects who are in the Union whose processing activities are related to the offering of goods or services, irrespective of whether a payment of the Data Subject is required, to such Data Subjects in the Union, or to the monitoring of their behaviour as far as their behaviour takes place within the Union, the Controller or the Processor should designate a representative, unless the processing is occasional, does not include processing, on a large scale, of special categories of personal data or the processing of personal data relating to criminal convictions and offences, and is unlikely to result in a risk to the rights and freedoms of Natural Persons, taking into account the nature, context, scope and purposes of the processing or if the Controller is a public authority or body. The representative should act on behalf of the Controller or the Processor and may be addressed by any Supervisory Authority. The representative should be explicitly designated by a written mandate of the Controller or of the Processor to act on its behalf with regard to its obligations under this Regulation. The designation of such a representative does not affect the responsibility or liability of the Controller or of the Processor under this Regulation. Such a representative should perform its tasks according to the mandate received from the Controller or Processor, including cooperating with the competent supervisory authorities with regard to any action taken to ensure compliance with this Regulation. The designated representative should be subject to enforcement proceedings in the event of non-compliance by the Controller or Processor.

Recital 81: To ensure compliance with the requirements of this Regulation in respect of the processing to be carried out by the Processor on behalf of the Controller, when entrusting a Processor with processing activities, the Controller should use only Processors providing sufficient guarantees, in particular in terms of expert knowledge, reliability and resources, to implement technical and organisational measures which will meet the requirements of this Regulation, including for the security of processing. The adherence of the Processor to an approved code of conduct or an approved certification mechanism may be used as an element to demonstrate compliance with the obligations of the Controller. The carrying-out of processing by a Processor should be governed by a contract or other legal act under Union or Member State law, binding the Processor to the Controller, setting out the subject-matter and duration of the processing, the nature and purposes of the processing, the type of personal data and categories of Data Subjects, taking into account the specific tasks and responsibilities of the Processor in the context of the processing to be carried out and the risk to the rights and freedoms of the Data Subject. The Controller and Processor may choose to use an individual contract or standard contractual clauses which are adopted either directly by the Commission or by a Supervisory Authority in accordance with the consistency mechanism and then adopted by the Commission. After the completion of the processing on behalf of the Controller, the Processor should, at the choice of the Controller, return or delete the personal data, unless there is a requirement to store the personal data under Union or Member State law to which the Processor is subject.

Recital 82: In order to demonstrate compliance with this Regulation, the Controller or Processor should maintain records of processing activities under its responsibility. Each Controller and Processor should be obliged to cooperate with the Supervisory Authority and make those records, on request, available to it, so that it might serve for monitoring those processing operations.

Recital 83: In order to maintain security and to prevent processing in infringement of this Regulation, the Controller or Processor should evaluate the risks inherent in the processing and implement measures to mitigate those risks, such as encryption. Those measures should ensure an appropriate level of security, including confidentiality, taking into account the state of the art and the costs of implementation in relation to the risks and the nature of the personal data to be protected. In assessing data security risk, consideration should be given to the risks that are presented by personal data processing, such as accidental or unlawful destruction, loss, alteration, unauthorised disclosure of, or access to, personal data transmitted, stored or otherwise processed which may in particular lead to physical, material or non-material damage.

Recital 84: In order to enhance compliance with this Regulation where processing operations are likely to result in a high risk to the rights and freedoms of Natural Persons, the Controller should be responsible for the carrying-out of a data protection impact assessment to evaluate, in particular, the origin, nature, particularity and severity of that risk. The outcome of the assessment should be taken into account when determining the appropriate measures to be taken in order to demonstrate that the processing of personal data complies with this Regulation. Where a data-protection impact assessment indicates that processing operations involve a high risk which the Controller cannot mitigate by appropriate measures in terms of available technology and costs of implementation, a consultation of the Supervisory Authority should take place prior to the processing.

Recital 85: A personal data breach may, if not addressed in an appropriate and timely manner, result in physical, material or non-material damage to Natural Persons such as loss of control over their personal data or limitation of their rights, discrimination, identity theft or fraud, financial loss, unauthorised reversal of pseudonymisation, damage to reputation, loss of confidentiality of personal data protected by professional secrecy or any other significant economic or social disadvantage to the Natural Person concerned. Therefore, as soon as the Controller becomes aware that a personal data breach has occurred, the Controller should notify the personal data breach to the Supervisory Authority without undue delay and, where feasible, not later than 72 hours after having become aware of it, unless the Controller is able to demonstrate, in accordance with the accountability principle, that the personal data breach is unlikely to result in a risk to the rights and freedoms of Natural Persons. Where such notification cannot be achieved within 72 hours, the reasons for the delay should accompany the notification and information may be provided in phases without undue further delay.

Recital 86: The Controller should communicate to the Data Subject a personal data breach, without undue delay, where that personal data breach is likely to result in a high risk to the rights and freedoms of the Natural Person in order to allow him or her to take the necessary precautions. The communication should describe the nature of the personal data breach as well as recommendations for the Natural Person concerned to mitigate potential adverse effects. Such communications to Data Subjects should be made as soon as reasonably feasible and in close cooperation with the Supervisory Authority, respecting guidance provided by it or by other relevant authorities such as law-enforcement authorities. For example, the need to mitigate an immediate risk of damage would call for prompt communication with Data Subjects whereas the need to implement appropriate measures against continuing or similar personal data breaches may justify more time for communication.

Recital 87: It should be ascertained whether all appropriate technological protection and organisational measures have been implemented to establish immediately whether a personal data breach has taken place and to inform promptly the Supervisory Authority and the Data Subject. The fact that the notification was made without undue delay should be established taking into account in particular the nature and gravity of the personal data breach and its consequences and adverse effects for the Data Subject. Such notification may result in an intervention of the Supervisory Authority in accordance with its tasks and powers laid down in this Regulation.

Recital 88: In setting detailed rules concerning the format and procedures applicable to the notification of personal data breaches, due consideration should be given to the circumstances of that breach, including whether or not personal data had been protected by appropriate technical protection measures, effectively limiting the likelihood of identity fraud or other forms of misuse. Moreover, such rules and procedures should take into account the legitimate interests of law-enforcement authorities where early disclosure could unnecessarily hamper the investigation of the circumstances of a personal data breach.

Recital 89: Directive 95/46/EC provided for a general obligation to notify the processing of personal data to the supervisory authorities. While that obligation produces administrative and financial burdens, it did not in all cases contribute to improving the protection of personal data. Such indiscriminate general notification obligations should therefore be abolished, and replaced by effective procedures and mechanisms which focus instead on those types of processing operations which are likely to result in a high risk to the rights and freedoms of Natural Persons by virtue of their nature, scope, context and purposes. Such types of processing operations may be those which in, particular, involve using new technologies, or are of a new kind and where no data protection impact assessment has been carried out before by the Controller, or where they become necessary in the light of the time that has elapsed since the initial processing.

Recital 90: In such cases, a data protection impact assessment should be carried out by the Controller prior to the processing in order to assess the particular likelihood and severity of the high risk, taking into account the nature, scope, context and purposes of the processing and the sources of the risk. That impact assessment should include, in particular, the measures, safeguards and mechanisms envisaged for mitigating that risk, ensuring the protection of personal data and demonstrating compliance with this Regulation.

Recital 91: This should in particular apply to large-scale processing operations which aim to process a considerable amount of personal data at regional, national or supranational level and which could affect a large number of Data Subjects and which are likely to result in a high risk, for example, on account of their sensitivity, where in accordance with the achieved state of technological knowledge a new technology is used on a large scale as well as to other processing operations which result in a high risk to the rights and freedoms of Data Subjects, in particular where those operations render it more difficult for Data Subjects to exercise their rights. A data protection impact assessment should also be made where personal data are processed for taking decisions regarding specific Natural Persons following any systematic and extensive evaluation of personal aspects relating to Natural Persons based on profiling those data or following the processing of special categories of personal data, biometric data, or data on criminal convictions and offences or related security measures. A data protection impact assessment is equally required for monitoring publicly accessible areas on a large scale, especially when using optic-electronic devices or for any other operations where the competent Supervisory Authority considers that the processing is likely to result in a high risk to the rights and freedoms of Data Subjects, in particular because they prevent Data Subjects from exercising a right or using a service or a contract, or because they are carried out systematically on a large scale. The processing of personal data should not be considered to be on a large scale if the processing concerns personal data from patients or clients by an individual physician, other health care professional or lawyer. In such cases, a data protection impact assessment should not be mandatory.

Recital 92: There are circumstances under which it may be reasonable and economical for the subject of a data protection impact assessment to be broader than a single project, for example where public authorities or bodies intend to establish a common application or processing platform or where several Controllers plan to introduce a common application or processing environment across an industry sector or segment or for a widely used horizontal activity.

Recital 93: In the context of the adoption of the Member State law on which the performance of the tasks of the public authority or public body is based and which regulates the specific processing operation or set of operations in question, Member States may deem it necessary to carry out such assessment prior to the processing activities.

Recital 94: Where a data protection impact assessment indicates that the processing would, in the absence of safeguards, security measures and mechanisms to mitigate the risk, result in a high risk to the rights and freedoms of Natural Persons and the Controller is of the opinion that the risk cannot be mitigated by reasonable means in terms of available technologies and costs of implementation, the Supervisory Authority should be consulted prior to the start of processing activities. Such high risk is likely to result from certain types of processing and the extent and frequency of processing, which may result also in a realisation of damage or interference with the rights and freedoms of the Natural Person. The Supervisory Authority should respond to the request for consultation within a specified period. However, the absence of a reaction of the Supervisory Authority within that period should be without prejudice to any intervention of the Supervisory Authority in accordance with its tasks and powers laid down in this Regulation, including the power to prohibit processing operations. As part of that consultation process, the outcome of a data protection impact assessment carried out with regard to the processing at issue may be submitted to the Supervisory Authority, in particular the measures envisaged to mitigate the risk to the rights and freedoms of Natural Persons.

Recital 95: The Processor should assist the Controller, where necessary and upon request, in ensuring compliance with the obligations deriving from the carrying out of data protection impact assessments and from prior consultation of the Supervisory Authority

Recital 96: A consultation of the Supervisory Authority should also take place in the course of the preparation of a legislative or regulatory measure which provides for the processing of personal data, in order to ensure compliance of the intended processing with this Regulation and in particular to mitigate the risk involved for the Data Subject.

Recital 97: Where the processing is carried out by a public authority, except for courts or independent judicial authorities when acting in their judicial capacity, where, in the private sector, processing is carried out by a Controller whose core activities consist of processing operations that require regular and systematic monitoring of the Data Subjects on a large scale, or where the core activities of the Controller or the Processor consist of processing on a large scale of special categories of personal data and data relating to criminal convictions and offences, a person with expert knowledge of data protection law and practices should assist the Controller or Processor to monitor internal compliance with this Regulation. In the private sector, the core activities of a Controller relate to its primary activities and do not relate to the processing of personal data as ancillary activities. The necessary level of expert knowledge should be determined in particular according to the data processing operations carried out and the protection required for the personal data processed by the Controller or the Processor. Such data protection officers, whether or not they are an employee of the Controller, should be in a position to perform their duties and tasks in an independent manner

Recital 98: Associations or other bodies representing categories of Controllers or Processors should be encouraged to draw up codes of conduct, within the limits of this Regulation, so as to facilitate the effective application of this Regulation, taking account of the specific characteristics of the processing carried out in certain sectors and the specific needs of micro, small and medium enterprises. In particular, such codes of conduct could calibrate the obligations of Controllers and Processors, taking into account the risk likely to result from the processing for the rights and freedoms of Natural Persons.

Recital 99: When drawing up a code of conduct, or when amending or extending such a code, associations and other bodies representing categories of Controllers or Processors should consult relevant stakeholders, including Data Subjects where feasible, and have regard to submissions received and views expressed in response to such consultations.

Recital 100: In order to enhance transparency and compliance with this Regulation, the establishment of certification mechanisms and data protection seals and marks should be encouraged, allowing Data Subjects to quickly assess the level of data protection of relevant products and services.

101:116 - Transfers to Third Countries or International Organisations

Recital 101: Flows of personal data to and from countries outside the Union and international organisations are necessary for the expansion of international trade and international cooperation. The increase in such flows has raised new challenges and concerns with regard to the protection of personal data. However, when personal data are transferred from the Union to Controllers, Processors or other recipients in third countries or to international organisations, the level of protection of Natural Persons ensured in the Union by this Regulation should not be undermined, including in cases of onward transfers of personal data from the third country or international organisation to Controllers, Processors in the same or another third country or international organisation. In any event, transfers to third countries and international organisations may only be carried out in full compliance with this Regulation. A transfer could take place only if, subject to the other provisions of this Regulation, the conditions laid down in the provisions of this Regulation relating to the transfer of personal data to third countries or international organisations are complied with by the Controller or Processor.

Recital 102: This Regulation is without prejudice to international agreements concluded between the Union and third countries regulating the transfer of personal data including appropriate safeguards for the Data Subjects. Member States may conclude international agreements which involve the transfer of personal data to third countries or international organisations, as far as such agreements do not affect this Regulation or any other provisions of Union law and include an appropriate level of protection for the fundamental rights of the Data Subjects.

Recital 103: The Commission may decide with effect for the entire Union that a third country, a territory or specified sector within a third country, or an international organisation, offers an adequate level of data protection, thus providing legal certainty and uniformity throughout the Union as regards the third country or international organisation which is considered to provide such level of protection. In such cases, transfers of personal data to that third country or international organisation may take place without the need to obtain any further authorisation. The Commission may also decide, having given notice and a full statement setting out the reasons to the third country or international organisation, to revoke such a decision

Recital 104: In line with the fundamental values on which the Union is founded, in particular the protection of human rights, the Commission should, in its assessment of the third country, or of a territory or specified sector within a third country, take into account how a particular third country respects the rule of law, access to justice as well as international human rights norms and standards and its general and sectoral law, including legislation concerning public security, defence and national security as well as public order and criminal law. The adoption of an adequacy decision with regard to a territory or a specified sector in a third country should take into account clear and objective criteria, such as specific processing activities and the scope of applicable legal standards and legislation in force in the third country. The third country should offer guarantees ensuring an adequate level of protection essentially equivalent to that ensured within the Union, in particular where personal data are processed in one or several specific sectors. In particular, the third country should ensure effective independent data protection supervision and should provide for cooperation mechanisms with the Member States' data protection authorities, and the Data Subjects should be provided with effective and enforceable rights and effective administrative and judicial redress.

Recital 105: Apart from the international commitments the third country or international organisation has entered into, the Commission should take account of obligations arising from the third country's or international organisation's participation in multilateral or regional systems in particular in relation to the protection of personal data, as well as the implementation of such obligations. In particular, the third country's accession to the Council of Europe Convention of 28 January 1981 for the Protection of Individuals with regard to the Automatic Processing of Personal Data and its Additional Protocol should be taken into account. The Commission should consult the Board when assessing the level of protection in third countries or international organisations.

Recital 106: The Commission should monitor the functioning of decisions on the level of protection in a third country, a territory or specified sector within a third country, or an international organisation, and monitor the functioning of decisions adopted on the basis of Article 25(6) or Article 26(4) of Directive 95/46/EC. In its adequacy decisions, the Commission should provide for a periodic review mechanism of their functioning. That periodic review should be conducted in consultation with the third country or international organisation in question and take into account all relevant developments in the third country or international organisation. For the purposes of monitoring and of carrying out the periodic reviews, the Commission should take into consideration the views and findings of the European Parliament and of the Council as well as of other relevant bodies and sources. The Commission should evaluate, within a reasonable time, the functioning of the latter decisions and report any relevant findings to the Committee within the meaning of Regulation (EU) No 182/2011 of the European Parliament and of the Council as established under this Regulation, to the European Parliament and to the Council.

Recital 107: The Commission may recognise that a third country, a territory or a specified sector within a third country, or an international organisation no longer ensures an adequate level of data protection. Consequently, the transfer of personal data to that third country or international organisation should be prohibited, unless the requirements in this Regulation relating to transfers subject to appropriate safeguards, including binding corporate rules, and derogations for specific situations are fulfilled. In that case, provision should be made for consultations between the Commission and such third countries or international organisations. The Commission should, in a timely manner, inform the third country or international organisation of the reasons and enter into consultations with it in order to remedy the situation.

Recital 108: In the absence of an adequacy decision, the Controller or Processor should take measures to compensate for the lack of data protection in a third country by way of appropriate safeguards for the Data Subject. Such appropriate safeguards may consist of making use of binding corporate rules, standard data protection clauses adopted by the Commission, standard data protection clauses adopted by a Supervisory Authority or contractual clauses authorised by a Supervisory Authority. Those safeguards should ensure compliance with data protection requirements and the rights of the Data Subjects appropriate to processing within the Union, including the availability of enforceable Data Subject rights and of effective legal remedies, including to obtain effective administrative or judicial redress and to claim compensation, in the Union or in a third country. They should relate in particular to compliance with the general principles relating to personal data processing, the principles of data protection by design and by default. Transfers may also be carried out by public authorities or bodies with public authorities or bodies in third countries or with international organisations with corresponding duties or functions, including on the basis of provisions to be inserted into administrative arrangements, such as a memorandum of understanding, providing for enforceable and effective rights for Data Subjects. Authorisation by the competent Supervisory Authority should be obtained when the safeguards are provided for in administrative arrangements that are not legally binding.

Recital 109: The possibility for the Controller or Processor to use standard data-protection clauses adopted by the Commission or by a Supervisory Authority should prevent Controllers or Processors neither from including the standard data-protection clauses in a wider contract, such as a contract between the Processor and another Processor, nor from adding other clauses or additional safeguards provided that they do not contradict, directly or indirectly, the standard contractual clauses adopted by the Commission or by a Supervisory Authority or prejudice the fundamental rights or freedoms of the Data Subjects. Controllers and Processors should be encouraged to provide additional safeguards via contractual commitments that supplement standard protection clauses.

Recital 110: A group of undertakings, or a group of enterprises engaged in a joint economic activity, should be able to make use of approved binding corporate rules for its international transfers from the Union to organisations within the same group of undertakings, or group of enterprises engaged in a joint economic activity, provided that such corporate rules include all essential principles and enforceable rights to ensure appropriate safeguards for transfers or categories of transfers of personal data.

Recital 111: Provisions should be made for the possibility for transfers in certain circumstances where the Data Subject has given his or her explicit consent, where the transfer is occasional and necessary in relation to a contract or a legal claim, regardless of whether in a judicial procedure or whether in an administrative or any out-of-court procedure, including procedures before regulatory bodies. Provision should also be made for the possibility for transfers where important grounds of public interest laid down by Union or Member State law so require or where the transfer is made from a register established by law and intended for consultation by the public or persons having a legitimate interest. In the latter case, such a transfer should not involve the entirety of the personal data or entire categories of the data contained in the register and, when the register is intended for consultation by persons having a legitimate interest, the transfer should be made only at the request of those persons or, if they are to be the recipients, taking into full account the interests and fundamental rights of the Data Subject.

Recital 112: Those derogations should in particular apply to data transfers required and necessary for important reasons of public interest, for example in cases of international data exchange between competition authorities, tax or customs administrations, between financial supervisory authorities, between services competent for social security matters, or for public health, for example in the case of contact tracing for contagious diseases or in order to reduce and/or eliminate doping in sport. A transfer of personal data should also be regarded as lawful where it is necessary to protect an interest which is essential for the Data Subject's or another person's vital interests, including physical integrity or life, if the Data Subject is incapable of giving consent. In the absence of an adequacy decision, Union or Member State law may, for important reasons of public interest, expressly set limits to the transfer of specific categories of data to a third country or an international organisation. Member States should notify such provisions to the Commission. Any transfer to an international humanitarian organisation of personal data of a Data Subject who is physically or legally incapable of giving consent, with a view to accomplishing a task incumbent under the Geneva Conventions or to complying with international humanitarian law applicable in armed conflicts, could be considered to be necessary for an important reason of public interest or because it is in the vital interest of the Data Subject.

Recital 113: Transfers which can be qualified as not repetitive and that only concern a limited number of Data Subjects, could also be possible for the purposes of the compelling legitimate interests pursued by the Controller, when those interests are not overridden by the interests or rights and freedoms of the Data Subject and when the Controller has assessed all the circumstances surrounding the data transfer. The Controller should give particular consideration to the nature of the personal data, the purpose and duration of the proposed processing operation or operations, as well as the situation in the country of origin, the third country and the country of final destination, and should provide suitable safeguards to protect fundamental rights and freedoms of Natural Persons with regard to the processing of their personal data. Such transfers should be possible only in residual cases where none of the other grounds for transfer are applicable. For scientific or historical research purposes or statistical purposes, the legitimate expectations of society for an increase of knowledge should be taken into consideration. The Controller should inform the Supervisory Authority and the Data Subject about the transfer.

Recital 114: In any case, where the Commission has taken no decision on the adequate level of data protection in a third country, the Controller or Processor should make use of solutions that provide Data Subjects with enforceable and effective rights as regards the processing of their data in the Union once those data have been transferred so that that they will continue to benefit from fundamental rights and safeguards.

Recital 115: Some third countries adopt laws, regulations and other legal acts which purport to directly regulate the processing activities of natural and legal persons under the jurisdiction of the Member States. This may include judgments of courts or tribunals or decisions of administrative authorities in third countries requiring a Controller or Processor to transfer or disclose personal data, and which are not based on an international agreement, such as a mutual legal assistance treaty, in force between the requesting third country and the Union or a Member State. The extraterritorial application of those laws, regulations and other legal acts may be in breach of international law and may impede the attainment of the protection of Natural Persons ensured in the Union by this Regulation. Transfers should only be allowed where the conditions of this Regulation for a transfer to third countries are met. This may be the case, inter alia, where disclosure is necessary for an important ground of public interest recognised in Union or Member State law to which the Controller is subject.

Recital 116: When personal data moves across borders outside the Union it may put at increased risk the ability of Natural Persons to exercise data protection rights in particular to protect themselves from the unlawful use or disclosure of that information. At the same time, supervisory authorities may find that they are unable to pursue complaints or conduct investigations relating to the activities outside their borders. Their efforts to work together in the cross-border context may also be hampered by insufficient preventative or remedial powers, inconsistent legal regimes, and practical obstacles like resource constraints. Therefore, there is a need to promote closer cooperation among data protection supervisory authorities to help them exchange information and carry out investigations with their international counterparts. For the purposes of developing international cooperation mechanisms to facilitate and provide international mutual assistance for the enforcement of legislation for the protection of personal data, the Commission and the supervisory authorities should exchange information and cooperate in activities related to the exercise of their powers with competent authorities in third countries, based on reciprocity and in accordance with this Regulation.

117:131 - Independent Supervisory Authorities

Recital 117: The establishment of supervisory authorities in Member States, empowered to perform their tasks and exercise their powers with complete independence, is an essential component of the protection of Natural Persons with regard to the processing of their personal data. Member States should be able to establish more than one Supervisory Authority, to reflect their constitutional, organisational and administrative structure.

Recital 118: The independence of supervisory authorities should not mean that the supervisory authorities cannot be subject to control or monitoring mechanisms regarding their financial expenditure or to judicial review.

Recital 119: Where a Member State establishes several supervisory authorities, it should establish by law mechanisms for ensuring the effective participation of those supervisory authorities in the consistency mechanism. That Member State should in particular designate the Supervisory Authority which functions as a single contact point for the effective participation of those authorities in the mechanism, to ensure swift and smooth cooperation with other supervisory authorities, the Board and the Commission.

Recital 120: Each Supervisory Authority should be provided with the financial and human resources, premises and infrastructure necessary for the effective performance of their tasks, including those related to mutual assistance and cooperation with other supervisory authorities throughout the Union. Each Supervisory Authority should have a separate, public annual budget, which may be part of the overall state or national budget.

Recital 121: The general conditions for the member or members of the Supervisory Authority should be laid down by law in each Member State and should in particular provide that those members are to be appointed, by means of a transparent procedure, either by the parliament, government or the head of State of the Member State on the basis of a proposal from the government, a member of the government, the parliament or a chamber of the parliament, or by an independent body entrusted under Member State law. In order to ensure the independence of the Supervisory Authority, the member or members should act with integrity, refrain from any action that is incompatible with their duties and should not, during their term of office, engage in any incompatible occupation, whether gainful or not. The Supervisory Authority should have its own staff, chosen by the Supervisory Authority or an independent body established by Member State law, which should be subject to the exclusive direction of the member or members of the Supervisory Authority.

Recital 122: Each Supervisory Authority should be competent on the territory of its own Member State to exercise the powers and to perform the tasks conferred on it in accordance with this Regulation. This should cover in particular the processing in the context of the activities of an establishment of the Controller or Processor on the territory of its own Member State, the processing of personal data carried out by public authorities or private bodies acting in the public interest, processing affecting Data Subjects on its territory or processing carried out by a Controller or Processor not established in the Union when targeting Data Subjects residing on its territory. This should include handling complaints lodged by a Data Subject, conducting investigations on the application of this Regulation and promoting public awareness of the risks, rules, safeguards and rights in relation to the processing of personal data.

Recital 123: The supervisory authorities should monitor the application of the provisions pursuant to this Regulation and contribute to its consistent application throughout the Union, in order to protect Natural Persons in relation to the processing of their personal data and to facilitate the free flow of personal data within the internal market. For that purpose, the supervisory authorities should cooperate with each other and with the Commission, without the need for any agreement between Member States on the provision of mutual assistance or on such cooperation.

Recital 124: Where the processing of personal data takes place in the context of the activities of an establishment of a Controller or a Processor in the Union and the Controller or Processor is established in more than one Member

State, or where processing taking place in the context of the activities of a single establishment of a Controller or Processor in the Union substantially affects or is likely to substantially affect Data Subjects in more than one Member State, the Supervisory Authority for the main establishment of the Controller or Processor or for the single establishment of the Controller or Processor should act as lead authority. It should cooperate with the other authorities concerned, because the Controller or Processor has an establishment on the territory of their Member State, because Data Subjects residing on their territory are substantially affected, or because a complaint has been lodged with them. Also where a Data Subject not residing in that Member State has lodged a complaint, the Supervisory Authority with which such complaint has been lodged should also be a Supervisory Authority concerned. Within its tasks to issue guidelines on any question covering the application of this Regulation, the Board should be able to issue guidelines in particular on the criteria to be taken into account in order to ascertain whether the processing in question substantially affects Data Subjects in more than one Member State and on what constitutes a relevant and reasoned objection.

Recital 125: The lead authority should be competent to adopt binding decisions regarding measures applying the powers conferred on it in accordance with this Regulation. In its capacity as lead authority, the Supervisory Authority should closely involve and coordinate the supervisory authorities concerned in the decision-making process. Where the decision is to reject the complaint by the Data Subject in whole or in part, that decision should be adopted by the Supervisory Authority with which the complaint has been lodged.

Recital 126: The decision should be agreed jointly by the lead Supervisory Authority and the supervisory authorities concerned and should be directed towards the main or single establishment of the Controller or Processor and be binding on the Controller and Processor. The Controller or Processor should take the necessary measures to ensure compliance with this Regulation and the implementation of the decision notified by the lead Supervisory Authority to the main establishment of the Controller or Processor as regards the processing activities in the Union.

Recital 127: Each Supervisory Authority not acting as the lead Supervisory Authority should be competent to handle local cases where the Controller or Processor is established in more than one Member State, but the subject matter of the specific processing concerns only processing carried out in a single Member State and involves only Data Subjects in that single Member State, for example, where the subject matter concerns the processing of employees' personal data in the specific employment context of a Member State. In such cases, the Supervisory Authority should inform the lead Supervisory Authority without delay about the matter. After being informed, the lead Supervisory Authority should decide, whether it will handle the case pursuant to the provision on cooperation between the lead Supervisory Authority and other supervisory authorities concerned ('one-stop-shop mechanism'), or whether the Supervisory Authority which informed it should handle the case at local level. When deciding whether it will handle the case, the lead Supervisory Authority should take into account whether there is an establishment of the Controller or Processor in the Member State of the Supervisory Authority which informed it in order to ensure effective enforcement of a decision vis-à-vis the Controller or Processor. Where the lead Supervisory Authority decides to handle the case, the Supervisory Authority which informed it should have the possibility to submit a draft for a decision, of which the lead Supervisory Authority should take utmost account when preparing its draft decision in that one-stop-shop mechanism.

Recital 128: The rules on the lead Supervisory Authority and the one-stop-shop mechanism should not apply where the processing is carried out by public authorities or private bodies in the public interest. In such cases the only Supervisory Authority competent to exercise the powers conferred to it in accordance with this Regulation should be the Supervisory Authority of the Member State where the public authority or private body is established.

Recital 129: In order to ensure consistent monitoring and enforcement of this Regulation throughout the Union, the supervisory authorities should have in each Member State the same tasks and effective powers, including powers of investigation, corrective powers and sanctions, and authorisation and advisory powers, in particular in cases of complaints from Natural Persons, and without prejudice to the powers of prosecutorial authorities under Member

State law, to bring infringements of this Regulation to the attention of the judicial authorities and engage in legal proceedings. Such powers should also include the power to impose a temporary or definitive limitation, including a ban, on processing. Member States may specify other tasks related to the protection of personal data under this Regulation. The powers of supervisory authorities should be exercised in accordance with appropriate procedural safeguards set out in Union and Member State law, impartially, fairly and within a reasonable time. In particular, each measure should be appropriate, necessary and proportionate in view of ensuring compliance with this Regulation, taking into account the circumstances of each individual case, respect the right of every person to be heard before any individual measure which would affect him or her adversely is taken and avoid superfluous costs and excessive inconveniences for the persons concerned. Investigatory powers as regards access to premises should be exercised in accordance with specific requirements in Member State procedural law, such as the requirement to obtain a prior judicial authorisation. Each legally binding measure of the Supervisory Authority should be in writing, be clear and unambiguous, indicate the Supervisory Authority which has issued the measure, the date of issue of the measure, bear the signature of the head, or a member of the Supervisory Authority authorised by him or her, give the reasons for the measure, and refer to the right of an effective remedy. This should not preclude additional requirements pursuant to Member State procedural law. The adoption of a legally binding decision implies that it may give rise to judicial review in the Member State of the Supervisory Authority that adopted the decision.

Recital 130: Where the Supervisory Authority with which the complaint has been lodged is not the lead Supervisory Authority, the lead Supervisory Authority should closely cooperate with the Supervisory Authority with which the complaint has been lodged in accordance with the provisions on cooperation and consistency laid down in this Regulation. In such cases, the lead Supervisory Authority should, when taking measures intended to produce legal effects, including the imposition of administrative fines, take utmost account of the view of the Supervisory Authority with which the complaint has been lodged and which should remain competent to carry out any investigation on the territory of its own Member State in liaison with the competent Supervisory Authority.

Recital 131: Where another Supervisory Authority should act as a lead Supervisory Authority for the processing activities of the Controller or Processor but the concrete subject matter of a complaint or the possible infringement concerns only processing activities of the Controller or Processor in the Member State where the complaint has been lodged or the possible infringement detected and the matter does not substantially affect or is not likely to substantially affect Data Subjects in other Member States, the Supervisory Authority receiving a complaint or detecting or being informed otherwise of situations that entail possible infringements of this Regulation should seek an amicable settlement with the Controller and, if this proves unsuccessful, exercise its full range of powers. This should include: specific processing carried out in the territory of the Member State of the Supervisory Authority or with regard to Data Subjects on the territory of that Member State; processing that is carried out in the context of an offer of goods or services specifically aimed at Data Subjects in the territory of the Member State of the Supervisory Authority; or processing that has to be assessed taking into account relevant legal obligations under Member State law.

131:140 - Cooperation and Consistency

Recital 132: Awareness-raising activities by supervisory authorities addressed to the public should include specific measures directed at Controllers and Processors, including micro, small and medium-sized enterprises, as well as Natural Persons in particular in the educational context.

Recital 133: The supervisory authorities should assist each other in performing their tasks and provide mutual assistance, so as to ensure the consistent application and enforcement of this Regulation in the internal market. A Supervisory Authority requesting mutual assistance may adopt a provisional measure if it receives no response to a request for mutual assistance within one month of the receipt of that request by the other Supervisory Authority.

Recital 134: Each Supervisory Authority should, where appropriate, participate in joint operations with other supervisory authorities. The requested Supervisory Authority should be obliged to respond to the request within a specified time period.

Recital 135: In order to ensure the consistent application of this Regulation throughout the Union, a consistency mechanism for cooperation between the supervisory authorities should be established. That mechanism should in particular apply where a Supervisory Authority intends to adopt a measure intended to produce legal effects as regards processing operations which substantially affect a significant number of Data Subjects in several Member States. It should also apply where any Supervisory Authority concerned or the Commission requests that such matter should be handled in the consistency mechanism. That mechanism should be without prejudice to any measures that the Commission may take in the exercise of its powers under the Treaties.

Recital 136: In applying the consistency mechanism, the Board should, within a determined period of time, issue an opinion, if a majority of its members so decides or if so requested by any Supervisory Authority concerned or the Commission. The Board should also be empowered to adopt legally binding decisions where there are disputes between supervisory authorities. For that purpose, it should issue, in principle by a two-thirds majority of its members, legally binding decisions in clearly specified cases where there are conflicting views among supervisory authorities, in particular in the cooperation mechanism between the lead Supervisory Authority and supervisory authorities concerned on the merits of the case, in particular whether there is an infringement of this Regulation.

Recital 137: There may be an urgent need to act in order to protect the rights and freedoms of Data Subjects, in particular when the danger exists that the enforcement of a right of a Data Subject could be considerably impeded. A Supervisory Authority should therefore be able to adopt duly justified provisional measures on its territory with a specified period of validity which should not exceed three months.

Recital 138: The application of such mechanism should be a condition for the lawfulness of a measure intended to produce legal effects by a Supervisory Authority in those cases where its application is mandatory. In other cases of cross-border relevance, the cooperation mechanism between the lead Supervisory Authority and supervisory authorities concerned should be applied and mutual assistance and joint operations might be carried out between the supervisory authorities concerned on a bilateral or multilateral basis without triggering the consistency mechanism.

Recital 139: In order to promote the consistent application of this Regulation, the Board should be set up as an independent body of the Union. To fulfil its objectives, the Board should have legal personality. The Board should be represented by its Chair. It should replace the Working Party on the Protection of Individuals with Regard to the Processing of Personal Data established by Directive 95/46/EC. It should consist of the head of a Supervisory Authority of each Member State and the European Data Protection Supervisor or their respective representatives. The Commission should participate in the Board's activities without voting rights and the European Data Protection Supervisor should have specific voting rights. The Board should contribute to the consistent application of this

Regulation throughout the Union, including by advising the Commission, in particular on the level of protection in third countries or international organisations, and promoting cooperation of the supervisory authorities throughout the Union. The Board should act independently when performing its tasks

Recital 140: The Board should be assisted by a secretariat provided by the European Data Protection Supervisor. The staff of the European Data Protection Supervisor involved in carrying out the tasks conferred on the Board by this Regulation should perform its tasks exclusively under the instructions of, and report to, the Chair of the Board.

141:152 - Remedies, Liabilities and Penalties

Recital 141: Every Data Subject should have the right to lodge a complaint with a single Supervisory Authority, in particular in the Member State of his or her habitual residence, and the right to an effective judicial remedy in accordance with Article 47 of the Charter if the Data Subject considers that his or her rights under this Regulation are infringed or where the Supervisory Authority does not act on a complaint, partially or wholly rejects or dismisses a complaint or does not act where such action is necessary to protect the rights of the Data Subject. The investigation following a complaint should be carried out, subject to judicial review, to the extent that is appropriate in the specific case. The Supervisory Authority should inform the Data Subject of the progress and the outcome of the complaint within a reasonable period. If the case requires further investigation or coordination with another Supervisory Authority, intermediate information should be given to the Data Subject. In order to facilitate the submission of complaints, each Supervisory Authority should take measures such as providing a complaint submission form which can also be completed electronically, without excluding other means of communication.

Recital 142: Where a Data Subject considers that his or her rights under this Regulation are infringed, he or she should have the right to mandate a not-for-profit body, organisation or association which is constituted in accordance with the law of a Member State, has statutory objectives which are in the public interest and is active in the field of the protection of personal data to lodge a complaint on his or her behalf with a Supervisory Authority, exercise the right to a judicial remedy on behalf of Data Subjects or, if provided for in Member State law, exercise the right to receive compensation on behalf of Data Subjects. A Member State may provide for such a body, organisation or association to have the right to lodge a complaint in that Member State, independently of a Data Subject's mandate, and the right to an effective judicial remedy where it has reasons to consider that the rights of a Data Subject have been infringed as a result of the processing of personal data which infringes this Regulation. That body, organisation or association may not be allowed to claim compensation on a Data Subject's behalf independently of the Data Subject's mandate.

Recital 143: Any natural or legal person has the right to bring an action for annulment of decisions of the Board before the Court of Justice under the conditions provided for in Article 263 TFEU. As addressees of such decisions, the supervisory authorities concerned which wish to challenge them have to bring action within two months of being notified of them, in accordance with Article 263 TFEU. Where decisions of the Board are of direct and individual concern to a Controller, Processor or complainant, the latter may bring an action for annulment against those decisions within two months of their publication on the website of the Board, in accordance with Article 263 TFEU. Without prejudice to this right under Article 263 TFEU, each natural or legal person should have an effective judicial remedy before the competent national court against a decision of a Supervisory Authority which produces legal effects concerning that person. Such a decision concerns in particular the exercise of investigative, corrective and authorisation powers by the Supervisory Authority or the dismissal or rejection of complaints. However, the right to an effective judicial remedy does not encompass measures taken by supervisory authorities which are not legally binding, such as opinions issued by or advice provided by the Supervisory Authority. Proceedings against a Supervisory Authority should be brought before the courts of the Member State where the Supervisory Authority is established and should be conducted in accordance with that Member State's procedural law. Those courts should exercise full jurisdiction, which should include jurisdiction to examine all questions of fact and law relevant to the dispute before them.

Where a complaint has been rejected or dismissed by a Supervisory Authority, the complainant may bring proceedings before the courts in the same Member State. In the context of judicial remedies relating to the application of this Regulation, national courts which consider a decision on the question necessary to enable them to give judgment, may, or in the case provided for in Article 267 TFEU, must, request the Court of Justice to give a preliminary ruling on the interpretation of Union law, including this Regulation. Furthermore, where a decision of a Supervisory Authority implementing a decision of the Board is challenged before a national court and the validity of the decision of the Board is at issue, that national court does not have the power to declare the Board's decision invalid but must refer the question of validity to the Court of Justice in accordance with Article 267 TFEU as interpreted by the Court of Justice, where it considers the decision invalid. However, a national court may not refer a question on the validity of the decision of the Board at the request of a natural or legal person which had the opportunity to bring an action for annulment of that decision, in particular if it was directly and individually concerned by that decision, but had not done so within the period laid down in Article 263 TFEU.

Recital 144: Where a court seized of proceedings against a decision by a Supervisory Authority has reason to believe that proceedings concerning the same processing, such as the same subject matter as regards processing by the same Controller or Processor, or the same cause of action, are brought before a competent court in another Member State, it should contact that court in order to confirm the existence of such related proceedings. If related proceedings are pending before a court in another Member State, any court other than the court first seized may stay its proceedings or may, on request of one of the parties, decline jurisdiction in favour of the court first seized if that court has jurisdiction over the proceedings in question and its law permits the consolidation of such related proceedings. Proceedings are deemed to be related where they are so closely connected that it is expedient to hear and determine them together in order to avoid the risk of irreconcilable judgments resulting from separate proceedings.

Recital 145: For proceedings against a Controller or Processor, the plaintiff should have the choice to bring the action before the courts of the Member States where the Controller or Processor has an establishment or where the Data Subject resides, unless the Controller is a public authority of a Member State acting in the exercise of its public powers.

Recital 146: The Controller or Processor should compensate any damage which a person may suffer as a result of processing that infringes this Regulation. The Controller or Processor should be exempt from liability if it proves that it is not in any way responsible for the damage. The concept of damage should be broadly interpreted in the light of the case-law of the Court of Justice in a manner which fully reflects the objectives of this Regulation. This is without prejudice to any claims for damage deriving from the violation of other rules in Union or Member State law. Processing that infringes this Regulation also includes processing that infringes delegated and implementing acts adopted in accordance with this Regulation and Member State law specifying rules of this Regulation. Data subjects should receive full and effective compensation for the damage they have suffered. Where Controllers or Processors are involved in the same processing, each Controller or Processor should be held liable for the entire damage. However, where they are joined to the same judicial proceedings, in accordance with Member State law, compensation may be apportioned according to the responsibility of each Controller or Processor for the damage caused by the processing, provided that full and effective compensation of the Data Subject who suffered the damage is ensured. Any Controller or Processor which has paid full compensation may subsequently institute recourse proceedings against other Controllers or Processors involved in the same processing

Recital 147: Where specific rules on jurisdiction are contained in this Regulation, in particular as regards proceedings seeking a judicial remedy including compensation, against a Controller or Processor, general jurisdiction rules such as those of Regulation (EU) No 1215/2012 of the European Parliament and of the Council[1] should not prejudice the application of such specific rules.

Recital 148: In order to strengthen the enforcement of the rules of this Regulation, penalties including administrative fines should be imposed for any infringement of this Regulation, in addition to, or instead of appropriate measures imposed by the Supervisory Authority pursuant to this Regulation. In a case of a minor infringement or if the fine likely to be imposed would constitute a disproportionate burden to a Natural Person, a reprimand may be issued instead of a fine. Due regard should however be given to the nature, gravity and duration of the infringement, the intentional character of the infringement, actions taken to mitigate the damage suffered, degree of responsibility or any relevant previous infringements, the manner in which the infringement became known to the Supervisory Authority, compliance with measures ordered against the Controller or Processor, adherence to a code of conduct and any other aggravating or mitigating factor. The imposition of penalties including administrative fines should be subject to appropriate procedural safeguards in accordance with the general principles of Union law and the Charter, including effective judicial protection and due process.

Recital 149: Member States should be able to lay down the rules on criminal penalties for infringements of this Regulation, including for infringements of national rules adopted pursuant to and within the limits of this Regulation. Those criminal penalties may also allow for the deprivation of the profits obtained through infringements of this Regulation. However, the imposition of criminal penalties for infringements of such national rules and of administrative penalties should not lead to a breach of the principle of ne bis in idem, as interpreted by the Court of Justice.

Recital 150: In order to strengthen and harmonise administrative penalties for infringements of this Regulation, each Supervisory Authority should have the power to impose administrative fines. This Regulation should indicate infringements and the upper limit and criteria for setting the related administrative fines, which should be determined by the competent Supervisory Authority in each individual case, taking into account all relevant circumstances of the specific situation, with due regard in particular to the nature, gravity and duration of the infringement and of its consequences and the measures taken to ensure compliance with the obligations under this Regulation and to prevent or mitigate the consequences of the infringement. Where administrative fines are imposed on an undertaking, an undertaking should be understood to be an undertaking in accordance with Articles 101 and 102 TFEU for those purposes. Where administrative fines are imposed on persons that are not an undertaking, the Supervisory Authority should take account of the general level of income in the Member State as well as the economic situation of the person in considering the appropriate amount of the fine. The consistency mechanism may also be used to promote a consistent application of administrative fines. It should be for the Member States to determine whether and to which extent public authorities should be subject to administrative fines. Imposing an administrative fine or giving a warning does not affect the application of other powers of the supervisory authorities or of other penalties under this Regulation.

Recital 151: The legal systems of Denmark and Estonia do not allow for administrative fines as set out in this Regulation. The rules on administrative fines may be applied in such a manner that in Denmark the fine is imposed by competent national courts as a criminal penalty and in Estonia the fine is imposed by the Supervisory Authority in the framework of a misdemeanour procedure, provided that such an application of the rules in those Member States has an equivalent effect to administrative fines imposed by supervisory authorities. Therefore, the competent national courts should take into account the recommendation by the Supervisory Authority initiating the fine. In any event, the fines imposed should be effective, proportionate and dissuasive.

Recital 152: Where this Regulation does not harmonise administrative penalties or where necessary in other cases, for example in cases of serious infringements of this Regulation, Member States should implement a system which provides for effective, proportionate and dissuasive penalties. The nature of such penalties, criminal or administrative, should be determined by Member State law.

153:165 - *Processing Relating to Specific Processing Situations*

Recital 153: Member States law should reconcile the rules governing freedom of expression and information, including journalistic, academic, artistic and or literary expression with the right to the protection of personal data pursuant to this Regulation. The processing of personal data solely for journalistic purposes, or for the purposes of academic, artistic or literary expression should be subject to derogations or exemptions from certain provisions of this Regulation if necessary to reconcile the right to the protection of personal data with the right to freedom of expression and information, as enshrined in Article 11 of the Charter. This should apply in particular to the processing of personal data in the audio/visual field and in news archives and press libraries. Therefore, Member States should adopt legislative measures which lay down the exemptions and derogations necessary for the purpose of balancing those fundamental rights. Member States should adopt such exemptions and derogations on general principles, the rights of the Data Subject, the Controller and the Processor, the transfer of personal data to third countries or international organisations, the independent supervisory authorities, cooperation and consistency, and specific data-processing situations. Where such exemptions or derogations differ from one Member State to another, the law of the Member State to which the Controller is subject should apply. In order to take account of the importance of the right to freedom of expression in every democratic society, it is necessary to interpret notions relating to that freedom, such as journalism, broadly.

Recital 154: This Regulation allows the principle of public access to official documents to be taken into account when applying this Regulation. Public access to official documents may be considered to be in the public interest. Personal data in documents held by a public authority or a public body should be able to be publicly disclosed by that authority or body if the disclosure is provided for by Union or Member State law to which the public authority or public body is subject. Such laws should reconcile public access to official documents and the reuse of public sector information with the right to the protection of personal data and may therefore provide for the necessary reconciliation with the right to the protection of personal data pursuant to this Regulation. The reference to public authorities and bodies should in that context include all authorities or other bodies covered by Member State law on public access to documents. Directive 2003/98/EC of the European Parliament and of the Council leaves intact and in no way affects the level of protection of Natural Persons with regard to the processing of personal data under the provisions of Union and Member State law, and in particular does not alter the obligations and rights set out in this Regulation. In particular, that Directive should not apply to documents to which access is excluded or restricted by virtue of the access regimes on the grounds of protection of personal data, and parts of documents accessible by virtue of those regimes which contain personal data the re-use of which has been provided for by law as being incompatible with the law concerning the protection of Natural Persons with regard to the processing of personal data.

Recital 155: Member State law or collective agreements, including 'works agreements', may provide for specific rules on the processing of employees' personal data in the employment context, in particular for the conditions under which personal data in the employment context may be processed on the basis of the consent of the employee, the purposes of the recruitment, the performance of the contract of employment, including discharge of obligations laid down by law or by collective agreements, management, planning and organisation of work, equality and diversity in the workplace, health and safety at work, and for the purposes of the exercise and enjoyment, on an individual or collective basis, of rights and benefits related to employment, and for the purpose of the termination of the employment relationship.

Recital 156: The processing of personal data for archiving purposes in the public interest, scientific or historical research purposes or statistical purposes should be subject to appropriate safeguards for the rights and freedoms of the Data Subject pursuant to this Regulation. Those safeguards should ensure that technical and organisational measures are in place in order to ensure, in particular, the principle of data minimisation. The further processing of personal data for archiving purposes in the public interest, scientific or historical research purposes or statistical purposes is to be carried out when the Controller has assessed the feasibility to fulfil those purposes by processing data which do not permit or no longer permit the identification of Data Subjects, provided that appropriate safeguards exist (such as, for instance, pseudonymisation of the data). Member States should provide for appropriate safeguards for the processing of personal data for archiving purposes in the public interest, scientific or historical research purposes or statistical purposes. Member States should be authorised to provide, under specific conditions and subject to appropriate safeguards for Data Subjects, specifications and derogations with regard to the information requirements and rights to rectification, to erasure, to be forgotten, to restriction of processing, to data portability, and to object when processing personal data for archiving purposes in the public interest, scientific or historical research purposes or statistical purposes. The conditions and safeguards in question may entail specific procedures for Data Subjects to exercise those rights if this is appropriate in the light of the purposes sought by the specific processing along with technical and organisational measures aimed at minimising the processing of personal data in pursuance of the proportionality and necessity principles. The processing of personal data for scientific purposes should also comply with other relevant legislation such as on clinical trials.

Recital 157: By coupling information from registries, researchers can obtain new knowledge of great value with regard to widespread medical conditions such as cardiovascular disease, cancer and depression. On the basis of registries, research results can be enhanced, as they draw on a larger population. Within social science, research on the basis of registries enables researchers to obtain essential knowledge about the long-term correlation of a number of social conditions such as unemployment and education with other life conditions. Research results obtained through registries provide solid, high-quality knowledge which can provide the basis for the formulation and implementation of knowledge-based policy, improve the quality of life for a number of people and improve the efficiency of social services. In order to facilitate scientific research, personal data can be processed for scientific research purposes, subject to appropriate conditions and safeguards set out in Union or Member State law.

Recital 158: Where personal data are processed for archiving purposes, this Regulation should also apply to that processing, bearing in mind that this Regulation should not apply to deceased persons. Public authorities or public or private bodies that hold records of public interest should be services which, pursuant to Union or Member State law, have a legal obligation to acquire, preserve, appraise, arrange, describe, communicate, promote, disseminate and provide access to records of enduring value for general public interest. Member States should also be authorised to provide for the further processing of personal data for archiving purposes, for example with a view to providing specific information related to the political behaviour under former totalitarian state regimes, genocide, crimes against humanity, in particular the Holocaust, or war crimes.

Recital 159: Where personal data are processed for scientific research purposes, this Regulation should also apply to that processing. For the purposes of this Regulation, the processing of personal data for scientific research purposes should be interpreted in a broad manner including for example technological development and demonstration, fundamental research, applied research and privately funded research. In addition, it should take into account the Union's objective under Article 179(1) TFEU of achieving a European Research Area. Scientific research purposes should also include studies conducted in the public interest in the area of public health. To meet the specificities of processing personal data for scientific research purposes, specific conditions should apply in particular as regards the publication or otherwise disclosure of personal data in the context of scientific research purposes. If the result of scientific research in particular in the health context gives reason for further measures in the interest of the Data Subject, the general rules of this Regulation should apply in view of those measures.

Recital 160: Where personal data are processed for historical research purposes, this Regulation should also apply to that processing. This should also include historical research and research for genealogical purposes, bearing in mind that this Regulation should not apply to deceased persons.

Recital 161: For the purpose of consenting to the participation in scientific research activities in clinical trials, the relevant provisions of Regulation (EU) No 536/2014 of the European Parliament and of the Council should apply.

Recital 162: Where personal data are processed for statistical purposes, this Regulation should apply to that processing. Union or Member State law should, within the limits of this Regulation, determine statistical content, control of access, specifications for the processing of personal data for statistical purposes and appropriate measures to safeguard the rights and freedoms of the Data Subject and for ensuring statistical confidentiality. Statistical purposes mean any operation of collection and the processing of personal data necessary for statistical surveys or for the production of statistical results. Those statistical results may further be used for different purposes, including a scientific research purpose. The statistical purpose implies that the result of processing for statistical purposes is not personal data, but aggregate data, and that this result or the personal data are not used in support of measures or decisions regarding any particular Natural Person.

Recital 163: The confidential information which the Union and national statistical authorities collect for the production of official European and official national statistics should be protected. European statistics should be developed, produced and disseminated in accordance with the statistical principles as set out in Article 338(2) TFEU, while national statistics should also comply with Member State law. Regulation (EC) No 223/2009 of the European Parliament and of the Council provides further specifications on statistical confidentiality for European statistics.

Recital 164: As regards the powers of the supervisory authorities to obtain from the Controller or Processor access to personal data and access to their premises, Member States may adopt by law, within the limits of this Regulation, specific rules in order to safeguard the professional or other equivalent secrecy obligations, in so far as necessary to reconcile the right to the protection of personal data with an obligation of professional secrecy. This is without prejudice to existing Member State obligations to adopt rules on professional secrecy where required by Union law.

Recital 165: This Regulation respects and does not prejudice the status under existing constitutional law of churches and religious associations or communities in the Member States, as recognised in Article 17 TFEU.

166:170 - Delegated Acts and Implementing Acts

Recital 166: In order to fulfil the objectives of this Regulation, namely to protect the fundamental rights and freedoms of Natural Persons and in particular their right to the protection of personal data and to ensure the free movement of personal data within the Union, the power to adopt acts in accordance with Article 290 TFEU should be delegated to the Commission. In particular, delegated acts should be adopted in respect of criteria and requirements for certification mechanisms, information to be presented by standardised icons and procedures for providing such icons. It is of particular importance that the Commission carry out appropriate consultations during its preparatory work, including at expert level. The Commission, when preparing and drawing-up delegated acts, should ensure a simultaneous, timely and appropriate transmission of relevant documents to the European Parliament and to the Council.

Recital 167: In order to ensure uniform conditions for the implementation of this Regulation, implementing powers should be conferred on the Commission when provided for by this Regulation. Those powers should be exercised in accordance with Regulation (EU) No 182/2011. In that context, the Commission should consider specific measures for micro, small and medium-sized enterprises.

Recital 168: The examination procedure should be used for the adoption of implementing acts on standard contractual clauses between Controllers and Processors and between Processors; codes of conduct; technical standards and mechanisms for certification; the adequate level of protection afforded by a third country, a territory or a specified sector within that third country, or an international organisation; standard protection clauses; formats and procedures for the exchange of information by electronic means between Controllers, Processors and supervisory authorities for binding corporate rules; mutual assistance; and arrangements for the exchange of information by electronic means between supervisory authorities, and between supervisory authorities and the Board.

Recital 169: The Commission should adopt immediately applicable implementing acts where available evidence reveals that a third country, a territory or a specified sector within that third country, or an international organisation does not ensure an adequate level of protection, and imperative grounds of urgency so require.

Recital 170: Since the objective of this Regulation, namely to ensure an equivalent level of protection of Natural Persons and the free flow of personal data throughout the Union, cannot be sufficiently achieved by the Member States and can rather, by reason of the scale or effects of the action, be better achieved at Union level, the Union may adopt measures, in accordance with the principle of subsidiarity as set out in Article 5 of the Treaty on European Union (TEU). In accordance with the principle of proportionality as set out in that Article, this Regulation does not go beyond what is necessary in order to achieve that objective.

171:173 - Final Provisions

Recital 171: Directive 95/46/EC should be repealed by this Regulation. Processing already under way on the date of application of this Regulation should be brought into conformity with this Regulation within the period of two years after which this Regulation enters into force. Where processing is based on consent pursuant to Directive 95/46/EC, it is not necessary for the Data Subject to give his or her consent again if the manner in which the consent has been given is in line with the conditions of this Regulation, so as to allow the Controller to continue such processing after the date of application of this Regulation. Commission decisions adopted and authorisations by supervisory authorities based on Directive 95/46/EC remain in force until amended, replaced or repealed.

Recital 172: The European Data Protection Supervisor was consulted in accordance with Article 28(2) of Regulation (EC) No 45/2001 and delivered an opinion on 7 March 2012.

Recital 173: This Regulation should apply to all matters concerning the protection of fundamental rights and freedoms vis-à-vis the processing of personal data which are not subject to specific obligations with the same objective set out in Directive 2002/58/EC of the European Parliament and of the Council[1], including the obligations on the Controller and the rights of Natural Persons. In order to clarify the relationship between this Regulation and Directive 2002/58/EC, that Directive should be amended accordingly. Once this Regulation is adopted, Directive 2002/58/EC should be reviewed in particular in order to ensure consistency with this Regulation.

- End of Recitals -

LIST OF EUROPEAN UNION DATA PROTECTION AUTHORITIES

The following is a list of the Supervisory Authorities for each EU Member State. Most Member States have one Supervisory Authority, however certain Members States devolve certain powers to other organisations.

AUSTRIA - ÖSTERREICHISCHE DATENSCHUTZBEHÖRDE
BELGIUM - COMMISSION DE LA PROTECTION DE LA VIE PRIVÉE
BULGARIA - COMMISSION FOR PERSONAL DATA PROTECTION
CROATIA - CROATIAN PERSONAL DATA PROTECTION AGENCY
CYPRUS - COMMISSIONER FOR PERSONAL DATA PROTECTION
CZECH REPUBLIC - THE OFFICE FOR PERSONAL DATA PROTECTION
DENMARK - DATATILSYNET
ESTONIA - ESTONIAN DATA PROTECTION INSPECTORATE (ANDMEKAITSE INSPEKTSIOON)
FINLAND - OFFICE OF THE DATA PROTECTION OMBUDSMAN
FRANCE - COMMISSION NATIONALE DE L'INFORMATIQUE ET DES LIBERTÉS - CNIL
GERMANY[183] - DIE BUNDESBEAUFTRAGTE FÜR DEN DATENSCHUTZ UND DIE INFORMATIONSFREIHEIT
GREECE - HELLENIC DATA PROTECTION AUTHORITY
HUNGARY - DATA PROTECTION COMMISSIONER OF HUNGARY
IRELAND - DATA PROTECTION COMMISSIONER
ITALY - GARANTE PER LA PROTEZIONE DEI DATI PERSONALI
LATVIA - DATA STATE INSPECTORATE
LITHUANIA - STATE DATA PROTECTION
LUXEMBOURG - COMMISSION NATIONALE POUR LA PROTECTION DES DONNÉES
MALTA - OFFICE OF THE DATA PROTECTION COMMISSIONER
NETHERLANDS - AUTORITEIT PERSOONSGEGEVENS
POLAND - THE BUREAU OF THE INSPECTOR GENERAL FOR THE PROTECTION OF PERSONAL DATA - GIODO
PORTUGAL - COMISSÃO NACIONAL DE PROTECÇÃO DE DADOS - CNPD
ROMANIA - THE NATIONAL SUPERVISORY AUTHORITY FOR PERSONAL DATA PROCESSING
SLOVAKIA - OFFICE FOR PERSONAL DATA PROTECTION OF THE SLOVAK REPUBLIC
SLOVENIA - INFORMATION COMMISSIONER
SPAIN - AGENCIA DE PROTECCIÓN DE DATOS
SWEDEN - DATAINSPEKTIONEN
UNITED KINGDOM - THE INFORMATION COMMISSIONER'S OFFICE

European Data Protection Supervisor
e-mail: edps@edps.europa.eu
Website: http://www.edps.europa.eu/EDPSWEB/

[183] The competence for complaints is split among different data protection supervisory authorities in Germany.

ABOUT THE AUTHOR

Stephen Massey is a highly respected Data Protection and Information Security Practitioner with over 20 years of experience. He has developed and directed international information security and operational risk functions in a range of sectors including financial services and commercial real estate. He is an acknowledged specialist in information risk & operational risk management, data protection, and third-party risk governance and has managed the successful implementation of global projects and business initiatives. Experienced with IT security controls and regulatory compliance auditing including business and IT service continuity planning, network and perimeter security, and data privacy.

Stephen originally studied Physics at the University of Manchester Institute of Science and Technology (UMIST), holds a 1st Class Honours Degree in Intelligence and Security from the University of Staffordshire and a Master's Degree in Business Continuity, Security and Emergency Management from Bucks University. In addition to Stephen's academic achievements, Stephen is a Fellow of Information Privacy (FIP) and a Certified Information Systems Security Professional (CISSP) in good standing.

When not writing and consulting, Stephen loves nothing more than to spend time with his best friend, his fox red Labrador, Cooper. Stephen also enjoys skiing and SCUBA diving.

Lightning Source UK Ltd.
Milton Keynes UK
UKHW050204101118
332085UK00005B/527/P